Distinctive Feature Theory

Phonology and Phonetics 2

Editor

Aditi Lahiri

Mouton de Gruyter
Berlin · New York

Distinctive Feature Theory

Edited by

T. Alan Hall

Mouton de Gruyter
Berlin · New York   2001

Mouton de Gruyter (formerly Mouton, The Hague)
is a Division of Walter de Gruyter GmbH & Co. KG, Berlin.

♾ Printed on acid-free paper which falls within the guidelines
of the ANSI to ensure permanence and durability.

Die Deutsche Bibliothek — Cataloging-in-Publication Data

Distinctive feature theory / ed. by T. Alan Hall. — Berlin ; New York :
Mouton de Gruyter, 2001
   (Phonology and phonetics ; 2)
   ISBN 3-11-017033-7

Printing & Binding: Hubert & Co, Göttingen.
Cover design: Christopher Schneider, Berlin.
Printed in Germany.

Contents

Contributors

Peter Avery
Department of Linguistics
York University
4700 Keele St
North York ON M3J1P3
Canada
pavery@yorku.ca

G. N. Clements
Universite de Paris 3
CNRS
19, rue des Bernardins
75005 Paris
France
clements@idf.ext.jussieu.fr

Janet Grijzenhout
Institut für Sprache und Information
Heinrich-Heine University
Universitätsstr. 1
40225 Düsseldorf
Germany
grijzenh@phil-fak.uni-duesseldorf.de

T. A. Hall
Institut für Linguistik
Brühl 34-50
University of Leipzig
04109 Leipzig
Germany
hall@rz.uni-leipzig.de

K. David Harrison
University of Pennsylvania /IRCS
3401 Walnut Street St 401
Philadelphia, Pennsylvania 19104
USA
kdh2@linc.cis.upenn.edu

William J. Idsardi
Department of Linguistics
University of Delaware
46 E. Delaware Av
Newark, DE 19716-2551
USA
idsardi@udel.edu

Michael Jessen
Bundeskriminalamt
Fachbereich Sprechererkennung,
Tonbandauswertung und
Linguistische Textanalyse
65173 Wiesbaden
Germany

Abigail Kaun
2017 Glendon Av
Los Angeles, California 90025
USA
kaun @pantheon.yale.edu

Bertus van Rooy
Research Unit for Phonetics and
Phonology
Potchefstroom University
Potchefstroom 2520
South Africa
nffajvr@puknet.puk.ac.za

Richard Wiese
Institut für Germanistische
Sprachwissenschaft
Philipps-Universität Marburg
Wilhelm-Roepke-Str. 6A
35032 Marburg
Germany
wiese@mailer.uni-marburg.de

Daan Wissing
Research Unit for Phonetics and Phonology
Potchefstroom University
Potchefstroom
2520
South Africa
nffdpw@puknet.puk.ac.za

Introduction: Phonological representations and phonetic implementation of distinctive features*

T. Alan Hall

1. Introduction

Current interest in Optimality Theory (henceforth OT; Prince & Smolensky 1993) has caused a shift of attention in recent years from questions regarding phonological representations, which concerned phonologists in the 1970's and 1980's, to topics pertaining to constraints and their interaction. At the same time we have witnessed a greater interest in phonetic explanations in phonology than in previous years. Thus, it is not uncommon for current phonological analyses to go to great lengths to demonstrate the phonetic naturalness of their proposed treatments. Sometimes the two developments go hand in hand, the most obvious example being the approach typified by linguists at UCLA, according to which output constraints in the OT model can refer to a considerable amount of phonetic detail (e.g. Kirchner 1997, Steriade 2000).

A consequence of the shift away from representational questions and the preoccupation with phonetic explanations is that there is at present much uncertainty concerning certain fundamental questions pertaining to both phonological representations and to the phonetics-phonology boundary. With respect to features, the most obvious question regarding the first topic is: What featural representations (e.g. feature geometry, underspecification) are necessary in a phonological theory? A similar query can be posed with respect to the second topic: Is there a difference between phonological and phonetic representations, especially pertaining to featural representations?

The purpose of this book is to address these two broad issues: (i) the nature of featural representations in the phonological component, e.g. feature geometry and underspecification, and (ii) the connection between featural representations in the phonological component and the interpretation, or implementation, of these features in the phonetics.

This introductory article is organized in the following way. In section 2 I discuss the featural aspects of phonological representations. Here I provide an overview of the history of various featural frameworks proposed throughout the past forty years within the general research program of Nonlinear Phonology, e.g. Autosegmental Phonology, Feature Geometry and theories of Underspecification. Section 3 considers some topics pertaining to the interface between phonology and phonetics. In the course of sections 2 and 3 I summarize briefly the content of the eight articles in this volume and show how they fit in to the respective theoretical frameworks. Section 4 concludes.[1]

The primary aim of this introductory article is to summarize some of the research that has been done on the two broad topics referred to above – featural representations and the phonology-phonetics connection – and to show how the following eight articles contribute to some controversial questions. A second goal of the present article is to provide a brief survey of the theories of distinctive features described in the preceding paragraph. This survey is intended to serve as a background for those readers who might not be familiar with the underpinnings of these theories.

2.   Phonological representations of distinctive features

The majority of the authors in this book presuppose some model of feature geometry as well as some degree of underspecification. In this section I discuss the claims linguists have made concerning these and other aspects of featural representations in the past 30 years, focussing on some of the current areas of controversy, and summarize the new analyses discussed by the authors in this volume.

2.1 The nature of distinctive features   — could be title

The idea that segments are composed of a bundle of features has a
long tradition in phonology. See, for example, Jakobson, Fant &
Halle (1952) for the first thorough treatment and Chomsky & Halle
(1968; henceforth SPE) – probably the single most influential post-
Jakobsonian work dealing with features from a phonological point of
view. Although SPE and Jakobson *et al.* disagree on a number of
issues, both approaches concur that each feature is defined in terms
of some phonetic property. For example, when we say that a segment
like /n/ is [+nasal] (as in SPE), then [+nasal] is taken to correspond
to the lowering of the velum. One of the ways in which the SPE and
Jakobsonian systems differ is that the former takes the point of view
that features are defined solely on articulatory terms, whereas the
latter argues that features have primarily acoustic definitions. In
general, phonologists have followed the SPE tradition by analyzing
features articulatorily, although there is a recent trend to allow
acoustic, or auditory definitions (see, for example, Flemming 1995,
Boersma 1998, Steriade 2000, Jessen this volume).[2]

The Jakobsonian and SPE systems also share the view that any
given segment is simply an abbreviation for an unordered bundle of
features. A sample phonological representation for the segment /n/ in
the SPE system is presented in (1), where I have only included five
features indicated below.[3]

(1)   SPE features for /n/:
$$\begin{bmatrix} \text{+consonantal} \\ \text{+sonorant} \\ \text{−continuant} \\ \text{+nasal} \\ \text{+coronal} \end{bmatrix}$$

According to the approach espoused by SPE morphemes and words
are composed of a string of the corresponding feature matrices and
boundary symbols. For this reason representations like the one in (1)
are usually referred to as *linear*. The linearity property of phonological representations is typical for featural representations in the SPE

tradition, but has been rejected by most phonologists, who have argued in favor of *nonlinear* representations (see section 2.2 and 2.3).

Another theoretical assumption shared in both the Jakobsonian and in the SPE systems is that distinctive features are *binary*. This approach to features means that each feature has two *values*, namely '+' and '−', e.g. /m n ŋ/ and /d b g/ are examples of [+nasal] and [−nasal] segments respectively.

The binarity hypothesis as described in the previous paragraph, although widely accepted in the years after SPE, has been questioned by a number of researchers. On the one hand, some linguists have argued that certain features are *multivalued*, or *scalar*, e.g. Williamson (1977), Gnanadesikan (1997). For example, Williamson (1977) argues that place of articulation among consonants is to be captured with the multivalued feature [place], e.g. [6 place], [5 place], and [4 place] are defined as the bilabial, labiodental and dental places of articulation respectively.[3] The second alternative to binarity hypothesis is that some (if not all) features are *privative*. The latter approach has proven to be the most influential in current theory; hence, I treat this topic below separately (see section 2.4.1).

An important argument for demonstrating the necessity of distinctive features is to capture natural classes. Thus, when we say that a segment like /d/ is marked for the two features [+voice, −sonorant], for example, we mean not only that /d/ belongs to the class of sounds that is [+voice], but also to the natural class of [−sonorant] segments. Thus, features allow one to classify /d/ together with /b g/ on the one hand and /b g t k f v/ on the other. Phonological evidence for natural classes typically take the form of some rule or phonotactic statement referring to the relevant feature(s). For example, the natural class of obstruents, defined featurally as [−sonorant], is necessary because rules of Final Devoicing in various languages (e.g. German) affect only these sounds and no others.

A second reason for the necessity of features is to capture contrasts in natural languages. For example, since there are many languages in which /p t k/ contrast with /pʰ tʰ kʰ/ the feature [±spread] is required, where the positive value of this feature corresponds to the spreading of the glottis characterized by aspirated sounds and the negative value to nonaspiration. The feature [±spread] is quite different from a feature we might call [±burst], where [+burst] corresponds to the brief period of noise following the release of closure in stops like /p t k/. Since no language distinguishes [+burst] stops vs. [−burst] stops, [±burst] does not capture a contrast in any known natural language. The standard way of explaining these two features is to say that [±spread] is a *distinctive feature* (or *phonological feature*), whereas [±burst] is a *phonetic feature*.

An important point regarding the distinction between phonological (i.e. distinctive) and phonetic features is that only those features which can potentially have a distinctive function in some language are classified as phonological. In the Jakobsonian view – also assumed by generative phonologists in the SPE and post-SPE traditions – such features serve a distinctive function in some languages and a nondistinctive function in others. For example, the phonological feature [±spread] referred to above is distinctive in Korean, which contrasts /p t k/ vs. /p^h t^h k^h/, but nondistinctive in English, since [p t k] and [p^h t^h k^h] do not contrast. In yet other languages the same feature may be *latent* in the sense that while not present at all, it may at some later historical stage be introduced by an allophonic rule, thereby becoming a nondistinctive feature. At a later stage further developments might cause this nondistinctive feature to become distinctive. By contrast, a parallel development involving a phonetic feature like [±burst] is unattested.

Although the authors of the eight articles presented below tend to agree with the standard approach as described in the preceding paragraph, a number of recent studies have questioned the distinction between phonological vs. phonetic features (see, for example, Flemming 1995, Kirchner 1997, Steriade 2000). Indeed, much of this current work is symptomatic of the general goal of eliminating the distinction between phonetics and phonology and of (re)introducing functional explanations into phonology (see Martinet 1964, Stampe 1973 for realier functional approaches to phonology).

2.2 Segmental structure: From linear to nonlinear representations

Much work in the late 1970's and in subsequent years argued against the linear view of segmental structure in (1), according to which segments are composed of unordered bundles of distinctive features. Some of the evidence levelled against linear representations like the one in (1) came from developments in Autosegmental Phonology (e.g. Goldsmith 1976, 1990, Pulleyblank 1986 and much subsequent work), in which it was shown that certain features behave phonologically as if they were independent of the others. Typical examples illustrating this phenomenon come from *tone languages*, in which various data require features like [±high tone] to be represented independently from the purely segmental features.

Subsequent work in Autosegmental Phonology demonstrated that languages with rules of *harmony* suggest that the relevant harmonizing feature should be represented independently from all other segmental features, e.g. [±back], [±Advanced Tongue Root] (henceforth [±ATR]) in *vowel harmony* systems and [±nasal] in languages with *nasal harmony*. A typical set of data exhibiting nasal harmony is illustrated in (2).

(2)   Nasal Harmony in Desano (Kaye 1971):
    a.   [w̃ãĩ]   'name'
          [sẽnãnũ]   'pineapple'
    b.   [wai]   'fish'
          [goru]   'ball'

The examples from Desano in (2) show that words in this language can be grouped into two classes, nasal in (2a) and oral in (2b). What these categories mean is that all segments within a word belonging to (2a) and (2b) are nasal and oral respectively but that no word of this language consists of nasal *and* oral segments.[4] The standard autosegmental treatment of the data in (2) is to analyze the feature [±nasal] in Desano not as a property of certain segments, but instead as a property of certain morphemes. This example therefore suggests that in languages like Desano the feature [±nasal] can be extracted from the bundle of features in (1) and be analyzed independently (see 3b below).

Autosegmental Phonology provides a formalism for capturing the independence of certain features from the remaining segmental features. According to this theory we can express the independence of the feature [+nasal], for example, by situating it on an independent *tier* from all other features. This formalism is expressed in (3a), where '∘' designates the *root node*, which for our purposes is simply an abbreviation for all other features that comprise the segment /n/, i.e. [+consonantal, +sonorant, −continuant, +coronal]. A slightly definition for root node is introduced in section 2.3. In (3a) the *autosegment* [+nasal] is linked to the root node by an *association line*. We say that the feature [+nasal] has been *autosegmentalized*, or alternatively *suprasegmentalized* because it is projected onto its own tier.

(3) a. Partial Autosegmental Representation for /n/

[+nasal]

  b. Autosegmental representations for Desano [w̃ãĩ] and [wai]:

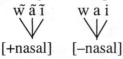

[+nasal] [−nasal]

In (3b) we see autosegmental representations for a nasal and an oral word respectively in Desano (recall 2).

By placing the feature [+nasal] (or some other feature) on an independent tier the assimilation of this feature is expressed by its *spreading* to another segment. Assimilation as (progressive) spreading is illustrated in (4):

(4) Assimilation as spreading of the feature [F]:

[F]

A number of authors have argued that *all* assimilations and not only those involving tones or harmony processes be analyzed as spreading (e.g. Hayes 1986). Thus, according to this approach, purely local assimilations are analyzed as spreading as in (4), e.g. the assimilation of the feature [+nasal] from a nasal consonant onto a preceding vowel in English (e.g. *den* /dɛn/ → [dɛ̃n]).

Analyzing individual features like [back] and [nasal] as if they occupied their own tier analogously allows phonological processes deleting some feature (e.g. neutralizations, dissimilations) to be formalized as the deletion of an association line. On this view the principle known as Stray Erasure (Steriade 1982) then ensures that features not anchored to some segment are deleted at the end of the derivation. The deletion of the feature [+F] as the deletion of an association line is depicted in (5a). An example of a language which has been argued to have a process like the one in (5a) is Standard German. For example, Wiese (1996: 204ff.) analyzes Final Devoicing in that language as the delinking of [+voice], e.g. *Rad* /ʀaːd/ → [ʀaːt] 'wheel'.

(5) a. Deletion of feature [+F]:   b.   Default addition of [−F]:

It is often assumed that languages undergoing a deletion operation like the one in (5a) require a *default rule* like the one in (5b), which adds the opposite value for the deleted feature. For example, Wiese (1996: 204ff.) argues that a default rule adding [−voice] follows the delinking of [+voice] by Final Devoicing, i.e. the 't' produced by delinking the feature [+voice] from the /d/ in /ʀaːd/ is 'incomplete' and needs the value [−voice] to receive the correct phonetic inter-pretation. Other linguists have argued that neutralizations like the one in (5a) do not require default rules like the ones in (5b) and that the output of operations like the one in (5a) remain *underspecified* for feature [A], or that feature [A] is privative (e.g. Lombardi 1991, Ghini this volume). The role of underspecification and default rules and privative features is dealt with below at length in sections 2.4 and 3.1.

2.3 Segmental structure: Feature geometry

Work done on Autosegmental Phonology was complemented by the observation that certain features function together as a unit in phonological processes, e.g. assimilations, dissimilations, neutralization. A textbook case of this phonemenomen is *place assimilation*, where all and only the place features spread. For example, in English and in many other languages the partial assimilation /np nb nk ng/ → [mp mb ŋk ŋg] involves the spreading of the place features from the oral stop leftward to the nasal consonant. Significantly, it is only the place features which spread and not other ones, e.g. [–sonorant], [±voice], etc.

The basic intuition behind the observation that certain groups of features function together as a unit is captured in the model that is usually referred to as Feature Geometry (see Clements 1985, Sagey 1986, McCarthy 1988, Halle 1995, Clements & Hume 1995). A typical feature geometric model presupposes that the segment is composed of a series of elements, usually referred to as *class nodes*, as well as the traditional features described in the preceding sections. The former, which are capitalized in (6) and below, are linked to other nodes and/or features by association lines. A typical example of a *feature tree* (after McCarthy 1988) is presented in (6):[5]

(6)   A feature tree:

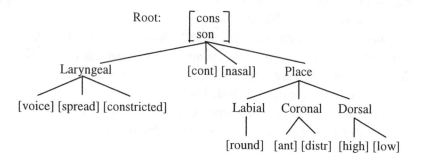

The highest entity in (6) is the Root node, which is usually assumed to consist of the major class features [cons] and [son] (see McCarthy 1988).[6] The Root node in (6) dominates Laryngeal and Place, as well as the features [cont] and [nasal], and Place dominates the Articulator nodes Labial, Coronal and Dorsal. Features are terminal elements in feature geometric models like the one in (6). They can be daughters of Laryngeal, Labial, Coronal, Dorsal, or the Root node itself.

In recent years many versions of the feature geometric model in (6) have been proposed (see references cited above). Although there are differences among all of these models, they all share the basic assumption that there is a hierarchical structure which is internal to the segment.

Given the feature geometric representation of segment structure as in (6) the assimilation of all and only the place features can be represented as the assimilation of a single constituent (recall 4 above), namely as the spreading of Place, as in (7):

(7)   Place assimilation as spreading of the Place node:

Place

Since Place dominates all of the Articulator nodes, which in turn dominate all of the terminal place features in (7), the spreading of Place entails the spreading of all and only its daughters. Hence, the assimilation of place features to nasal consonants referred to above, i.e. /np nb nk ng/ → [mp mb ŋk ŋg], cannot spread individual place features *and* nonplace features, e.g. [son], because non-place features are not dominated by Place.

Two of the articles in this book (Avery & Idsardi, Clements) make concrete proposals concerning various aspects of the Feature Geometry model given in (6). In the remainder of this section I summarize their respective modifications.

Avery & Idsardi (this volume) argue in favor of a refinement of earlier approaches to feature geometry. Focussing on the laryngeal phonology, they propose that the Laryngeal node and its three dependents in (6) be modifed as in (8):

(8)

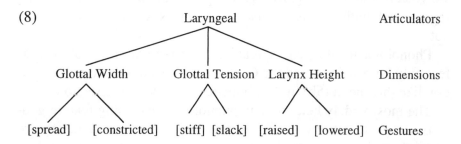

According to the feature tree in (8) there are three layers of organizational structure: Articulators, Dimensions, and Gestures. The first are basically the same as the corresponding nodes in standard approaches to Feature Geometry in (6); Dimensions and Gestures require some comment.

There are three laryngeal Dimensions in (8), namely Glottal Width, Glottal Tension and Larynx Height. The Dimensions refer to muscle groups forming antagonistic pairs; thus, only a single muscle within a Dimension can be active in any given speech sound. This is expressed in phonological representations by restricting the Dimensions to be non-branching. Given this requirement, Avery & Idsardi can capture the generalization that there are sounds like /tʰ/ that are [spread] and ones like /t'/ that are [constricted], but none that are both [spread] and [constricted].

The Gestures in (8) are motor instructions to the Articulators which represent the smallest articulatory action, i.e. the action of a single muscle group. The Gestures [constricted] and [spread] are basically the same as the equivalent features used by other writers (see the model in 6). The Glottal Tension Gestures [stiff] and [slack] (first proposed by Halle & Stevens 1971) serve a similar function to [voice] in other theories. The Gestures [raised] and [lowered] refer to the height of the larynx; the former is necessary for ejectives and the latter for implosives.

The Gestures in (8) form the ultimate constituents of phonological representations but they are unlike the traditional features in (6) because the Gestures are not used to express phonological contrasts.

Contrasts are expressed in the model in (8) at the level of Dimensions. For example, in a language like Spanish which opposes voiced vs. voiceless sounds, e.g. /b d g/ vs. /p t k/, the former segments are represented with 'Glottal Tension', whereas voiceless sounds are not.

Phonological rules, e.g. spreadings like the one in (7) above, affect only Dimensions, and the Gestures are added by a default operation like the one in (5b) in the phonetic component (see section 3.1).

The most widely held view in phonology concerning feature geometric representations in (6) is that the features and nodes are situated on their respective tiers regardless of how they pattern in a given phonological system. For example, [nasal] is situated on the [nasal] tier not only in nasal harmony languages like Desano (recall 2) but also in languages which have no phonological processes involving this feature. Clements (this volume) observes that this approach introduces superfluous representational elements in the sense that there are some tiers which play no role at all in certain languages. He proposes that this superfluity be eliminated with a principle he calls the Prominence Criterion:

(9)   The Prominence Criterion:
       In any language, all and only prominent features and nodes are
       projected onto separate autosegmental tiers.

Features and nodes are 'prominent' if, for example, they spread. A corollary of the Prominence Criterion is that if a language has no prominent features at all then nothing is projected and all of the features are grouped together under the Root node – not unlike the SPE representation in (1).

Clements applies his proposal to several languages, e.g. Tahltan, Basque, Zoque. In the latter language there is evidence that certain features restricted to the Coronal node can be projected onto their own tier, while others cannot be. The dependents of Coronal assumed by Clements are [±strident], [±apical] and [±posterior].[7] Clements shows that in Zoque there is a rule of coronal palatalization converting an underlying sequence /t͡s + j/ into [t͡ʃ], which he analyzes as the spreading of [+posterior], e.g. /me?t͡s-jah-u/ [me?t͡ʃahu] 'they sought it'. In (10a) and (10b) I have shown the segmental structure involved in this process below the Root node in the input (i.e. /t͡s + j/) and output (i.e. [t͡ʃ]) respectively.

(10) a.

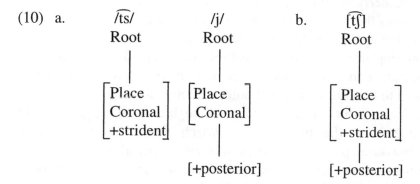

In (10) we see that only [+posterior] is projected onto its own tier, but not [+strident], which forms a 'feature bundle' with the Place and Coronal nodes. Support for this comes from processes of Zoque like coronal palatalization, in which [posterior] but not [strident] spreads.

Clements speculates that the (universal) maximal expansion of the Coronal node is as in (11):

(11) $\begin{bmatrix} \text{Coronal} \\ \pm\text{strident} \end{bmatrix}$
$\quad\quad |$
$\begin{bmatrix} \pm\text{posterior} \\ \pm\text{apical} \end{bmatrix}$

The structure in (11) makes two important predictions: (i) there are no languages with rules assimilating or dissimilating [±strident] alone; and (ii) [±posterior] and [±apical] form a unit together in the sense that no language can spread or delink one of these two features without the other one also being affected.

2.4   Underspecification

Underspecification is traditionally understood as an approach in which underlying representations lack some feature. In rule-based approaches there are often assumed to be default rules like the one in (5b) which apply in a derivation which have the function of filling in the missing unmarked feature values. This approach is similar but not identical to one in which features are privative (or *unary*) as opposed to binary. Most of the authors in the present volume assume some degree of underspecification, although they all suggest various refinements to the traditional approach described above; some authors assume privative features, whereas others adopt binary ones.

In the present section I discuss first the way in which underspecification as it is traditionally understood is expressed in phonological representations and compare this approach with one with privative features (section 2.4.1). As I point out in that section underspecified structures require that the commonly assumed definition for distinctness (recall section 2.1) be rethought. I then consider two of the arguments for underspecified representations, namely redundancy (section 2.4.2) and the transparency of segments with respect to spreading rules (section 2.4.3). In the latter section I also summarize Grijzenhout's (this volume) approach to nasal harmony. I conclude section 2.4 by comparing some of the models of underspecification that have been influential in the literature, namely Radical and Contrastive Underspecification with the approach taken by Ghini (this volume) (section 2.4.4) and Archiphonemic Underspecification in the framework of Inkelas (1995) in OT and the treatment proposed by Harrison & Kaun (this volume) (section 2.4.5).

2.4.1 Underspecified representations, privative features and distinctness

The traditional approach to underspecification in generative phonology can be illustrated with the representations in (12a) and (12b):

(12)   a.   /z/   b.   /d/   c. $\begin{bmatrix} +\text{cons} \\ -\text{son} \end{bmatrix}$

$\begin{bmatrix} +\text{cons} \\ -\text{son} \end{bmatrix}$ $\begin{bmatrix} +\text{cons} \\ -\text{son} \end{bmatrix}$

[+cont]   [−cont]

In (12a) and (12b) we see the underlying representation for /z/ and /d/ respectively. In these structures I have only considered the major class features [±cons] and [±son], which are part of the Root node, and the binary feature [±cont], which is situated on ist own tier. In (12a) /z/ is specified for [+cont] but in (12b) /d/ is not marked for continuancy. (12b) is therefore referred to as *underspecified* for the feature [cont]. An example of a default rule which adds [−cont] to representation (12b) in the derivation is presented in (12c).

According to this approach underspecification is only temporary because it is only in the underlying form that underspecified representations exist. When the default rule in (12c) applies, the segment /d/ is no longer underspecified for the feature [−cont]. Thus, the underspecified representation in (12b) is transformed into the fully specified representation in (13b).[8]

(13)   a.   /z/   b.   /d/

$\begin{bmatrix} +\text{cons} \\ -\text{son} \end{bmatrix}$ $\begin{bmatrix} +\text{cons} \\ -\text{son} \end{bmatrix}$

[+cont]   [−cont]

Many phonologists in the 1980's argued that binary features can be underspecified and that default rules fill in the missing values, e.g. Archangeli (1988).

The underspecified representation in (12b) is similar but not identical to the privative approach to features referred to briefly in section 2.1. If [cont] is analyzed as a privative (i.e. unary) feature then segments like /z/ are [cont] and stops like /d/ have no feature at all on the [cont] tier. The two contrasting representations are illustrated in (14a) and (14b) respectively:

(14)   a.   /z/   b.   /d/

$$\begin{bmatrix} +cons \\ -son \end{bmatrix} \qquad \begin{bmatrix} +cons \\ -son \end{bmatrix}$$

|

[cont]

The crucial difference between the binary analysis of [cont] in (12) and the privative analysis of the same feature in (14) is that the latter approach assumes no default rule like the one in (12c). Hence, in the phonetic representation the binary approach treats [d] as [−cont], whereas the privative approach treats the same segment as in (14b) because there is no feature [−cont]. For obvious reasons, the privative approach described above is sometimes referred to as *permanent underspecification*.

In the approach illustrated in (12) underspecification refers to particular values of distinctive features, e.g. the '+' value of [cont] is specified and the '−' value of the same feature is underspecified. In the privative approach phonological representations can also be underspecified, but here entire features can be absent. For example, a large literature on the phonology of coronals has proposed that labials and velars are marked for Place and the respective Articulator node but that coronals like /t/ are underspecified for Coronal (see the articles in Paradis & Prunet 1991a), as shown in (15):

(15) /p/   /t/   /k/

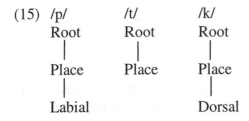

The assumption is that Coronal is added to /t/ by a later default rule (see, for example, Paradis & Prunet 1991b).

The privative approach to distinctive features has proven to be very influential. For example, in almost all versions of Feature Geometry (recall 6), the Articulator nodes Labial, Coronal and Dorsal are assumed to be unary.[9] Some linguists have proposed that certain of the terminal features in (6) are privative as well, e.g. Mester & Itô (1989) for [voice] and Lombardi (1991) [voice] and the laryngeal features [spread] and [constricted], whereas others have taken the more radical position that *all* features are privative, e.g. Avery & Rice (1989).[10]

The controversy regarding which features are binary or privative is reflected in the contributions to the present volume. For example, Avery & Idsardi adopt a model of Feature Geometry (recall 8), in which all features are privative. Grizenhout similarly proposes that [nasal] is unary, and in his analysis of vowel features, Ghini argues that [high] and [low] are privative. By contrast, Clements and Harrison & Kaun presuppose that the daughters of Coronal and the feature [back] respectively are binary.

Representations lacking some element – be they underspecified, as in (12b), or unary, as in (14b) – bring up the question of how distinctness is to be interpreted. In SPE it was assumed that [0F] and [αF] are nondistinct and that only [−F] and [+F] can be referred to in phonological rules. Were one to extend this definition of distinctness to some of the representations discussed above, then one would have to conclude – incorrectly – that they are nondistinct. For example, in (14a) /z/ is [cont] and /d/ lacks this feature. However, the traditional SPE definition of distinctness is usually not assumed to hold for privative features or underspecified representations (see Paradis & Prunet 1991b).

In the preceding paragraphs I have sketched the mechanics of underspecified and unary representations without motivating these structures. Why would one want to underspecify a segment in the first place? Two of the most common arguments cited in favor of underspecified representations are (i) underspecification allows one to eliminate redundancies and (ii) underspecification explains transparency to spreading and the failure to initiate spreading. In sections 2.4.2 and 2.4.3 I consider (i) and (ii) respectively.[11]

2.4.2 Redundancy

One argument that segments lack certain feature values in the underlying form is that such 'incomplete' representations capture redundancies, i.e. predictable information.

An example of a redundancy that can be eliminated with an underspecified representation is illustrated in a language like Spanish, in which all non-low back vowels are rounded. Thus, in contrast to other languages Spanish has no vowels like high back unrounded /ɯ/. Put differently, if a vowel has the features [+back, –low] then it must be [+round]. Since the feature [+round] is not distinctive for non-low back vowels, it can therefore be underlyingly underspecified. The feature value [+round], as a *redundant* feature, is predictable and hence can be introduced in the derivation by the following rule (sometimes referred to as a *redundancy* rule):[12]

(16)   [–low, +back] → [+round]

For proponents of underspecification (e.g. Archangeli 1988) rule (16) implies that a segment like /u/ is underlyingly [–low, +back, 0round] and that (16) applies in the derivation to fill in the blank.

2.4.3 Underspecification in autosegmental representations

A second reason often advanced for underspecified representations is that they can account for the fact that certain segments are either transparent to autosegmental spreading rules, e.g. processes of vowel harmony, or that they fail to initiate spreading. The most common explanation for these two situations is to analyze the relevant sound as underspecified for the feature that spreads.

A typical example for a language in which certain segments are transparent to a rule of harmony comes from Finnish (see van de Hulst & van de Weijer 1995). In Finnish all vowels within a word agree in terms of the feature [±back], e.g. [pöytä] 'table' vs. [pouta] 'fine weather', where [ö y ä] are [–back] and [o u a] [+back]. Assuming that both values of this feature spread iteratively then one needs to explain why certain segments (i.e. *neutral vowels* like /i/; recall note 5) allow the backness feature to spread across them, e.g. [palttina] 'linen cloth'. The spreading of [+back] in this word is illustrated in (17)

(17)   p   a   l   tt   i   n   a
              L_____
         [+back]

Were /i/ to be specified [–back] then one would not expect [+back] to spread to /a/, otherwise the resulting representation would violate the No Crossing Constraint (see Goldsmith 1976 and much subsequent work).[14] One commonly assumed explanation for the behavior of transparent neutral vowels like /i/ in Finnish is to posit that they are underspecified for the feature that spreads, in this case [+back].

In her analysis of nasality, Grijzenhout (this volume) invokes permanent underspecification in order to account for why certain segments which should apparently trigger a spreading rule do not. She proposes that there are two universal representations for nasal consonants, namely the one in (18a), which she dubs 'plain nasal stops' and the 'light nasal stops' in (18b). A comparison of these two representations reveals that the feature [nasal] is lacking altogether in (18b).

(18)   a. [+son, +cons]   b.   [+son, +cons]
          |
       [nasal]

In (18a), nasalization is phonologically active in the sense that it can trigger the spreading of [nasal], as illustrated below. In (18b), nasalization appears merely as a phonetic consequence of [+son], and accordingly, does not function in the phonology. In such consonants, nasalization occurs because [+son] requires airflow across the glottis and the noncontinuancy prevents this airflow from channeling through the oral cavity. Hence airflow through the nasal cavity is required.

Grijzenhout argues that languages which participate in nasal harmony (e.g. Brazilian Portuguese) choose (18a) and those which do not participate in such processes (e.g. European Portuguese) have the structure in (18b). Some languages, e.g. Acehnese, can have both representations. An assimilated representation for the word [mãw̃ʌ̃] (/mawʌ/) 'rose' in the latter language is presented in (19).

(19)   m   ã   w̃   ʌ̃

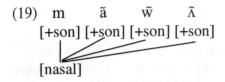

In Acehnese there are also nasal segments that do not trigger harmony, e.g. [m̊on] 'dew' (*[m̊õn]), where [m̊] is a 'light nasal stop'. Grijzenhout proposes that these light nasal stops have the representation in (18b), in which nasal is permanently underspecified. Significantly, the two contrastive representations in (18) derive some phonetic support as well: Durie (1985) observes that airflow measurements for Acehnese plain nasal stops have a higher degree of airflow through the nose than the light nasal stops. This observation was confirmed by Ladefoged & Maddieson (1996: 104-106), who determined a measurable difference in velic opening between the two types of nasal stops.

2.4.4   Radical vs. Constrastive Underspecification

In the 1980's two competing theories of underspecification arose, namely Radical Underspecification (Archangeli 1984, 1988) and Contrastive Underspecification (Steriade 1987, Clements 1988, Mester & Itô 1989).

Let us consider the vowel system /i u e o ɑ/ as an illustration of these two theories. Fully specified matrices for these five segments have been provided in (20), where I only consider the four features indicated below and no others.

(20) Fully specified matrices:

	i	u	e	o	ɑ
[high]	+	+	−	−	−
[low]	−	−	−	−	+
[back]	−	+	−	+	+
[round]	−	+	−	+	−

The system in (20) has a number of redundancies, four of which are captured with the rules in (21):

(21) a. [+low]   →   [−high]
          [+high] →   [−low]
      b. [+low]   →   [+back]
          [−back] →   [−low]

Consider first (21a). Given the marked feature values [+low] and [+high] we can assume that unmarked [−high] and [−low] are redundant values introduced by the respective rules. In (21b) we see rules expressing the generalization that all low vowels are [+back] and all front vowels are non-low. Subtracting the redundant values in (21) from the fully specified matrices in (20) obtains the underspecified matrices in (22):

(22) Contrastively underspecified matrices:

	i	u	e	o	ɑ
[high]	+	+	−	−	
[low]				−	+
[back]	−	+	−	+	

The approach to underspecification in (22) is called Contrastive Underspecification.

Contrastive Underspecification assigns specific values to a feature in underlying representations only when that feature is used to distinguish segments in the respective contexts; by contrast, noncontrastive features are left blank. In the vowel system /i u e o ɑ/ the two front vowels contrast in terms of the feature [high]; therefore /i/ and /e/ are marked for the respective values for this feature. By contrast, the vowel /ɑ/ does not have a high counterpart and is therefore underspecified for this feature. The same procedure can be applied to /u/ vs. /o/; they contrast and therefore they are marked for [+high] and [–high] respectively. A comparison of the two pairs /i/ vs. /u/ and /e/ vs. /o/ shows that the feature [±back] is distinctive. Hence, each of these four vowels is marked for its respective value for [±back].[14] Since /ɑ/ contrasts with /o/, these two segments are marked [–low] and [+low] respectively.

It is possible to eliminate additional redundancies in (22) as well. For example, if /i u/ are specified as [+high] in the underlying representations then /e o ɑ/ need not be marked [–high]. Consequently, the rule in (23a) introduces the value [–high]. The same point can be made regarding [low] and [back] as well: Given the feature values [+low] and [+back], [–low] and [–back] can be introduced by (23b) and (23c) respectively.

(23)   a.   [ ]   →   [–high]
        b.   [ ]   →   [–low]
        c.   [ ]   →   [–back]

The matrices that result from the procedure of underspecifying the five vowels /i u e o ɑ/ implies the underspecified matrices in (24):

(24)   Radically underspecified matrices:

	i	u	e	o	ɑ
[high]	+	+			
[low]					+
[back]		+		+	

The matrices in (24) are called radically underspecified because each feature is underlyingly specified for a single value, i.e. in this case only the '+' values are present.[15]

Ghini (this volume) proposes a set of procedures for determining which features are distinctive in any given language, which is similar but not identical to the Radical Underspecification model in (24). Restricting his discussion to vowel features, he dubs his approach Place of Articulation First.

Ghini assumes a model of Feature Geometry as in (25), in which the Place node dominates an Articulator node as well as an Aperture node (see Lahiri & Evers 1991 for a similar model).

(25)

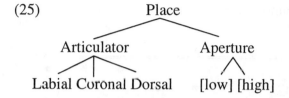

Place of Articulation First says that the features under the Articulator node are assigned before the Aperture features.

Ghini's approach is illustrated with the short vowel system of Migliola Ligurian: /i e æ y ø ɑ o u/. The five features Dorsal, Labial, [low], [high] and Coronal are assigned in the following order:

(26) i.   Insertion of Dorsal
      ii.   Insertion of Labial
      iii. Insertion of [low]
      iv.   Insertion of [high]
      v.   Insertion of Coronal and Labial

To see how the set of procedures in (26) works, let us compare (i)-(v) with the respective line of the distinctive feature matrices in (27). Here '•' indicates the presence of a privative feature.

According to (26), Dorsal is assigned first (by i); thus, the back vowels /ɑ o u/ receive this feature and the front ones do not. Ghini assumes that Labial, as a secondary feature in vowels, is only inserted onto vowels that are marked for Dorsal, namely /o u/ (by step ii). (By contrast, the front vowels /y ø/ receive this feature by step v). Place of Articulation First is overridden in the case of Coronal, due to the universally unmarked status of this feature (see Paradis & Prunet 1991b). Step (iii) assigns [low]. Among the front vowels, /æ/ undergoes (iii) because it is the lowest front vowel. Among the back rounded vowels /u o/, the latter segment is assigned [low] because it is the lower of the two vowels. By contrast, /ɑ/ does not get this feature (or any other) because it does not contrast with any other vowel in its place of articulation. At this point all of the back vowels are distinct and no other features are necessary. Among the front vowels, the feature [high] is inserted by step (iv) to /i/ and /y/. The final step in (26) (=26v) is the assignment of Coronal and Labial to the two front rounded vowels /y ø/:

(27)

	i	e	æ	y	ø	ɑ	o	u
Dorsal						●	●	●
Labial				●	●		●	●
[low]			●			●		
[high]	●			●				
Coronal				●	●			

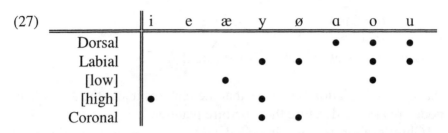

The feature matrices in (27) are understood to be the underlying, or distinctive features necessary for this language.

An examination of the distinctive feature matrices in (27) reveals that this system is clearly at odds with Contrastive Underspecification. For example, since [high] is a distinctive feature for the vowels in (27), Contrastive Underspecification would analyze /i u/ as [+high] and /e o/ as [–high], but in (27) the negative value of this feature (and all others) is absent.

Ghini also emphasizes that Place of Articulation First predicts underlying feature matrices like the ones in (27) which differ from the ones predicted by Radical Underspecification. For example, Ghini assumes that the assignment of a feature [F] requires that the node immediately dominating [F] be specified both for the segments marked for [F] but also for those where it is not specified. For example, when [low] is assigned by step (26iii) to /æ/ the Aperture node will automatically be assigned both to this vowel as well as to all other vowels. According to Ghini, this is the main difference between his approach and Radical Underspecification.

2.4.5   Underspecification and Optimality Theory: Archiphonemic Underspecification

Generally speaking OT emphasizes the role of constraint interaction as opposed to representations (recall section 1). Hence, the approaches to underspecification described in the previous two sections have been criticized in various OT accounts (e.g. Itô, Mester & Padget 1995, Inkelas 1995), where it is argued that constraint interactions not requiring underspecification are superior. Nevertheless, there is some room for underspecification in OT, as proposed, for example, by Inkelas's (1995) theory of Archiphonemic Underspecification. In this section I describe this approach and compare it with the one proposed by Harrison & Kaun (this volume).

Within the framework of OT, the principle known as Richness of the Base bans systematic exclusion of featural specifications from input representations (see Prince & Smolensky 1993, Smolensky 1995). The input is assumed to be infinite and therefore unrestricted; by contrast, the lexicon is understood to be finite. According to Prince & Smolensky (1993) a learner's construction of lexical representations is determined by the principle of Lexicon Optimization, which heavily prefers fully specified inputs. According to Prince & Smolensky a speaker will choose the most harmonic input-output mappings, i.e. the fullest specified. Thus, given two competing input forms, one fully specified and the other being partially specified, the former is preferred. However, under certain circumstances the OT model leaves room for underspecified lexical entries.

Archiphonemic Underspecification (Inkelas 1995) is an attempt to predict under what circumstances underspecified inputs in OT are employed. According to Inkelas, predictable feature values will be underspecified only when they occur in surface alternations. Thus, underspecification in her model can only arise when there are fully regular and predictable alternations, as shown in the table in (28) (from Inkelas 1995: 290):

(28)

	Alternating	Non-alternating
Predictable	underspecified	specified
Unpredictable	specified	specified

Archiphonemic Underspecification can be illustrated with Turkish front-back vowel harmony. Only those vowels that are involved in these alternations are predicted to be underspecified for backness in underlying representations. This is illustrated with the two examples in (29a), in which the value of [back] for the suffix depends on the backness of the preceding stem vowels: [im] surfaces after [–back] vowels and [ɨm] after [+back] vowels.

(29)   a.   [kilim-im]   'rug'   b.   /kilim-Im/
            [kɨlɨc-ɨm]   'sword'   /kɨlɨc-Im/

Archiphonemic Underspecification predicts that the vowel in the suffix in (29a) is underspecified for backness, as in (29b). In (29b) /i/ and /ɨ/ represent vowels specified for [–back] and [+back] respectively. /I/ is a high vowel underspecified for [back]. By contrast, Archiphonemic Underspecification also predicts that root vowels are always specified for backness, even when the two vowels of the root seem to obey harmony, e.g. the vowels of the respective roots in (29a). For example, Inkelas predicts that the root in [kɨlɨc-ɨm] 'sword' is /kɨlɨc/ and not /kIlIc/. [16]

   Harrison & Kaun (this volume) argue against the claim made by Archiphonemic Underspecification that root vowels cannot be under-specified for harmonic features. They hold that speakers can under-specify not only alternating vowels in affixes, as in (29b), but also non-alternating vowels within roots. What is more, Harrison & Kaun contend that in some languages alternating and/or non-alternating predictable features demand fully specified inputs. Harrison & Kaun therefore conclude that (28) must be revised along the lines of (30):

(30)

	Alternating	Non-alternating
Predictable	underspecified or specified	specified or underspecified
Unpredictable	specified	specified

Examples of a predictable non-alternating segments that need to be underspecified – contrary to the prediction made by Archiphonemic Underspecification – are drawn from vowel harmony in Tuvan and

Finnish. Harrison & Kaun contend that underspecification in such contexts is necessary to predict the harmonic vs. disharmonic vowels in reduplication and re-harmonization.

2.5 Prosodic features

Many features once held to be segmental – as described in the previous sections – are now assumed to be captured by certain other entities in phonological representations. Three well-known examples illustrating this reanalysis are [±syllabic], [±long], and [±stress]. For example, contrasts between syllabic vs. nonsyllabic segments, e.g. /u/ vs. /w/, were once assumed to involve the binary feature [±syllabic] (see SPE: 354) but are now captured in terms of syllable- and or moraic structure. Moraic structure (or, alternatively, skeletal structure) similarly captures contrasts between short vs. long segments, e.g. /a/ vs. /aː/, thereby eliminating the necessity for [±long]. The feature [±stress] is also superfluous given that prominence is a relational property and not one inherent to individual segments. Stress distinctions are therefore best captured in representations cast in Metrical Phonology (e.g. Hayes 1995). What these three examples have in common is that they involve not segmental features but *prosodic* ones. One question for future research is whether or not any of the segmental features commonly employed today will in the future be captured prosodically.

One proposal along these lines for the major class features [±cons] and [±son] (as well as [±syllabic]) was made by Selkirk (1984).[17] She argues that all major class features should be eliminated from phonological theory and that they be replaced by the Sonority Hierarchy and the assigment of a *sonority index* to individual segments that captures the point they occupy on that hierarchy. An example of such sonority hierarchy for English (see Selkirk 1984: 112) is provided in (31):

(31) *Sound*   *Sonority index*

Sound	Sonority index
a	10
e, o	9
i, u	8
r	7
l	6
m, n	5
s	4
v, z, ð	3
f, θ	2
b, d, g	1
p, t, k	.5

Given the hierarchy in (31) natural classes such as [+son] and [−son] can be captured by referring to adjacent sonority indices. For example, [+son] and [−son] sound have sonority indices ≥ 5 and ≤ 5 respectively. Thus, a consequence of Selkirk's analysis is that not all natural classes are captured in terms of segmental features.

Wiese (this volume), following Walsh-Dickey (1997) and Hall (1997), argues that the class of rhotics – a group of sounds sub-suming trills, central approximants, flaps and, for Wiese, certain fricatives – is an example of a natural class which is defined not in terms of some segmental feature(s), but instead prosodically. Although Wiese believes that the individual stricture types comprising the rhotics, as well as the individual r-sounds themselves, are composed of segmental features, the entire natural class of rhotics is defined in his approach prosodically. From a formal point of view Wiese captures his claim that r-sounds are a 'prosody' by analyzing this class of sound as an abstract point on the sonority hierarchy, similar to the approach taken by Selkirk (1984) in (31). Note that this proposal is at odds with the commonly made assumption that (all) of the points on the sonority hierarchy are definied featurally (see, for example, Levin 1985, Clements 1990, Grijzenhout this volume).

3. Phonetics-phonology connection

The representations discussed in the preceding section are usually
assumed to hold only in the phonological component and a mapping
process is presupposed – usually referred to as *phonetic implementation* – which converts these structures into phonetic reality. In this
section I discuss the connection between featural representations in
the phonology and their phonetic implementation. In section 3.1 I
outline the traditional generative approach to the phonetics-phonology interface and compare it with the one proposed by Clements
(this volume). In 3.2 I describe the implementation of phonological
features, focussing specifically on the proposals by Van Rooy &
Wissing (this volume) and Jessen (this volume) concerning voicing
contrasts.

3.1 Representational levels

Traditionally generative phonology draws a distinction between
various levels of representation, as shown in (32):

(32) Traditional generative approach to representational levels:

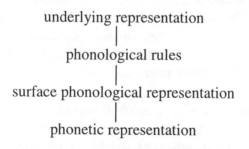

According to (32) the underlying representation is the input to the
phonological component, where phonological rules apply. The output of the phonological component is the surface phonological
representation, which is mapped onto phonetic reality (= the
phonetic representation) by the process referred to above as phonetic
implementation. Note that the model in (32) is very different from

the one presupposed in most approaches to OT (e.g. Prince & Smolensky 1993), in which output candidates are evaluated at a single representational level, which is usually assumed to correspond roughly to the surface phonological representation.

Many earlier writers assume that underspecifed representations (e.g. the one in 12b for /d/) hold only for an early stage in the phonological component and the default rules that add the missing values (which might be interspersed with phonological rules) gradually build up these representations so that the surface phonological representation (and the phonetic representation) are fully specified. Evidence against this approach comes from some of the experimental studies in the literature demonstrating that certain features are underspecified in *phonetic* representations (see, for example Keating 1988b and Cohn 1993). For this reason many current researchers do not believe that the surface phonological representation or the phonetic representation necessarily have to be fully specified. An example of this kind of 'surface underspecification' can be seen in the privative approach in (13), in which /d/ lacks specification for [cont] throughout the entire phonology. In the present volume several authors similarly propose models in which various features are (permanently) underspecified in the phonological component, e.g. Avery & Idsardi, Ghini, Grijzenhout.

As in the traditional generative view sketched above, Clements (this volume) assumes that fewer features are necessary at the underlying level than at the surface phonological (or phonetic) levels. For Clements only *distinctive* features are present at the underlying level; features necessary in the phonological component due to their presence in natural classes and phonological rules are introduced derivationally. Unlike the traditional view, Clements rejects default/redundancy rules, which insert predictable feature values. Instead, the insertion of redundant features is accomplished with his Activation Criterion:

(33) The Activation Criterion
      In any language, redundant feature values are specified in all and only the segments in which they are active.

A feature is 'active' in any segment or segment class which satisfies a term in a constraint mentioning that feature.

Clements illustrates the Activation Criterion with examples from Zoque. In that language voicing is nondistinctive for sonorants and obstruents. However, the feature values [–voice] and [+voice] are both active in Zoque. This is the case for [–voice], since Zoque has a constraint banning [+nasal] [–voice, –cont] sequences, as in (34a); we also know that [+voice] is active because Zoque has the repair operation in (34b) which has the function of inserting [+voice].

(34) a.   *[+nasal] [–voice, –cont]
     b.   Insert([+voice])

Rule (34a) is necessary to account for the voicing of /p t k/ after a nasal consonant, e.g. /n-tatah/ [ndatah] 'my father'. Restricting our attention to this example, Clements proposes that all segments in a word like /n-tatah/ are unspecified for [voice] in the underlying representation. Since Zoque has the constraint in (34a), the Activation Criterion ensures that /p t k/ receive [–voice] in the phonological component; hence both /t/'s in /n-tatah/ are [–voice] at this representational level. At the surface phonological representation the first /t/ in /tatah/ becomes [+voice] by (34b).

3.2 Phonetic implementation of phonological features

Most generative approaches recognize a difference between distinctive features, which are understood to be abstract phonological entities, and their concrete *articulatory* or *acoustic correlates* (see, for example, Jakobson, Fant & Halle 1952, Halle 1983: 94ff.). Thus, according to this view, distinctive features form the link between articulatory and acoustic properties of speech sounds. This approach is illustrated in (35) with respect to the feature [labial]. The first of the acoustic correlates, namely the downward transition of all vowel formants, is evident when labials occur next to vowels and the second one, i.e. the falling burst spectrum, when labials occur between consonants.

(35) *acoustic correlate*   *feature*   *articulatory correlate*
      negative F transition ———→ [labial]——— lip constriction
      falling burst spectrum

The translation of discrete phonological representations – like the feature [labial] in (35) – into real life physiological activity, by it articulatory or acoustic, is accomplished by phonetic implementation (see Pierrehumbert 1990, Keating 1990).

Two contrastive approaches to the implementation of the distinctive feature [voice] have been proposed in the literature. According to the broad interpretation (Lisker & Abramson 1964), a contrast between two stops at the phonological level can be implemented phonetically in three different ways: (i) voice onset precedes stop release (negative voice onset time), (ii) voice onset immmediately follows stop release (short-lag voice onset time), or (iii) voice onset substantially lags behind stop release (long-lag voice onset time). According to the narrow interpretation (Jakobson 1949) [voice] is employed as a distinctive feature only when actual vocal fold vibration is present in the production of the marked member of the voiced vs. voiceless pair.

Both approaches have been defended in recent studies. For example, on the basis of lowering and raising effects of [+voice] and [–voice] on the fundamental frequency of adjacent vowels, Kingston & Diehl (1994) argue in favor of the broad interpretation. On the other hand the narrow interpretation of [voice] is defended by Keating (1990), Iverson & Salmons (1995), and Jessen (1998). Two studies in the present volume also defend the narrow interpretation, namely Van Rooy & Wissing, and Jessen.

Van Rooy & Wissing (this volume) offer phonological and phonetic evidence in support of the narrow interpretation of [voice], namely rules of regressive voicing assimilation. Specifically, the authors argue that the existence of the distinctive feature [voice] – defined narrowly above – implies the existence of regressive voicing assimilation in the same language. The authors investigate languages commonly assumed to have contrasts between voiced vs. voiceless obstruents, e.g. Dutch, Polish, Armenian, Tswana, Afrikaans, and show that in these languages there are productive processes of regressive voicing assimilation. Apparent counterexamples (i.e. languages with voicing oppositions in which no regressive voicing assimilation occurs) are accounted for by analyzing the voicing distinctions not with the feature [voice], but instead with [spread]. For example, all of the languages listed above employ [voice] as a distinctive feature to distinguish between the stops usually transcribed as /p t k/ vs. /b d g/. By contrast, a language like English does not distinguish /p t k/ vs. /b d g/ with [voicc], but instead with [spread] (see also Iverson & Salmons 1995, Avery & Idsardi this volume and Jessen this volume, who have a similar view).

Jessen (this volume) discusses the phonetic (i.e. acoustic/auditory) correlates of the feature [voice] (as well as [tense]) in stop consonants.[18] An important innovation of Jessen's contribution is his distinction between 'basic correlates' and 'non-basic correlates' of any given feature (see figure 1 below). The former are those correlates which are unique to a particular feature, and which have particularly high contextual stability and perceptual saliency. The term 'contextual stability' means that in the majority of contexts in the language in question the relevant distinction is expressed by the basic correlate.

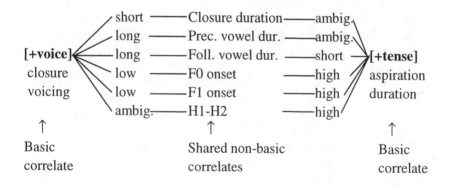

Figure 1.

Figure 1. Model of the range of acoustic/auditory correlates of [tense] and [voice]

In contrast to the basic correlates, the non-basic correlates have less perceptual saliency and less contextual stability. Jessen proposes that the non-basic correlates for [voice] are the same as those for [tense].

For example, in German the difference between /p t k/ and /b d g/ is expressed in almost all contexts as a significantly longer aspiration for the former set. Jessen argues that the basic correlates such as [tense] in the /p t k/ vs. /b d g/ contrast is characterized by high perceptual saliency. This can be demonstrated by manipulating the basic correlate by itself in a speech perception experiment. As Jessen shows, such experiments lead to a categorical perception.

Notes

* This article has benefitted from comments by Laura Downing, Silke Hamann, Aditi Lahiri and Marzena Rochoń. All errors are my own.
1 The articles in the present volume are a selection of the papers presented at the Conference on Distinctive Theory held in October 1999 at the Zentrum für Allgemeine Sprachwissenschaft in Berlin. I would like to take this opportunity to thank all of the anonymous reviewers for the time they took to evaluate all of the submitted papers.
2 In some earlier studies acoustic/auditory features have been proposed, e.g. Lahiri & Blumstein (1984).
3 Since there are several studies in which individual features in the Jakobsonian, SPE and post-SPE systems are discussed (e.g. Keating 1988a, Clements & Hume 1995), I do not provide an entire set of features in this introductory article. Instead, I introduce individual features when they become relevant.
4 For one of the earliest approaches to features along these lines see Trubetzkoy (1939), who proposed that certain oppositions are 'gradual'.
5 Voiceless segments like [s] in the second example in (2a) are *neutral* in the sense that they are not capable of bearing the feature [+nasal].
6 The structure in (6) only includes certain features, whereas others have been ignored, e.g. [±strident], [±lateral].
   In (6) and below a number of features have been abbreviated: [±cons] = [±consonantal], [±son] = [±sonorant], [±cont] = [±continuant], [±spread] = [±spread glottis], [±constricted] = [±constricted glottis], [±ant] = [±anterior], and [±distr] = [±distributed].
7 See, however, Kaisse (1992), who argues that [cons], as a feature that can spread in assimilations, is linked to the Root node by an association line.
8 [±apical] and [±posterior] serve a similar function to the features [±distr] and [±ant] respectively in (6).
9 Recall that I am only considering three features in the representations in (12) and (13) and no others.

10 By contrast, Cho (1991) and Lombardi (1996) argue that Coronal is a binary feature. According to Lombardi only rules that apply late in a derivation can make reference to the minus value.

11 The equivalent of 'features' in Dependency Phonology (e.g. Anderson & Ewen 1987, van der Hulst 1989) and Government Phonology (e.g. Kaye *et al.* 1985) are also asumed to be unary.
By contrast, one also finds in the literature a defense of certain binary features, e.g. Ní Chiosáin (1991, 1994) argues that [±back] is binary and not privative.

12 Underspecified phonological representations are not without controversy. Some of the studies in which underspecification theory has been challenged include Clements (1988), Christdas (1988), McCarthy & Taub (1991), and Mohanan (1991).

13 Rule (16) is stated linearly. One could alternatively recast the rule in a non-linear fashion, as in (5b), where [+round] is added to a segment that is [–low, +back]

14 Note that any analysis also needs to account for why the /i/ in the representation in (17) does not undergo spreading.

15 One could alternatively argue that [±round] and not [±back] is distinctive.

16 The arguments that have been presented in the literature for and against Contrastive and Radical Underspecification will not be discussed here. See Kenstowicz (1994) and van der Hulst & Ewen (2001) for recent overviews.

17 A similar position on the full specification of roots in Turkish is taken by Clements & Sezer (1982).

18 See also Hankamer & Aissen (1974), Dogil & Luschützky (1990), van der Hulst & Ewen (1991) for various proposals concerning the elimination of [cons] and/or [son].

19 The latter feature is basically used in the same way other phonologists use [spread] (see above). One of the major differences between [spread] as described in the preceding sections and Jessen's feature [tense] is the scope of possible phonetic correlates of these features. For most researchers [spread] refers simply to aspiration in stops (which is interpreted to mean that the glottis is spread), whereas [tense] refers both to aspiration and to the durational events of the relevant consonant in its context.

References

Anderson, J. & C. Ewen
   1987   *Principles of Dependency Phonology*. Cambridge: Cambridge University Press.
Archangeli, D.
   1988   Aspects of underspecification theory. *Phonology* 5.2: 183-207.

Avery, P. & K. Rice
1989   Segment structure and coronal underspecification. *Phonology* 6: 179-200.

Boersma, P.
1998   *Functional Phonology. Formalizing the Interactions between Articulatory and Perceptual Drives.* The Hague: LOT.

Cho, Y. - M. Y.
1991   On the universality of the coronal articulator. In: Paradis, C. & J.-F. Prunet (1991a: 159-179)

Chomsky, N. and M. Halle
1968   *The Sound Pattern of English.* New York: Harper & Row.

Christdas, P.
1988   The phonology and morphology of Tamil. Ph.D. dissertation, Cornell University.

Clements, G. N.
1985   The geometry of phonological features. *Phonology Yearbook* 2: 225–252.

1988   Toward a substantive theory of feature specification. *Proceedings of the Northeast Linguistic Society* 18: 79-93.

1990   The role of the sonority cycle in core syllabification. In Kingston, J. and M. Beckman (eds), *Papers in Laboratory Phonology I: Between the Grammar and Physics of Speech*, 283-333. Cambridge: Cambridge University Press.

Clements, G. N. and E. V. Hume
1995   The internal organization of speech sounds. In: J. Goldsmith (ed.), *The Handbook of Phonological Theory*, 245-306. Oxford: Blackwell.

Clements, G. N. & E. Sezer
1982   Vowel and consonant disharmony in Turkish. In H. van der Hulst & N. Smith (eds.), *The Structure of Phonological Representations, Part II*, 213-255. Dordrecht: Foris.

Cohn, A.
1993   The status of nasalized continuants. In: M. K. Huffman and R. A. Krakow (eds.), *Phonetics and Phonology 5: Nasals, Nasalization and the Velum*, 329-367. San Diego: Academic Press.

Dogil, G. & H. C. Luschützky
1990   Notes on sonority and segmental strength. *Rivista di Linguistica* 2.2: 3-54.

Durie, M.
1985   *A Grammar of Acehnese.* Verhandelingen van het Koninklijk Instituut voor Taal-, Land- en Volkenkunde 112. Dordrecht: Foris.

Flemming, E.
  1995   Auditory representations in phonology. Ph.D. dissertation, UCLA.
Gnanadesikan, A.
  1997   Phonology with ternary scales. Ph.D. dissertation, University of
            Massachusetts at Amherst.
Goldsmith, J.
  1976   Autosegmental phonology. Ph.D. dissertation, MIT.
  1990   *Autosegmental and Metrical Phonology.* Oxford: Blackwell.
Hall, T. A.
  1997   *The Phonology of Coronals.* Amsterdam: Benjamins.
Halle, M.
  1983   On distinctive features and their articulatory implementation.
            Natural Language and Linguistic Theory 1: 91-105.
  1995   Feature geometry and feature spreading. *Linguistic Inquiry* 26: 1-46.
Halle, M. and K. N. Stevens
  1971   A note on laryngeal features. *MIT Research Laboratory of
            Electronics Quarterly Progress Report* 101: 198–213.
Hankamer, J. & J. Aissen
  1974   The sonority hierarchy. In: A. Bruck *et al.* (eds.) *Papers from the
            Parasession on Natural Phonology*, 131-145. Chicago.
Hayes, B.
  1986   Assimilation as spreading in Toba Batak. *Linguistic Inquiry* 17: 467-
            499.
  1995   *Metrical Stress Theory: Principles and Case Studies.* Chicago: Uni-
            versity of Chicago Press.
Hulst, H. van der
  1989   Atoms of segmental structure: components, gestures and depen-
            dency. *Phonology* 6: 253-303.
Hulst, H. van der & C. Ewen
  1991   Major class and manner features. In: P. M. Bertinetto, M. Kensto-
            wicz & M. Loporcaro (eds.) *Certamen Phonologicum II: Papers
            from the 1990 Cortona Phonology Meeting*, 19-41. Torino:
            Rosenberg & Sellier.
  2001   *The Phonological Structure of Words.* Cambridge: Cambridge Uni-
            versity Press.
Hulst, H. van der & J. van de Weijer
  1995   Vowel harmony. In: J. Goldsmith (ed.) *The Handbook of Phonolo-
            gical Theory*, 495-534. Oxford: Blackwell.
Inkelas, S.
  1995   The consequences of optimization for underspecification. In: E.
            Buckley & S. Iatridou (eds.), *Proceedings of the Twenty-Fifth*

Northeastern Linguistics Society I, 287-302. Amherst, Mass.: GLSA.

Itô, J., R. A. Mester & J. Padgett
1995   Licensing and underspecification in Optimality Theory. *Linguistic Inquiry* 26: 571-614.

Iverson, G. K. and J. C. Salmons
1995   Aspiration and laryngeal representation in Germanic. *Phonology* 12: 369–396.

Jakobson, R.
1949   On the identification of phonemic entities. *Selected Writings I: Phonological Studies,* 418-425. s'Gravenhage: Mouton.

Jakobson, R., G. Fant and M. Halle
1952   *Preliminaries to Speech Analysis.* Cambridge, Mass.: The MIT Press [sixth printing, 1965].

Jessen, M.
1998   *The Phonetics and Phonology of Tense and Lax Obstruents in German.* Amsterdam: Benjamins.

Kaisse, E.
1992   Can [consonantal] spread? *Language* 68: 313-332.

Kaye, J.
1971   Nasal harmony in Desano. *Linguistic Inquiry* 2: 37-56.

Kaye, J., J. Lowenstamm & J.-R. Vergnaud
1985   The internal structure of phonological elements: a theory of charm and government. *Phonology Yearbook* 2: 305-328.

Keating, P. A.
1988a   A survey of phonological features. Bloomington: Indiana University Linguistics Club.

1988b   Underspecification in phonetics. *Phonology* 5.2: 275-292.

1990   Phonetic representation in a generative grammar. *Journal of Phonetics* 18: 321–334.

Kenstowicz, M.
1994   *Phonology in Generative Grammar.* Oxford: Blackwell.

Kingston, J. and R. L. Diehl
1994   Phonetic knowledge. *Language* 70: 419-454.

Kirchner, R.
1997   Contrastiveness and faithfulness. *Phonology* 14: 83-111.

Ladefoged, P. & I. Maddieson
1996   *Sounds in the World's Languages.* Oxford: Blackwell.

Lahiri, A. and S. Blumstein
1984   A re-evaluation of the feature coronal. *Journal of Phonetics* 12: 133-146.

Lahiri, A. and V. Evers
1991   Palatalization and coronality. In: C. Paradis & J.-F. Prunet (eds.), *The Special Status of Coronals,* 79-100. San Diego, Academic.
Levin, J.
1985   A metrical theory of syllabicity. Ph.D. dissertation, MIT.

Lisker, L. and A. S. Abramson
1964   A cross-language study of voicing in initial stops: acoustic measurements. *Word* 20: 384-422.
Lombardi, I.
1991   Laryngeal features and laryngeal neutralization. Ph.D. dissertation, University of Massachussetts at Amherst [published 1994, New York/London: Garland].
1996   Postlexical rules and privative features. *Phonology* 13: 1-38.
Martinet, A
1964   *Elements of General Linguistics.* Chicago: University of Chicago Press.
McCarthy, J.
1988   Feature geometry and dependency: a review. *Phonetica* 43: 84-108.
McCarthy, J. and A. Taub
1992   Review of C. Paradis & J.-F. Prunet (eds.), *Phonetics and Phonology: The Special Status of Coronals. Phonology* 9.2: 363-70.
Mester, R. A. & J. Itô
1989   Feature predictability and underspecification: Palatal prosody in Japanese mimetics. *Language* 65: 258-293.
Mohanan, K. P.
1991   On the bases of radical underspecification. *Natural Language and Linguistic Theory* 9: 285-325.
Ní Chiosáin
1991   Topics in the phonology of Irish. Ph.D. dissertation, University of Massachusetts at Amherst.
1994   The representation of place features. *Phonology* 11: 89-106.
Paradis, C. & J.-F. Prunet (eds.)
1991a   *Phonetics and Phonology. The Special Status of Coronals. Internal and External Evidence.* San Diego: Academic Press.
1991b   Introduction: asymmetry and visibility. In: C. Paradis & J.-F. Prunet (1991a: 1-28).
Pierrehumbert, J.
1990   Phonological and phonetic representation. *Journal of Phonetics* 18: 375–394.
Prince, A. & P. Smolensky
1993   Optimality Theory. Ms. Rutgers University & University of Colorado.

Pulleyblank, D.
    1986   *Tone in Lexical Phonology*. Dordrecht: Reidel.
Sagey, E.
    1986   The representations of features and relations in nonlinear phonology. Ph.D. dissertation, MIT.
Selkirk, E.
    1984   On the major class features and syllable theory. In: M. Aronoff & R. T. Oehrle (eds.), *Language Sound Structure: Studies in Phonology Presented to Morris Halle by his Teacher and Students*, 107-136. Cambridge, Mass.: MIT Press.
Smolensky, P.
    1995   The initial state and the „richness of the base" in Optimality Theory. Technical report, Cognitive Science Department, Johns Hopkins University, Baltimore, Md.
Stampe, D.
    1973   *A Dissertation on Natural Phonology*. New York: Garland.
Steriade, D.
    1982   Greek prosodies and the nature of syllabification. Ph.D. dissertation, MIT.
    1987   Redundant values. *Papers from the Annual Regional Meeting, Chicago Linguistic Society* 23: 339-369.
    2000   Paradigm uniformity and the phonetics-phonology boundary. In: M. Broe & J. Pierrhumbert (eds.), *Papers in Laboratory Phonology 5*, 313-334. Cambridge: Cambridge University Press.
Trubetzkoy, N. S.
    1939   *Grundzüge der Phonologie*. Prague. [1989 Göttingen: Vandenhoeck & Ruprecht].
Walsh Dickey, L.
    1997   The phonology of liquids. Ph.D. dissertation, University of Massachusetts at Amherst.
Wiese, R.
    1996   *The Phonology of German*. Oxford: Clarendon Press.
Williamson, K.
    1977   Multivalued features for consonants. *Language* 53: 843-871.

Laryngeal dimensions, completion and enhancement

Peter Avery and William J. Idsardi

1. Introduction

In this article we present a new model of phonological representations, concentrating on laryngeal systems. Our proposals are embedded in a theory of phonology in which representational economy is an axiomatic principle. Representational economy forces the phonology to be non-redundant in the sense that phonological representations are minimally specified. Deviations from the requirements of representational economy arise only in circumstances where independent complexity requirements force additional structure to be present. Apart from these cases, representations will always be specified only to the degree necessary to represent contrast within the system. This view of phonology must be contrasted with our view of the *phonetic* representations. Unlike the phonological representations, the phonetic representations are tremendously over-specified, containing information far beyond what is necessary for the simple maintenance of contrast. This extra information is useful, but it is not required from the point of view of the phonology. In our model the phonological system *per se* makes use of only very general phonetic information, indeed the features have a much more limited role in our system. The phonological representations provide specification for the phonetic *dimensions* and not for the phonetic *features* (modulo headedness, see section 2.3). In section 2 we will introduce our model of phonological representation and sketch our theory of phonetic implementation, using laryngeal systems as our focus. We illustrate various principles in sections 3-5 with case studies of laryngeal systems: English, Japanese and Korean. In section 6 we provide some conclusions and implications of our theory. Speculations regarding the rest of the feature geometry can be found in the Appendix.

2.   Theoretical preliminaries

In (1) we contrast our model, (1b), with the current standard model of laryngeal organization, (1a) (as in Lombardi 1991 and others).

(1)   a.

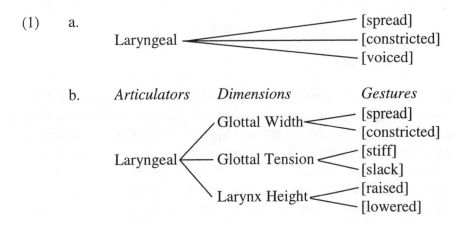

Because we depart from standard assumptions in several ways, we will explain the various aspects of the new organizational system, especially the extra layer of organizational structure.

As this paper is primarily concerned with laryngeal phonology, and indeed with only a subset of the laryngeal dimensions, we will restrict our attention to that system. Our speculations on the application of these principles of organization to the entire feature system are contained in the Appendix.

2.1.   Laryngeal motor instructions and gestures

The terminal elements in (1b) – those enclosed in square brackets – are to be interpreted as motor instructions to the articulators. Thus, they share much in common with the *gestures* of Browman and Goldstein (1989), and so we will co-opt their term. They differ from Browman and Goldstein's gestures in that in our model the gestures play a very reduced role in the *phonology*, being in general absent from the phonological representation. In our view a gesture is the smallest independent articulatory action, the action of a single muscle or muscle group. As Kim (1972: 338) states: "Speech production involves a large number of muscles, the majority of which are capable of independent control."

We carry over the features for glottal adduction, [constricted], and abduction, [spread], from previous researchers.

The features [±stiff] and [±slack] were introduced by Halle and Stevens (1971). Criticisms of these features have often focussed on the over-generation in the theory with respect to the number of systems allowed using two binary features [±stiff] and [±slack] (Lombardi 1991; Keating 1988). The theory proposed here does not suffer from such shortcomings for two reasons: 1) the gestures are privative and 2) only *dimensions* can be contrastive in obstruents (discussed in section 2.2). We are able to correctly constrain the number of phonological systems through the use of *dimensions*, discussed in section 2.2. Furthermore, some of the criticism has clearly been misplaced. Halle and Stevens explicitly intend their system to also represent tonal features – high tone is [+stiff], low tone is [+slack] – and most of the criticisms do not weigh this extra explanatory power against the added complexity. We also believe that laryngeal features capture both phonation type and tone, for details see Avery and Idsardi (2000b).

Following Ladefoged (1973), we include the two phonetic gestures that control the height of the larynx. Although common in phonetic works, these features have been largely absent from phonological models. The gesture [raised] is operative in certain ejectives and raises FØ. The gesture [lowered] is the primary gesture for implosives and lowers FØ. We will ignore larynx height in the rest of this article, but we note in passing that there are two sources of tone in this model – glottal tension and larynx height. These issues are discussed further in Avery and Idsardi (2000b; in preparation).

2.2. Laryngeal dimensions

We go beyond previous models, however, in acknowledging explicitly that muscle groups form antagonistic pairs. This constitutes the *pre-terminal* organization of the gestures, a layer that we will call the *dimensions.* Our inspiration for dimensions comes from more general studies of motor control (e.g. Sherrington 1947; Gallistel 1980; Zemlin 1998). Sherrington's crucial insight is that muscles are organized into antagonistic pairs:

"The muscles of the claw of *Astacus* are striated, and the case is interesting as one in which the co-ordination of action of two antagonistic muscles of the skeletal type is effected by the peripheral inhibition of one through the same nerve-trunk that induces active contraction of the other. But the similar co-ordination in the taxis of the skeletal musculature of vertebrates exerts its inhibition not at the periphery but in the nerve-centres. It occurs within the grey matter of the central nervous system." (Sherrington 1947: 85)

"A stimulus that excites a muscle on one side of a joint invariably inhibits excitation of the antagonistic muscle on the other side of the joint, and vice versa. Sherrington called this the principle of reciprocal inhibition." (Gallistel 1980: 58)

"... we shall be concerned chiefly with the actions of striated muscles. There are about 329 of them in the human body, and *all but two are paired muscles.* ... A muscle can exert a force in just one direction, and it is incapable of exerting any force in the opposite direction. Thus, either muscle in a functional pair may be the antagonist of the other." (Zemlin 1998: 18-27)

In our model the dimensions organize antagonistic pairs. The reciprocal antagonism of the muscles is modeled by restricting the dimensions to be non-branching. Thus, only a single muscle within a dimension can be active in any given speech sound. As stated previously, the gestures, which are the ultimate constituents of the phonological representation, do not bear the major contrastive burden and are in many ways unlike the features in traditional feature theory. They cannot be binary, as the muscle is either activated or inhibited by the activation of its antagonistic partner. For the most part, the phonology begins at one level removed from the gesture – the dimension, and this is the level that is largely responsible for contrast (see section 2.3).

The laryngeal gestures are dependents of three dimensions: Glottal Width (GW), Glottal Tension (GT) and Larynx Height (LH).

The dependents of GW are [spread] and [constricted], which are familiar from most recent theories. Our theory, however, makes different predictions about the nature of the contrasts between GW segments. Other theories allow for a contrast between [spread] and [constricted] segments at the phonological level. We, on the other hand, do not allow for such a contrast. This necessitates a reanalysis of those systems that have been analyzed using [spread] and [constricted] contrastively, for example, Korean. In section 5 we present a case study of Korean and show that the contrast of [spread] versus [constricted] is not basic but is instead derived in the phonetics. We will argue that the 'tense' consonants of Korean are in fact long segments that are enhanced with [constricted] in phonetic implementation. This is a case of phonetic over-differentiation where the underlying contrast is obscured by phonetic enhancement.

The dependents of GT are [stiff] and [slack]. Being mutually antagonistic, they cannot both be present in the same representation. Because obstruent contrasts are limited to dimensions (section 2.3), we limit the number of potential contrasts, and in this way respond to criticisms of over-generation. Because GT is normally completed with [slack] (section 2.4), the dimension node GT acts similarly to the feature [voice] in other theories. The principal difference is that we will allow more latitude in the phonetic implementation of GT.

The dependents of LH are [raised] and [lowered]. We will not consider this dimension in this article.

2.3. Contrast

We follow what we refer to as the Toronto School of Contrast (Dresher, Piggott and Rice 1995; Avery 1996). Under this view, contrasts are always of the type ∅/Marked, so that in any two-term system there is an element that has no marking and an element that has some specification. This means that for any contrasting pair, at the phonological level they differ only by the presence versus the absence of a single node.

In obstruents, only the dimensions are contrastive, not the gestures themselves. The contrastive use of gestures is severely limited.

They contrast only when they are the designated articulator (the *head* of a segment), see section 2.5 and section 5.4. The dimensions are the primary interface between the phonology and the phonetics. Gestures are progressively added to the representations as they become more phonetic. All structure above the gesture is phonological and purely cognitive in nature.

Restricting ourselves to GT and GW systems, we predict that the basic two-way systems will involve a Ø/GT or a Ø/GW contrast. Of course, a length contrast is also available phonologically, and the dimensions can be combined. In (2) we outline the predicted systems which employ the GW and GT dimensions.

(2) Predicted phonological systems

	Contrasts	*Example*	*Typical characteristics*
a.	Ø	Tamil	no contrast
b.	Ø/GT	Spanish	fully voiced versus unmarked
c.	Ø/GW	English	aspirated versus unmarked
d.	Ø/GT/GW	Thai	fully voiced, aspirated and plain
e.	Ø/GT/GW /GT+GW	Hindi	full cross-classification including voiced aspirate

In other languages, such as Korean and Swiss German, length is also used contrastively. In more complex systems, such as Igbo, the LH dimension is recruited contrastively as well.

In sections 3-5 we illustrate the workings of the theory through case studies of three rather different laryngeal systems: English, Japanese and Korean. It is in the study of these systems that the validity of our theoretical assumptions will be evaluated.

2.4.   Phonetic completion and enhancement

Our theory of minimal contrast ensures that phonological representations are generally incomplete (i.e. underspecified). Thus, phonological representations are not by themselves pronounceable. In order to become pronounceable, the mapping from phonology to phonetics must add the missing gestural specifications. We will call this process *completion*. Bare dimension nodes are completed through the insertion of a dependent gesture.

We distinguish completion from *enhancement*. While completion merely involves the additions of gestural information to the already present dimensions, enhancement involves the addition of a dimension node, turning a phonological Ø/X contrast into a phonetic equipollent (X/Y) contrast. Enhancement leads to the widely observed phonetic over-differentiation of contrast.

As the bare dimension nodes are generally the phonologically contrastive elements in the system, we must leave it to completion and enhancement to give the segment its phonetic content. Each bare dimension has a *default* completion, which is universal. For GT and GW the default completions are [slack] and [spread] respectively. This accords with the fact that in most languages with a two-way laryngeal contrast either a plain versus voiced distinction or a plain versus aspirated distinction is found. However, there are also context-sensitive completions, also universal, which are sensitive to inter-articulator phasing. One of the principles governing gestural completion is Kingston's Law, given in (3).

(3) Kingston's Law: a gesture ↔ phasing bi-directional relation
     a. GW in phase with stop ↔ [constricted]
     b. otherwise (GW out of phase with stop) ↔ [spread]

We draw here on the important research conducted by Kingston (1985, 1990) in specifying the relation between phasing and GW completion, though Kingston does not formulate a law in these terms. Kingston's Law is particularly prevalent in laryngeal completions. When GW is phased with the closure of a stop it is completed with [constricted], otherwise it will be completed with [spread] (the default). This is in accord with Kingston's finding that aspiration is generally not associated with the closure of a stop but that glottalization is. Under special circumstances, such as assimilation (see section 5.4) stops can become [spread]. In this case GW spreads until it is out of phase with the stop closure. Languages may also completely exclude the use of certain gestures, leading to language-particular violations of Kingston's Law. Japanese (section 4) presents such a case, eschewing [constricted].

Our second principle, building directly on Vaux (1998), is Vaux's Law, (4).

(4) Vaux's Law: [fricative] → GW

Vaux's Law is not a principle of completion, but rather defines an obligatory enhancement relation. Recall that enhancement differs from completion in that enhancement adds a new dimension leading to phonetic over-differentiation. Vaux's Law ensures that fricatives are enhanced with GW whenever possible. If a system has a contrast between an unmarked fricative and a GT fricative, as in Japanese, then the unmarked fricative will be enhanced with GW. The net result is that the unmarked fricative will be completed with [spread]. If, instead, the contrast is between an unspecified fricative and a GW fricative, as in English, then the GW fricative is completed with [spread] and the unmarked fricative will not receive GW. That is, Vaux's Law is suspended in cases where GW is contrastive for fricatives. In general, enhancement is restricted to introducing non-contrastive dimensions. Consequently, the only systems in which we would expect to find true plain fricatives are those in which GW is not available for enhancement, i.e. systems that employ GW contrastively.

2.5. Heads

There are cases in which terminal gestures can be employed contrastively. Such cases can be succinctly explained, once the notion of *head* is introduced. Following Dresher and van der Hulst (1999), all segments have a head, which is the locus of greatest constriction in the segment. Thus, the notion "head" takes on the function of the "designated articulator" in other models (Sagey 1986; Halle 1995). As Dresher and van der Hulst document, heads can have greater structure than dependents. This implies that not only can heads contain more specification but also the corollary – dependents have less specification. Therefore, since in obstruents laryngeal dimensions are always dependents, the laryngeal dimensions must be less specified, and consequently there are no contrastive laryngeal gestures in obstruent systems. In segments containing only a laryngeal component, there is no oral constriction and thus the laryngeal dimension node must be the head. Heads must have at least a minimal amount of structure, and in this case the only available structure are the gestural dependents. When GW is the head, it must be specified for [spread] or [constricted], yielding the pure laryngeals /h/ and /ʔ/, respectively. Unlike GW, it is apparently the case that GT and LH cannot function as segmental heads. We know of no language that has independent segments that are only specified for GT or LH, but we must leave this question to further research.

3.   English: GW invariance

In this section we establish two points: 1) the laryngeal contrast in English stops is of the Ø-GW type, and 2) English provides strong support for the claim that it is the *dimension* rather than the *gesture* that is contrastive. Space limitations prevent us from presenting more than a sketch of the laryngeal phonology of English, see Avery and Idsardi (in prep.) for details.

3.1.   English as a Ø/GW system

Iverson and Salmons (1995) present both synchronic and diachronic evidence that the voicing contrast in Germanic languages is best analyzed as a two-way distinction between an unmarked segment and one that is commonly aspirated. We agree that the glottal opening gesture involved in making an aspirated segment signals the marked member of the contrast, but we propose that the contrast is at the level of the GW dimension node, rather than the [spread] gesture. Support for this claim can be found in English in the stability of the phonetic cues for the GW segments as opposed to the unmarked segments. We see this in the relative lack of consistent cues found in the unmarked (that is, the so-called voiced) segments and their phonological inertness (especially as assimilation triggers). These are the properties we take to be the hallmarks of the unmarked member of a contrastive pair and the central cues in acquisition. Clearly, phonological inertness must be a primary guide to the child in the setting up of underlying contrasts. If there is no phonological evidence for the presence of a feature through its activity in the phonological processes of the language, then there is no reason for the child to utilize the feature in constructing the inventory. While we believe that phonological inertness is a necessary condition for the unmarked status we are also convinced that inertness alone is not sufficient. The marked member of an opposition should also be relatively tightly distributed around a set of acoustic and auditory cues for the dimensional contrast: that is, the marked feature should display something that we refer to as *dimensional invariance*. This is not to deny that there could be contexts where contrasts are weakened or even completely neutralized, as clearly this is a common occurrence. Rather what we intend by this is that there will be contexts where the contrast is sharply indicated by the distributional properties of the acoustic and/or articulatory cues for the marked member of the contrast pair, and that such cues will be a signal to the contrastive *dimension*. Let us take for example the distinction between sounds such as /p/ and /b/ in English in onset position before a stressed syllable. In this case, the cues for the /p/ are consistent, the /p/ being marked by the presence of aspiration. On the other hand, the /b/ is sometimes fully voiced, sometimes partially voiced, and sometimes completely voiceless. While there is no overlap between the two segments, the distribution of the /b/ is quite scattered as compared to the /p/ (for phonetic studies see Docherty 1992). It is this scattering that must be compared to the invariant cues that signal the marked member of the contrast.

3.2. English fricatives

The obstruents of English contrast unmarked segments with GW segments. We will justify this claim first with a brief examination of the fricatives. The primary evidence comes from phonetic studies of

/s/ and /z/ but we are confident that these results extend to the other fricatives as well. Smith (1997) studied /s/ and /z/ in connected discourse (see also Scully 1971, 1979, 1992). She found that /z/ is variably realized as voiced or plain depending on surrounding phonetic context, while /s/ is consistently realized as voiceless. The oral airflow is consistently higher for /s/ than /z/, even when acoustically the distinction with the fricative is neutralized, e.g. *bus/buzz* (a 'near merger' effect). This higher airflow of /s/ is best explained by a larger glottal opening, which is also confirmed from trans-illumination studies. This dimensional invariance of /s/ indicates it is underlyingly specified for the dimension node GW and subject to completion with the gesture [spread], the default GW completion. That /z/ varies is entirely consistent with the claim that it has no active laryngeal specification and thus receives *contextual voicing* (see Avery 1996).

In phonetic implementation, the plain fricatives of English do not acquire the gesture [spread] by Vaux's Law because Vaux's Law is suspended in cases where GW is the contrastive dimension. In general contrastive dimensions cannot be used for enhancement.

3.3. English stops

Of more interest to us than the realization of the fricatives is the behavior of the stops. Like the fricatives, we find that it is the so-called 'voiceless' series that is always realized with the GW dimension, while the 'voiced' series varies depending on the surrounding segmental environment (again, see Docherty 1992 for a detailed review of the phonetics literature). What is most interesting in English, however, is the phonetic completion of the GW stops. In this case, they appear to be sensitive to phasing relations and thus subject to Kingston's Law.

The basic facts are: 1) when GW stops are initial in an onset, they are aspirated and the peak of aspiration is coordinated with the release of the stop, devoicing any following sonorant, (5a-f), 2) in syllable final position, these stops are generally unreleased and

glottalized, (5g-i). This aspiration is realized either on the offset of the stop or on a following sonorant.

(5) Syllable initial stops
    a. [pʰe]   'pay'   b. [tʰi]   'tea'   c. [kʰi]   'key'
    d. [pʰr̥e]   'pray'   e. [tʰr̥e]   'tray'   f. [kʰr̥e]   'cray'
    Syllable-final stops
    g. [hiˀp]   'heap'   h. [hiˀt]   'heat'   i. [huˀk]   'hook'

Thus, when an obstruent stop is in a position that allows for release, as in onset position, it is completed with [spread]. This gesture is realized on the offset of the stop and may even overlap with a following onset consonant. If the stop is unreleased, as it often is in syllable final position, then the stop is completed with the gesture [constricted]. This is in accord with Kingston's Law but most importantly from our perspective it shows that the dependents of the GW are not behaving contrastively. They are clearly alternate realizations of a single contrastive dimension.

3.4. Conclusion

In English we see two types of variable behavior in the stops. The unmarked stops are realized as voiced or voiceless depending on the precise phonetic context. On the other hand, the GW stops can be either aspirated or glottalized depending on phasing relations. Crucially, the bare GW dimension node in the representation of the GW stops of English allows us to account for the alternation between [spread] and [constricted], without any use of deletion processes. Also, by restricting contrast to dimension nodes we cannot create incompatible specifications which would then have to be identified and resolved through a constraint such as *[spread constricted].

As stated at the outset of this section, we are only presenting a thumbnail sketch of the English system as a full analysis would take us far beyond the concerns of this paper. We have ignored the status of foot-medial stops, flapping and reduction to glottal stop after glottalization. We must refer the reader to Avery & Idsardi (in prep.) for the full analysis of the English system.

4.   Japanese: GW Enhancement of a GT system

In section 3 we saw that GW is a contrastive dimension in English, marking the voiceless obstruents. In this section, we discuss the laryngeal system of Japanese in which GW is used as an enhancement.

In Japanese, the interaction between a phonological process known as *rendaku* (sequential voicing) and a morpheme structure constraint known as Lyman's Law (Lyman 1885, 1894; Mester and Itô 1986; Clements this volume) demonstrates that the primary contrast must be Ø/GT. *Rendaku*, illustrated in (6), is a process by which the initial consonant of the second member of certain compounds becomes voiced.

(6) *Rendaku*
    a.   ori   +   kami   → origami
         'fold'   'paper'   'origami'
    b.   yama   +   tera   → yamadera
         'mountain'   'temple'   'mountain temple'

Rendaku is blocked by Lyman's Law, a constraint operating on the native vocabulary of Japanese that disallows the occurrence of two voiced obstruents in the same morpheme. Therefore, if the target morpheme already contains a voiced obstruent, the initial obstruent of the second member of the compound will not be voiced as illustrated in (7).

(7) *Rendaku* blocked by Lyman's Law

    kami   +   kaze   → kamikaze
    'god'   'wind'   'divine wind'

The fact that *rendaku* creates voiced obstruents, and that it is blocked by the presence of other voiced obstruents in the same domain indicates that the voiced series is marked in Japanese. Therefore, *ren-daku* is the insertion of a floating GT dimension node in conjunction with the compounding process. The floating GT is then associated with the initial consonant of the second member of the compound. The fact that *rendaku* requires grammatical information (i.e. that it is restricted to a particular type of compound), shows that *rendaku* is phonological rather than phonetic. This phonological evidence decides in favor of a Ø/GT system.

In Japanese, we also find a process of high-vowel devoicing. This involves the devoicing of a high vowel especially between two voiceless obstruents as shown in (8).

(8) a. [kippu] 'ticket'   b. [kiku] 'hear'

Tsuchida (1997) shows that vowel devoicing in Japanese is due to the presence of a [spread] gesture in voiceless obstruents, indicating the presence of GW phonetically (see also Varden 1998). EMG, glottographic and trans-illumination studies (Hirose and Ushijima 1978; Yoshioka, Löfqvist and Hirose 1982) confirm the presence of [spread] on Japanese voiceless obstruents. Thus, phonetically Japanese voiceless obstruents are [spread] not plain. However, we have argued above that the primary contrast, based on the phonology of Japanese is Ø/GT. Our theory, constrained by the principle of *representational economy*, eschews phonological overdifferentiation, thus excluding an analysis in which the contrast in a two-way system is equipollent, GW/GT. We propose instead that the Ø/GT phonological system is enhanced by the insertion of the non-contrastive GW dimension, leading to the subsequent introduction of [spread]. GW will spread onto neighboring vowels to satisfy its phasing requirements, leading to vowel devoicing through trajectory smoothing. Our account agrees with Tsuchida's other findings, namely that vowel devoicing is highly variable, just as would be expected of a phonetic, rather than a strictly phonological process.

5. Korean: [constricted] is not distinctive

In Korean there is a three-way distinction among the stops. The series are traditionally described as plain voiceless, aspirated and tense (or fortis). The analysis of the tense series has long been controversial. Phonetically these segments have both a [constricted] gesture and long closure duration, making it unclear which aspect is the primary contrast, since in previous theories both length and [constricted] are available as distinctive properties. Thus, Lombardi (1991) has proposed that the feature [constricted] is present underlyingly on the tense series. Then, presumably, the length of the closure duration is supplied by a phonetic rule of Korean, though Lombardi does not discuss this. For others (e.g. Martin 1952) the difference between the tense consonants and the other series is length, an analysis that is also reflected in the Hangul orthography.

Our theory prevents us from adopting Lombardi's analysis, as this would require a sub-dimensional contrast, something that is prohibited when the dimension is not the head. We are thus forced to look elsewhere for the contrastive property, and length is the obvious candidate. Moreover, there is striking phonological evidence confirming the primacy of length as the contrastive property when all of the relevant segments are considered. We begin by discussing the fricatives (section 5.1) and then consider the stops (section 5.2) and the interactions with /h/ (section 5.3). Taken together, the facts show that the length analysis is clearly superior to the [constricted] analysis.

5.1. Korean fricatives

Our analysis of the Korean fricative system owes a tremendous debt to Iverson (1983), which explains the phonetics and phonology of the fricatives very clearly. The fricative system is much simpler than the stop system, as Korean has only two fricatives (we ignore the palatalized allophonic variants). Phonetically, the Korean fricatives are aspirated, [s^h], and long [s:]. This is clearly an example of phonetic over-differentiation as the fricatives differ in *both* aspiration and length. Importantly, [s:] is *not* constricted, although its glottal width is about half that of [s^h] (Kagaya 1974; Iverson 1983). Spectrograms (Kagaya 1974, Lee 2000) show that the aspiration following [s^h] covers a substantial part of the following vowel. This is a general fact about aspiration in Korean, as there is also an inverse correlation between the length of aspiration and the length of the following vowel (Oh and Lee 1997; Roberts and Lee 1997). We conclude that GW is always bipositional in Korean, a fact that will be crucial in our analysis. Formally, this is a condition requiring that a singly linked GW node spread, as in (9).

(9) GW spreading:

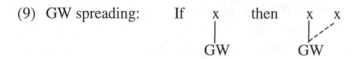

Since fricatives normally receive GW through Vaux's Law, and we know of no phonetic reason for lengthening one of the fricatives, we analyze the phonological contrast in the fricatives to be one of length. Underlyingly, [s^h] is /s/, and [s:] is /s:/. The laryngeal properties of both segments follow from Vaux's Law, (repeated in (10)), GW spreading, (9), and GW completion, (11).

(10) Vaux's Law: [fricative] → GW

(11) GW completion:

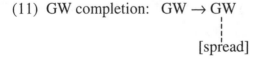

The underlying fricatives are shown in (12). (The C and V timing nodes are used here for expository purposes only. We also omit irrelevant intervening structure, in particular the Oral Place node).

(12) Underlying representations

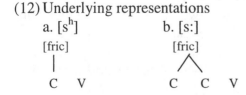

The application of Vaux's Law creates the structures in (13). Although GW is contrastive for Korean stops (see below), it is not contrastive in the fricatives. Therefore, Vaux's Law can apply in (13).

(13) Vaux's Law

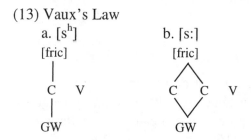

To meet the bipositional requirement, GW spreads in (14a) onto the following vowel position, ultimately devoicing the initial portion of the vowel. Since GW is already bipositional in (14b), no spreading is necessary.

(14) GW spreading

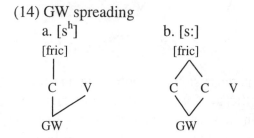

Finally, GW is phonetically completed with [spread] as in (15).

(15) GW completion

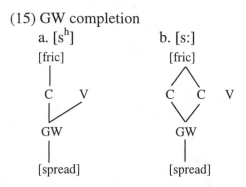

Notice that phonetically both the length of the [fricative] gestures and the relative timing of the [spread] gesture differ for the two fricatives and that this is captured representationally. Our analysis requires only a single statement that is specific to Korean: that GW must be bipositional. We now turn to the stops.

5.2. Korean stops

Given the existence of a length contrast in the simpler system of the fricatives, the most parsimonious analysis will also employ length in the stop system. Thus, we propose that Korean has the three-way contrast Ø/long/GW as shown in (16).

(16) Underlying representations

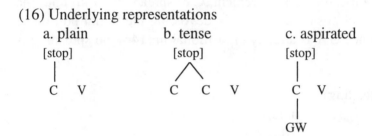

    a. plain   b. tense   c. aspirated

As noted above, phonetically the tense stops are both long and [constricted]. This property is specific to Korean, and not universal, as other languages, such as Italian, have plain long stops. So Korean contains a language-specific process which inserts GW onto bipositional stops, (17). This process also conforms to the bipositional requirement on GW, (9).

(17) GW insertion on long stops

Because the GW feature is in phase with the closure of the stop, Kingston's Law requires completion with [constricted]. The phonetic representation of the stops is given in (18).

(18) Phonetic representations

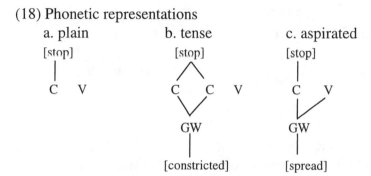

a. plain	b. tense	c. aspirated

In (18a) the plain stop receives no additional features and is realized as plain. In (18b), the long stop receives GW, and is completed with [constricted]. In (18c) GW spreads onto the vowel, devoicing the initial portion of the vowel, yielding the "heavy" aspiration characteristic of Korean. We are thus able to derive the phonetic properties of the long stops from independent principles. We will now discuss additional support from the process of tensification.

5.3. Post-obstruent tensification

In Korean, plain obstruents become tense after another obstruent, as shown in (19). Because (19a) is a compound, an analogous monomorphemic example with /p^h + k/ is also provided.

(19)

Cluster	Result	Example
a. /k^h + p/	→ [kp']	/puʌk^h patak / → [puʌkp'adak] 'kitchen floor'
/p^h + k/	→ [pk']	/tʌp^{h}kæ/ → [tʌpk'æ] 'cover'
b. /k + p^h/	→ [kp^h]	/cakp^{h}um/ → [cakp^{h}um] 'a piece of work'
c. /k + p/	→ [kp']	/kikpinca/ → [kikp'inja] 'poor person'

Tensification is the result of three more general processes – Oral Place spread, GW spread and GW insertion. We provide derivations below. The underlying representations are shown in (20).

(20)   a. /kʰ + p/   b. /k + pʰ/   c. /k + p/

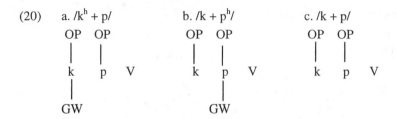

The obstruents come to share manner features through the spreading of the Oral Place node, which dominates the manner feature [stop] (see the Appendix). This, coupled with GW spreading, gives the results shown in (21). In other cases, such as /p + k/ the Oral Place node of the left-hand stop is then deleted, and the result is total assimilation (see Iverson and Lee 1995).

(21) Oral Place and Glottal width spreading
     a. /kʰ + p/   b. /k + pʰ/   c. /k + p/

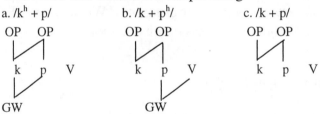

After OP spreads, [stop] will be shared, so the structural description for GW insertion, (17), is met in (21c).

(22) GW insertion
     a. /kʰ + p/   b. /k + pʰ/   c. /k + p/

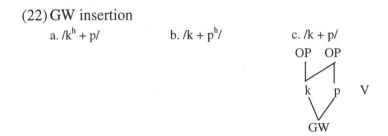

As GW is in phase with [stop] in (21a) and (22c), it is completed with [constricted]. In (21b), GW is out of phase with [stop], and therefore it is completed with [spread].

(23) GW completion

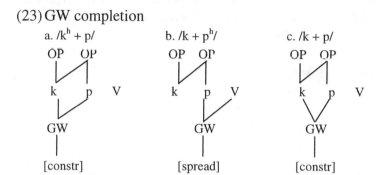

Note that our analysis requires no deletion whatsoever, only realization.[1] Korean shows the same result as in English, that the GW series can show up as either [spread] or [constricted] depending on its phasing relations.

5.4. Korean /h/

Our analysis receives striking support from the behavior of /h/ when it is in contact with obstruents (Oh 1997; Kang, Lee and Lee 1997). We will consider /h/ in two contexts: prior to fricatives and prior to stops. We show that the properties of /h/ follow from the fact that it is a GW-headed segment, and therefore is gesturally specified with [spread] underlyingly, as in (24).

(24) Representation of /h/

C
|
GW
|
[spread]

Now consider the realization of /hC/ clusters in Korean, (25).[2]

(25) a. h + s → s: /noh + sumnita/ → [nos:umnita] 'put formal'
 b. h + t → t^h /coh + ta/   → [cot^{h}a]   'good (indic.)'

Under the analysis we have so far developed, in both cases in (25) the feature [spread] has been retained. The underlying representations for these cases are shown in (26).

(26) Underlying representations
   a. h + s   b. h + t

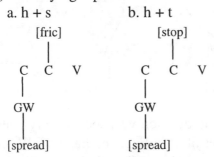

Oral Place and GW spreading apply in both cases, (26). In (26b) this yields a [spread] gesture in phase with the [stop] closure, a configuration disfavored by Kingston's Law. Korean remedies this situation by spreading GW onto the vowel, so that [spread] will be out of phase with [stop].

(27) Oral Place and GW spreading, Kingston's Law
   a. h + s   b. h + t

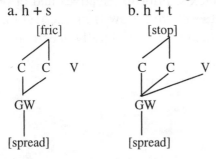

If /h/ did not have a GW dependent, then the GW dependent appropriate to the existing phasing relations would have been added, as with the aspirated stops, (23a). Notice that the aspirated stops do not contribute aspiration to the following stop in syllable contact, but /h/ does. So the aspirated stops are "less" aspirated than /h/ and we capture this by giving the stops a bare GW node, but giving /h/ both GW and [spread]. What is invariant in Korean is the presence of GW rather than one of its dependents. The gestures [spread] and [constricted] are introduced to satisfy phasing requirements, and the gesture [spread] is maintained if it is underlyingly present.[3]

5.5. Further work

We acknowledge that the above analysis does not provide a complete picture of Korean laryngeal phonology. For instance, we have not provided an account of the neutralization of coda obstruents to stops in Korean. Most researchers claim that the final stops are plain and unreleased, but Baek (1992) claims that final stops are glottalized. Contrary to previous researchers, Kim and Jongman (1996) found that "83% of the word-final stops ... were followed by a brief burst." More recently, Kim and Rhee (1997) extended the Kim and Jongman study, and found a smaller proportion of very weakly released stops. They interpret these as "inaudibly released" stops, and conclude that such release is phonologically irrelevant.

While the non-release of stops in phrase-final and pre-stop position may explain the *origin* of neutralization in Korean, there are two additional phenomena which favor a *phonological* neutralization to plain stops independent of phonetic release. First, final stops in the first member of a compound can become voiced when the second member begins with a sonorant: /pat^h + ilaŋ/ → [padiraŋ] 'field-ridge'. Second, in verbs which take *–hata* the final obstruent becomes aspirated: /k'æk'is + hata/ → [k'æk'it^{h}ada] '(be) clean'. Both of these changes point to an intermediate plain stage as the result of neutralization, as glottalized variants should not become either voiced or aspirated. Note, further, that the neutralized stops are, of course, phonetically released when followed by a vowel, as in these two cases.

We speculate that the laryngeal neutralization found in Korean is the result of the unavailability of GW spread in final position, given the lack of a subsequent position at that point in the derivation. Conceivably, being unable to spread GW to be bi-positional would trigger deletion of the GW dimension as an alternative 'repair'.

Another aspect of Korean neutralization is that both /s/ and /h/ become [t] in final position. Given the presence of [spread] on /h/ underlyingly, this neutralization strongly points to the deletion of either [spread] or GW in final position. The neutralization of /s/ also points to the loss of the [fricative] gesture word-finally. Finally, Kim (1997, 1999) has shown that Korean /c c' c^h/ are primarily affricates phonologically (and only secondarily palatal), and since they also neutralize to [t] word-finally, the word-final neutralization must also accomplish de-affrication.

We believe that the correct analysis will relate these disparate facts to the phasing of gestures and the bi-positional nature of GW in Korean. Such an analysis is similar to, but distinct from, aperture-based analyses. Word-finally, only a single position is available, and therefore GW is illicit in this position. Without the possibility of GW in this position, /h/ and /s/ are also illicit. By a corollary to Vaux's Law, /s/ must lose [fricative] if it cannot have GW, turning into [t]. Similar considerations apply to /h/, which will then acquire the default Coronal place (Avery and Rice 1989).

6.   Conclusion

We have seen that a model of feature organization that groups [spread] and [constricted] into a single GW dimension allows for a more explanatory account of the alternations observed between [spread] and [constricted] segments in the languages investigated thus far. Previously, such alternations were generally ignored and the intimate connection between the features [spread] and [constricted] was missed. Our theory of segment structure, in which antagonistic gestures are grouped into dimensions, allows us to revisit the connections between different gestural pairs. For us, non-contrastive variation between [spread] and [constricted] realizations is simply a matter of completing a bare GW dimension node. In theories where [spread] or [constricted] is used to implement the contrast, languages such as English or Korean have to be analyzed as changing one feature, e.g. [spread] into a diametrically opposed feature.

Furthermore, because dimensions organize antagonistic gestures we have a direct structural explanation for impossible combinations. We do not require extrinsic filters such as *[spread constricted] as in Lombardi (1991).

We have seen in Japanese that enhancement can lead to phonetic over-differentiation but that phonological processes can provide the answer as to the true nature of the phonological contrast in the language. The child, in setting up the contrastive dimensions in the language then, draws not only on the phonetic information but also the phonological patterning of the language.

We have also demonstrated the necessity for both underspecification and for feature geometry. It is the underspecified dimension nodes that allow us to provide maximally simple analyses of laryngeal alternations in the languages investigated. Only through the employment of a hierarchically organized segment are we able to implement a theory of gestural completion that can make the right predictions about the behavior of laryngeal features.

The theory and analyses given above also offer strong support to a modular approach to the phonetics-phonology interface. Better explanations are achieved with our reticulated model, marshalling elements from both the phonetics and the phonology. At the same time sharp boundaries must be established between these two aspects of language, as it is the *phonological* contrasts not the phonetic manifestations that must be acquired by the child (Avery and Idsardi 2000a).

Appendix

In Figure 1 we give a speculative model of segmental organization based on the theory and ideas presented in this article. The organization suggested in Figure 1 gives the reader a flavor of the theory that we are assuming, although at this point many of the details follow from nothing more than a desire for symmetry throughout the system. At the terminal level are the motor instructions, actions that can be executed by articulators. This includes the articulator-free gestures [stop] and [fricative], which plausibly involves antagonistic differences between ballistic and controlled movements in the closure and release phases (stops being ballistic in both phases, fricatives having a controlled closure and affricates having a controlled release). Antagonistic gestures are organized into dimensions, these features cannot co-occur in a single representation. There is minimal structure above this. Antagonistic relations do not generally hold at the upper layers, for example [high front] is a valid gesture complex, though Curl and Groove may indeed be antagonistic. Groups of dimensions sharing the same articulator are grouped together into the organizational nodes Larynx, Dorsal, and Coronal. The Oral Place node provides the grouping for the dimensions and articulators of the mouth proper. These are the only gestures which can be performed with complete or near-complete closure, and thus correspond to the class of possible obstruents. For this reason, the gestures dealing with obstruency are dependents of the Oral Place node, and sounds will be sonorant unless specified for an obstruent gesture.

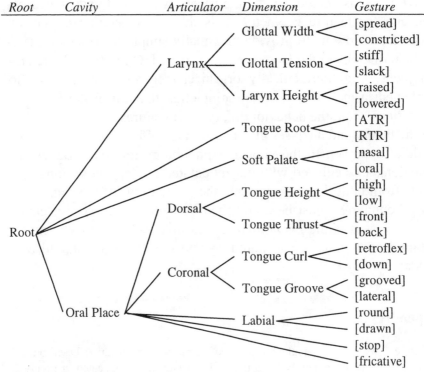

Figure 1. Segmental organization

Notes

1   We recognize that there must be word-final deletion in Korean to get the various neutralizations. All theories will have to posit multiple neutralization pro-

cesses in word-final position. For further discussion see Avery and Idsardi (in preparation).

2 Some speakers report additional variants of /h+s/ with [...ts:...]. Space considerations preclude discussion of this issue here.

3 Alternatives analyses of the Korean (Sohn 1987) which employ rule-ordering (with coda-neutralization feeding tensification) have to neutralize aspirated stops but not /h/ in syllable contact, a poorly motivated difference. For further discussion see Avery and Idsardi (in preparation).

References

Avery, Peter
  1996   The representation of voicing contrasts. Ph.D. dissertation, University of Toronto.
Avery, Peter and William J. Idsardi
  2000a   Issues in the acquisition of contrast. Paper presented at the First North American Phonology Conference, Concordia University, Montréal, April 28-30, 2000.
  2000b   Tonal Representation and Consonant-Tone Interactions. Paper presented at 5th Annual International Tromsø Workshop in Linguistics, Universitetet i Tromsø, June 5-7, 2000.
  in prep. Laryngeal phonology.
Avery, Peter and Keren Rice
  1989   Segment structure and coronal underspecification. *Phonology* 6: 179-200.
Baek, Eung-Jin
  1992   Unreleasing in Korean: a phonetic explanation. *Harvard Studies in Korean Linguistics* IV: 29-35.
Browman, Catherine and Louis Goldstein
  1989   Articulatory gestures as phonological units. *Phonology* 6: 201-251.
Docherty, Gerard J.
  1992   *The Timing of Voicing in British English Obstruents.* Berlin: Foris.
Dresher, Elan, and Harry van der Hulst
  1999   Head-dependent asymmetries in phonology: complexity and visibility. *Phonology* 15: 317-352.
Dresher, Elan, Glynn Piggott and Keren Rice
  1995   Contrast in phonology: overview. In Carrie Dyck, (ed.), *Toronto Working Papers in Linguistics* 13.1: iii-xvii.
Gallistel, C. R.
  1980   *The Organization of Action.* Hillsdale: Lawrence Erlbaum Associates.

Halle, Morris
    1995   Feature geometry and feature spreading. *Linguistic Inquiry* 26: 1-
            46.
Halle, Morris and Kenneth Stevens
    1971   A note on laryngeal features. *Quarterly Progress Report of the Re-
            search Laboratory of Electronics* 101: 198-213.
Hirose, Hajime and Tatsujiro Ushijima
    1989   Laryngeal control for voicing distinction in Japanese consonant
            production. *Phonetica* 35: 1-10.
Iverson, Gregory
    1983   Korean s. *Journal of Phonetics* 11: 191-200.
Iverson, Gregory and Shinsook Lee
    1995   Variation as Optimality in Korean cluster reduction. *Proceedings of
            the Eastern States Conference on Linguistics* 11: 174-185.
Iverson, Gregory and Joseph Salmons
    1995   Aspiration and laryngeal representation in Germanic. *Phonology* 12:
            369-396.
Kagaya, Ryohei
    1974   A fiberscopic and acoustic study of the Korean stops, affricates and
            fricatives. *Journal of Phonetics* 2: 161-180.
Kang, Seok-keun, Borim Lee and Ki-jeong Lee.
    1997   A correspondence account of Korean /h/. *Proceedings of the Seoul
            International Conference on Linguistics* IV: 684-696. Seoul: The
            Linguistics Society of Korea.
Keating, Patricia
    1988   A survey of phonological features. Indiana University Linguistics
            Club
Kim, Chin-Wu
    1972   Directionality of voicing and aspiration in initial position. *Actes du
            Septième Congrès International des Sciences Phonétiques*, 338-343.
            The Hague: Mouton.
Kim, Chin-Wu and Seok-Chae Rhee
    1997   Non-release and neutralization in Korean revisited. *Harvard Studies
            in Korean Linguistics*, VII: 121-137. Cambridge, MA: Harvard Uni-
            versity Department of Linguistics.
Kim, Hyunsoon
    1997   The phonological representation of affricates: evidence from Ko-
            rean and other languages. Ph.D. dissertation, Cornell University.
    1996   The place of articulation of Korean affricates revisited. *Journal of
            East Asian Linguistics* 8: 313-347.

Kim, Hyunsoon and Allard Jongman
1996   Acoustic and perceptual evidence for complete neutralization of manner articulation in Korean. *Journal of Phonetics* 24: 295-312.

Kingston, John
1985   The phonetics and phonology of the timing of oral and glottal events. Ph.D. dissertation, University of California, Berkeley.
1990   Articulatory binding. In John Kingston and Mary E. Beckman (eds.), *Papers in Laboratory Phonology I: Between the Grammar and Physics of Speech,* 406-434. Cambridge: Cambridge University Press.

Ladefoged, Peter
1973   The features of the larynx. *Journal of Phonetics* 1: 73-83.

Lee, Kyung-Hee
2000   Kukŏwe /s/-ŭn phyŏng'ŭminga kyŏgŭminga. Talk presented at Hangukŏnŏhakhwe kyŏwuyŏnguhwe palphyomun, Seoul, January 2000.

Lombardi, Linda
1991   Laryngeal features and laryngeal neutralization. Ph.D. dissertation, University of Massachusetts at Amherst.

Lyman, Benjamin Smith
1885   On the Japanese nigori of composition. *Journal of the American Oriental Society* 11: cxlii-cxliii.
1894   The change from surd to sonant in Japanese compounds. *Oriental Studies: a Selection of the Papers read before the Oriental Club of Philadelphia 1888-1894,* 160-176. Boston: Ginn and Company.

Martin, Samuel
1952   *Korean Morphophonemics.* Baltimore: Linguistic Society of America.

Mester, Armin and Junko Itô
1986   The phonology of voicing in Japanese. *Linguistic Inquiry* 17: 49-73.

Oh, Mira
1994   A reanalysis of consonant cluster simplification and *s*-neutralization. In: Young-Key Kim-Renaud (ed.), *Theoretical Issues in Korean Linguistics,* 157-174. Stanford: Center for the Study of Language & Information.

Oh, Mira and Seunghwan Lee
1997   The phonetics and phonology of aspirated consonants in Korean. *Proceedings of the Seoul International Conference on Linguistics,* IV: 247-255. Seoul: The Linguistics Society of Korea.

Roberts, E. Wyn and Kyoung-Ja Lee.
    1997   VOT in Korean, with particular reference to CV transitions and phonological segmentation. *Proceedings of the Seoul International Conference on Linguistics,* IV: 256-265. Seoul: The Linguistics Society of Korea.
Sagey, Elizabeth
    1986   The representation of features and relations in non-linear phonology. Ph.D. dissertation, Massachusetts Institute of Technology.
Scully, Cecilia
    1971   A comparison of /s/ and /z/ for an English speaker. *Language and Speech* 14: 187-200.
    1979   Model prediction and real speech: fricative dynamics. In: Bjorn Lindblom and Sven E. G. Öhman (eds.), *Frontiers of Speech Communication Research,* 35-48. London: Academic Press.
    1992   Articulatory actions within a phonological system and resulting complexity of speech signals. *Phonetica* 49: 212-221.
Sherrington, Charles
    1947   *The Integrative Action of the Nervous System* (Second edition). New Haven: Yale University Press.
Smith, Caroline L.
    1997   The devoicing of /z/ in American English: effects of local and prosodic context. *Journal of Phonetics* 25: 471-500.
Sohn, Hyang-Sook
    1987   Underspecification in Korean phonology. Ph.D. dissertation, University of Illinois at Urbana-Champaign.
Tsuchida, Ayako
    1997   Phonetics and phonology of Japanese vowel devoicing. Ph.D. dissertation, Cornell University.
Varden, John
    1998   On high vowel devoicing in standard modern Japanese: Implications for current phonological theory. Ph.D. dissertation, University of Washington.
Vaux, Bert
    1998   The laryngeal specifications of fricatives. *Linguistic Inquiry* 29: 497-511.
Yoshioka, Hirohide, Anders Löfqvist and Hajime Hirose
    1982   Laryngeal adjustments in Japanese voiceless sound production. *Journal of Phonetics* 10: 1-10.
Zemlin, Willard R.
    1998   *Speech and Hearing Science: Anatomy and Physiology* (Fourth edition). Boston: Allyn and Bacon.

Representational economy in constraint-based phonology*

G. N. Clements

"We are to admit no more causes of natural things
than such as are both true and sufficient to explain
their appearances." — Isaac Newton

1. Introduction

The linguist setting out to describe the phonological system of a
language attempts to find an account that captures all significant
regularities of sound patterning, including both memorized and
productive features. From a cognitive point of view, the aim is to
discover not only the system of internalized grammatical rules
shared by the members of the speech community, but also the representational elements, including phonological features and their
modes of combination.

With the rise of constraint-based phonological theories in the
1990s as an alternative to rewrite-rule-based theories, the main focus
of accounting for linguistic generalizations has shifted from the
study of rules and representations to the study of constraints and
their interactions. This shift of attention has been salutary in that it
has turned attention to the nature of the substantive principles that
underly phonological patterns, and has shown that a better understanding of these principles can lead to greater insight into the nature
of the patterns themselves. However, one less desirable consequence
has been an increasing uncertainty regarding such fundamental
questions as: What is a lexical representation? What is a phonological representation? Of what features or feature specifications do
they consist? How do these features combine? What is the trade-off
between constraints and representations in understanding phonological regularities?

Underlying the present study is the conviction that in much recent
work, phonological representations are encumbered with representational elements – features and feature values, nodes and tiers –

72   *G. N. Clements*

that play no essential role in understanding the sound patterns of the languages to which they are attributed. It will be maintained here that phonological representations should be freed of superfluous representational elements, leaving only those that are essential to an understanding of lexical, phonological, and phonetic generalizations.

Economy is not just a matter of theoretical elegance, but is reflected in empirical data. One area in which economy can be observed is the widely-noted preference for the economical use of features in phoneme systems. Phoneme systems are typically structured by the use of just a few features to create a large number of phonemic contrasts (see e.g. Trubetzkoy 1939, Martinet 1955, Hockett 1955, Maddieson 1984). Thus, for example, a stop system such as /p b t d c ɟ k g/, making economical use of a single phonation contrast (voicing), is strongly preferred to one like /b ɓ t tʰ c ɟ k k'/, which makes use of several.

The aim of the present study is to raise the question: What *minimal* assumptions about phonological feature representations must the constraint-based description of a language make if it is to satisfy widely-accepted criteria of simplicity, generality, and explanatory adequacy? It argues for a general principle of representational economy according to which features are specified in a given language only to the extent that they are needed in order to express generalizations about the phonological system. The features thus present in lexical and phonological representations are those members of the universal feature set that can plausibly be assumed to be discovered by speakers as a result of their linguistic experience, via their role in distinguishing lexical items (distinctivity) or in defining regular phonotactic pattern and alternations.

Following a similar logic, this paper explores the view that features and feature sets are autosegmentalized in a given language only to the extent needed to express generalizations in that language. Autosegmentalized features are those that acquire prominence by virtue of their special behavior, in essentially the sense defined by the earlier literature in Autosegmental Phonology.

In this perspective, phonological representations are not uniform across languages, but vary in ways that reflect the specific differences in their sound patterning, a view for which Sapir (1925) provides the classical antecedent. Particular grammars can be viewed as drawing their representational elements from the pool provided by universal grammar. Features, nodes, or tiers that are not employed in a given language remain *latent* in the sense that they are always potentially available, and may subsequently become distinctive or active as a result of language contact, internal historical change, and other dynamic factors influencing language development.

This paper is organized as follows. After a preliminary review of background assumptions (section 2), a contrast-based model of lexical representation is developed in the context of a universal theory of feature accessibility (section 3). Section 4 takes up the notion of phonological feature activation, specifying conditions under which features not present in the lexicon may be inserted into phonological representations; this model is illustrated by phonological patterns involving nondistinctive features in Zoque. Section 5, dealing with tier projection, outlines conditions under which feature values present in the phonology may be autosegmentally projected onto tiers, with further illustrations from Zoque.

Sections 6 and 7 illustrate this approach to feature representation with case studies, showing how a number of well-known problems involving feature transparency can be solved without appealing to special assumptions. Section 6 reviews the phenomenon of coronal transparency and proposes analyses of coronal harmony in Basque and Tahltan. Section 7 outlines a new analysis of Sequential Voicing in Japanese, with special attention to the problem raised by voicing transparency. Section 8 discusses a recent alternative to the approach proposed here, and section 9 offers a brief conclusion.

2. Background assumptions

Some background assumptions are summarized in (1):

(1) a. phonological processes are constraint-driven
    b. constraints are universal (recurrent across languages)
    c. constraints may be rank-ordered
    d. constraints may be violated in surface representations

  e.   representations are changed only to eliminate constraint
        violations (derivational economy)

This set of assumptions, most of which are shared by current constraint-based frameworks such as Optimality Theory (OT), may be
implemented in various ways depending on one's theoretical preferences. To a significant extent, the choice among these different implementations will be irrelevant to the representational issues raised
below. A serial approach to constraint-based phonology is assumed
here (see Clements 2000 for motivation); however, questions of
constraint formalization will be raised only to the extent that they are
crucial to matters at issue. The analyses proposed below are to some
degree intelligible in (and translatable into) a variety of alternative
frameworks.

The following, simplified view of the organization of the lexicon
and phonology will be sufficient for the purposes of the following
discussion:

(2)

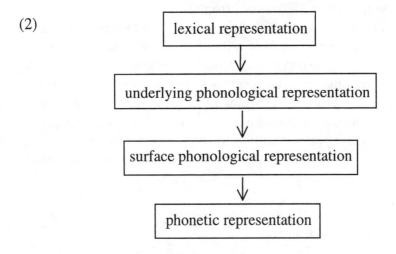

This view proposes a minimum of four levels in phonological description. A more complete model of phonology and morphology
would provide a word formation component, further levels of representation (such as root-, stem-, word- and phrase-level strata),
several types of phonetic representation (articulatory, acoustic, etc.),

and further links among these components, some reversing the top-to-bottom directionality expressed by the arrows. The following discussion abstracts from these distinctions insofar as they do not appear to bear directly on issues discussed here.

3.   Lexical Feature Specification

3.1 Underspecification Theory

We now take up the question of lexical feature specification. Much phonological work in the 1980s was directed toward the study of underspecification theory, according to which nondistinctive or predictable feature values are omitted from lexical or underlying representation and inserted by redundancy rules in the course of derivations. These positions came under severe attack due to problems such as the following (see e.g. Steriade 1987, 1995, Clements 1988, 1993a, Christdas 1988, Mohanan 1991, Odden 1992, and Calabrese 1995 for critical discussion):

(3)   Some problems in underspecification theory:
- insufficiency of many of the arguments adduced for under-specification (e.g. assumed limitations on lexical storage capacity)
- excessive complexity of grammars containing redundancy rules, and the consequent burden on the language learner
- indeterminacy in choosing among alternative ways of under-specifying a given phoneme inventory
- conflicting evidence arguing in some cases for one model of underspecification, and in other cases for another
- technical problems, such as the potential use of zero as a third value, or the characterization of underspecified natural classes

As a result of this critique, underspecification theory has been largely abandoned at the present time in favor of approaches which disallow the use of redundancy rules. This result is accepted here.

The OT literature has cast these questions in a different light. In an early study of this question, Itô, Mester, and Padgett (1995) maintained that underspecification is incompatible with OT's output-oriented perspective. In contrast, Inkelas (1995) advocated retaining a restricted version of it (see also Harrison and Kaun, this volume). Most more recent work in the OT framework, however, appears to have endorsed the view that underspecification is incompatible with the Richness of the Base hypothesis, which holds that no constraints hold exclusively of underlying representation (Prince and Smolensky 1993, Smolensky 1996, Smolensky *et al.* 2000). In this view, no constraints are available to enforce underspecification, or indeed, any particular condition on underlying representations. Nevertheless, underspecification could be imposed, if one wished, by general principles belonging to the architecture of the theory itself, rather than to the constraint system as such. Thus, whether Richness of the Base actually enforces fully-specified underlying representations depends on what further principles we adopt (or fail to adopt).

One popular approach has invoked the principle of Lexicon Optimization, which, all else being equal, favors the closest possible match between the underlying and surface representation of any given form, eventually including allophonic detail (see Prince and Smolensky 1993: 192-4, and Kager 1999 for further discussion). This principle rules out underspecified lexical representations in most cases. However, the question of to what extent Lexicon Optimization is actually supported by empirical considerations remains open. Other principles bearing directly on lexical specification (e.g. formal simplicity, contrast, markedness) make different predictions concerning the nature of lexical representation, and cannot be dismissed on a priori grounds. The theory of Active Feature Specification to be presented below offers one such alternative to Lexicon Optimization.[1]

It is important to keep in mind that even if we reject underspecification theory as such, it does not follow that lexical or underlying representations must be fully specified for all theoretically possible feature values; we must only be sure that feature values which are absent underlyingly are not inserted later on. One can entertain the idea that some feature values are absent both underlyingly and on the surface. In fact, there is a certain amount of evidence from phonetic studies that redundant or predictable feature values are unspecified in surface representations in at least some cases (see Pierrehumbert and Beckman 1988, Keating 1988, Cohn 1993). The consequences of this result have still not been fully explored in current theory. Thus, the nature of feature specification at all levels (lexical, underlying, surface-phonological) remains an open question at the present time.

The approach developed below, according to which all and only those features that are active in a given language occur in its lexical and phonological representations, will be termed *Active Feature Specification*. The term 'active feature' is used to designate a feature or feature value that is required for the expression of lexical contrasts or phonological regularities in a language, including both static phonotactic patterns and patterns of alternation. In this view, whet.ier or not a given feature or feature value is specified in a given language can only be determined from an examination of its system of contrasts and sound patterns. In this sense, feature representation is relativized to each phonological system.

3.2　Active Feature Specification

Three fundamental conditions for feature specification are stated in (4), corresponding to the lexical, phonological and phonetic levels of representation, respectively:

(4)　Conditions for feature specification
  a.　lexical level: distinctiveness
  - a feature or feature value is present in the lexicon if and only if it is distinctive (in a sense to be defined)
  b.　phonological levels: feature activity
  - a feature or feature value is present at a given phonological level if it is required for the statement of phonological patterns (phonotactic patterns, alternations) at that level

    c. phonetic level: pronounceability
- feature values are present in the phonetics if required to account for relevant aspects of phonetic realization

Any features and feature values meeting these conditions are specified. A carry-over principle is further assumed according to which all features present in the lexicon are carried into the phonology, and all features present in the phonology are carried into the phonetics. Features present at the phonetic level are interpreted in the acoustic and articulatory domains. But in this logic, the mere fact that a given segment bears a certain feature phonetically does not entail that it bears that feature phonologically; evidence for phonological specification can come only from evidence of lexical or phonological activity. Thus, for example, the fact that [t] is realized phonetically as a voiceless coronal stop in a given language does not require us to assign it the feature [coronal] in the phonology; for such an assignment to be justified, it must further be shown that this feature is distinctive or active in the sense of (4).

    The notion of distinctiveness can be intuitively defined as follows: *Thus allowed thanks features*

(5)   A feature is *distinctive* in a given segment if it is required to distinguish that segment from another.

More specifically, two segments S_i, S_j are distinct if a feature present in one is absent in the other. Distinctness in this sense is illustrated in the schematic example in (6), in which feature F is present only in segment S_1 and feature G is present only in segment S_2; all three segments are distinct.

(6) S_1, S_2, S_3 are distinct:

    S_1 S_2 S_3
    | |
    F   G

It is assumed here that all features other than the articulator features [coronal], [labial], and [dorsal] are potentially binary. How-

p──➤ new

ever, following the strategy of simplifying feature representation to a maximum, only one value of any distinctive feature is entered in the lexical representation of any segment class. Where the marked value of a feature can be established by reliable criteria, it is this value that is present. In cases where markedness criteria diverge or are indeterminate, phonological activity is taken as the deciding factor. In case neither value of such a feature is active in a given phonological system, the choice of which value to specify is arbitrary, with no other consequences, however, for the grammar as a whole.

Given the model in (4), an interesting question is whether one can maintain the following strong hypothesis:

(7)   Lexical feature representations are identical to phonological feature representations

(7) maintains that the features and feature values needed for lexical specification are sufficient for the purposes of phonological specification; in other words, only lexically distinctive values are phonologically active. (7) would entail, for example, that if the feature [coronal] is not required to distinguish /t/ from other phonemes in a given system, it will not be phonologically active in that system.[2] This hypothesis is attractive in that, if true, it would place strong constraints on the nature of feature representation. However, we shall see below that some features that are absent in lexical specification are active, and necessarily present, in the phonology, showing that (7) cannot be maintained in its strong form.

Let us now consider how feature values are entered in lexical representations. It will be recalled that in underspecification theories, there are usually many ways to underspecify a phoneme system; the problem of deciding among them can be called the Indeterminacy Problem (see especially Mohanan 1991 and Odden 1992 for discussion). The Indeterminacy Problem carries over, in principle, to any model which proposes to specify less than the full set of features, whether distinctive or redundant.

The proposed solution to this problem draws on the notion that features can be ranked according to a universal hierarchy of accessibility. At the top of the hierarchy are features that are highly favored in the construction of phoneme systems, while at the bottom are features that are highly disfavored. In between these extremes are features that fall on a scale from more to less favored. For example, nearly all known consonant systems include a contrast between at least one obstruent and at least one sonorant, and most have several members of both categories. The [±sonorant] contrast is acquired early in the course of language acquisition, and one or both values of the feature are very often active in defining phonological patterns. We thus consider [±sonorant] to be a highly accessible feature. In contrast, the feature [±apical] (or [±distributed]) is a less accessible feature, since only a minority of languages make distinctive use of it (and then often in a limited way).

A partial ranked scale of some of the more accessible consonant features is proposed in (8):

(8) Partial ranked scale of feature accessibility for consonants

	feature:	*in:*
a.	[coronal]	
b.	[sonorant]	
c.	[labial]	
d.	[dorsal]	[−sonorant]
e.	[strident]	
f.	[nasal]	
g.	[posterior]	[+sonorant, −nasal]
h.	[lateral]	[+sonorant]
i.	[voice]	[−sonorant]

Some of the features on this list are restricted to certain contexts, as indicated on the right. Thus, [dorsal] is highly accessible in obstruents, as indicated by the high ranking of statement (d), but much less accessible in sonorants (/ŋ/ is much less common than /k/ in the world's languages). Similarly, [posterior] is accessible in approximant systems where it commonly distinguishes the palatal approximant /y/ from the liquids /l/ or /r/, but is less common in nasal systems (/ɲ/ vs. /n/) or obstruent systems (/ʃ/ vs. / /s/).

Plausible phoneme systems can be constructed from the complete accessibility scale, of which (8) shows just a portion. To do this, we proceed through the scale from top down without skipping, introducing appropriate phoneme contrasts to instantiate each feature as we go. The entry-level feature [coronal] yields a coronal consonant. In an imaginary system with no other consonant, this would typically be realized as [t]. The next feature on the scale, [sonorant], introduces a contrast between a coronal obstruent and a coronal sonorant, such as /t/ vs. /n/, as is found in most languages. The following feature, [labial], introduces a contrast between a labial and nonlabial obstruent, on the one hand, and a labial and nonlabial sonorant, on the other; a typical realization of such a system would be /p t m n/. A contrast involving a [dorsal] sound appears next, but only in obstruents; a system accessing just these features would typically have the phoneme set /p t k m n/. These five sounds are the commonest consonants in the world's languages. Proceeding down the list, we build up larger and larger phoneme sets as more and more features are accessed. Many phoneme systems can be constructed without skipping any point in the scale, but there are exceptions; for example, Klao and Pirahã are reported to have no sonorant consonants, Vanimo no dorsal consonants, and Wichita no labial consonants. Although these cases are very exceptional, they are sufficient to show that the scale in (8) represents widely-observed crosslinguistic trends rather than strict laws of solidarity in the sense of Jakobson (1968).

This proposal draws upon work by a number of earlier writers on markedness and accessibility hierarchies, especially Jakobson (1968), Jakobson and Halle (1956), and Calabrese (1994), all of whom provide fuller discussion of the empirical considerations supporting the choice of one particular scale as opposed to another. Accessibility statements in the sense understood here define the set of admissable segments both in the lexicon and at the point of entry to a phonological system. Following Calabrese (1994, 1995) in particular, it is assumed that statements which are passed over in constructing the phoneme inventory of a language – for example "[labial]" (8c) in the case of Wichita – are present in the grammar in negated form (e.g. "*[labial]") where, depending on their relative rank with respect to other constraints, they may play a role in defining patterns of structure-preservation in the sense of Kiparsky (1985).

The major empirical claim underlying a scale such as the one proposed in (8) is that the presence of a phoneme representing a lower-ranked feature contrast in a given system generally entails the presence of a phoneme representing a higher-ranked contrast. Thus, for example, a language having a /t/ vs. /c/ contrast, representing the less accessible contrast involving [posterior] in [–sonorant] (not shown in 8), generally has a /t/ vs. /s/ contrast representing the more accessible contrast involving [strident], (8e). The reverse entailment is much less likely to be true.

The following list reports the most common consonant types in Maddieson's (1992) genetically-balanced sample of 451 languages.

(9) Consonant types occurring in at least two-thirds of the world's languages, in rank order (source: Maddieson 1992)

T	98%	S	82%
K	98	W	80
N	96	L	77
M	95	B	71
P	90	R	71
Y	84	D	69

By 'consonant type' we mean, roughly, any sound that would ordinarily be transcribed by the lower-case variant of the symbol designating the type. Thus a T-sound is any voiceless dental or alveolar nonaffricated stop, whether apical or dental, aspirated or plain, an S-sound is any voiceless strident dental or alveolar fricative, whether apical or laminal, slit or grooved, palatalized or plain, while L- and R-sounds are any voiced lateral or central liquids, whether trills, taps, or approximants, and so forth. An extension of the list would include H-sounds (65%) and G-sounds (63%).

While the particular choices presented in (8) are based primarily on phoneme frequency data, other criteria tend to provide supporting evidence. Thus in language acquisition, higher-level contrasts are often observed to be mastered before lower-level ones. Higher-level features tend to be easy to implement in articulatory terms, and to correlate with efficient acoustic indices (Stevens and Keyser 1989). Cooccurrence constraints involving lower-level features are often restricted to classes defined by higher-level features, such as [sonorant], as is suggested by the contextual conditions in (8).

The predictions of (8) regarding phoneme accessibility can be more readily visualized in the form of a branching tree (Figure 1, next page). The tree is rooted in a simple consonant, bearing no features other than [+consonantal]. Each lower-level node represents a segment class defined by the features developed up to that point.

The choice of symbol on each node represents the class of sounds defined by the features developed to that point. Thus, for example, P in the third ([labial]) row stands for a labial obstruent, whose least marked member is [p]. Phoneme types are arrayed in order of decreasing accessibility as we proceed down the tree. For instance, the high-level split between an obstruent and a sonorant, represented by the branching from the root node T to its daughters T and N, represents the claim that a contrast between an obstruent such as /t/ and a sonorant such as /n/ is highly accessible, and likely to be found in the vast majority of phoneme systems. Lower-level branches represent less accessible contrasts.

In Figure 1, the order in which consonant types branch off does not exactly replicate the order of phoneme frequency in (9). This is because the categories of Figure 1 refer to sets of consonant types, instead of to individual consonants. Thus, for example, P in row 3 represents not p-sounds, but all labial obstruents, while K in row 4 represents not k-sounds but all velar obstruents. These two more general sets of sound types show only negligible differences in frequency across Maddieson's survey (98.9% vs. 99.8% respectively). Thus the relative ranking of P- and K-type obstruents in Figure 1 is arbitrary as far as phoneme frequency counts are concerned, and must be based on supplementary criteria (here, we have drawn on the commonly-observed fact that the /t/ vs. /p/ contrast commonly emerges before the /t/ vs. /k/ contrast in language acquisition.)

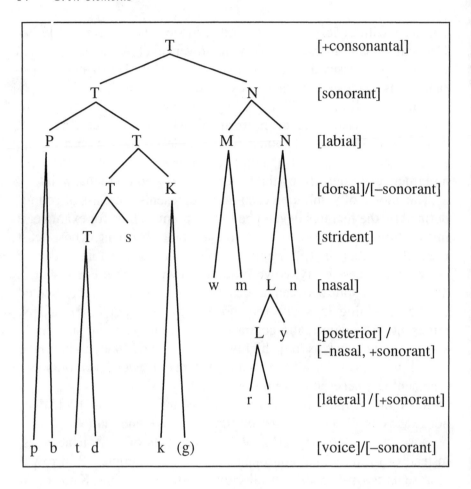

Figure 1. Consonant accessibility, as determined by the scale of feature accessibility (8).

Is the feature hierarchy in (8), as illustrated in Figure 1, universal across languages? While it is possible that the hierarchy is simply given as such in universal grammar, it is not unreasonable to suppose that it can be recovered, at least in large part, from the speaker's linguistic experience through massive exposure to data allowing a calculation of relative phoneme frequencies and other phenomena related to feature accessibility. If this is true, it is possible that universally-given feature rankings might be contradicted in certain languages, giving rise to language-particular rerankings. However, such reversals should be relatively limited, given that the constraints on production and perception that underlie the notion of accessibility are presumably the same, or very similar, for all normal speakers. We expect, then, that the ranking in (8) or one similar to it should be largely respected from one language to another.

A method will now be presented for entering feature specifications in lexical representations. The basic principle is that passing down the hierarchy of feature accessibility (8) one step at a time, all and only the marked feature specifications are entered that are needed to distinguish one phoneme from another. This procedure is essentially identical to an algorithm proposed by Dresher *et al.* (1995) and Dresher (1998) and further developed in work by Dresher (2000) and Ghini (1998; this volume).[3]

As an illustration, (10) specifies the consonant phoneme system of Hawaiian, based on the description in Elbert and Pukui (1979).

(10) lexical feature specification of Hawaiian consonants

	p	m	w	n	l	k	h	?
[sonorant]		+	+	+	+		+	+
[labial]	+	+	+					
[nasal]		+		+				
[spread]							+	
[constricted]								+

This table specifies Hawaiian phonemes in terms of a minimal set of marked feature values, giving priority to those that appear higher on the scale in (8). Feature specifications are entered into an initially empty table in the following way. First, following in particular Ghini (1998), since [coronal] is the unmarked place feature (see e.g. Kiparsky 1985, Paradis and Prunet 1991a, b, Rice 1996), no values for [coronal] are entered. The first feature specifications that can be entered, therefore, are those for [+sonorant], which is the marked value of the feature [sonorant] in consonants. Proceeding down the list in (8), we next enter specifications for [labial]. Once these are entered, /p/ and /k/ are distinct from all other sounds. (8d) next allows [dorsal] to be entered in obstruents, but as the two obstruents

/p k/ are now distinct, this feature is redundant, and so is not entered. [strident] is also redundant, and so no specifications for this feature are entered either. (Hawaiian is of course atypical among the world's languages in not having contrasts involving these two features.) Passing on to (8f), the feature [nasal] next distinguishes /m/ and /n/ from all other sounds, and so these are marked [+nasal]; notice that /w/ is now also fully distinct, since at this point, it is the only sound specified only as [+sonorant, labial] in the system. It remains to distinguish /l h ʔ/, which are so far specified only as [+sonorant]. The features [posterior], [lateral], and [voice] are useless for this purpose, as they are all lexically redundant in Hawaiian. We therefore pass on to the lower-ranked features [spread glottis] and [constricted glottis], not included in (8), whose specifications accomplish this purpose. The lexical specification of Hawaiian consonant phonemes is now complete. All phonemes are distinct according to the account in (5) and (6) above. Any further feature specifications would introduce redundancy.

Massively productive patterns of adaptation of English loanwords into Hawaiian support the feature analysis in (10). The more important of these patterns are summarized in (11).

(11)   coronal obstruents, [g] > /k/
        [b], [f] > /p/
        [w], [v] > /w/
        [ŋ] > /n/

The superficially surprising interpretation of coronals as /k/, illustrated by examples such *ticket > kikiki, diamond > kaimana, Peter > Pika, Samuel > Kamuela, rose > loke, George > Keoki, thousand > kaukan,* follows from the fact that both [t] and [k] are nonlabial obstruents, identical in terms of the distinctive feature specifications in (10). Hawaiian differs from most other languages in interpreting a featurally unspecified obstruent as a dorsal, rather than coronal sound in the phonetics. The only other surprising element in the pattern, given the feature characterizations in (10), is the interpretation of [v] as /w/ instead of the expected /p/. This fact can be understood in terms of the fact that /w/ varies in pronunciation between [w] and what is described by Judd *et al.* (1945) as a 'soft' *v*, distinct from the 'hard' *v* of English. Since English [v] itself has frictionless realizations, it would appear that Hawaiian speakers categorize English *v* as a sonorant sound, identifying it with the labio-dental variant [ʋ] of their own /w/.

To summarize, the model of lexical feature specification presented in this section represents the hypothesis that the lexical units of speech are categorized and distinguished by a minimal set of marked features and feature values, selected according to a universal scale of feature accessibility. The assumption that features are minimally specified in the lexicon does not rest on doubtful *a priori* assumptions about constraints on storage capacity in memory, which have been correctly criticized in the earlier literature, but from the notion of representational economy, which requires that representational entities such as features and tiers can only be postulated at a given level if there is explicit empirical evidence for their presence.

4. Phonological Feature Activation

4.1 Overview

We next take up the question of feature activation in the phonology. We have seen that features are present in the lexicon only to the extent that they are required to distinguish phonemes. These lexically specified features are carried over into the phonology. In addition, phonological representations may contain further, redundant feature specifications that are required to express phonological patterning generalizations. This principle is stated as the Activation Criterion:

(12) The Activation Criterion:
      In any language, redundant feature values are specified in all and only the segments in which they are active

A feature value is *active* in any segment or segment class which satisfies a term in a constraint mentioning that feature. For example, a constraint SPREAD([nasal]) will activate the feature [nasal] in all segments bearing it in their full phonological feature description, whether this feature is present in their lexical representation or not.

One rather far-reaching consequence of the notion of feature activation is that not all members of the set of universal constraints are present in all grammars. If they were, all features would be activated in all languages, including many that play no distinctive or phonological role. The view is therefore taken that only those constraints that are actually operative in a given language – that is, those that play a crucial role in defining phonotactic patterns or alternations – are present in its grammar. Other universal constraints, just like inactive redundant features, are latent in they sense that they may become activated in the process of loanword adaptation, linguistic change, and so forth. Language acquisition therefore involves not only discovering which features are active in a given language, but also which constraints are operative.

A further principle of Feature Inertia excludes context-free insertion of redundant features within a phonological level. This principle excludes the effect of redundancy and default rules.

(13) Feature Inertia
      A feature unspecified in the input to a level cannot be inserted to satisfy a context-free feature constraint.

Under this principle, which implements a form of derivational economy, no constraints may have the effect of inserting redundant features in a given segment class unless a context is specified.

4.2 Illustration: Stop Voicing in Zoque

We illustrate the notion of feature activation with an example drawn from the phonology of Copainalá Zoque, a Mixe-Zoque language spoken in Chiapas, Mexico (Wonderly 1951-2; Dell 1985; Hall 2000). Speakers of this language tend to be bilingual in Spanish, and as a consequence, many phonological features of Spanish have been incorporated into the lexicon through loanword adaptation (Wonderly 1946). The following discussion concerns the native phonological stratum except as otherwise noted.[4]

The native lexicon contains the following distinctive consonants:

(14) Native Zoque consonant phonemes

p	t	ts	tʃ	c	k	ʔ
		s	ʃ			h
m	n			ɲ	ŋ	
w	l			y		

As the choice of symbols in (14) suggests, the oral stops /p t ts tʃ c k/ are usually realized as voiceless. However, they are regularly voiced after nasals, as is shown in (15):

(15) a. pama   'clothing'   m-bama   'my clothing'
          tatah   'father'   n-datah   'my father'
          tsima   'calabash'   n-dzima   'my calabash'
          tʃoʔngoya 'rabbit'   ɲ-dʒoʔngoya 'my rabbit'
          kama   'cornfield'   ŋ-gama   'my cornfield'

      b. tih-u   'he arrived'   min-u   'he came'
          tih-pa   'he arrives'   min-ba   'he comes'
          tih-keʔtu 'he arrived again' min-geʔtu 'he came again'

(The prefix illustrated in (15a) is the 1st or 2nd person possessive /n-/, and the suffixes in (15b) are /-u/ 'completive', /-pa/ 'incompletive', and /-keʔtu/ 'again, also.') Although the voicing feature is nondistinctive in the native stratum, it is thus required by a phonotactic pattern which is exceptionless in the native stratum, and which creates regular patterns of alternation in both the native and Spanish strata.

The Zoque consonants in (14) are lexically specified as shown in (16) below, following the procedure outlined earlier.[5]

(16) lexical feature specification of Zoque consonants

	p	t	ts	tʃ	c	k	s	ʃ	m	n	ɲ	ŋ	w	l	y	h	ʔ
[sonorant]									+	+	+	+	+	+	+	+	+
[labial]	+								+				+				
[dorsal]					+							+					
[strident]			+	+			+	+									
[nasal]									+	+	+	+					
[posterior]				+	+			+			+			+			
[spread]																+	
[constricted]																	+
[continuant]							+	+									

In the native stratum, specifications for [voice] and [lateral] are non-distinctive and so are not entered. In contrast, not all Zoque phonemes are distinguished by the accessibility statements in (8). The following further statements, all ranked below those in (8), are sufficient for this purpose:

(17)   j.   [spread (glottis)]
       k.   [dorsal]   in [+nasal]
       l.   [posterior]   in [+strident]
       m.   [constricted (glottis)]
       n.   [continuant]   in [−voice, −sonorant]
       o.   [posterior]   in [+nasal]
       p.   [posterior]   in [−sonorant]

It is assumed that these statements are ranked approximately as given, though further statements, not relevant to Zoque, may be interspersed among them.

Now let us consider the pattern illustrated in (15). This pattern exemplifies a constraint prohibiting voiceless sounds after nasal stops (*NT), resolved in Zoque by the redundant (nonneutralizing) voicing of the stop. Though this voicing is nondistinctive, it provides a redundant cue to the presence of a nasal, which commonly represents the grammatical prefix /n-/ (cf. 15a).

How is this pattern to be analyzed? Pater (1999) observes that NT clusters are disfavored in many genetically unrelated languages.

As he points out, such sequences are often altered by voicing the postnasal stop, as in Zoque, but other remedies are found as well, including the following:

- nasal substitution (e.g. Indonesian)
- nasal deletion (e.g. Swahili)
- denasalization (e.g. Toba Batak)

This variety of repair operations argues for disassociating the diagnosis – the *NT constraint itself – from the remedy. As Pater notes, especially strong evidence for this view comes from the existence of languages such as (Oshi)Kwanyama in which two of these processes (in this case nasal substitution and voicing) conspire to eliminate NT clusters. Frameworks treating postnasal voicing as a spreading operation (voicing assimilation) would not generalize to the full range of *NT effects.

The repair operation chosen by Zoque is stop voicing. There can be little doubt that postnasal voicing is indeed a phonological process in Zoque, rather than a matter of phonetic implementation. Voicing is not only obligatory but categorial, in the sense that the [d] produced by voicing is the same as the [d] which realizes the phoneme /d/ occurring in Spanish loanwords; thus, redundant [d] and distinctive [d] are identical. Note as well that although voicing inserts a redundant feature in native words, it has a neutralizing effect in inflected forms of Spanish roots, merging voiceless stops with voiced stops, as in the following examples:

(18)   paloma   'bird'   m-baloma   'my bird'
   cf. burru   'burro'   m-burru   'my burro'
        trampa   'trap'   n-drampa   'my trap'
   cf. disko   'disk'   n-disko   'my disk'
        kwarto   'room'   ŋ-gwarto   'my room'
   cf. gallu   'rooster'   ŋ-gallu   'my rooster'

The following constraints describe this system:

(19) a. *NT: *[+nasal][–voice, –cont]
      b. INSERT([+voice])

The first of these constraints identifies the ill-formed feature sequence, and the second specifies the repair operation. The latter can
be viewed in this case as a universal input-output constraint, requiring that a segment lacking a [+voice] specification in the input
must correspond to a segment containing such a specification in the
output. Such *antifaithfulness constraints* apply only to eliminate constraint violations. This restriction follows from the principle of derivational economy (1e), which disallows gratuitous changes to representations (cf. Chomsky 1993, 1995; Prince and Smolensky 1993).[6]

*NT activates the feature complex [–voice], [–cont] in voiceless
stops. Voiceless stops following nasals violate *NT and trigger the
application of INSERT([+voice]). By the principle of derivational economy, this constraint inserts [+voice] only in stops presenting *NT
violations. The following examples illustrate (only features of concern to the present discussion are shown):

(20) a. lexical representation: contains only distinctive values

		t	a	t	a	h		n	-	t	a	t	a	h
nasal								+						
cont														
voice														

    b. phonological input (activated features are also present):

		t	a	t	a	h		n	-	t	a	t	a	h
nasal								+						
cont			–		–						–		–		
voice			–		–						–		–		

    c. phonological output :

		t	a	t	a	h		n	-	t	a	t	a	h
nasal								+						
cont			–		–						–		–		
voice			–		–						+		–		

It is reasonable to ask whether the choice of INSERT([+voice]) (19b) needs to be stipulated as the operation used to repair *NT violations in Zoque, or whether the choice of this repair is predictable. It appears that among the various repair operations used cross-linguistically to eliminate *NT violations, postnasal voicing is the commonest (see discussion of a similar Japanese case in section 7). Other imaginable strategies for eliminating *NT violations, such as metathesis and vowel epenthesis, seem rarely if ever attested. It would be theoretically unsatisfactory to simply list which repair operations are commonly used to satisfy which constraints, e.g. in terms of universal default rankings. As Pater points out, "Persistent links between marked configurations and the processes used to repair them would seem to force a more fundamental shift in theoretical assumptions" (Pater 1999: 334).

Addressing this problem, Paradis (1996 and elsewhere) has suggested that repair strategies apply at the lowest phonological level to which the violated constraint refers (this statement forms part of a more general Minimality Principle). The hierarchy of levels assumed in this statement is: metrical level > syllabic level > skeletal level > root node > non-terminal feature > terminal feature. This proposal is not arbitrary, but reflects the intuition that repairs apply in such a way as to perform minimal changes in phonological form. Applying this principle to the case at hand, it suggests why the feature-changing operation INSERT([+voice]) should be preferred in Zoque, and widely across languages, to more drastic repair operations such as segment epenthesis, deletion, and metathesis: by affecting only a single feature value (and in Zoque, a redundant one at that), it is the minimal way in which the constraint can be satisfied. However, the fact that other, more drastic repair operations are also used on occasion to repair *NT violations shows that the Minimality Principle represents at best a widely-observed trend, which may be overridden by other factors.

94   G. N. Clements

4.3 Phonetic specification

We finally take up, though only briefly, the topic of conditions on feature specification at the phonetic level. The discussion so far has assumed that phonological features that are distinctive in the lexicon and/or active in the phonology are carried over into the phonetic level, where they form part of integrated phonological/phonetic representations (see e.g. Clements and Hertz 1996 for one such model). However, the pronounceability criterion (4c) states that non-distinctive and inactive features may also appear in phonetic representations, if needed to ensure the correct phonetic output.

That nondistinctive, inactive features might be needed at the phonetic level is perhaps not obvious at first sight. Take the case of a hypothetical language in which [coronal] is both lexically non-distinctive and phonological inactive in the apico-alveolar sound [t]. To account for its articulation, it might be assumed that the features [coronal], [–posterior] and [+apical] must be inserted at the entry to phonetic interpretation. However, it is well known that phonological features are generally too coarse to provide for all aspects of segment realization (see e.g. Ladefoged and Maddieson 1996). More appropriate candidates for insertion at the entry to the phonetics might be multivalued phonetic features of the sort proposed by Ladefoged and Maddieson, articulatory gestures as proposed by Browman and Goldstein (1989 and elsewhere), acoustic parameter targets as proposed by Hertz (1991), or any of a variety of other proposals to be found in the phonetic literature. Since the details of phonetic realization must be implemented in terms of such fine-grained phonetic specifications in any case, default values for incompletely specified segments can be given directly in phonetic terms, and additional phonological features would be superfluous.

However, the observation that some predictable feature specifications may still have to be added to account for aspects of phonetic realization has been suggested in work by Keating (1988), Cohn (1993), and others. The basic idea underlying these studies is that the presence or absence of a feature value in a given segment can be detected by phonetic patterns: features present in a segment are correlated with intrinsic acoustic or articulatory target values, while those that are absent are not. In this view, whenever a phonetic vector associated with some feature F appears to follow the shortest path between two target values lying in nonadjacent segments, the intervening segment is regarded as unspecified for F, but where the vector appears to aim at an appropriate intervening target lying off this path, a value of F must be present.

In support of this view, Cohn (1993) cites a regular difference in the interpretation of French and English oral vowels in nasal contexts. In French, which has a lexical contrast between oral and nasal vowels, oral vowels are robustly oral in all contexts, while in English, which lacks such a contrast, oral vowels tend to be realized with a gradually increasing nasal ramp before syllable-final nasal consonants, as in words like *bent*. Cohn assumes, following earlier underspecification models, that both values of [±nasal] are lexically present in French vowels, while neither value is present in English vowels. The presence of [−nasal] in French oral vowels would thus explain their robustly oral realization, while the absence of this feature in English vowels explains the apparent absence of an oral target.

In the present framework, in which only marked values of features are present in lexical representations, precluding [−nasal] in the lexical specification of French (and English) vowels, a different explanation must be offered. To account for the apparent presence of [−nasal] in French (but not in English) vowels at the phonetic level, we must assume that it is inserted at the entry to the phonetic level. A suitable principle for this purpose might be one of complementary feature value insertion, according to which the second value of a lexically distinctive binary feature may be inserted at the entry to the phonetic level. As a result, French vowels would be specified for both values of [±nasal] at the phonetic level. This principle is of course functionally motivated, since it has the effect of reinforcing the perceptual distinction between oral and nasal vowels in languages in which, like French, they are lexically distinctive.[7]

What is crucial to the present account is that purely phonetic generalizations, such as the fact that [t] is typically apical in one language but typically laminal in another, or that oral vowels are robustly oral in one language but gradiently nasal in another, have no direct consequences for the level of phonological feature representation itself. A minimalist approach of the sort adopted here requires that features are present at only those levels where they are required to express generalizations. It follows that features required only to express phonetic generalizations are present, if present at all, only at the phonetic level.

5.   Tier Projection

5.1 Overview

We now consider an application of the principle of representational economy to the notion of autosegmental tier projection. Perhaps the standard view in phonology at present is that most or all features are assigned to independent autosegmental tiers according to a universal schema, usually given in the form of an inverted rooted tree whose terminal elements are features (see e.g. Sagey 1990, Halle 1991, Clements and Hume 1995). The structure of the tree is held to be the same in all languages, regardless of differences in phonological patterning. However, this view introduces superfluous representational elements in the form of tiers that play no role at all in given languages. Following the principle of representational economy, we wish to eliminate all representational elements that play no role in the phonological system of a given language. This principle applies to nodes and tiers as well as to features.

In order to eliminate this superfluity, a Prominence Criterion for autosegmental projection is proposed:

(21) Prominence Criterion:
      In any language, all and only prominent features and nodes are projected onto separate autosegmental tiers

The effect of this principle is that tier projection, like feature specification, is relativized to the system of each particular language. The notion of prominence unites several functional properties of features, all of which provide motivation for autosegmental representation. The more important of these are summarized below:

(22) Prominence

An active feature value or node X is said to be *prominent* if it satisfies at least one of the following conditions:

   a. X is the argument in a constraint SPREAD(X), AGREE(X), or OCP(X)

   b. X is a floating feature

   c. X forms part of a monosegmental contour

   d. X constitutes a morpheme

(All the constraint types in (22a) will be exemplified below.) Features and feature sets not meeting one of these conditions, or others that may have to be included in a complete list, are nonprominent and are not projected.

The restriction of tier projection to prominent features and nodes, in the above sense, follows the logic, if not always the practice, of earlier Autosegmental Phonology. An important precedent can be found in McCarthy (1988), who observed that the features [sonorant] and [consonantal] differ from all other features in that they arguably never spread, delink, or exhibit OCP effects independently of other features.[8] The placement of these features on independent autosegmental tiers fails to predict this behavior. Consequently, McCarthy proposed to group them together on the root node, dominating all features of a segment, where they form an indissociable bundle, as shown in McCarthy's figure (16), reproduced in (23) below:

(23)   McCarthy (1988):

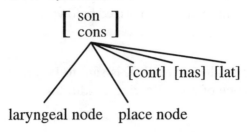

$$\begin{bmatrix} \text{son} \\ \text{cons} \end{bmatrix}$$

[cont] [nas] [lat]

laryngeal node   place node

The prediction made by this mode of representation is that [sonorant] and [consonantal] do not behave independently of each other, or of the root node upon which they are bundled. Consequently, they spread from one segment to another only if the root node itself spreads, as in total segmental assimilation. Generalizing this idea, Clements and Hume (1995: 267) propose a set of criteria for feature organization, requiring among other things that if the spreading or delinking of either of two nodes x and y always entails the spreading or delinking of the other, x and y form a single node. This principle allows a given feature to be autosegmentalized only when it displays genuine autonomous behavior with respect to operations such as spreading and delinking, i.e. prominence in the sense in which this term is used here. If we now take the further step of applying this principle to individual languages, it entails that features are autosegmentalized only in languages in which they are prominent. In the limit case, if no features display prominence in a given language, all are entered on the root node, and no further tiers are projected.

It might at first seem that this move toward additional representational economy undermines the strong predictions that follow from a universal feature geometry. To maintain these predictions, we propose to incorporate the universal geometry as a constraining condition on the features and feature sets that may be autosegmentally extracted in any language:

(24) Projection Condition:
    All constituents in the feature representations of a given language must be constituents of the universal feature hierarchy.

(A constituent is defined as any node in the rooted tree, including its dependents, if any.)

This principle can be illustrated schematically as follows. Let us assume a universal feature hierarchy represented as in (25), where A is the root node, B, C, and D are intermediate (class) nodes, and f, g, h, i, j are features:

(25)

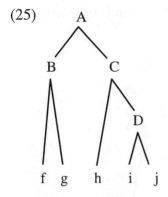

The Projection Condition (24) allows the following features and feature sets to be extracted, among others:

(26)   a.   b.   c.   d.   e.

$\begin{bmatrix} A \\ fghij \end{bmatrix}$ $\begin{bmatrix} A \\ fg \end{bmatrix}$ $\begin{bmatrix} A \\ fg \end{bmatrix}$ $\begin{bmatrix} A \\ fg \end{bmatrix}$ $\begin{bmatrix} A \\ fg \end{bmatrix}$

            $\begin{bmatrix} C \\ hij \end{bmatrix}$ $\begin{bmatrix} C \\ h \end{bmatrix}$ $\begin{bmatrix} C \\ h \end{bmatrix}$ $\begin{bmatrix} C \\ h \end{bmatrix}$

                        $\begin{bmatrix} D \\ ij \end{bmatrix}$ $\begin{bmatrix} D \\ i \end{bmatrix}$ $\begin{matrix} D \\ \diagup \diagdown \\ i \quad j \end{matrix}$

                                    j   i

In the first of these representations, nothing has been extracted; all features are bundled on the root node. Here there is a single constituent, A, which corresponds to constituent A in (25). In the second, the features constituting node C have been extracted as a unit, but none of its individual features h, i, j have been separately projected. Here there are two constituents, A and C, each corresponding to constituents in (25). Each remaining representation illustrates fuller degrees of tier projection, in which all constituents still conform to the Projection Condition (24). (25) itself represents the full or maximal projection of the universal hierarchy.

Other imaginable representations *not* meeting the Projection Condition are shown in (27a-c).

(27)   a.   b.   c.   d.

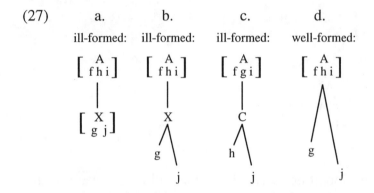

In (27a), only g and j have been extracted as a constituent, bundled onto a new node X; this node matches no constituent in (25). Extracting g and j on separate tiers as shown in (27b) still fails to satisfy the Projection Condition. A representation in which not all members of a constituent have been projected, as in (27c) where h and j have been extracted under a node C but i has been left behind, equally violates the Projection Condition. But a representation in which g and j have each been extracted as individual constituents, as shown in (27d), is well-formed, as it satisfies the Projection Condition; the constituents in this representation are A, g, and j, all of which are constituents in (25).

Let us consider a concrete illustration in which, for example, B of (25) is interpreted as the Laryngeal node, C the Oral Cavity node, and D the Place node in the sense of Clements and Hume (1995), and features f-j are interpreted as [spread], [constricted], [cont], [labial], and [coronal], respectively. Projectable feature and nodes include the Laryngeal node, the Oral Cavity node, the Place node, the individual features, and any well-formed combinations of these. The following languages are permitted by the Projection Condition, among others:

(28) a. Language A has no prominent features. In this language nothing is projected; all features are bundled on the Root node. For example, if /p/ is specified only for the feature [labial], as in Hawaiian (10), /p/ is represented as follows:

Root
[labial]

b. Language B differs from Language A in that only [labial] is prominent. Only [labial] is projected, and /p/ is represented as follows:

Root
|
[labial]

c. Language C differs from Language B in that only the set of place features is prominent, as a group. Just the Place node is projected, and /p/ is represented as follows:

Root
|
Place
[labial]

d. Language D differs from Language C in that [labial] is also prominent. Here, both the Place node and [labial] are projected, and /p/ is accordingly represented as follows:

Root
|
Place
|
[labial]

In sum, only those nodes needed to express prominence-related generalizations are projected.

A principle of Tier Inertia parallels that of Feature Inertia (13):

(29) Tier Inertia

A tier unprojected in the input to a level cannot be inserted later in that level.

As a result, tier structure is stable throughout a phonological level. In parallel to the carry-over principle governing feature specifications, it is further assumed that tier structure present at one level is carried over into the next level. Thus, successive levels may become progressively enriched in tier structure.

The notion of prominence, as defined above, is related to those of distinctiveness and markedness. A feature that is prominent at a given level must satisfy the criteria of either distinctiveness or activity (or else it would be absent). As a result of the feature specification procedure discussed earlier, distinctive feature specifications present in the lexicon (and carried over into the phonology) are marked values, and tend to be drawn from features higher on the accessibility hierarchy. Prominent feature values are a subset of active values (including distinctive) values, and so will tend to consist of marked values of higher-level features (excluding of course those which, like [±sonorant], are universally unprojectable). But as unmarked values may sometimes be active and prominent as well – such as L tones in two-level tone systems, which commonly spread, float and contour – it cannot be stipulated that only marked values can be projected.

However, it appears to be the case that not all unmarked feature values are projectable. Phonological behavior requiring the projection of unmarked values such as [–nasal], [–spread], [–constricted] and certain other features is hard to come by, as these features apparently do not spread, dissimilate, contour, float, or exhibit other properties of prominence. The unmarked values of these features are apparently required only to delimit the natural classes to which constraints apply.[9]

Since projected vs. nonprojected features differ in terms of their 'visibility' to prominence-sensitive processes, prominence theory makes predictions with respect to possible and impossible feature behavior:

(30) Within any phonological level,
  a. prominent features will block long-distance spreading and OCP effects
  b. nonprominent features will be transparent to long-distance spreading and OCP effects

5.2   Some Assimilation Processes in Zoque

As a concrete illustration of the theory of tier projection presented above, let us consider further processes in Zoque, whose lexically specified consonants were shown in (16). Zoque has a process of nasal place assimilation, according to which an affix-final labial or coronal nasal assimilates in place to a following stop (Wonderly 1951-2). This process applies both in words containing native roots and in Spanish loans. Examples involving the 1st/2nd person singular possessive prefix /n-/ were shown in (15a) and (18). Further examples, showing that this process also affects the labial nasal /m/, are given in (31), illustrating the suffixes /-tam/ (31a) and /-aʔm/ (31b), as well as the 1st and 2nd person transitive subject prefix /n-/.

(31) a. /n-ken-tam-u/   →   ŋgendamu   'you (pl.) saw it'
    /n-ken-tam-keʔt-u/   →   ŋgendaŋgeʔtu   'you (pl.) also saw it'
    /n-ken-tam-tʌʔ-u/   →   ŋgendandʌʔu   'you (pl.) intended to see it'
    /y-ʔʌŋ-tam-coʔy-u/   →   ʔyʌŋdaɲɟoʔyu   'you (pl.) were sleepy'
  b. /min-u-aʔm-ʌh/   →   minwaʔmʌh   'I already came'
    /min-u-aʔm-tʌh/   →   minwaʔndʌh   'we already came'

Velar nasals do not assimilate: thus for example, /aʔŋ-pʌhk-/ 'to invite' is realized [aʔŋbʌhk]. Nor does /m/ assimilate in the exceptional suffix /-num/ 'impersonal'. The full set of assimilations is summarized in (32), which includes the effect of postnasal voicing:

(32) Nasal place assimilation before stops:

m or n	+	p	→	mb
"	+	t	→	nd
"	+	ts	→	dz
"	+	tʃ	→	dʒ
"	+	c	→	ɲɟ
"	+	k	→	ŋg

(See 15a, 18 for further examples). These processes apply only before stops, including affricates. The prefix /n/ is otherwise realized as nasalization of a following [w y h], and deletes without a trace in all other contexts. Affix-final /m/ is realized as [m] before [w] and vowels, and appears to be unattested in other contexts.[10]

Place assimilation will be expressed as a two-level constraint, PL-ASSIM. An informal statement is given in (33).

(33) PL-ASSIM: Given a nonhomorganic [+nasal] + [−continuant] sequence occurring in an input, spread the Place node of the stop to the nasal in the output.

This constraint, like other members of the SPREAD family, requires the insertion of an association line as its repair operation. Given representations such as (34a) or (34b) satisfying its input condition,

(34) a.   [+nasal] [−cont]   b.   [+nasal] [−cont]

          | | |
        Place_i   Place_j   Place_j

the output representation must be (35):

(35) [+nasal] [−cont]

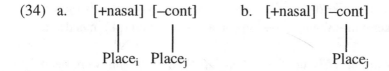

          Place_j

Unlike in our earlier analysis of *NT, we have built the repair operation, in this case spreading (association line insertion), directly into the statement of PL-ASSIM, by formulating it as a two-level constraint with the repair specified in the output. This is because spreading appears to be the overwhelmingly favored way of eliminating nonhomorganic NC sequences like (34a) and (34b). Other conceivable repair operations, such as epenthesis, metathesis, segment deletion, Place node deletion, or a change of the features [+nasal] or [–continuant], seem rarely if ever attested.[11] This might at first sight appear to provide support for the Minimality Principle (Paradis 1996) as discussed above if we place association lines at the very bottom of the hierarchy of levels, but as we have already noted this principle expresses only preferences, and does not categorically exclude other types of repair operations. Two-level constraints have, of course, been proposed elsewhere in the literature (e.g. the bilevel rules of Goldsmith (1993), or the Input-Output Faithfulness Constraints of standard OT), and appear to be the appropriate way to express nasal place assimilation.[12] The expression of PL-ASSIM as a two-level constraint instead of a one-level markedness constraint such as ALIGN(PLACE) has the desirable effect of constraining the class of possible repairs to just the attested one.

Nasal place assimilation can be illustrated by the example *mbama* 'my clothing', from underlying /n-pama/:

(36)   Nasal place assimilation : n-pama → mbama

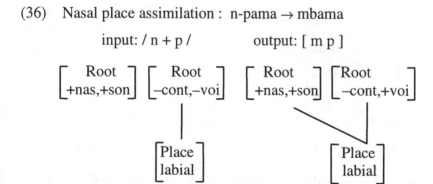

All distinctive and active features are displayed in both segments in these representations. The lexical feature specifications given in (16)

provide [+nasal, +sonorant] in /n/ and [labial] in /p/. In addition, *NT (19a) activates [–voice] in /p/, and both *NT and PL-ASSIM activate [–continuant] in /p/. No other features are present in these segments. PL-ASSIM renders the Place node prominent and triggers its projection onto a separate tier, respecting the Projection Condition (24). Since [labial] itself is not rendered prominent by PL-ASSIM nor by any other phenomena of Zoque under consideration here, it is not projected onto a separate tier of its own, and remains bundled on the Place node as shown in (28c). Given these representations, the input form satisfies the input condition of PL-ASSIM, and the ill-formed configuration is repaired by spreading the Place node from the stop to the nasal in the output. (The violation of *NT is at the same time eliminated by INSERT([+voice]).)

A further assimilation process of importance in Zoque is Palatal Substitution, according to which anterior coronals fuse with a following [y] to become the corresponding posterior sound. Palatal Substitution is illustrated by the forms in (37):

(37) /wiht-yah-u/   →   wihcahu   'they walked'
      /y-meʔts-yah-u/   →   myeʔtʃahu   'they sought it'
      /y-sohs-yah-u/   →   ʃohʃahu   'they cooked it'
      /ken-yah-u/   →   keɲahu   'they looked'

Other Cy sequences remain unfused.[13] The full set of changes is as follows:

(38) Palatal Substitution:

      t + y   →   c
      ts + y   →   tʃ
      s + y   →   ʃ
      n + y   →   ɲ

(Palatal Substitution does not affect prefixal /n-/ before y, which, as noted earlier, drops out after nasalizing the y.) Following the feature characterization of Zoque consonants given in (16), Palatal Substitution spreads [+posterior] from the [y] to the preceding coronal and eliminates the [y]. No other features change. In particular, affricates remain affricates and plosives remain plosives; following the analysis in Kim (1997) and Clements (1999), this is taken as evidence that specifications of [+strident] remain constant.

To account for these changes, we factor Palatal Substitution into two constraints, posteriorization (POST) and y-deletion (Y-DEL), as stated informally in (39):

(39) a. POST: Given an unassimilated coronal + y sequence occurring in the input, spread the [+posterior] node of y to the coronal in the output
   b. Y-DEL: Delete [y] in a place-linked coronal cluster

Let us briefly comment these two constraints. POST characterizes the shift of an anterior coronal sound to its posterior counterpart in terms of the spreading of the feature [+posterior] (Lahiri and Evers 1991). [+posterior] is the appropriate feature for this task, as spreading of [–back] or [+high] would create an anterior palatalized segment instead.[14] POST is formulated as a two-level input-output constraint just like PL-ASSIM, for the same reasons: assimilation is the overwhelmingly favored way of repairing the ill-formed input configuration. While y is often deleted in this context, it typically disappears only after palatalizing the coronal sound, as in Zoque. Other imaginable repair operations for eliminating Cy sequences, such as epenthesis, metathesis, deletion of [+posterior], or deletion of the coronal consonant are unattested, at least in this writer's experience, except when forming part of more general phenomena such as cluster simplification.[15]

Y-DEL is also stated as a two-level constraint, with deletion incorporated as the unique repair operation; again, other imaginable repair operations seem unattested. Y-DEL is stated separately from POST since POST may apply independently. A striking example is [yoʃyoʃɲayu] 'he puttered (or tinkered) around', from underlying /yohs-yohs-nay-u/ (Wonderly 1951-2: 111, 150); in this form, the requirements of reduplicative identity appear to have resulted in both the overapplication of POST to the second (underlying) /s/ and the underapplication of Y-DEL to the second /y/.

Palatal Substitution is illustrated in (40), showing the example *wihcahu* 'they walked' from underlying /wiht-yah-u/.

(40)   Palatal Substitution: wiht-yah-u → wihcahu

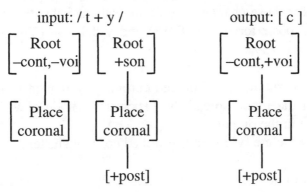

As before, all distinctive and active features are displayed in each segment: [+sonorant] and [+posterior] are distinctive in /y/, [–continuant] and [–voice] are activated in /t/ by *NT, as discussed earlier, and [coronal] is activated by POST and Y-DEL. No other features are present in the representation, at least on the basis of the evidence discussed in this paper. The Place node is projected due to its appearance as a spreading node in PL-ASSIM (33), and [+posterior] due to its role as a spreading node in POST.[16]

Representation (40) conflates two steps. In the first, [+posterior] spreads leftward; in the second, the remaining features of [y] delete.

To summarize, this section has shown how certain features and nodes are rendered prominent and autosegmentally projected, as a result of their occurrence in constraints of the type SPREAD(X). Features and nodes that are unprominent remain unprojected, as illustrated in (40). Although languages accordingly differ in terms of which nodes are autosegmentally projected, all projections are strongly constrained by the Projection Condition (24).

We return to further aspects of place assimilation and palatalization in Zoque in the next section, after examining the structure of the coronal node in fuller detail.

6. Coronal transparency

This section applies the framework developed in sections 1-5 to a problem arising in the recent phonological literature involving the treatment of coronal transparency. After a preliminary examination of the structure of the coronal node (section 6.1), a new analysis of coronal transparency phenomena is proposed, explaining how sounds whose [coronal] feature is present in representations can nevertheless be transparent to coronal spreading processes (section 6.2).

6.1 The structure of the coronal node

The coronal place features shown in (41), describing four places of coronal articulation further subcategorized by [±strident], have been motivated in the recent literature (Hume 1994, Hall 1997, Clements 1999).

(41)

	t	t͜s	t̪	t̪͜s̪	ʈ	ʈ͜ʂ	c	tʃ, tɕ
[posterior]	−	−	−	−	+	+	+	+
[apical]	+	+	−	−	+	+	−	−
[strident]	−	+	−	+	−	+	−	+

Typical realizations, as suggested by the symbols at the head of each column, are (proceeding from left to right): apical denti-alveolar plosives, apical denti-alveolar affricates, laminal denti-alveolar plosives, laminal denti-alveolar affricates, retroflex plosives, retroflex affricates, palatal plosives, and postalveolar affricates.

How are the three features of (41) organized? The view that the first two, at least, are dependents of the Coronal node (Sagey 1990, based on unpublished work by Steriade 1986), is well supported and has been widely adopted. However, the place of [strident] in the feature hierarchy remains a matter of controversy. Two principal views have been expressed:

- [+strident] is a Root node dependent
- [+strident] is a Coronal node dependent

The second view has come to receive rather convincing support from a number of observations. First, if [+strident] characterizes only coronal sounds, as a number of linguists have suggested, then it should not be treated as a root-dependent feature, where it could potentially characterize other sounds as well. Second, a number of facts show that [+strident] forms a functional unit with the other coronal features. For example, Shaw (1991) cites facts involving consonant harmony in Tahltan showing that [+strident] spreads as a unit with other coronal features (we consider these facts in more detail below). Rubach (1994) similarly observes that [+strident] spreads with other coronal features in Polish.

If [+strident] is analyzed as a member of the coronal node, we strongly predict that when coronal features spread as a unit in rules of coronal assimilation or place assimilation, [+strident] should spread with them. However, there is a major counterexample to this claim. As Rubach (1994) has observed, rules of place assimilation never spread [+strident] from sibilants onto nasals. In Zoque, for example, as seen in the examples in (15a) above, the application of place assimilation to the underlying form /n-tsima/ 'my calabash' yields [ndzima], in which the nasal remains nonstrident. Rubach suggests two possible solutions to this problem: "Either we can adopt a universal convention that erases [strid] whenever it has been spread to a sonorant or we can assume that [strid] is not interpreted phonetically when it appears on a sonorant" (p. 139).

The first of these proposals raises a formal problem, since any universal convention erasing [+strident] under a multilinked Place (or coronal) node would eliminate stridency in the oral stop as well. The second solution does not raise this problem, but seems ad hoc: why should we require a special phonetic principle for just this particular case? Aren't we forced to concede, after all, that [+strident] is linked to the Root node, where it will be unaffected by Place node spreading?

That the answer is negative can be appreciated in the light of a further observation. In many languages, geminated affricates are realized as long stops with a single affricated release, as the following forms from Kabyle Berber illustrate (Elmedlaoui 1993):

(42)

	perfect	*imperfect*	
β / bb	əsβəʁ	səbbəʁ	'to paint'
θ / tt	əfθəl	fəttəl	'to roll out (couscous)'
χ / dd	əχðəm	χəddəm	'to work'
s / tts	əχsi	χəttsi	'to go off (fire) '
z / ddz	ənzər	nəddzər	'to blow one's nose'
ʃ / ttʃ	əkʃəm	kəttʃem	'to come in'
ʒ / ddʒ	əmʒər	məddʒər	'to harvest'

As these forms show, [+strident] is distinctive in Kabyle stops according to the feature analysis in (41). When the sibilant [s] is geminated, the result is a long stop with a strident release [tts] rather than two successive affricates [tsts]. These facts raise the same problem as the assimilation of [n] to [ts] in Zoque: [+strident] formally characterizes both members of the cluster, but is realized only in the second. In the case of affricate gemination, however, the failure of [+strident] to be realized in the first member cannot be solved by moving [+strident] up to the Root node, since the spreading of the Root node to form the geminate carries all its dependents, including [+strident], along with it.

Instead, developing Rubach's second suggestion we propose the following principle of phonetic interpretation:

(43) The feature [+strident] is realized phonetically in the turbulence noise associated with obstruents.

Since stridency is defined acoustically as high-amplitude, high-frequency noise, it is not surprising that it should be manifested in the turbulence noise associated with obstruent production. This analysis readily explains the facts cited above. In Kabyle, as the first component of the geminate [tts] is unreleased, turbulence noise only occurs at the release of the second component; consequently, only the release can bear the acoustic manifestation of stridency. The failure of the nasal to become strident in the place-assimilated sequence [nts] can therefore be understood as a special case of a more general principle.[17]

Now let us consider how the three coronal features are organized under the coronal node. In earlier frameworks, it was assumed that these features, like all others, lie on independent tiers. If this analysis were correct, it would predict that each of the three features can spread independently of the others. But this does not appear to be the case. A survey of the literature suggests the following generalizations:

(44)   Solidarity patterns among coronal features:
a. [±strident] cannot spread independently of [±posterior] and [±apical]
b. [±posterior] and [±apical] can spread independently of [±strident]
c. [±posterior] and [±apical] cannot spread independently of each other

Full evidence for these generalizations cannot be reviewed here, but a few illustrative examples can be offered.

First, in support of (44a), [+strident] has been observed to spread as a unit with other coronal features, as noted by Shaw (1991) in Tahltan and by Rubach (1994) in Polish. A further case of sibilant harmony in Basque will be reviewed below. I am unfamiliar with cases in which [+strident] spreads to the exclusion of other coronal features. A putative example would be a case in which /t/ is realized as the affricate [ts] before [ʃ ʒ], or in which an alveopalatal stop [c] becomes the corresponding affricate [tɕ] before [s z].

The independence of [±posterior] with respect to [+strident] has already been illustrated by Palatal Substitution in Zoque, in which [+posterior] spreads without affecting [+strident]; thus, /y-meʔts-yah-u/ 'they sought it' is realized [myeʔtʃahu], in which the assimilated [tʃ] retains its underlying stridency. This is shown in (45), paralleling (40).

(45) Palatal Substitution: y-me?ts-yah-u → mye?tʃah-u

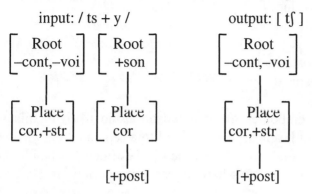

input: / ts + y /   output: [tʃ]

$$\begin{bmatrix} \text{Root} \\ -\text{cont,}-\text{voi} \end{bmatrix} \begin{bmatrix} \text{Root} \\ +\text{son} \end{bmatrix} \qquad \begin{bmatrix} \text{Root} \\ -\text{cont,}-\text{voi} \end{bmatrix}$$

$$\begin{bmatrix} \text{Place} \\ \text{cor,}+\text{str} \end{bmatrix} \begin{bmatrix} \text{Place} \\ \text{cor} \end{bmatrix} \qquad \begin{bmatrix} \text{Place} \\ \text{cor,}+\text{str} \end{bmatrix}$$

[+post]   [+post]

If the nonstridency of [y] had been carried along with its feature [+posterior] as a single unit, we would have expected [tʃ] to shift to its nonstrident counterpart [c].[18]

I am unaware of cases in which [±posterior] and [±apical] spread independently of each other, and none are revealed in the surveys of Hamilton (1993) and Gnanadesikian (1994). In a language in which both features are distinctive or active, the spread of one without the other would yield hypothetically possible, but unattested effects like those shown in (46) (symbols are as defined in 41):

(46)   ṭ → c / __ t̪

(i.e. [+posterior] spreads from a retroflex to a laminal without concurrent spread of [+apical])

t̪ → ṭ / __ t̪

(i.e. [+apical] spreads from a retroflex to a laminal without concurrent spread of [+posterior])

In consequence, it appears that the coronal node has the following maximal expansion:

(47)
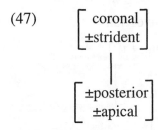

This structure embodies the generalizations in (44). In this view, [±posterior] and [±apical] are assigned to a separate tier, where they can spread independently of [±strident]. [±strident] is bundled onto the coronal node itself, where it can spread only if all coronal features spread.

6.2 Case studies in coronal transparency

"Coronal transparency" refers to the fact that the place features of coronal sounds, including [coronal] itself, are frequently invisible to long–distance coronal spreading. An early attempt to explain this fact, developing a suggestion by Kiparsky (1985), was the idea that coronal sounds are unspecified for [coronal] at early points in a derivation, acquiring this feature only later in the derivation (see the papers collected in Paradis and Prunet 1991a). As Paradis and Prunet themselves observe in their overview of this problem, however, "none of the present underspecification theories can account for the full range of the properties identified as constituting the special status of coronals" (1991b: 24). In particular, a major problem facing the treatment of coronal transparency in terms of any universal theory of coronal underspecification is that fact that morpheme structure constraints and early rules of the phonology often make crucial reference to [coronal] (Paradis and Prunet 1991b: 13, Mohanan 1991, McCarthy and Taub 1992). This problem is compounded in monostratal versions of OT since the constraints accounting for both of these contradictory sets of facts must be defined on the output, where coronal features cannot be both present and absent at the same time. As a result of these problems, analyses treating coronal transparency in terms of coronal underspecification have tended to become discredited. However, no alternative solution has yet received wide acceptance.

The present framework allows a new approach to this problem. As we saw in section 3, the feature [coronal] is absent in lexical specifications, following the principle that unmarked features and feature values are lexically unspecified. The feature [coronal] is specified in the phonology only if it figures as a term in constraints, and is projected to a separate tier only if it is phonologically prominent. Coronal transparency phenomena can therefore be expressed in either of two ways: 1) in terms of the absence of [coronal] (in segment classes in which this feature is fully inactive), and 2) in terms of the nonprojection of [coronal] (in segment classes in which the feature is active but unprojected). We thus obtain the advantages of coronal underspecification (the expression of transparency effects) without incurring its disadvantages (the inability to refer to the features needed to express morpheme structure constraints and early rules applying at the same level).

It is here proposed that the marked values of coronal features are [+strident], [+posterior], [+apical] in posterior coronals (i.e. retroflex as opposed to (alveo)palatal sounds), and [–apical] in anterior coronals (i.e. laminal as opposed to apical dentals and alveolars). This analysis assumes the pairings of representative stops shown in (48):

(48) | *marked* | *unmarked* |
|---|---|
| ts (strident) | t (nonstrident) |
| c (posterior) | t (anterior) |
| ṭ (apical) | c (laminal) |
| t̪ (laminal) | ṭ (apical) |

When just one value of a feature is projected, it is typically the marked value. This means that an unprojected coronal will normally be one of the unmarked nonstrident apical dentals or alveolars such as *t*, *n*, *r*, or *l*. Such sounds are expected to be transparent to long-distance spreading. However, in a language in which unmarked values are prominent as well, all coronal sounds should be opaque.

6.2.1 Sibilant Harmony in Baztan Basque

An interesting example of long-distance coronal harmony involving all three marked coronal features can be cited from Baztan Basque (N'diaye 1970, Hualde 1991). This language requires all sibilants to agree in place of articulation within the root. Baztan coronal consonants are shown below in both phonetic and orthographic transcription:

(49)

	phonetic:					orthographic:				
1	2	3	4	5		1	2	3	4	5
t				c		t				tt
d						d				
	t̪s̪	t̠s̠	tʃ				tz	ts	tx	
	s̪	s̠	ʃ				z	s	x	
n			ɲ			n				ñ
l			ʎ			l				ll

A feature description of these sounds is given in (50), following the feature framework in (41) (articulatory labels are from N'diaye):

(50)

		[posterior]	[apical]	[strident]	
1.	t, d, n, l	–	+	–	dental
2.	t̪s̪, s̪	–	–	+	predorsal alveolar
3.	t̠s̠, s̠	–	+	+	retroflex
4.	tʃ, ʃ	+	–	+	palatoalveolar
5.	c, ɲ, ʎ	+	–	–	palatal

According to Hualde's description, Sibilant Harmony requires all sibilants to agree in all coronal features within the root. Examples include the following:

(51) asots, eltsuntse, urtxintx, samats, zuzen, azazkal, zimitz,
      sasoin, eskasi, osasun, zintzur, itseso, sasi, zorrotz, zortzi, zize,
      zurruzte, zapelatz

As these examples illustrate, nonsibilant consonants are transparent to Sibilant Harmony. Sibilant Harmony is also active in the adaptation of Castillian words containing apical [s] and laminal [θ] (Hualde 1991). From regular sound correspondences we would expect *frantzes* 'French', with disagreeing sibilants, corresponding to the modern Castillian *francés* [franθés]. Instead we find the harmonized *frantses*. Similarly, Castillian *sazón* has been adopted in Basque as *sasoi* 'season'. As Hualde points out, although Sibilant Harmony does not yield synchronic alternations today, regular patterns of loanword adaptation suggest that a spreading process was active historically.[19]

To express static harmony such as this, which produces no alternations, a constraint of the type SPREAD(X) is inappropriate: this is a case of similtude, not assimilation. Here, a different constraint family, AGREE(X), is more appropriate. Members of this family require all nodes meeting a certain condition to be identical; but there is no requirement that they share a spreading node. In the case of Basque Sibilant Harmony, the following constraint is proposed:

(52) AGREE(SIBILANT): Within the root, [coronal, +strident] nodes must be identical.

In the native lexicon, AGREE(SIBILANT) is satisfied by avoidance, and no repair operation need be specified. In loanwords, AGREE (SIBILANT) violations are repaired by node copy, which requires that the full content of one [+strident] coronal node, including all dependent structure, be copied onto another. AGREE(SIBILANT) renders [+strident] coronal nodes prominent, and requires them to be projected onto a separate tier. Only strident coronal nodes are projected since only these are specified in the constraint.

Other considerations, involving phonetic interpretation, support the choice of AGREE(SIBILANT) with its associated repair operation of node copy as the operative constraint in Sibilant Harmony. Spreading nodes in autosegmental representations can usually be interpreted as single, uniform articulatory gestures extending over several segments. Besides being strongly supported by phonology-internal arguments (see e.g. Odden 1986, Hayes 1986, Clements and

Hume 1995), this interpretation renders autosegmental representations congruent with the overlapping gestural representations sometimes thought to represent the articulatory level of phonetic interpretation (see e.g. Browman and Goldstein 1989). In contrast, however, sequences of identical, independent nodes should be interpreted phonetically as sequences of rearticulated gestures.

Certain Basque forms show that Sibilant Harmony does not involve a single, uniform spreading gesture superimposed over intervening gestures with which they are compatible, as a spreading analysis would require. In the verb [siɲet̪s̪i] 'to believe', the harmonizing sequence [s̪ ... t̪s̪] consists of apico-alveolar sounds. This sequence is interrupted by the incompatible palatal segment [ɲ], differing from it in terms of both apicality and posteriority. If we adopted an analysis spreading the coronal node from [s̪] to [t̪s̪], we would expect (under the uniform interpretation principle) that the intervening [ɲ] would merge with the apico-anterior [n]. But this is not the case. The use of AGREE(SIBILANT) allows us to maintain the uniform interpretation principle in such cases.[20]

An analysis incorporating AGREE(SIBILANT) is illustrated with the form [siɲet̪s̪i] in (46). (Irrelevant segments are omitted.)

(53)   s̪   ...   ɲ   ...   t̪s̪

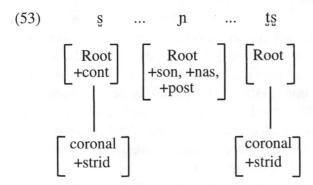

Following the lexical specification procedure presented earlier (section 3), [+strident] and [+continuant] will be lexically specified in /s̪/, [+sonorant], [+nasal] and [+posterior] in /ɲ/, and [+strident] in /t̪s̪/. No other features are lexically present in these segments. [coronal], though not distinctive, is activated and made prominent in [s̪] and [t̪s̪] by AGREE(SIBILANT). Crucially, this constraint does not refer to nonstrident coronal nodes, and therefore does not project or activate [coronal] in [ɲ]. Thus this sound, though bearing the coronal feature [+posterior] distinctively, is transparent, and AGREE (SIBILANT) applies to the tier-adjacent [coronal, +strident] nodes, consistently with requirements of locality.

If we are correct in believing that constraints of the AGREE family apply locally on their tier, there could be no other processes in Basque belonging to the same stratum as Sibilant Harmony rendering coronal nodes prominent in intervening segments, for if such processes existed, these nodes would be projected into the tier structure between the two target nodes, blocking AGREE(SIBILANT).

A possible case of this type turns out not to be one on closer inspection. Baztan Basque has two lexical palatalization processes which assign [+posterior] to sonorants in certain contexts (Hualde 1991, 37-9, 114-23). The first of these, Palatalization, posteriorizes /n l/ in the context i̯ __ V, triggering loss of the glide, and creating alternations such as [aɾai̯n] 'fish', [aɾaɲ-e] 'the fish'. As this example shows, Palatalization applies to the output of morphological affixation. A similar process of Word-initial Palatalization palatalizes /n/ in the context #i__V; this too applies to the output of the morphology, creating alternations such as [nola] 'how', [i-ɲola] 'anyhow'.

These processes parallel the analogous process POST in Zoque (cf. 39), and we must assume that they render [+posterior] prominent in the vocoid [i] in Basque, from whence it spreads onto a following /n/, creating derived [ɲ]. It will be recalled, however, that the projection of [+posterior] does not, by itself, entail the projection, or even the activation, of [coronal] in the present framework. Thus these palatalization processes, even if belonging to the stratum in which Sibilant Harmony holds, are not expected to interact with it.[21]

6.2.2 Coronal Harmony in Tahltan

Let us consider a further case of long-distance coronal assimilation in the Telegraph Creek variety of Tahltan, an Athapaskan language described by Shaw (1991). This case has stimulated much discussion, and continues to present an anomaly for most current feature frameworks, which are required to posit more or less ad hoc solutions. It will be shown that given the present framework, the original analysis of these facts proposed by Shaw, employing coronal transparency, can be maintained with no essential modification.

Coronal obstruents occur in five series:

(54)   *(simple)   lateral   apical   laminal   palato-alveolar*

d	dl	dz	dð	dʒ
t	tɬ	ts	tθ	tʃ
t'	tɬ'	ts'	tθ'	tʃ'
	ɬ	s	θ	ʃ
	l	z	ð	ʒ

According to Coronal Harmony, any apical, laminal, or palato-alveolar obstruent assimilates all coronal place features of any following member of the same class, within the word. As Shaw (1991) points out, what these sounds have in common is that they all bear distinctive specifications for a marked value of one of the coronal place features. These are shown below (using present feature terminology):

(55)   [strident] [apical] [posterior]

    apical: ts, dz   +
    laminal: tθ, dð   −
    palato-alveolar: tʃ, dʒ   +

(Recall from (48) that [−apical] is the marked value of [apical] in anterior sounds.) It can easily be verified that these specifications, proposed by Shaw, are just the ones produced by the feature specification procedure outlined in section 3, nomenclature aside. In contrast, members of the remaining series bear no marked values for these features.

Coronal harmony creates alternations such as the following (target segments are separated by dashes):

(56) /-s-/ '1st sg. subject marker'

    s → θ: θɛ-θ-ðɛɬ   'I'm hot'
             dɛ-θ-kʷʊθ   'I cough'
             ɛ-θ-duːθ   'I whipped him'
             na-θ-tθ'ɛt   'I fell off (horse) '
    s → ʃ: hudi-ʃ-tʃa   'I love them'
             ɛ-ʃ-dʒɪni   'I'm singing'
             ya-ʃ-tɬ'ɛtʃ   'I splashed it'
    s → s: (elsewhere)
             ɛ-s-k'aː   'I'm gutting fish'
             ɛ-s-dan   'I'm drinking'

(57) /-θ-/ '1st dual subject prefix'

    θ → s: dɛ-s-idzɛl   'we shouted'
             xa-s-iːdɛts   'we plucked it'
             dɛ-s-it'ʌs   'we are walking'
    θ → ʃ: i-ʃ-itʃotɬ   'we blew it up'
             u-ʃ-idʒɛ   'we are called'
    θ → θ: (elsewhere)
             dɛ-θ-igɪtɬ   'we threw it'
             na-θ-ibaːtɬ   'we hung it'

As these and further examples show, the members of the first two series in (54) are transparent to coronal harmony.

Turning now to the analysis, we must first determine whether we are dealing with a SPREAD or AGREE constraint. The phonetic considerations discussed above argue for the latter choice, since in an example like [xasiːdɛts] 'we plucked it' (57), the spreading features of the sibilant [ts] must cross the articulatorily incompatible features of the nonsibilant [d]. Under the feature analysis assumed here (see Kim 1997, Clements 1999), if [d] acquired the spreading feature [+strident], it would be realized as [dz], since [d] differs from [dz] only in lacking the marked feature [+strident]. Consequently, we cannot maintain that a single, uniform articulatory gesture spreads across the whole sequence. We propose the following variant of the AGREE constraint proposed earlier for Basque (52):

(58) AGREE (MARKED CORONAL): Within the word, [coronal] nodes
bearing marked feature values must be identical.

Only marked coronal nodes are activated and projected to a separate
tier by this constraint. Violations are repaired by Node Copy. The
analysis of [xasiːdɛts] is thus as shown in (59):

(59) Coronal harmony: xa-θ-iːdɛts → xasiːdɛts

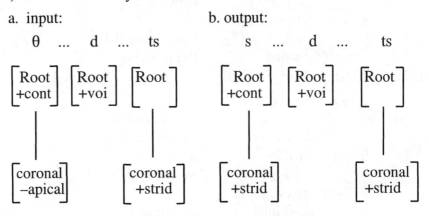

    a. input: b. output:

This analysis expresses the major features of Shaw's analysis,
without requiring any ad hoc assumptions about feature representation. In Tahltan, the /t/ and /tɬ/ series are transparent to coronal
harmony because their unmarked [coronal] features are neither
lexically specified nor active, and thus absent.

6.2.3 Summary

This section has shown how several well-known cases of coronal
harmony can be explained under the assumptions developed here.
Transparent coronals are typically the anterior, apical, nonstrident
sounds [t d l r], which bear the unmarked values for these three
coronal place features, and hence are unspecified for them in the
lexicon. Unless these features are activated and projected in the phonology, they will not be available to block long-distance assimilation.

Unlike previous approaches to coronal underspecification as represented by the papers collected in Paradis and Prunet (1991a), this account is consistent with the observation that transparent coronals do sometimes bear lexically distinctive or phonologically active coronal features. An example was cited from Basque, in which the incompatible sound [ɲ], bearing a lexically distinctive specification for [+posterior], occurs internally to the harmony domain in [siɲetṣi]. Under most approaches to coronal underspecification, such specifications necessarily block long-distance harmony. But in the present framework, such segments remain transparent as long as they are not rendered prominent by other constraints.

7. Transparence of [voice] in Japanese

As a final case study, we take up another unresolved anomaly in current phonological theory involving interactions between the well-known rules of Rendaku (Sequential Voicing) and Postnasal Voicing in Japanese. We first review the relevant facts (section 7.1), and then develop an analysis (section 7.2).

7.1 The Problem

Native Japanese consonant phonemes are give in (60), following standard sources such as Vance (1987) and Shibatani (1987):

(60) Japanese consonant phonemes (native or Yamato stratum):

	t	k
b	d	g
	s	h
	z	
m	n	
w	r	y

Of these sounds, /z/ is variably realized as the affricate [dz] or the fricative [z]. /h/ has several contextual variants including weak labial and palatal fricatives, and so is classed here among the obstruents; according to Itô and Mester (1999), it can be derived from underlying /p/, which debuccalizes as a singleton consonant but is realized as [pp] when geminate.

Lexical feature specifications for these consonants are given in (61), following the accessibility hierarchy in (8) and (17)):

(61)

	t	k	b	d	g	s	z	h	m	n	w	r	y
[sonorant]									+	+	+	+	+
[labial]			+						+		+		
[dorsal]		+			+								
[strident]						+	+						
[nasal]									+	+			
[posterior]													+
[voice]			+	+			+						
[spread]								+					

Notice that [lateral] and [continuant] are fully nondistinctive. Following the specification procedure stated earlier, [voice] is redundant in /b/ and so does not form part of its feature composition, although if we reanalyze /h/ as /p/ as suggested by Itô and Mester, [voice] would become distinctive in /b/.

According to the phenomenon known as Rendaku, initial obstruents are voiced in the second member of right-headed native compounds (see Itô and Mester 1986, Vance 1987, Itô, Mester, & Padgett 1995, 1999, Labrune 1999 and references therein). Representative examples are given in (62). The element represented by the symbol N, indicating the voicing trigger, will be discussed below.

(62) yu 'hot water' + N + toofu 'tofu' → yu doofu 'boiled tofu'
      iro 'color' + N + kami 'paper' → iro gami 'colored paper'
      yo 'night' + N + sakura 'cherry' → yo zakura 'blossoms at night'
      mizu 'water' + N + seme 'torture' → mizu zeme 'water torture'

According to a constraint known as Lyman's Law, Rendaku systematically fails to apply when the second member of the compound contains a voiced obstruent anywhere to the right; see the examples in (63). /b/ triggers Lyman's Law just as do the other voiced obstruents, as witnessed by the first form *siro-tabi*. As the last three examples show, Lyman's Law applies even if a nasal consonant or voiceless stop intervenes.

(63) siro + N + tabi   →   siro tabi   'white tabi'
      mono + N + šizuka   →   mono šizuka   'tranquil'
      onna + N + kotoba   →   onna kotoba   'feminine speech'
      taikutsu + N + šinogi   →   taikutsu šinogi 'time-killing'
      širooto + N + kaŋgae   →   širooto kaŋgae   'layman's idea'

Lyman's Law also applies as a morpheme-level constraint prohibiting two voiced obstruents in native roots; thus we find *buta* 'pig', *futa* 'lid', *fuda* 'sign', but not **buda*, etc.

A process of Postnasal Voicing similar to the one observed in Zoque voices obstruents after nasals in native and mimetic roots. This process gives rise to alternations such as those involving the suffixes /-te/ and /-ta/ in (64) as well as verbal compounds formed with /fum/ 'step on', shown in (65):

(64) verbal inflection

	stem		*gerund*	*past*
a.	mi	'see'	mi-te	mi-ta
	tor	'take'	tot-te	tot-ta
	kaw	'buy'	kat-te	kat-ta
	tok	'solve'	toi-te	toi-ta
b.	kam	'chew'	kan-de	kan-da
	šin	'die'	šin-de	šin-da
	tob	'fly'	ton-de	ton-da

(65) verbal compounds

tsukeru	'attach'	fun-dzukeru	'trample on'
kiru	'cut'	fuŋ-giru	'give up'
šibaru	'tie'	fun-ĵibaru	'immobilize'

Postnasal Voicing applies also within native (Yamato) roots as a static constraint: thus we find forms like *tombo* 'dragonfly', *tumbo* 'deaf', but no forms like **tompo*.[22]

These are the facts that will concern us here. We now turn to the well-known visibility paradox described by Itô, Mester, and Padgett (1995) and discussed by others since, notably Calabrese (1995) and Pater (1999). As Itô, Mester, and Padgett present it, nasals behave inconsistently in regard to the feature [voice]. In some forms, this feature appears to be invisible, as shown in (66):

(66) [+voice] is invisible in nasals:

    a. mizu 'water'

    b. iro + N + kami → iro gami
        ([m] does not trigger Lyman's Law, and Rendaku applies)

    c. taikutsu + N + šinogi → taikutsu šinogi
        (Lyman's Law blocks Rendaku across [n])

In (66a), the nasal does not create a violation of Lyman's Law. This shows that Lyman's Law is sensitive to voicing in obstruents, but does not detect voicing in nasals. In (66b), Rendaku applies in spite of the following (voiced) nasal; here again, Lyman's Law is insensitive to the voicing of the nasal. In (66c), Lyman's Law blocks voicing of the initial [š], in spite of the intervening voiced nasal; once again, its voicing specification appears to be invisible. These facts are simply explained on the theory that voicing is not specified in the class of nasals, where it is lexically nondistinctive.

However, another set of observations might suggest that this analysis cannot be maintained:

(67) [+voice] is apparently visible in nasals:
    a. tombo 'dragonfly', but *tompo
    b. kam+te → kan-de 'chewing'
    c. širooto + N + kaŋgae → širooto kaŋgae 'layman's idea'

In (67a), Postnasal Voicing requires the obstruent to be voiced after the nasal, ruling out forms like **tompo*. (67b) shows the same effect across a morpheme boundary. (67c), exhibiting a failure of Rendaku, shows that stops voiced by Postnasal Voicing trigger Lyman's Law. Itô, Mester, and Padgett (1995) attribute these effects to the spread of the redundant voicing feature of the nasal to the obstruent.

Here, then, is the paradox as Itô, Mester, and Padgett present it: to explain the effects in (66), we must assume that voicing is unspecified in nasals, but to explain those in (67), we must assume that voicing is specified in nasals. Itô, Mester, and Padgett show that this contradiction cannot be resolved by a judicious ordering of Rendaku and a redundancy rule inserting voicing in nasals. The generalization, as they put it, is that "nasals appear to receive voice only where necessary to trigger NC voicing" (p. 577).[23]

For reasons already discussed in connection with similar voicing patterns in Zoque, Pater's (1999) proposal to analyse Postnasal Voicing in terms of the constraint *NT will be adopted here. *NT violations are resolved in Japanese by the insertion of voicing. Under this view, as Pater points out, the paradox disappears: [+voice] need never be specified in nasals.

However, under the present framework a new problem arises. As we have seen, feature values are activated by constraints that mention them. *NT mentions the feature [−voice], and thus activates it in Japanese. Indeed, this is not the only constraint that does so; another constraint, referred to as *P, excludes nongeminate [−voice] labial stops in native and Sino-Japanese morphemes (Itô and Mester 1999). Thus [−voice], on our assumptions, must be present in the native stratum of the phonology.

Here, then, is the problem: it will be recalled from examples like *onna-kotoba* 'feminine speech' (63) that voicelessness is transparent to Lyman's Law. Thus the intervening voiceless stop [t] in *kotoba* does not prevent the following voiced stop [b] from blocking the voicing of the initial stop [k]. In standard autosegmental theory, both [+voice] and [−voice] occupy the same autosegmental tier. If Lyman's Law is expressed via the OCP, ruling out adjacent occurrences of [+voice] as proposed by Itô and Mester (1986), then the intervening [–voice] value should incorrectly block Lyman's Law in *onna-kotoba*, as shown in (68):

(68) onna + N + k   o   t   o   b   a
         | | |
       [–voi] [–voi] [+voi]

Hence we expect the incorrect form **onna-gotoba*.

Itô and Mester (1986) took these facts as arguing for the under-specification of [–voice] in the stratum in which Rendaku applies, and Mester and Itô (1989) took the further step of proposing that [voice] is universally one-valued. Under either account, the values [–voice] of (68) would be absent, and Lyman's Law would correctly block the voicing of [k]. But as we have seen, this solution is not available in a theory including the principle of feature activation. The feature [–voice] is crucially required to define the natural class of voiceless obstruents in Japanese. Following familiar arguments, we cannot identify the class of relevant [–voice] sounds by referring to the class of sounds *lacking* [voice] specifications, since this class incorrectly includes sonorants, in which voicing is redundant and inactive (see Clements 1988, 1993a for discussion of the general problem of designating natural classes by reference to zero-speci-fications). Mester and Itô (1989: 280-1) take a strong stand on this point:

> Universally privative voicing means that voicelessness will remain phono-logically inert and can play no role in the phonology. Phonological rules cannot (a) insert, (b) spread, or (c) delete [–voiced], and (d) they cannot use it as a context predicate in nonassimilatory rules. We are not familiar with any cases crucially involving (c) and (d).

However, the constraint *NT provides just such an example of a context predicate, and requires, following this logic, that [–voice] be explicitly specified in voiceless obstruents in Japanese.[24]

7.2 A solution

The present framework allows a natural solution to this problem. The crucial insight is that while [+voice] is prominent in voiced stops due to Lyman's Law (viewed, following Itô and Mester, as an OCP constraint on [+voice]), the negative value [–voice], though activated by the phonotactic constraint *NT, is not rendered prominent by it, and is accordingly not projected onto the Voice tier. Consequently, though [–voice] can trigger *NT, it cannot block Rendaku.

Drawing upon the recent discussion by Labrune (1999), we shall regard the Rendaku trigger as a morphological affix consisting of a nasal autosegment, represented in the earlier examples as the element N. This element, restricted to certain compounds in the native lexical stratum, is the fossilized reflex of the nasal particles *no* and perhaps *ni* that earlier appeared in the Rendaku context and are thought to have triggered voicing. In the synchronic grammar, this element continues to trigger voicing to eliminate *NT violations, and then, at least in the standard dialect, deletes. This element is no more abstract than the placeless [voice] feature postulated by Itô and Mester (1986), and besides enjoying historical support, allows a significant unification of the analysis. In effect, Postnasal Voicing and Rendaku can now be viewed as two aspects of the same phenomenon. Labrune points to further facts in support of this analysis, including the observation that voiced stops, which are usually thought to have originated historically from prenasalized stops (*nd > d, etc.), are still prenasalized in some dialects (see also Vance 1982).[25]

The following constraints are proposed for the native stratum:

(69) a. *NT: *[+nasal][–voice, –son]
      b. INSERT([+voice])
      c. OCP([+voice]) in [–son]

*NT as stated here differs from the corresponding constraint in Zoque (19a) by the replacement of [–cont] with [–son], reflecting the fact that fricatives as well as stops undergo voicing. *NT violations do not arise in the lexicon due to the strategy of avoidance (Clements 2000), and are eliminated across morpheme boundaries by INSERT ([+voice]), accounting both for Postnasal Voicing and Rendaku. OCP([+voice]) expresses Lyman's Law. It must outrank *NT, since in forms to which both are potentially applicable, violations of *NT are tolerated in order to avoid violations of OCP([+voice]) (recall the examples in 63).

OCP([+voice]) is a rarely-attested constraint, and deserves more comment than can be given it here. Following the historical account of Vance (1982), this constraint may have originally applied to sequences of prenasalized stops, initiating their subsequent development into voiced stops. Labrune (1999) surmises that it is the complexity of sequences of prenasalized stops rather than that of voiced obstruents as such that originally motivated the constraint. This hypothesis can be supported by the rarity of morpheme-internal sequences of prenasalized stops in other languages, which contrasts strikingly with the high acceptability of voiced stop sequences. In this view, OCP([+voice]) would represent the synchronic relic of a historically plausible earlier constraint, which, under Labrune's own analysis (see note 25), would continue to survive in essentially this form in the modern grammar. This scenario would of course directly explain the restriction of the constraint to [−sonorant] sounds: sonorants were never prenasalized, and so could not have triggered a constraint involving prenasalized stop sequences.

Under the analysis in (69), then, *NT activates [−voice] and [−sonorant] in voiceless obstruents. OCP([+voice]) activates [+voice] in /b/, even if we assume this feature to be lexically absent, as suggested in feature chart (61). Moreover, OCP([+voice]) projects all occurrences of [+voice] onto an independent voicing tier. Crucially for the analysis, the negative value [−voice] is not prominent and so is not projected to the [voice] tier. It therefore remains transparent to the long reach of OCP([+voice]).

(70)-(76) show how this analysis applies to representative examples discussed above. The input forms shown here are phonological, not lexical, and therefore reflect the effect of feature activation and node projection. In the interest of simplicity, only the features [+voice] and [−voice] are shown.

(70)   m i z u
            |
       [+voi]

      (there is no OCP violation, as [+voice] is unspecified in nasals)

(71)   iro + N + kami → iro gami
           [−voi]
                  |
               [+voi]

      (INSERT([+voice]) is triggered on /k/ by *NT, where it does not violate the OCP)

(72)   taikutsu + N + š i n o g i
                [−voi]
                     |
              [+voi]

      (INSERT([+voice]) is blocked on /š/ by the OCP)

(73)   onna + N +   k o t o b a
                    [−voi]   [−voi]
                              |
                      [+voi]

      (INSERT([+voice]) is blocked on /k/ by the OCP; /t/ is crucially transparent)

(74)   t o m b o
    [−voi]
               |
        [+voi]

      ([+voice] is activated and projected in /b/ by its mention in the OCP)

(75)   k a m + t e   → k a n + d e
      [−voi]   [−voi]   [−voi]
                              |
                        [+voi]

      (*NT triggers INSERT([+voice]) on /t/)

(76)   širooto + N + k a ŋ g a e
           [–voi] |

                          [+voi]

(the OCP blocks INSERT([+voice]) in /k/)

Under this analysis of sequential voicing in Japanese, the transparency of voicing in nasals follows from the fact that [+voice] is not specified on nasals, while the transparency of [–voice] in obstruents follows from the fact that it is unprojected, even though active.

In sum, the theory of feature activation and feature projection proposed here accounts naturally for the Japanese data. We can draw a parallel between Japanese Rendaku and Sibilant Harmony in Basque. In both languages, long-distance processes were observed to operate across segments bearing incompatible specified feature values: [+posterior] in the case of Basque, [–voice] in the case of Japanese. The explanation is the same in both cases: the transparent values, though necessarily present for lexical or phonological purposes, are nonprominent, and so cannot interact with processes involving prominent values of the same features.

8.   Discussion of Calabrese (1995)

Let us finally consider what is perhaps the most carefully-worked-out alternative to the present feature representation framework in the recent literature. Calabrese (1995) proposes a feature representation system designed to express the view that lexically distinct feature values, marked feature values and redundant values all play a role in defining phonological patterns and processes, though not necessarily at the same time or in regard to all phenomena. Calabrese develops a system for defining marked and distinctive values comparable to the one expressed above, though differing from it in significant details.

In Calabrese's view, phonological rules can access any of three types of feature representation: contrastive, marked, or full feature representation. Unless specifically noted, rules access only contrastive values, as determined by a specific algorithm. In addition, however, rules can be specially marked to access marked values, or all values. Calabrese proposes examples of all three types of rules. Compared to previous versions of autosegmental feature representation, therefore, Calabrese's theory is an exceptionally powerful one. Calabrese himself recognizes this fact, and attempts to justify it by showing that the extra descriptive power is required to express linguistic generalizations.

One strong prediction of this theory is that rules accessing each of these projections may be interspersed in the rule ordering. As Calabrese puts it (1995: 430):

> In the approach proposed here, a rule sensitive to all specifications could in principle precede a rule sensitive to contrastive or marked features, since feature visibility is a property of rules and not of levels of representation ... The point is that there are facts that require the greater flexibility required by the present theory.

Thus, unlike the more traditional view (which has been retained in the present study), there is no unidirectional progression from sparse underlying representations to more and more fully specified representations in the course of derivation; this is because all modes of representation are accessible at all times.

In support of this extra flexibility, Calabrese alleges two cases in which a rule accessing full feature representations appears to precede a rule accessing marked feature specifications. He characterizes them as follows:

(77) Japanese Rendaku
- an early rule (Postnasal Voicing) requires [+voice] to be specified in nasals, requiring access to an unmarked, non-contrastive feature, and thus to full feature representation;
- a later rule (Rendaku) requires [+voice] to be absent in nasals, thus requiring access to marked feature specifications only

(78) English coronal place assimilation
- early phonotactic rules require the unmarked place feature [coronal] to be present in representations, requiring access to full feature specification (it is assumed that [coronal] is unmarked and noncontrastive in English)
- a later rule of place assimilation requires [coronal] to be absent in representations, requiring access to marked features, to express the fact that only coronals assimilate to following stops in colloquial speech; thus we find te[n] 'ten', te[m] pounds, te[ŋ] kings (showing assimilation of unmarked coronal stops), but so[m]e 'some', so[m]etime, so[m]e kings, as well as ki[ŋ] 'king', ki[ŋ] Tom, Ki[ŋ] Babar (showing no assimilation of labial and velar stops)

We have already discussed Japanese, and seen that the analysis upon which Calabrese's claim rests, that of Itô, Mester, and Padgett (1995), cannot be maintained. Postnasal voicing does not require [+voice] in nasals.

The example from English is equally inconclusive. Let us admit, following Hayes (1992), that the assimilations in question are truly phonological even if they sometimes involve articulator overlap; and let us also agree that early phonotactic rules of English access the unmarked feature [coronal] in alveolar stops. Calabrese's argument then rests on the assumption that assimilation rules target only segments unspecified for the spreading feature. But this assumption runs up against many well-known counterexamples. For example, we have seen that nasal place assimilation targets [m] as well as [n] in Zoque. We cannot assume that place features of Zoque nasals delete in coda position, since [m] retains its labiality both word-finally, as in *kom* 'post', and before stops, as in *ki?mdamu* 'you (pl.) went'; nasal place assimilation only affects nasals in affix-final position. Many other examples of neutralizing assimilation rules can be cited. The generalization in English seems instead to be that only marked coronal nodes are prominent, just as in Tahltan. Unmarked coronal features are bundled on the Place node, which, bearing no prominent features at all, constitutes a privileged target for [labial] and [dorsal] place spreading.

One must conclude that the framework proposed in Calabrese (1995) is excessively powerful, and that phonological rules (or constraints) should not have the power to access different modes of feature specification.

9. Conclusions

This paper offers a framework of feature representation which eliminates superfluous features and tiers, and is at the same time constrained and strongly predictive. A central notion is that of representational economy, according to which only those features and nodes are present in representations at any given level that can be shown to be necessary for capturing generalizations at that level. The major components of this approach include a procedure of lexical feature specification, a principle of feature phonological feature activation, and a principle of tier projection.

This framework has been applied to problem cases involving feature transparency that have proven difficult to solve, if not intractable, in other frameworks without calling upon ad hoc or suspect principles and special assumptions. It has been shown that these cases receive a natural treatment, requiring no special assumptions, in the present framework. Incidentally to the main discussion, a substantive proposal regarding feature accessibility has been proposed, and a new account of the structure of the coronal node has been offered. It is hoped that the approach outlined here will stimulate fresh study of the nature of lexical and phonological feature representation.

Notes

* I would like to acknowledge several sources that have particularly stimulated my thinking on the issues raised in this paper, including most notably the Minimalist Program for syntax (Chomsky 1993, 1995), Optimality Theory (Prince & Smolensky 1993), and Calabrese's Theory of Phonological Inventories (Calabrese 1994, 1995). If I have not adopted the familiar parallel implementation of Optimality Theory in the present exposition, it is because a number of fundamental questions raised by this framework still remain unanswered (cf. Clements 2000). Following the initial presentation of this paper at the Conference on Distinctive Feature Theory, Berlin, October 1999, several recent and still unpublished studies in the framework of the Toronto school of contrast were brought to my attention, including Dresher, Piggott, and Rice 1995; Avery 1996; and Dresher 1998, 2000 (see also Ghini 1998). This work, with its strong emphasis on representational economy, presents significant parallels to some of the basic ideas developed here. Other versions of this paper have been presented at the Workshop on Features, Schloss Freudental (Konstanz), December 2000, at HILP (Holland Institute of Linguistics Phonology Conference) 5, Potsdam, January 2001, and at various talks and seminars in Paris. I thank the participants at these various gatherings for useful discussion, in particular François Dell, Elan Dresher, Bill Idsardi, Paula Fikkert, Paul Kiparsky, and Keren Rice, as well as Laurence Labrune for electronic correspondence; the usual disclaimers apply.

1 Special thanks go to Bill Idsardi, Elan Dresher and other members of the Workshop on Features at Schloss Freudental (Konstanz), December 2000, for stimulating discussion of these issues.

2 This state of affairs is possible under the definition of distinctness given in (6) if we allow S_1, S_2, and S_3 to be stops, F to be [labial] and G to be [dorsal]. In this case, S_1 can be interpreted as /p/, S_2 as /k/, and S_3 as (underspecified) /t/. All three are distinct, and [coronal] is superfluous.

3 This algorithm is stated by Dresher as follows (1998, 2000):
   a. In the initial state, all sounds are assumed to be variants of a single phoneme.
   b. If the set is found to have more than one phoneme, a binary distinction is made on the basis of one of the universal set of distinctive features; this cut divides the inventory into a marked set and an unmarked set
   c. Repeat step (b) in each set, dividing each remaining set until all distinctive sounds have been differentiated.
   Dresher's approach differs from the one developed here primarily in that features are not ranked in a universal hierarchy. Instead, features are ordered in a given language in such a way that following application of the Successive Binary Algorithm, the effective natural classes of the language are definable in the most general terms. Thus the order of features can theoretically vary from one language to another. I thank Elan Dresher for bringing his work to my attention at the Workshop on Features, December 2000.

4 The distinction between native and loanword strata is strongly motivated in Zoque and many other languages on the basis of various morphological and phonological criteria; see e.g. Itô and Mester (1999) for discussion of Japanese.

5 The sounds /c ɲ/, described as nonaffricated alveopalatal stops and transcribed

t^y $\tilde{n}$ by Wonderly (1951-2), are entered as posterior sounds, implying that they are [coronal]; see Hume (1994) and Hall (1997) for justification. See further Kim (1997) and Clements (1999) for the analysis of affricates as strident stops, with no [+continuant] component.

6 "The principle of economy of derivation requires that computational operations must be driven by some condition on representations, as a "last resort" to overcome a failure to meet such a condition" (Chomsky 1995, 28).

7 Other approaches to this problem, not involving feature insertion, are no doubt available as well. In the interest of avoiding what would necessarily be a long digression from the central issues of this paper, I will leave this question open here.

8 See Kaisse (1992) for discussion of apparent cases of [consonantal] spread, and Hume and Odden (1996) for alternative analyses.

9 In the past, the failure of such feature values to spread, etc., has sometimes been taken as evidence that the features in question are one-valued. However, these feature values are sometimes required to define natural classes. We return to this point in the discussion of Japanese voicing in section 7.

10 Hall (2000) argues that NC sequences should be analyzed as prenasalized stops in word-initial position, but points out that they pattern as bisegmental sequences word-internally.

11 Most exceptionally, place spreads from the nasal onto the following stop in the Roermondsch dialect of Dutch, e.g. /kom-t/ → [komp] 'come' (imp. pl.). While nasals do delete before voiceless stops in some languages, as observed earlier in the discussion of *NT, deletion is better viewed in such cases as a way of repairing *NT violations than as a rectification of Spread(Place) violations. This analysis is supported by the observation that unassimilated nasals are rarely if ever found to delete before voiced and voiceless stops alike.

12 Place assimilation always appears to apply locally in languages having this process, and this condition is explicitly included in the statement in (33). However, the class of source and target segments is not always predictable, nor is directionality. Favored sources are stops, favored targets are nasals and laterals (with a preference for affixes over roots), and the favored direction of assimilation is right-to-left. Nevertheless, all of these statements have known exceptions in the literature (for example, nasal place assimilation applies progressively in German, as in /leːbən/ → ['leːbm̩] 'to live'; Kohler 1992), and require parameterization in one form or another. The parameters observed by Zoque have been included directly in statement (33), but these might possibly be derived from separate constraints in a more detailed study.

13 Evidence that word-internal Cy sequences are indeed bisegmental, rather than single fused palatalized segments, is provided by a process of h-Deletion, which deletes [h] before a syllable-final consonant (e.g. /nihp-kuy/ → [nip.kuy] 'planting'), including those followed by [y] (e.g. /kihp-yah-u/ → [kip.ya.hu]

138   *G. N. Clements*

'they fought'. [h] is not deleted before an onset consonant: /y-nihp-u/ →
[ɲih.pu] 'you are planting'. Palatal Substitution bleeds h-Deletion, as is shown
by examples like [wih.ca.hu] 'they walked' from underlying /wiht-yah-u/. (See
Wonderly 1951: 119-20; syllabifications follow Wonderly 1951:115-6). This
evidence does not apply to word-initial Cy sequences, which might be analyzed
as simple palatalized segments (see Hall 2000 for an OT analysis of word-
initial morphophonemics).

14 The feature analysis of coronal stops assumed here is further discussed and
motivated in section 6.1.

15 For example, occasionally attested metatheses of the form VCy → VyC apply
in the context of all consonants, not just coronals, and appear to be motivated
by syllable structure constraints.

16 It is provisionally assumed here that a node projected in a segment class by one
constraint is projected into all representations in that segment class, even those
that do not satisfy the description of the constraint which triggered projection.
Thus POST projects [+posterior] in [y] in the cluster *ky* as well as in the cluster
ty, etc. This principle assures that a given feature or node occurs consistently
on the same tier in a given segment class.

17 In other languages, however, both components of a geminated affricate have a
release burst, and in this case stridency is manifested twice; an example is the
optional realization of the Hungarian phrase [somse:d tˢɔlɑ:d] 'neighboring
family' as [somse:tˢtˢɔlɑ:d], created by a rule totally assimilating stops to following affricates (Vago 1980). Since nasals (and voiced sonorants) never have
a turbulent release burst, they cannot employ this option.

18 A further example can be cited from Coronal Assimilation in English, in which
coronal stops assimilate to the marked values of [posterior] and [apical] (but
not [strident]) of adjacent coronal consonants. Thus, for example, the phrase
size 8 shoes is realized with the sequence [...t̠ ʃ...], where t̠ is the posteriorized
counterpart of [t]. In this writer's speech, this phrase remains distinct from *size
H shoes* [...tʃ ʃ...], showing that the *t* of *eight* remains nonstrident.

19 Other dialects of Basque, including the Standard, have a less thorough-going
pattern of Sibilant Harmony in which words of the form *tx ... sC ...* are regular
exceptions: *txistu* 'flute', *tximista* 'lightning', *txosten* 'report'.

20 Ní Chiosáin and Padgett (1997) discuss an alternative way of accommodating
long-distance consonant assimilation over nonuniform domains within a theory
of strict locality. Gafos (1998) proposes to reinterpret selected cases of long-
distance assimilation as segmental reduplication; however, his specific proposals concern root-affix interactions and do not extend directly to cases of
root harmony such as the one discussed here.

21 A stylistic rule of Affective Palatalization causes all coronal consonants,
including sonorants, to become palatal, creating related pairs of words such as
lagun ~ llagun 'friend'. However, this process, which inserts [+posterior]

under the coronal node of anterior coronals, applies in the postlexical (or phrase-level) phonology, as is shown by phrasal examples like *zer da ~ xerdda* 'what is it?'.

22 Keren Rice (1997 and personal communication) has questioned the synchronic motivation for the recognition of a native or Yamato stratum in Japanese. Itô and Mester (1999) and Itô, Mester, and Padgett (1999) have provided a reasoned reply to Rice's challenge which appears to successfully address the points she has raised. I accept their view here, pending any further arguments that might be advanced for the alternative.

23 We need not review Itô, Mester, and Padgett's proposal to resolve the paradox by a theory of Redundant Feature Licensing, according to which features are licensed in segments in which they are redundant only if they are also linked to segments in which they are distinctive, since this approach has been adequately criticized on typological grounds by Pater (1999: 328-34). Equally significantly, it does not extend to postnasal voicing in languages like Zoque, where, as seen earlier, voicing is redundant in stops as well as nasals.

24 Mascaró and Wetzels (2000) provide independent arguments for the binary nature of [voice].

25 Space limitations preclude a full review of Labrune's analysis here. I do not here adopt Labrune's analysis of all voiced obstruents as underlying prenasalized stops in the native stratum of the standard dialect, though as Labrune points out to me, some support could be offered for this position in distributional constraints (in particular, the virtual absence of morpheme-internal contrasts between voiced obstruents and NC sequences.).

References

Avery, Peter
   1996   The representation of voicing contrasts. Ph.D. dissertation, University of Toronto. [not seen]
Browman, Catherine P. & Louis Goldstein
   1989   Articulatory gestures as phonological units. *Phonology* 6.2: 201-251.
Calabrese, Andrea
   1994   A constraint-based theory of phonological inventories. In: W. U. Dressler, M. Prinzhorn, and J. R. Rennison (eds.) *Phonologica 1992: Proceedings of the 7th International Phonology Meeting*, 35-54. Torino: Rosenberg & Sellier.
   1995   A constraint-based theory of phonological markedness and simplification procedures. *Linguistic Inquiry* 26.3: 373-463.

Chomsky, Noam
  1993   A minimalist program for linguistic theory. In: K. Hale and S. J.
          Keyser (eds.) *The View from Building 20*. Cambridge, Mass.: MIT
          Press.
  1995   *The Minimalist Program*. Cambridge, Mass.: MIT Press.
Christdas, Prathima.
  1988   The phonology and morphology of Tamil.   Ph.D. dissertation,
          Cornell University, Ithaca, N.Y.
Clements, George N.
  1988   Toward a substantive theory of feature specification. In: J. Blevins
          and J. Carter (eds.) *Proceedings of NELS 18*: 79-93. Amherst:
          GSLA.
  1993a   Underspecification or nonspecification? In: M. Bernstein and A.
          Kathol (eds.) *ESCOL '93 (Proceedings of the Tenth Eastern States
          Conference on Linguistics)*, 58-80. Ithaca, N.Y.: Cornell University,
          Department of Linguistics.
  1993b   Lieu d'articulation des consonnes et des voyelles: une théorie unifée.
          In: B. Laks and A. Rialland (eds.) *L'Architecture des Représen-
          tations Phonologiques*, 101-145. Paris: Editions du C.N.R.S.
          [English version: *Working Papers of the Cornell Phonetics
          Laboratory* 5, 1991, 77-123. Ithaca, N.Y.: Cornell University,
          Department of Linguistics.]
  1999   Affricates as noncontoured stops. In: O. Fujimura, B. Joseph, and B.
          Palek, (eds.) *Proceedings of LP '98: Item Order in Language and
          Speech*, 271-299. Prague: The Karolinum Press.
  2000   In defense of serialism. *The Linguistic Review* 17.2-4: 181-197.
Clements, George N. & Susan R. Hertz
  1996   An integrated approach to phonology and phonetics. In: J. Durand
          and B. Laks (eds.) *Current Trends in Phonology: Models and
          Methods, vol. 1,* 143-74. Salford: University of Salford Publications.
Clements, George N. & Elizabeth Hume
  1995   The internal structure of speech sounds. In: John Goldsmith (ed.)
          Handbook of Phonological Theory, 245-306. Oxford: Blackwell.
Cohn, Abigail C.
  1993   Nasalization in English: phonology or phonetics? *Phonology* 10.1:
          43-81.
Dell, François
  1985   *Les règles et les sons: Introduction à la phonologie générative.* 2nd
          corrected edition. Paris: Hermann.

Dresher, Elan
  1998   On contrast and redundancy. Paper presented at the annual meeting of the Canadian Linguistic Association, Ottawa, Ms., University of Toronto.
  2000   Contrastive features: Manchu to Miogliola. Paper presented at the Workshop on Features, Schloss Freudental (Konstanz), December 7-9, 2000.
Dresher, Elan, Glynn Piggott, & Keren Rice
  1995   Contrast in phonology: overview. In: Carrie Dyck (ed.) *Toronto Working Papers in Linguistics* 13.1: iii-xvii. [not seen]
Elbert, Samuel H & Mary K Pukui
  1979   *Hawaiian Grammar*. Honolulu: University Press of Hawaii.
Elmedlaoui, Mohamed
  1993   Gemination and spirantization in Hebrew, Berber and Tigrinya: a 'Fortis-Lenis Module' analysis. *Linguistica Communicatio.*
Gafos, Diamandis
  1998   Eliminating long-distance consonantal spreading. *Natural Language and Linguistic Theory* 16.2: 223-278.
Ghini, Mirco
  1998   Asymmetries in the phonology of Miogliola. Doctoral dissertation, Universität Konstanz.
Gnanadesikan, Amalia E.
  1994   The geometry of coronal specifications. In: Mercè Gonzàlez (ed.) *NELS 24: Proceedings of the North East Linguistic Society*, 125-139. Amherst: GLSA, University of Massachusetts.
Goldsmith, John
  1993   Harmonic phonology. In: John Goldsmith (ed.) *The Last Phonological Rule: Reflections on Constraints and Derivations*, 21-60. Chicago: University of Chicago Press.
Hall, T. Alan
  1997   *The Phonology of Coronals*. (Current Issues in Linguistic Theory, 149). Amsterdam: Benjamins.
  2000   Syllabically conditioned coalescence and deletion in Zoque: an Optimality-theoretic approach. *Linguistics* 38.4: 711-738.
Halle, Morris
  1991   Phonological features. In: W. Bright (ed.), *Oxford International Encyclopedia of Linguistics*, 207-212. N.Y.: Oxford University Press.
Hamilton, Philip
  1993   On the internal structure of the coronal node: evidence from Australian languages. Unpublished ms., University of Toronto.

Hayes, Bruce
    1986   Inalterability in CV Phonology. *Language* 62.2: 321-51.
    1992   Comments on chapter 10. In: Gerard J. Docherty and D.Robert
              Ladd (eds.) *Papers in Laboratory Phonology II: Gesture, Segment,
              Prosody*, 280-286. Cambridge: Cambridge University Press.
Hertz, Susan R.
    1991   Streams, phones, and transitions: toward a new phonological and
              phonetic model of formant timing. *Journal of Phonetics* 19: 91-109.
Hockett, Charles F.
    1955   *A Manual of Phonology*. (Memoire 11 of *IJAL* 21.4, Part 1.)
              Baltimore: Waverley Press. Reprinted by the University of Chicago
              Press, 1974.
Hualde, José
    1991   *Basque Phonology*. London: Routledge.
Hume, Elizabeth
    1994   *Front Vowels, Coronal Consonants and their Interaction in
              Nonlinear Phonology*. New York: Garland Publishing, Inc.
Hume, Elizabeth & David Odden
    1996   Reconsidering [consonantal]. *Phonology* 13.3: 345-376.
Inkelas, Sharon
    1995   The consequences of optimization for underspecification. In: J.
              Beckman (ed.) *Proceedings of the North East Linguistic Society* 25,
              287-302. Amherst, MA: GLSA. [Also available as ROA-40]
Itô, Junko & Armin Mester
    1986   The phonology of voicing in Japanese: theoretical consequences for
              morphological accessibility. *Linguistic Inquiry* 17.1: 49-73.
    1999   The phonological lexicon. In: Natsuko Tsujimura (ed.) *The Hand-
              book of Japanese Linguistics*, 73-100.
Itô, Junko, Armin Mester, & Jaye Padgett
    1995   Licensing and underspecification in Optimality Theory. *Linguistic
              Inquiry* 26.4: 571-614.
    1999   Lexical classes in Japanese: a reply to Rice. *Phonology at Santa
              Cruz* 6: 39-46.
Jakobson, Roman
    1968   *Child Language, Aphasia and Phonological Universals*. Mouton:
              The Hague. [Original German edition 1941]
Jakobson, Roman & Morris Halle
    1956   *Fundamentals of Language*. Mouton: The Hague.
Judd, Henry P., Mary K. Pukui, & John F. G. Stokes
    1945   *Introduction to the Hawaiian Language*. Honolulu: Tongg
              Publishing Co.

Kager, René
1999   *Optimality Theory.* Cambridge: Cambridge University Press.
Kaisse, Ellen
1992   Can [consonantal] spread? *Language* 68: 313-332.
Keating, Patricia
1988   Underspecification in phonetics. *Phonology* 5.2: 275-292.
Kim, Hyunsoon
1997   The phonological representation of affricates: evidence from Korean and other languages. Ph.D. dissertation, Cornell University, Ithaca, N.Y.
Kiparsky, Paul
1985   Some consequences of lexical phonology. *Phonology Yearbook* 2: 85-138.
Kohler, Klaus J.
1992   Gestural reorganization in connected speech: a functional viewpoint on 'Articulatory Phonology'. *Phonetica* 49: 205-211.
Labrune, Laurence
1999   Variation intra et inter-langue: morpho-phonologie du *rendaku* en japonais et du *sai-sios* en coréen. In: J. Durand and C. Lyche (eds.) *Phonologie et Variation (Cahiers de Grammaire* 24), 117-152.
Ladefoged, Peter & Ian Maddieson
1996   *The Sounds of the World's Languages.* Oxford: Blackwell.
Lahiri, Aditi & Vincent Evers
1991   Palatalization and coronality. In: Paradis & Prunet (1991a: 79-100).
McCarthy, John
1988   Feature geometry and dependency: a review. *Phonetica* 45: 84-108.
McCarthy, John & Alison Taub
1992   Review of Paradis & Prunet 1991a. *Phonology* 9: 363-370.
Maddieson, Ian
1984   *Patterns of Sounds.* Cambridge: Cambridge University Press.
1992   UCLA phonological segment inventory database, version 1.1. Los Angeles: Department of Linguistics, UCLA.
Martinet, André
1955   *Economie des changements phonétiques: Traité de phonologie diachronique.* Berne: Francke.
Mascaró, Joan & W. Leo Wetzels
2000   The typology of voicing and devoicing. To appear in *Language.*
Mester, Armin & Junko Itô
1989   Feature predictability and underspecification: palatal prosody in Japanese mimetics. *Language* 65: 258-93.

Mohanan, K.P.
  1991   On the bases of radical underspecification. *Natural Language and Linguistic Theory* 9.2: 285-326.
Ní Chiosáin, Moira, & Jaye Padgett
  1997   Markedness, segment realization, and locality in spreading. Ms., University of California at Santa Cruz.
N'diaye, Geneviève
  1970   *Structure du dialecte basque de Maya.* The Hague: Mouton.
Odden, David
  1986   On the role of the Obligatory Contour Principle in phonological theory. *Language* 62: 353-383.
  1992   Simplicity of underlying representation as motivation for under-specification. In: Elizabeth Hume (ed.) *Papers in Phonology* (OSU Working Papers in Linguistics 41), 85-100.
Paradis, Carole
  1996   The inadequacy of filters and faithfulness in loanword adaptation. In: J. Durand and B. Laks (eds.) *Current Trends in Phonology: Models and Methods,* vol. 2, 509-534. Salford: University of Salford Publications.
Paradis, Carole, & Jean-François Prunet, eds.
  1991a   *Phonetics and Phonology*, vol. 2: *The Special Status of Coronals: Internal and External Evidence.* San Diego: Academic Press.
  1991b   Introduction: asymmetry and visibility in consonant articulations. In: Paradis and Prunet (1991a: 1-28).
Pater, Joe
  1999   Austronesian nasal substitution and other NÇ effects. In: René Kager, Harry van der Hulst, and Wim Zonneveld (eds.) *The Prosody-Morphology Interface,* 310-343. Cambridge: Cambridge University Press.
Pierrehumbert, Janet & Mary Beckman
  1988   *Japanese Tone Structure.* (LI Monograph Series No. 15). Cambridge, Mass.: MIT Press.
Prince, Alan & Paul Smolensky
  1993   Optimality theory: constraint interaction in generative grammar. Ms. Rutgers University & Johns Hopkins University.
Rice, Keren
  1996   Default variability: the coronal-velar relationship. *Natural Language and Linguistic Theory* 14.3: 493-543.
  1997   Japanese NC clusters and the redundancy of postnasal voicing. *Linguistic Inquiry* 28.3: 541-551.

Rubach, Jerzy
  1994   Affricates as strident stops in Polish. *Linguistic Inquiry* 25.1: 119-144.
Sagey, Elizabeth
  1990   *The Representation of Features in Nonlinear Phonology: the Articulator Node Hierarchy.* N.Y.: Garland.
Sapir, Edward
  1925   Sound patterns in language. *Language* 1: 37-51.
Shaw, Patricia
  1991   Consonant harmony systems: the special status of coronal harmony. In: Paradis and Prunet (1991a: 125-157).
Shibatani, Masayoshi
  1987   Japanese. In: Bernard Comrie (ed.) *The World's Major Languages*, 855-880. New York: Oxford University Press.
Smolensky, Paul
  1996   The initial state and "Richness of the Base" in Optimality Theory. Technical Report JHU-Cogsci-96-4. Baltimore: Department of Cognitive Science, Johns Hopkins University.
Smolensky, Paul, Lisa Davidson, & Peter Jusczyk
  2000   The initial and final states: theoretical implications and experimental explorations of richness of the base. Ms., Johns Hopkins University.
Steriade, Donca
  1986   A note on coronal. Ms., MIT, Cambridge, Ma.
  1987   Redundant values. In: Anna Bosch, Barbara Need, and Eric Schiller (eds.), *CLS 23: Papers from the 23rd Regional Meeting of the Chicago Linguistic Society. Part Two: Parasession on Autosegmental Phonology*, 339-362. Chicago: Chicago Linguistic Society.
  1995   Underspecification and markedness. In: John Goldsmith (ed.) *Handbook of Phonological Theory*, 114-174. Oxford: Basil Blackwell.
Stevens, Kenneth & Samuel Jay Keyser
  1989   Primary features and their enhancements in consonants. *Language* 65: 81-106.
Trubetzkoy, Nicolai S.
  1939   *Grundzüge der Phonologie.* Göttingen: Vandenhoeck & Ruprecht. (English edition: *Principles of Phonology*, tr. C.A.M. Baltaxe. Berkeley and Los Angeles: University of California, 1969.)
Vago, Robert M.
  1980   *The Sound Pattern of Hungarian.* Washington: Georgetown University Press.
Vance, Timothy J.
  1982   On the origin of voicing alternation in Japanese consonants. *Journal of the American Oriental Society* 102: 333-341.

1987   *An Introduction to Japanese Phonology.* Albany: State University
         of New York Press.
Wonderly, William L.
    1946   Phonemic acculturation in Zoque. *International Journal of American
             Linguistics* 12: 92-95.
    1951-2   Zoque (parts I-V). In *International Journal of American Linguistics*
             17 (1951), 1-9, 105-123, 137-162, 235-251; *International Journal of
             American Linguistics* 18 (1952), 35-48.

Place of articulation first[*]

Mirco Ghini

1. Introduction

Consider a five vowel system /a e i o u/. In such a system the occurrence of the feature [Labial] can be predicted on the basis of backness and height: Back non-low vowels are predictably round, i.e. labial. In an underspecification framework this normally means that the feature [Labial] is unspecified in the underlying representation, due to its redundancy.[1] However, such an analysis can only hold if, during the acquisition of the the contrast system of a language, the representation of the feature [Labial] in the underlying representation does not precede the representation of the features which categorize the vowels according to height and backness (Dresher *et al.* 1994; Ghini 1998; Dresher 1998). This means that the redundancy of [Labial] in the system being considered can only be established by taking into account the system as a whole. If feature specification in the lexicon is acquired stepwise, different redundancy pictures may arise.[2] Consider the possibility that place of articulation distinctions (such as [Dorsal]) have precedence over height distinctions (such as [Low]). In such a scenario [Labial] is assigned/acquired when height distinctions are not yet available. In the five vowel system above [Labial] is therefore no longer redundant, thus requiring ist underlying specification, whereas backness is redundant and not represented.

Consider now an asymmetric vowel system of the type /a ɛ e i o u/. In such a system, if place of articulation distinctions have precedence over height distinctions in the acquisition path, a possibility arises in the assignment of height features in the lexicon to /o u/, which is ruled out otherwise: In a bottom up procedure of unfolding the contrast system in which [Low] is assigned before [High] within preexisting place of articulation distinctions, /o u/ would be marked as a [Low-Ø] contrast, and would therefore be phonologically paired with the front vowels /ɛ e/, and not /e i/, clearly mismatching the phonetic pairings and correspondences between front and back vowels.

It is the goal of this paper to show that Place of Articulation First is indeed a principle in the acquisition of contrast representations in the mental lexicon. Redundancies and related underspecification patterns are established accordingly. The phonological pairings and correspondences needed to account for the facts mismatch the phonetics exactly in the way predicted by categorizing height contrasts within place of articulation contrasts. Place of Articulation First makes predictions regarding the featural specification of lexical entries and the patterning of contrastive phonemes in phonological rules. The natural classes of segments that undergo certain rules are predicted to be the ones defined by the distinctive features and not by features defined according to their respective phonetic values.

Evidence for Place of Articulation First is drawn from the Gallo-Italian dialect spoken in the community of Miogliola, a small village located on the Ligurian-Piedmontese border, in Northwest Italy. Although Miogliola lies on the Piedmontese side of the border, its dialect belongs to Ligurian, and therefore displays the typical Ligurian palatalization of Vulgar Latin obstruent+[l] clusters, e.g. *blanku* → *dʒaŋk* (Ghini 1998).

2. Assumptions

Phonology is the model of the shape, i.e. of the grammar, that the human mind projects on the physical sound continuum language makes use of. Phonology is abstract. The shaping of the phonetic reality is guided by Universal Grammar, the set of predispositions allowing the acquisition of a natural language and constraining its shape. Categorization of the sound continuum consists, among other things, of the following:

(1) Categorizing the sound continuum
    a.   distinctive, unpredictable information is separated from redundant, predictable information
    b.   distinctive units are compared and their *relative* phonetic values phonologized and represented in underlying representation
    c.   contrasting pairs are labeled in a zero/marked fashion.

Let us provide an example. A given language contrasts the two sounds [o] and [u]. The two sounds must therefore be represented as /o/ and /u/ and their phonetic height difference phonologized, as in (1a). Needless to say, phonology does not have the freedom of subverting the phonetic height values of the pair being considered here by, say, marking /o/ as [High] and leaving /u/ unspecified or, even worse, marking it [Low]. However, the height difference of the two distinctive units is weighed in relative terms, as in (1b), and the fact that /u/ is a phonetically high vowel, does not translate automatically into a phonological specification [High]. Of course, a possible way of phonologizing the height difference contrasting /u/ and /o/ is to mark /u/ as [High] as opposed to /o/. However, if there is no other back rounded vowel in the system lower than /o/, than /o/ can, and arguably must, be marked as [Low] as opposed to /u/, the assumption being that feature assignment gives [Low] preference over the feature [High].

On the assumption that height distinctions are made within place of articulation distinctions, the number of height contrasts among the non-dorsal vowels does not affect the representation of height in the case of /o/ and /u/. In any x-constituent system, the number of constituents with feature specification necessary is $x-1$, as in (1c), where one constituent being left unspecified. So in a two-height system [Low] suffices to express the contrast between the lower and the higher phonological constituent. Even if the higher unit is phonetically high, it need not be phonologically high, given that [High] does not fulfill any distinctive function in this example. By contrast, in a three-height system both [Low] and [High] are necessary to make the three phonological constituents distinct, one being marked [Low], one [High] and one is left unmarked.

Contrary to monostratal models of phonology (Prince and Smo-lensky 1993, Steriade 1995 and the OT literature in general), I assume the phonological component of the language to be deriva-tional (Kiparsky 2000), with Lexical Minimization governing the shape of underlying representations in the sense they are redundancy free. Full specification characterizes the acoustic signal perceived by the language listener (Lahiri 1991, 1999a, b; Reetz 1999, Lahiri and Reetz 2001).

Redundant and predictable featural information, which have no place in mental/underlying representations, become available during the construction work performed by the phonological component of the language at the different levels, to be maximally specified in the acoustic signal generated by the speaker and perceived by the listener.

The mapping process of maximally specified incoming signals and minimally specified mental representations is at the core of language comprehension, cf. the FUL-model (Featurally Unspecified Lexicon; Reetz 1998, 1999, Lahiri 1999a, b, Lahiri and Reetz 2001). Underspecification in the mental representation implies a three-way matching process with the signal: *match, mismatch* and *no-mismatch*. This last mode plays a crucial role in language understanding, since it allows finding a lexical entry despite the variation in the acoustic signal corresponding to a morpheme. This variation can, for exam-ple, be due to phonological alternation processes such as assimi-lations. Consider the case of the feature [Coronal] as an illustration. [Coronal] is the universally unmarked place of articulation feature. As such, [Coronal] is often argued to be unspecified in the under-lying representations of both vowels and consonants (Rice 1996). This treatment is intended to account for why /n/ but not /m/ can undergo place assimilation, e.g. *train prices > trai[m] prices*, vs. *lame duck*, where [m] does not change.

Lack of [Coronal] specification in mental representations has found strong support in the experimental work reported in (Lahiri 1999a, b, Lahiri and Reetz 2001). A cross-modal priming experiment was used to test underspecification.[3] Listeners showed a faster reaction time to a lexical decision task to a word like *bee* when a semantically related word preceded it such as *honey*, in contrast to an unrelated word like *stone*. The labial variant **homey* (this time a non-word) had the same priming effect on *bee*. In contrast, although *hammer* primed the semantically related word *metal,* the coronal variant **hanner* did not. Thus, labiality in the incoming acoustic signal did not prevent accessing words that actually contained /n/ in the underlying representation, as is evidenced by the priming effect for semantically related words. The reverse does not hold true: only incoming [m], not [n], allows accessing a lexical entry containing /m/. So no priming effect was observed in cases where [n] was present acoustically where an [m] was expected. This asymmetry in priming effects holds true for onsets and codas (**trai[m]* primes *engine, *fla[n]e* does not prime *candle*). If surface representations are fully specified and underlying representations lack specification for [Coronal] the results are straightforward: both [m] and [n] do not mismatch /n/, but only [m] does not mismatch (and in fact matches) underlying /m/, [n] does create a mismatch and thus prevents accessing the lexical entry (Lahiri and Reetz 2001). Thus the abstract mental representations the language learner develops according to the principles dictated by Universal Grammar allows for a more robust recognition of words in the acoustic stream despite variation.

The structure provided by Universal Grammar around which featural information is organized is assumed to be represented as a feature tree where monovalent features (Avery & Rice 1989) are hierarchically organized (Clements 1985). The sub-component of the tree relevant to the issue at stake here is the Place node, shown in (2). The Place node dominates the Articulator node, which organizes the place of articulation features, and the Aperture node, which organizes the height features (Lahiri and Evers 1991, Ghini 1998).

(2)

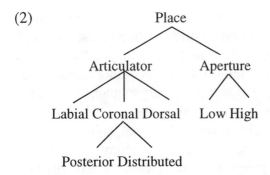

Vowels and consonants share the same features (Clements 1989, 1991; Clements and Hume 1995), as well as the same organizing nodes (Lahiri and Evers 1991, Ghini 1998), but are subject to different well-formedness constraints (Ghini 1998). Vowels, for example, can only be specified for [Labial] if another place of articulation feature has been previously specified, e.g. [Coronal] for front vowels and [Dorsal] for back vowels. This gives [Labial] the status of a secondary feature for vowels. The constraint on the occurrence of [Labial] in vowels is expressed in (3).

(3)   Constraint on [Labial] (Ghini 1998):
      Vowels can be specified for [Labial] iff another place of
      articulation feature is already available.

The presence of [Coronal] is not banned altogether in underlying representations. If a system contrasts units within the coronal space of articulation, then [Coronal] is activated (Avery and Rice 1989). A system can even contrast underlying coronals with units lacking underlying specification for place of articulation (Ghini 1998). In sum, the underlying presence of [Coronal] is marked and is taken to directly mirror the markedness of the systems which make use of it underlyingly.

   I turn now to the illustration of the vowel system in Miogliola Ligurian.

3.   Miogliola Ligurian Vowels

The chart in (4) shows the Miogliola Ligurian short vowel phonemes
in stressed position organized according to phonetic principles.

(4)   Phonetic chart of the stressed short vowel phonemes

	Place of articulation			
	front	front rounded	back	back rounded
high	i	y		u
mid	e	ø		o
low	æ		ɑ	

The long vowels in stressed position are shown in the chart in (5).
Observe that the long vowel inventory outnumbers its short counterpart by one unit, namely /ɔː/ in (5), which does not have a short
counterpart in (4).

(5)   The phonetic chart of the stressed long vowel phonemes

	Place of articulation			
	front	front rounded	back	back rounded
high	iː	yː		uː
higher mid	eː	øː		oː
lower mid				ɔː
low	æː		ɑː	

The inventories in (4) and (5) undergo two different patterns of
reduction. One is found in unstressed position, where length distinctions are neutralized and segmental contrasts appear as in (6). The
reduced vowel inventory contains vowels of a phonetic quality
unattested in the non-reduced vowel inventory. The mapping
between phonology and phonetics in the case of reduced and unre-
duced vowel inventories will be discussed in section 6.

(6)   Vowels in unstressed position[4]
   a. alternating with stressed   b. alternating with stressed
      short vowels   long vowels

i	y		u
ε		a	

i	y		u
ε		a	ɔ

The details of how neutralization works can be observed by looking at stress alternations of the type shown in (7).

(7)   Stress alternations and patterns of neutralization

   a. /e æ/ → [ε]   pǽʃka, peʃkέ   'fishing, to fish'
                        bέʃtja, beʃtjéŋ   'true, truth'

   b. /eː æː/ → [ε]   léːtʃ, letʃéŋ   'bed, bed demons'
                        bǽːlː, bɛl ǽtsa   'beautiful, beauty'

   c. /u o ø/ → [u]   rus, rusǽt   'red, lipstick'
                        óse, usǽte   'bones, little bones'
                        vøɾ, vurǽt   'flight, little flight'

   d. /oː ɔː/ → [ɔ]   kóːsa, kɔséŋ   'thing, wothless thing'
                        maróːt, marɔtýts   'sick, sick dem.'
                        róːba, rɔbéŋ   'dress, light dress'
                        sɔːt, sɔtέ   'jump, to jump'
                        kɔːts, kɔtsóŋ   'kick, big kick'
                        fɔːts, fɔtsóŋ   'false, liar'

The alternations in (7) show that neutralization in unstressed position affects the height contrast of the pairs /e æ/ and /u o/ in the short inventory, /eː æː/ and /oː ɔː/ in the long inventory. Another pattern of neutralization is exhibited by /ø/, which is 'displaced' from front to back. No unstressed counterpart of /øː/ is available.

   A second pattern of reduction is found in stressed position before /N/, a nasal phoneme with an underlyingly unspecified Place node.

This nasal surfaces as [n] or [ɲ] in onset position, and as [ŋ] in coda position and contrasts with three nasals specified for place underlyingly (Ghini 1998: section 2.5). The reduced inventory before /N/ is shown in (8).

(8)   Vowels before /N/
      a. before [ŋ]#   b. elsewhere (= before [n] and [ŋC]

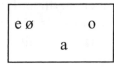   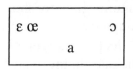

feŋ, fέ:na	'fine.m./f.'	fɛŋdz	'to pretend'
øŋ, œ́:na	'one.m./f.'	rœŋp	'to break'
saŋ, sá:na	'healthy.m./f.'	ʃpaŋdz	'to spill'
boŋ, bɔ́:na	'good.m./f. '	fɔŋdz	'mushroom'

The question which arises now is what feature specification can account for the patterns of reduction observed in Miogliola Ligurian. In what follows I assign features to the underlying representations of Miogliola vowels in a principled way and I show that by giving place of articulation precedence over height and by underspecifying all and only the redundancies which arise in following this principle a feature specification is derived that allows us to capture the reduction facts in a very simple, straightforward, and insightful way.

4.   A Principled Procedure of Feature Assignment

The claim that place of articulation distinctions have precedence over height distinction is expressed in (9).

(9)   Place of Articulation First:
     Place of articulation features are assigned before height features.

Needless to say, Place of Articulation First cannot ignore the other principles dictated by Universal Grammar. In particular, Place of

Articulation First interacts with the universally unmarked status of the place of articulation feature [Coronal] and with the constraint on the occurrence of the feature [Labial] in vowels stated in (3). In the following, I show the interaction of these principles in the assignment of features to the Miogliola Ligurian vowels. Due to the asymmetry between the short and long vowel inventories different, and phonetically unexpected results are bound to arise. I proceed by assigning features first to short vowels, then to their long counterparts.[5] The reader is also referred to Clements (this volume), for a procedure of feature assignment which operates on different principles than the ones in my analysis.

4.1 Assigning Features to the Short Vowels

[Dorsal] is the first feature assigned among the dependents of the Articulator node; it is introduced in the lexical representation of all vowels when the first contrast dependent of the Articulator node is acquired (cf. Ghini 1998: section 1.1.3.). This falls out from the unmarked status of the feature [Coronal], and from the constraints on the occurrence of [Labial] in vowels stated in (3). The assignment of the feature [Dorsal] is shown in (10). The result of [Dorsal] assignment results in a two-way split – represented in (10) with a vertical double line – between front and back vowels. A two-way phonemic contrast exists at this point in the acquisition of the inventory.

(10)   Vowel feature specification
        Step 1: insertion of [Dorsal]

	i	e	æ	y	ø	ɑ	o	u
[Dorsal]						•	•	•

The insertion of [Labial] is the second step in the feature assignment procedure adopted here. The feature [Labial] is assumed in (3) to be a secondary feature in vowels, and its specification implies the presence of another place of articulation feature. Therefore, [Labial] insertion can only apply in the back area of the vowel inventory, where the feature [Dorsal] has already been marked. In the front area of the vowel inventory no specification is available so far, and [Labial] insertion cannot take place. The assignment of [Labial] before [Coronal] falls out from the unmarked status of the latter feature, which is a last resort in my proposed procedures for feature assignment. [Labial] insertion is shown in (11). The resulting system is tripartite, with a back, a back round, and a front vowel phoneme.

(11)   Short vowel feature specification
        Step 2: Insertion of [Labial]

	i	e	æ	y	ø	ɑ	o	u
[Dorsal]						•	•	•
[Labial]							•	•

The place of articulation feature we are left with is [Coronal]. The Place of Articulation First principle is overridden by the universally unmarked status of [Coronal], the representation of which is therefore avoided if possible. The specification of features in the underlying representations of the vowels proceeds therefore with [Low], the insertion of which applies within the tripartite system in (11). Among the front vowels, which constitute a three height system, /æ/ undergoes [Low] insertion as the lowest vowel in the sub-system. So does /o/, which is the lower vowel in the two-height system of back rounded vowels. By contrast, /ɑ/ does not get any further specification because it does not contrast with any other vowel in its place of articulation with respect to height. The result of [Low] insertion is shown (12). This system consists of five vowel phonemes: a low and a non-low front vowel (i.e. /æ/ and /e/, the latter of which being underspecified), a back vowel (i.e. /ɑ/), and a low and non-low back rounded vowel (i.e. /o u/).

(12)   Short vowel feature specification
        Step 3: Insertion of [Low]

	i	e	æ	y	ø	ɑ	o	u
[Dorsal]						•	•	•
[Labial]							•	•
[Low]			•			•		

At this point all the vowels in the back area are distinct from each other; hence, no further feature specification is necessary. In the front area, though, a three height sub-system exists and therefore [High] insertion is required. The assignment of [High] results in the picture in (13), where six vowel phonemes are available for the mental representation of lexical entries: low, high and mid front, back, low and non-low back rounded. No phonemic distinction exists yet between front rounded and front unrounded vowels.

(13)   Short vowel feature specification
        Step 4: Insertion of [High]

	i	e	æ	y	ø	ɑ	o	u
[Dorsal]						•	•	•
[Labial]							•	•
[Low]			•			•		
[High]	•			•				

The vowel system generated so far is an unmarked one. It has been generated by assigning place of articulation features before height features and by leaving out the universally unmarked feature [Coronal]. In this system no front rounded vowels are available. To make them available, a further step is necessary, i.e. the insertion of the feature [Coronal], yielding a marked system. Although this feature is ultimately redundant, it is necessary in order to comply with with the [Labial] constraint in (3): [Coronal] insertion gives [Labial] the possibility to be represented, and coronal-labial vowels can be generated. The final step in the feature specification of the Miogliola Ligurian vowels is illustrated in (14). The newly introduced feature specifications are highlighted by using a diamond symbol instead of a circle.

(14) Short vowel feature specification
Step 5: Insertion of [Coronal] + [Labial]

	i	e	æ	y	ø	a	o	u
[Dorsal]						•	•	•
[Labial]				♦	♦		•	•
[Low]			•				•	
[High]	•			•				
[Coronal]				♦	♦			

I assume that [Coronal] is only inserted in the representation of front rounded vowels. It may be possible that once [Coronal] is activated in the system, all coronal vowels undergo [Coronal] insertion. The Miogliola Ligurian vowel patterns have no bearing on this issue. As will be seen, it is crucial that features are assigned in the way they have been assigned in order to account for the patterns of neutralization displayed by the vowels in (7) and (8), but no difference falls out from having front unrounded vowels specified for [Coronal] or not.

The phonetic organization of the eight short vowel phonemes in (4) can now be given the phonological organization in (15).

(15) Phonological chart of the short vowel phonemes

Articulator→ Height ↓		[Coronal] [Labial]	[Dorsal]	[Dorsal] [Labial]
[High]	i	y		
	e	ø	a	u
[Low]	æ			o

Observe now the positional switches that phonology has operated on the phonetic values of the vowel phonemes plotted in (4). Within the categories generated by the procedures adopted and illustrated above, vowels are specified for a given feature [F] in underlying representation iff they are phonetically 'more F' than others from which they have not been distinguished through other feature specifications at the moment in the acquisition path at which [F]-insertion takes place. If the second term of comparison is not available, then phonological specification of the phonetic value [F] does not take place and the vowel remains unspecified in the mental lexical entries. Consequently, the vowel /o/ is phonologically marked low, in spite of its being phonetically mid. The reason for this is that there is no other vowel which is lower in its place of articulation, and that there is another vowel, /u/, which is not as low. /u/ is only phonetically high, but not phonologically high, because within the category within which it is considered there is no second dorsal phoneme from which /u/ must be differentiated: /u/ is therefore left unspecified for height. The same holds true for /ɑ/, which is alone in its place of articulation and for which any height specification is totally redundant. The main point is that feature specification – and, in general phonological representations – arise from the set of relationships holding within a system, not from absolute phonetic values. Crucially, the set of relationships holding within the long vowel system is different from the set of relationships holding within the short vowel system, due to the presence of /ɔː/ and the absence of /ɔ/. Let us now turn to the relevant steps in the feature specification of the long vowels and see how the asymmetry between the two vowel systems, the short and the long, is mirrored in their feature specification.

4.2 Assigning Features to the Long Vowels

The chart in (16) shows the first three steps in the assignment of features to the long vowels: Insertion of [Dorsal], [Labial] and [Low].

(16)   Long vowel feature specification
        Steps 1-3: Insertion of [Dorsal], [Labial] and [Low]

	iː	eː	æː	yː	øː	ɑː	ɔː	oː	uː
[Dorsal]						●	●	●	●
[Labial]							●	●	●
[Low]			●				●		

In (16), [Dorsal] and [Labial] insertion work in exactly the same way as for the short vowels. When [Low] insertion applies, though, because place of articulation distinctions have already been made available, the dorsal-labial vowels display a two-height system in the short inventory, but a three-height system in the long one. The vowel /o/, which is the lower in its two-height system, therefore receives specification for [Low], in spite of its being phonetically mid (recall 12). However, its phonetic counterpart in the long inventory is part of a three-height system, within which /oː/ has both a higher and a lower counterpart. Therefore it cannot be specified for the feature [Low], which is assigned to /ɔː/ instead, the lowest among the long dorsal-labial vowels.

Feature specifications for the long vowels then proceed then as indicated in (17).

(17)   Long vowel feature specification
        Steps 4-5: Insertion of [High] and [Coronal] + [Labial]

	iː	eː	æː	yː	øː	ɑː	ɔː	oː	uː
[Dorsal]						●	●	●	●
[Labial]				◆	◆		●	●	●
[Low]			●				●		
[High]	●			●					●
[Coronal]				◆	◆				

Once [Low] has been assigned, [High] insertion takes place within the long vowels in (17), but not within the short dorsal-labial sub-system (recall 13). The long vowels require one more height specification because, unlike their short counterparts, they form, a three height-system. In the short inventory, this results in /u/ – already distinct from the phonologically low /o/ – being unspecified for height. By contrast, in the long inventory /uː/ undergoes [High] insertion, so that this vowel can be made distinct from /oː/. The final step in (17), i.e. the insertion of [Coronal] and [Labial], applies in a parallel fashion to the short and long vowel inventories.

The phonological chart resulting from the feature specification of the long vowels in (17) looks like (18).

(18)   Phonological chart of the long vowel phonemes

Articulator→ Height ↓		[Coronal] [Labial]	[Dorsal]	[Dorsal] [Labial]
[High]	iː	yː		uː
	eː	øː	ɑː	oː
[Low]	æː			ɔː

To conclude this section, I would like to point out once more how phonetics and phonology lead to different categorizations of the asymmetry between short and long vowels in Miogliola Ligurian. From the perspective of phonetics, /ɔː/ lacks a short counterpart, whereas higher up in the back rounded region the short and long inventories are symmetrical, cf. /o oː/ and /u uː/. From the phonological perspective, however, a different picture arises. For phonology, not /ɔː/, but rather /uː/ is singled out as the long vowel that does not have a short counterpart. While /uː/ is phonologically high, /u oː/ are phonologically mid and /o ɔː/ phonologically low.

Phonetics and phonology also predict different front/back correspondences. Whereas phonetics and phonology agree in pairing the front and back long vowels because they do not differ in height, a different picture arises for the short vowels. This is a consequence of the fact that in the short inventory the front unrounded vowels outnumber the back rounded ones. The front unrounded counterpart of /u/ is therefore /e/, not /i/, and the front unrounded counterpart of /o/ is /æ/, not /e/. An examination of the phonetic charts in (4) and (5), and the corresponding phonological charts in (15) and (18) may clarify the asymmetry. In what follows I show that the phonological perspective provides an adequate account for the two patterns of reduction seen above, whereas the phonetic perspective fails to do so.

5.   Comparing Radical and Contrastive Underspecification

My assumptions concerning the specification of contrasts in the underlying representation are:

(19) a.   features can be underspecified even if they are contrastive.

   b.   an algorithm assigning features to underlying representa-
         tions in a given order determines which features are speci-
         fied in underlying representation and which are not. That
         is, lexical minimality is not the overriding principle.

   c.   when a feature is assigned, its organising node is assigned
         not only for the feature which is specified but also for the
         segments where it is not specified.

We discuss each point with an example from Miogliola and point out
where Radical and Contrastive Underspecification theories differ.

On the basis of (19a), the feature assignment described in section
4 can be distinguished from Contrastive Underspecification. Consider the table (17). The feature [High] is contrastive for long vowels. The vowels [iː], [yː] and [uː] are specified as [High] while all
other non-high vowels remain unmarked. These need to be specified
as [–High] in Contrastive Underspecification (Steriade 1995: 141). In
addition, if we compare the short vowels in (14), only [i] and [y], but
not [u] are specified for [High]. Radical Underspecification would
predict that all three vowels are marked for this feature.

As mentioned in (19b), there is an order in the assignment of
features, in particular place of articulation features are assigned first.
Furthermore, for the feature [Labial] to be introduced, one of the
'main' place features [Dorsal] or [Coronal] has to be assigned. In
Miogliola, [yː] has both [Labial] and [Coronal], although on the
surface, one of the features would have been sufficient. Note that [iː]
is not specified for [Coronal]. Thus, presumably in Radical Underspecification, [yː] would only by marked [Labial]. The redundancy
proposed in our analysis would not be permitted (see Steriade 1995:
129). In Contrastive Underspecification, if [yː] has the feature [Coro-
nal], [i] should have it to – there is no way of keeping these distinct
in terms of the presence vs. absence of [Coronal].

Our third assumption is that when a contrastive feature is
assigned, its organising node must be present everywhere (see 19c).
This means that at the point when the feature [Low] is assigned to
[æ] (as in 12), the organising node Aperture will be automatically
assigned to all other vowels it now contrasts with by virtue of this

feature. We believe that this distinguishes our approach from Radical Underspecification. As discussed in Ghini (1998), in a language with voiceless and voiced obstruents, the Laryngeal node will be present in both obstruents, but not in the predictably voiced sonorants, because there is no laryngeal contrast among the sonorants and the laryngeal distinction is introduced only after the sonorant/obstruent distinction has already been established. Thus, in a language with [t d l] where [voice] is contrastive, [d] has a Laryngeal node with [voice] as a dependent, [t] has only a Laryngeal node, and [l] has nothing. Presumably, both Radical Underspecification (due to redundancy) and Contrastive Underspecification (due to feature co-occurrence) would see no [voice] specification for [l]. However, Radical Underspecification would have no difference between [t] and [l] with respect to laryngeal specification, whereas Contrastive Underspecification would specify [t] as [–voice], thereby not encoding a markedness asymmetry between [t] and [d].

The differences between our assumptions and that of Radical and Contrastive Underspecification are clearest when we compare the short and long high vowels in Miogliola. As we mentioned above, our feature assignment algorithm allows [uː] but not [u] to be [High] and [o] but not [oː] to be [Low] (cf. 15 and 18). While these asymmetries follow naturally from our algorithm and are necessary to account for the phonological alternations (as we will see in the next section), neither Radical nor Contrastive Underspecification can account for these generalisations.

6.   Accounting for the Patterns of Vowel Reduction

The patterns of neutralization in (7) show that in unstressed position four pairs undergo height neutralization: /e æ/, /eː æː/, /u o/ and /oː ɔː/. These neutralizations all involve a mid vowel which merges with a height neighbour in its place of articulation. What is striking about the height neutralizations at issue is that in three cases /e æ/, /eː æː/, and /oː ɔː/ the mid vowel neutralizes with its lower counterpart, whereas in one case, /u o/, the mid vowel neutralizes with its higher counterpart. Interestingly, the height contrast singled out by vowel neutralization in unstressed position is exactly the one which is part of a two-height system, assuming that height is analysed within its own place of articulation, as proposed here. If feature specification proceeds as illustrated, then the pair /u o/ is the height parallel of /e æ/, /e: æ:/, and /o: ɔ:/ in the back round area of the short vowel inventory: all these pairs of phonemes are distinguished by the presence/absence of the feature [Low].

If feature specification simply transposes the phonetic values of the vowel phonemes into phonological representations, such parallelism is lost, and no clear pattern of reduction can be seen. It is only phonologically that the lower vowel of *all* of the four pairs undergoing height neutralization is marked as [Low]. Making this feature unavailable in unstressed position gets all the observed neutralization facts: the loss of [Low] makes them identical with their higher counterparts. The delinking of [Low] in unstressed position is shown in (20).

(20)   Vowel reduction in unstressed position

Rule (20) correctly leaves the pairs /y ø/ and /y: ø:/ unaffected. These pairs are phonologically represented as a [High]/[Ø] contrast, not as a [Ø]/[Low] one, in spite of the fact that they form a two-height system within their place of articulation. This is due to the fact that their representations involve the presence of the feature [Coronal], the last feature to be assigned under the Place node. This delays the formation of a coronal-labial place of articulation until after height features have been assigned. Thus, /y ø/ and /y: ø:/ have the same height features as /i e/ and /i: e:/, from which they are phonemically nondistinct at the point of height feature specification, and with which they share membership to a three-height system including the low front vowel /æ/. The correctness of the strategies adopted here in assigning features to underlying representations is borne out by the data: /y/ and /ø/ do not merge. Unfortunately no data are available to see how stressed /øː/ patterns in unstressed position.

As for the displacement of the vowel /ø/ from front to back in unstressed position (see 7), this is assumed here to be a consequence of the shift in phonological relations caused by the delinking of [Low] in unstressed position. [Low] delinking in (20) leaves the short vowel inventory with two front vowels, but just one back rounded one. The cross-linguistic examination of phonological inventories shows that front rounded vowels never outnumber their back counterparts. Therefore, the backing of the vowel /ø/ can be seen as a repair strategy necessary to rebalance the system. This view makes the prediction that no rebalancing should take place in the long inventory, where, after the delinking of [Low], front and back rounded vowels are equal in number. As already pointed out, it is unfortunate that the very few examples of /øː/ available do not exhibit unstressed alternants which would allow for a verification of this prediction.

Height neutralization, only partial in unstressed position, appears to be more radical in the pattern of neutralization exhibited by Miogliola Ligurian vowels in (8). Before /N/, only place of articulation distinctions are available. This can be expressed formally by delinking the Aperture node altogether, so as to make height contrasts impossible. Total height neutralization is expressed in (21).

(21)   Total height neutralization before /N/

Place

Aperture

Observe that total height neutralization before /N/ results in a four-way contrast, not in a three-way contrast, as was shown in (8). This pattern of neutralization shows that there are four and not three places of articulation in Miogliola Ligurian, and that feature assignment must proceed so as to view labiality for the back vowels as non redundant. This is possible iff [Labial] is assigned at the point when height distinctions are not available yet, as predicted by Place of Articulation First. If redundancies and relative patterns of under-specification are established by looking at the system as a whole, [Labial] is redundant for the back vowels and should be left un-marked. However, this view makes incorrect predictions concerning the expected pattern of neutralization. Once height distinctions are neutralized, three places of articulations and not four, should result. [Labial] is therefore not redundant in Miogliola Ligurian back vowels, as predicted by Place of Articulation First.

7. Phonetic Implementation

The core of this paper is devoted to the question of how phonetics is translated into phonology, that is, the way phonology looks at the phonetic facts and categorizes them. The patterns of neutralization in Miogliola Ligurian show that phonology does not translate absolute phonetic values into phonological representations, but rather that phonology looks at relative values within given categories. More specifically, in Miogliola Ligurian phonological height values are established by taking into consideration what vowels are higher and lower with respect to each other within their respective place of articulation categories. Moreover, the assignment of phonological height features gives the feature [Low] precedence over the feature [High]. It falls out that in the case of a height contrast within a given place of articulation there will always be a phonologically low vowel, be it phonetically low or not.

An issue complementary to the question examined in this paper is the following. If the phonology looks at the phonetics in the way illustrated above, how does the phonetics looks at the phonology? That is, what are the principles that the phonetic component of the language resorts to in implementing the instructions coming from the phonological component? A theory of phonetic implementation is far beyond the scope of this paper. Therefore, I limit myself here to some general considerations Miogliola Ligurian seems to point to. The charts in (22) summarize the facts and the analyses outlined in the preceding sections by giving the overview of the phonological contrasts and their phonetic implementation in the vowel inventories in Miogliola Ligurian. Considerations on the ways phonetics implements phonology follow.

(22) Overview of the Miogliola Ligurian Vowels
      Phonological contrasts and phonetic implementation
      C = Coronal; L = Labial; H = High; L = Low; D = Dorsal

a. Stressed short vowels

i. phonological contrasts

		CL	D	DL
H	i	y		
	e	ø	ɑ	u
L	æ			o

ii. phonetic implementation

	c	cl	d	dl
high	i	y		u
mid	e	ø		o
low	æ		ɑ	

b. Stressed long vowels

i. phonological contrasts

		CL	D	DL
H	iː	yː		uː
	eː	øː	ɑː	oː
L	æː			ɔː

ii. phonetic implementation

	c	cl	d	dl
high	iː	yː		uː
mid	eː	øː		oː
mid				ɔː
low	æː		ɑː	

c. Unstressed vowels alternating with stressed short vowels

i. phonological contrasts

		CL	D	DL
H	i	y		
	ɛ		a	u

ii. phonetic implementation

	c	cl	d	dl
high	i	y		u
mid	ɛ			
low			a	

d. Unstressed vowels alternating with stressed long vowels

i. phonological contrasts

		CL	D	DL
H	i	y		u
	ɛ		a	ɔ

ii. phonetic implementation

	c	cl	d	dl
high	i	y		u
mid	ɛ			ɔ
low			a	

e. Stressed vowels before /N/

i. phonological contrasts

		CL	D	DL
	e/ɛ	œ/ø	a	ɔ/o

ii. phonetic implementation

	c	cl	d	dl
mid	e/ɛ	œ/ø		ɔ/o
low			a	

Let me turn first to what appear to be the general directions of phonetic implementation suggested by the Miogliola system. The only vowel specified as just dorsal is consistently realized as low and unrounded. By contrast, the other places of articulation appear to be consistent in avoiding the low region of the phonetic space and in using it only when absolutely necessary, that is to implement a three-height contrast. Such directions of phonetic implementation are paralleled in the analysis of Yawelmani proposed by Stevens el al. (1986). The input to the phonetic component they assume is the phonological feature specification in (23).

(23)   Yawelmani vowels (Stevens *et al.* 1986: 462)

	i	u	o	a
[high]			–	–
[round]		+	+	
[back]				
[low]				

The phonological specification assumed by Stevens *et al.* is couched within the framework of Radical Underspecification (Archangeli 1984), which differs in a number of ways from the assumptions made here (recall section 5). Nevertheless, as in the present analysis, phonological feature specifications in radically underspecified matrices like the one in (23) are assumed to be minimal and free of redundancies, and therefore raise the question how such abstract representations are implemented phonetically. Stevens *et al.* suggest that redundancies are filled in by rules which follow general principles related to auditory perception and to articulatory and acoustic phonetics. One of these principles is that the non-high vowel in the vowel triangle that is perceptually most distinct from all other vowels is the vowel labeled as [+low, +back, –round], that is, the vowel [ɑ] (Stevens *et al.* 1986: 462). Therefore, reasons of perceptual saliency justify, or even require, the presence of [ɑ] across vowel inventories. In Yawelmani, it is the vowel phoneme which is specified as [–high] which is closest to the surface feature specification of [ɑ], whereas the corresponding vowel phoneme in Miogliola is the one which is underlyingly specified as [Dorsal] only. At the same time, a clustering of low vowels should be avoided in a sparse vowel system, given that low vowels are perceptually rather close to each other. Again, perceptual distinctiveness predicts that vowels other than [ɑ] are can be realized as non-low. This is the case in both Yawelmani and Miogliola, where vowels in their respective places of articulation shift away from [ɑ] towards the top of the vowel chart. Such vowel shift is evident in Miogliola in the short back rounded vowels, where the underlying contrast [Low/Ø] is not realized as [ɔ o], but rather as [o u]. Needless to say, no shift takes place where three-way contrasts exist. In these cases, the presence of the phonetically low vowels [æ æː ɔː] cannot be done away with.

It is interesting to observe that the operations performed by the phonetic component of the language are different in a fundamental way with respect to the operations performed by phonology. The former look at the system as a whole, the latter operate within the different sub-domains of the system as they are being created. Thus, unlike the phonological component of the language, which marks the contrast /o-u/ as [Low]/[Ø], rather than [Ø]/[High] by looking at the dorsal-labial place of articulation in isolation, the phonetic component of the language operates according to different principles. By realizing [Low]/ [Ø] as phonetically mid/high, neither are the phonological height values of each member of the pair enhanced nor is their height contrast within the dorsal labial place of articulation.

The switch involving phonological height contrast to one position higher up only makes sense if seen across places of articulations and not within its own sub-system. Unlike the phonological component of the language, the phonetic component looks at the 'neighbours', and enhances the phonological distinctions in place of articulation by making them even more distinct through phonetic height.

Let us now turn to the phonetic implementation of the Miogliola vowels before /N/. In this position, the shift along the sides of the vowel space towards the top is only partial, since the low dorsal vowel contrasts with phonetically mid, not high, vowels. This counterexample to the stretching out towards the periphery of the vowel space is only apparent, since it finds an explanation within the phonology of the language. In stressed position, the presence of [ɛ œ a ɔ] signals the presence of a following /N/. This information is redundant when the following /N/ is in coda position and realized as [ŋ], because the velar nasal is the surface realization of a single underlying phoneme: /N/. However, when the following /N/ is in onset position, it is realized as [n], i.e. it is phonetically identical to the surface realization of another consonantal phoneme of the language, /n/, also realized as coronal. The contrast between /N/ and /n/ is therefore neutralized on the surface, but recoverable through the phonetics of the preceding stressed vowels. For the details of the phonology of /N/ → [n^1] and /n/ → [n^2], the interested reader is referred to Ghini (1998). The bottom up shift along the sides of the vowel space therefore stops at the relevant height not exploited by the other inventories, so as to preserve the recoverability of a phonological contrast neutralized by the phonetics. In Savonese, a Ligurian dialect closely related to Miogliola of which I am a native speaker, /N/ after a stressed vowel is always realized as /ŋ/ and no neutralization between the underlyingly placeless and the underlyingly coronal nasals occur on the surface. Not surprisingly, the reduced vowel inventory before /N/ corresponding to the Miogliola one undergoes a complete bottom up switch along the sides of the vowel chart, thus contrasting the phonetically low vowel [a] with the phonetically high vowels [i y u].

To conclude this paragraph, observe once more how the phonetic component of the language, in contrast to the phonological one, operates across categories. It has already been pointed out that phonetic implementation looks across places of articulation within an inventory in order to enhance perceptual saliency and distinctiveness. Now it has become clear that the phonetic component of the language looks across inventories as well. The phonetic contrast in stressed position before /N/ between the low vowel on the one hand

and the lower mid vowels on the other makes only sense if the other inventories are taken into consideration as well. If this is so, it becomes clear that the lower mid area of the phonetic space is left unexploited by the other stressed inventories and can be used as the target of phonetic implementation in order to maintain the recoverability of a phonological contrast.[6]

A last observation concerns the 'displacement' of the dorsal vowel, which is realized as [ɑ] in the full inventories, and as [a] in the reduced inventories. This is quite obviously in relation to the presence in the full inventories and absence in the reduced ones of the front low vowel [æ]. The dorsal vowel is articulated further back in the former case, where it contrasts with [æ] at the same height; it is centralized in the latter, where it is alone in its height range. In the specific case of the vowel inventory in stressed position before /N/, the centralization of the low vowel also serves the distinctive purposes already highlighted for the nonlow vowels: it signals that a following [n] is underlyingly /N/, not /n/.

8.   General concluding remarks

The Miogliola Ligurian vowel patterns support the Place of Articulation First principle, that is a phonological marking procedure whereby place of articulation features are assigned first and phonological height is analysed within the previously created place of articulation categories. What remains to be investigated is whether Place of Articulation First is a universal principle, or other conceivable procedures of feature assignment are adopted cross-linguistically. Lahiri (1999b) argues that Place of Articulation First is necessary to account for the vowel patterns in Bengali.

The phonological classification that the feature assignment algorithm predicts when Place of Articulation First is assumed holds true in Miogliola whether underspecification is assumed or not. The phonological height marking of the pair /o u/ must be parallel to the phonological height marking of the pairs /æ e/, /æː eː/, /ɔː oː/, simply because they pattern together in height neutralization patterns. Therefore, the classification into natural classes predicted by Place of Articulation First holds true independent of the underspecification assumptions made here. Notice, however, that a full specification approach with binary features should mark as [+Low, –High] the lower, as [–Low, –High] the higher member of the pairs /æ e/, /æː eː/, /o u/, and /ɔː oː/. Turning then [+Low] into [–Low] in the desired environment would capture the height neutralization facts. However, the [–High] marking for the vowel /u/ is a totally ad hoc stipulation in order to capture the facts, it does not follow from anything else. If phonology translates phonetics by looking at relative values, as the Miogliola vowel clearly suggest, then it is not clear what it may mean to mark the vowel /u/ as [–High]. The vowel /u/ is not less high than anything else in the Miogliola Ligurian vowel system, nor is it or can it be in any conceivable vowel system in the world languages. If, on the other hand, phonology translates phonetics by looking at absolute values, things get even worse: Miogliola /u/ (=[u]) is simply a high vowel, not a mid one.

A last remark on underspecification is in order at this point. Even if the Miogliola vowel patterns, at least from a pure computational point of view, can be accounted for by assuming full specification, Miogliola consonants cannot. (Ghini 1998). Within the consonant system /p t ts tʃ k b d dz dʒ g f s ʃ v z ʒ m n ɲ N l ɾ r/, where /N/ is a coronal-velar alternating nasal, a subset of consonants is singled out by the prosodic system of the language: /t d N l ɾ/. This subset of consonants can only be captured as a class if they are underlyingly unspecified for place of articulation. Crucially, it is *not* the nasal that surfaces invariably as coronal [n] that is part of the natural class, but the one alternating between [n] and [ŋ]. A full specification approach would have to specify the alternating nasal as underlyingly dorsal, given the presence of a coronal nasal in the system. In this scenario, it remains a complete mystery why a dorsal nasal patterns with a subset of coronals /t d l ɾ/ to the exclusion, among other things, of the plain coronal nasal /n/, and not with the dorsals /k g/. Of course, one might want to give up the idea that classes have to be captured by means of representations, but it is far from obvious how to explain the observed classifications alternatively. For a principled way to account for underlying lack of specification in just /t d N l ɾ/ see Ghini (1998).

To conclude, Miogliola vowels tell us that place of *articulation* is categorized in the lexicon prior to height, and that only the redundancies arising from such a procedure should be left unspecified in underlying representation.

Notes

*   Mirco Ghini passed away in January 2001 before he was able to incorporate all the changes he wanted to in response to the comments by the reviewers. We (Aditi Lahiri and Michael Wagner) had discussed most of the changes with Mirco before he died and have tried to revise the manuscript according to his wishes. Following the editor's suggestions, we have added a section comparing Mirco's theory with Contrastive and Radical Underspecification. We have done so by refering to his dissertation (Ghini 1998), where he discusses these issues in depth.

1   Section 5 clarifies how the assumptions about underspecification compare with Radical and Contrastive underspecification. One reviewer points out that there are several criticisms of underspecification such as Mohanan (1991), McCarthy and Taub (1992), and Steriade (1995). These and other criticisms are discussed in detail in Ghini (1998: chapter 1).

2   'Step-wise' does not refer to a 'derivation' as the filling in of features by default rules, as was understood by one of the reviewers. Rather it relates to the acquisition path by which the language learner establishes the system of contrasts in the underlying representation.

3   The experiments were run in German. We give English examples just for illustration.

4   In unstressed position, the dorsal vowel /ɑ/ surfaces as [a]. The underlying segment has in fact 6 surface allophones. This issues will be addressed at the end of section 7. For an in depth discussion cf. Ghini (1998: chapter 6).

5   Dresher (1998) has a similar theory of assigning contrastive features. His Successive Binary Algorithm is spelt out in detail in his paper. My analysis and Dresher (1998) differ in which feature is assigned first, but the basic principles are the same.

6   Why the phonetically non-low vowels are raised by one position in this specific case in which they precede a word final, but not a word internal, /N/ = [ŋ] is not clear.

References

Archangeli, Diana
    1984   Underspecification in Yawelmani phonology and morphology. Ph.D. dissertation, MIT.
Avery, Peter and Keren Rice
    1989   Segment structure and coronal underspecification. *Phonology* 6: 179-200.
Clements, G. N.
    1985   The geometry of phonological features. *Phonology Yearbook* 2: 225-252.
    1989   A unified set of features for consonants and vowels. Ms. Cornell University.
    1991   Place of articulations in consonants and vowels. *Working Papers of the Cornell Phonetics Laboratory* 5: 77-123.
Clements, G. N. and Elizabeth V. Hume
    1995   The internal organization of speech sounds. In: John Goldsmith (ed.), *The Handbook of Phonological Theory,* 245-306. Oxford: Blackwell.
Dresher, B. Elan
    1998   Child phonology, learnability, and phonological theory. In Tej Bhatia and William C. Ritchie (eds.), *Handbook of Language Acqusition,* 299-346. New York: Academic Press.
Dresher, B. Elan, Glynne Piggott, and Keren Rice
    1994   Contrast in phonology: overview. *Toronto Working Papers in Linguistics* 13(1): iii-xvii.
Ghini, Mirco
    1998   Asymmetries in the phonology of Miogliola. Doctoral Dissertation, University of Konstanz   [To appear 2001, Berlin: Mouton de Gruyter].
Kiparsky, Paul
    2000   Paradigms effects and opacity. In: Aditi Lahiri (ed.), *Analogy, Levelling, Markedness,* 15-46. Berlin: Mouton de Gruyter.
Lahiri, Aditi
    1991   Anteriority in sibilants. In: *XIIth International Congress of Phonetic Sciences.*
    1999a   Speech recognition with phonological features. In: O. John, T. Hasegawa, M. Ohala, D. Granville and A. Bailey (eds.), *14th International Congress of Phonetic Sciences,* 715-722. University of California, Berkeley.

1999b   Feature specification in processing and change. Talk given at the Conference on Distinctive Feature Theory: ZAS, Berlin, 7-9 October 1999.

Lahiri, Aditi and Vincent Evers
1991   Palatalization and coronality. In: C. Paradis & J.-F. Prunet (eds.), *The Special Status of Coronals,* 79-100. San Diego, Academic.

Lahiri, Aditi and Henning Reetz
2001   Underspecified recognition. In: Carlos Gussenhoven, Natasha Warner and Toni Rietveld (eds.), *Papers in Laboratory Phonology 7.* Berlin: Mouton de Gruyter.

McCarthy, John and A. Taub
1992   Review of C. Paradis & J.-F. Prunet (eds.), *The Special Status of Coronals. Phonology* 9, 2: 363-70.

Mohanan, K. P.
1991   On the bases of radical underspecification. *Natural Language and Linguistic Theory* 5: 485-518.

Prince, Alan and Paul Smolensky
1993   Optimality theory: constraint interaction in generative grammar, Ms. Rutgers University & University of Colorado.

Reetz, Henning
1998   Automatic speech recognition with features. Universität des Saarlandes.
1999   Converting speech signals to phonological features. In: O. John, T. Hasegawa, M. Ohala, D. Granville and A. Bailey (eds.), *14 International Congress of Phonetic Sciences,* 1733-6. University of California, Berkeley.

Rice, Keren
1996   Default variability: the coronal-velar relationship. *Natural Language and Linguistic Theory* 14(3): 493-543.

Steriade, Donca
1995   Underspecification and markedness. In: John Goldsmith (ed.), *The Handbook of Phonological Theory,* 114-174. Oxford: Blackwell.

Stevens, Ken N., Samuel J. Keyser and H. Kawasaki
1986   Toward a phonetic and phonological theory of redundant features. In: J. Perkell & D. Klatt (eds.) *Invariability and Variability in Speech Processes.* Hillsdale: Erlbaum.

Representing nasality in consonants[*]

Janet Grijzenhout

1. Introduction

Among the processes in which nasal consonants or the nasalization of consonants are involved, we find phonological processes such as nasal harmony and nasal insertion between vowels as well as morphological processes such as nasal affixation. An account of these processes crucially relies on the representation of nasality. In the literature on nasality in consonants, the two featural representations for nasal stops in (1a) and (1b) have been proposed. The most obvious way to represent a nasal consonant is to use the feature [nasal] (as in 1a). The other possibility to represent nasality in consonants is a combination of a feature that expresses sonority (i.e. [+son] or "SV" for Sonorant Voicing) and [–cont], or – under the assumption that features are monovalent – the absence of a feature for continuancy (as in 1b). In this paper, I argue that the representation with the feature [+nasal] should be used for nasal consonants that are involved in nasal harmony. To distinguish these nasal consonants from the ones that are not involved in nasal harmony processes, I will refer to the former as "plain nasal stops" and to the latter as "light nasal stops":[1]

(1) Two featural representations for nasal consonants

   a. plain nasal stop: [+son, +cons]
                              |
                           [nasal]

   b. light nasal stop: [+son, +cons]

The feature value [+son] indicates airflow from the lungs across the glottis and the feature value [–cont] (or the absence of [cont]) implies that the airflow cannot pass through the oral cavity due to closure.

The result is nasal airflow. In this paper, I present evidence for both representations for nasality in consonants from languages which exhibit nasal harmony, nasal affixation, and nasal epenthesis.

Nasal harmony is the result of spreading the feature [nasal] within a given morphological or prosodic domain. I argue that in those cases where nasal stops do not trigger harmony (as in e.g. European Portuguese), the stop in question is best represented without the feature [nasal]. Conversely, in those instances where nasal stops induce harmony of a neighboring segment (as in e.g. Brazilian Portuguese), the nasal stop is always specified for the feature [nasal]. The Indonesian language Acehnese is special in that it has both kinds of nasal stops; those specified for [nasal] are always followed by nasal vowels and those unspecified for [nasal] are followed by oral vowels.

Nasal affixation results from the introduction of a nasalizing feature into some domain by a morphological process. The phonological changes that segments undergo under nasal affixation vary and are determined by their sonority level. In Navajo, for example, vowels are nasalized, fricatives are voiced, and the less sonorant stops are not changed under nasal affixation. I argue that nasalization in Navajo results from the introduction of the affixal features SV (Sonorant Voicing) and [nasal]. I furthermore show that the same features play a role in Terena. In stems with an initial obstruent, Terena nasal affixation involves prenasalization of that obstruent. In all other cases, nasal affixation involves nasalization of all vowels and approximants preceding the first obstruent (which is prenasalized). Section 3.3 provides a detailed account of this phenomenon.

In languages with nasal epenthesis (e.g. High Alemannic and Dutch), the feature [nasal] never spreads. Following Ortmann (1998), I argue that in these languages, the nasal stop is best represented without the nasal feature.

The structure of this paper is as follows. Section 2 describes the behavior of nasal stops in languages with nasal harmony. Section 3 discusses voicing processes and nasal affixation in Navajo and Terena. Section 4 considers *n*-epenthesis in High Alemannic and *n*-insertion across a clitic boundary in Dutch. Section 5 concludes.

2. Nasal harmony

Nasal harmony affects different segments in different languages (see, e.g. Piggott 1992, Walker 1994, 1998). This paper discusses nasal harmony in Acehnese and Brazilian and European Portuguese. Acehnese is interesting because it has two types of nasal consonants; one type induces nasal harmony, whereas the other type does not. In Brazilian Portuguese, all nasal segments (including the nasal stops) trigger nasal harmony. This is not the case in European Portuguese. In European Portuguese, nasal harmony is triggered by nasal vowels only and nasal harmony affects non-consonantal segments, i.e. vowels and glides. Whether or not the feature [nasal] actually associates to a potential target under nasal harmony is determined by the sonority level of the target segment. The sonority requirement for nasality is language-specific and different languages may have different requirements concerning the sonority level of the target segments.

2.1. Acehnese nasal harmony

Acehnese is spoken by about 1,500,000 speakers in north Sumatra, Indonesia. Durie (1985: 19) gives the following inventory of consonant phonemes:

(2)   Acehnese consonant inventory (Durie 1985)

	labial	alveolar	palatal	velar	laryngeal
voiceless stops	p	t	c	k	ʔ
voiced stops	b	d	ɟ	g	
voiceless fricatives		s	ʃ		h
nasal stops	m	n	ɲ	ŋ	
approximants	w	l r	j		

According to Durie (1985), oral and nasal vowels are contrastive in stressed – i.e. word-final syllables. Nasal vowels in stressed syllables are preceded by nasal stops or nasalized /h w j/ and may be followed by unreleased stops (indicated by C', see 3):[2]

(3)   [c a . ɦ ɛ̃ t']   'sever with a knife attached to the end of a
                            pole'

Other segments do not co-occur in the same syllable with nasal
vowels, except in expressives such as *bɛ̃h* 'calf's cry' (Durie 1985:
21). This observation receives a straightforward explanation if we
assume that the feature [nasal] originates in vowels and spreads to
adjacent nodes specified for [+son] within the same syllable.
Throughout this paper, I use a feature-geometric structure (e.g.
Clements & Hume 1995) in which the root node contains the features
[cons] and [son] (e.g. McCarthy 1988) and in which the features
[cont], [strident], and [nasal] branch directly from the root. I furthermore assume that – except for the features in the root node – all
phonological features are monovalent. In this paper, stops are thus
characterized by the absence of the feature [cont] (see 1a, b, 5a), but
nothing crucial depends on this assumption.

(4)   A feature geometric representation of consonants

Root node
$$\begin{bmatrix} \pm \text{son} \\ \pm \text{cons} \end{bmatrix}$$

Manner features   [cont]   [nasal]

Laryngeal node   Laryngeal

                                                           C-Place

[spread] | [voice]
        [constricted]

                                            Labial | Dorsal
                                                  Coronal

Below, I will ignore place features, because they are irrelevant for the
point at hand (although see Clements this volume and Ghini this
volume for discussion). Acehnese oral stops and strident fricatives
are represented as in (5a) and (5b), respectively.

(5)   Representation of oral stops and strident fricatives:

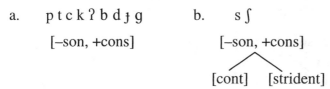

a.   p t c k ʔ b d ɟ g   b.   s ʃ

    [−son, +cons]   [−son, +cons]

                                        [cont]   [strident]

Under nasal harmony, the feature [nasal] does not spread to oral
stops, i.e. segments specified as [−son] without the feature [cont] (see
6a). I assume without further discussion that strident continuants are
represented by the feature [strident] (see 5b) and that the feature
[nasal] does not spread to segments specified for stridency, because
the features [strident] and [nasal] are incompatible (see 6b).

(6)   No nasalization of oral stops and strident fricatives:

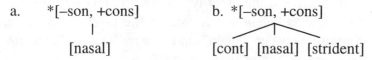

a.   *[−son, +cons]   b. *[−son, +cons]

        |

        [nasal]   [cont] [nasal] [strident]

Nasal stops and approximants are represented by the feature value
[+son]. The segments /l r/ differ from /h w j/ in that the former are
[+cons] and the latter are [−cons] (see, e.g. Chomsky & Halle 1968:
302-303):

(7)   Representation of approximants:

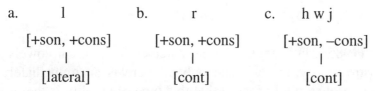

a.   l   b.   r   c.   h w j

    [+son, +cons]   [+son, +cons]   [+son, −cons]
        | | |
    [lateral]   [cont]   [cont]

The feature [nasal] does not associate to the segment /l/, presumably
because this segment is specified for the feature [lateral], which is
incompatible with [nasal]. The segments /h r w j/ are represented by
the features [+son] and [cont] (see 7b, 7c) and are possible targets for
the nasal feature (see 8).[3]

(8)   Nasalization of approximants:

ɦ r̃ w̃ j̃

[+son, ±cons]

[cont]   [nasal]

The question remains how nasal stops are to be represented. Before we answer this question, consider first that when the initial consonant of an unstressed – i.e. non-final – syllable is a nasal stop, we sometimes find that nasality spreads rightward through approximants and vowels until it reaches an obstruent or the right word-edge (9a-d). We also find cases where nasal stops occur in the environment of a following oral vowel (see 10a, b). Durie (1985: 22) concludes from this observation that there are two kinds of nasal stops; one type triggers harmony and the other type does not. Durie (1985) refers to the former type as "plain nasals" and to the latter as "funny nasals" (to distinguish between "plain" and "funny" nasals Durie uses the symbol ^ over the "funny" nasal stop):

(9)   a. [p ɯ ɲ ã m p o h]   'broom'
       b. [m ã n d r ɛ t]   'spicy drink'
       c. [m ã w̃ ʌ̃]   'rose'
       d. [m ũ ɦ ã j̃]   'expensive'

(10)   a. [m̂ o n]   'dew'
       b. [ŋ̂ r a m]   'angry'

Durie (1985: 21) is explicit in his statement that "nasal vowels occur in unstressed syllables if and only if there is an immediately preceding nasal stop". I propose that this type of nasality is the result of spreading the feature [nasal] from a nasal stop to [+son] segments:

(11)   m   ã   w̃   ʌ̃
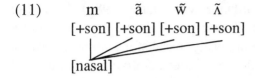

The question arises how the so-called "funny" – or "light" – nasal stops should be specified. One way to represent a nasal consonant is to use the feature [nasal] and the other possibility that emerges is the representation without the nasal feature. These possibilities are presented below as (12a) and (12b), respectively. The feature [+son] indicates that the airflow is not disrupted enough to inhibit voicing. When the airflow from the lungs passes the vibrating vocal cords and cannot escape through the oral cavity due to complete oral closure – represented by the absence of the feature [cont] – the air escapes through the nasal cavity. This means that the configuration in (12b) with a feature expressing a high level of sonority, but without the feature [cont] can only be interpreted as nasality.

(12)   a. plain nasal stop: [+son, +cons]
                                          |
                              [nasal]

       b. light nasal stop: [+son, +cons]

According to Durie (1985), airflow measurements reveal that one type of nasal stops in Acehnese has a higher degree of airflow through the nose than the other type and that vowels are allophonically nasalized after the former, but not after the latter. Ladefoged & Maddieson (1996: 104-106) confirm that there is a measurable difference in velic opening between the two nasal stops in Acehnese. In contrast to Durie (1985), Ladefoged & Maddieson (1996) only consider nasal stops in final stressed syllables and they ignore important data where a nasal stop in another syllable triggers nasal harmony (cf. the data in 9a-d). Their statement that "at this time we continue to believe that no linguistically distinctive use is made of nasals which differ in manner of articulation of the velum" is therefore based on a sub-set of relevant data. In contrast to Ladefoged &

Maddieson (1996) and in accordance with Durie (1985), I propose that the two ways to realize nasal stops in Acehnese correlate with a phonological distinction. More precisely, nasal stops which involve a relatively small velic opening do not trigger iterative rightward nasal spread, whereas nasal stops with a relatively large velic opening induce nasal harmony. We capture these distinctions by different phonological representations (12a versus 12b). The presence of the [nasal] feature accounts (i) for the relatively large velic opening and (ii) for the allophonic nasalization after "plain" nasals (see 9a-d, 11). The absence of the [nasal] feature in the representation of "light" nasals represents (i) a relatively small velic opening and (ii) explains why they are never involved in nasal harmony processes (see 10a, b).

The phonological motivation to assume the feature [nasal] is to account for nasal harmony. Moreover, in Acehnese the representation for nasal stops with and without the feature [nasal] correlates with the degree of airflow. This correlation is not a regular phonetic manifestation of the different representations and the choice of phonetic implementation is language specific (cf. Rice 1993: 311 for a similar proposal; according to her, a coronal consonant may be realized as dental or alveolar and segments with a feature for sonorant voicing – see 3.1 below – may be realized as nasals, prenasal stops, or voiced oral stops).

To summarize, I propose that in Acehnese, nasal stops which have a relatively high degree of airflow through the nose are specified for the feature [nasal] and this feature always spreads to adjacent segments. In contrast, nasal stops which have a lesser degree of nasal airflow are permanently unspecified for the feature [nasal] and due to the fact that there is no nasal feature to spread, they are always followed by oral segments. Furthermore, in Acehnese, the feature [nasal] spreads to vowels, approximants, and nasal stops, but it does not spread to strident fricatives (due to its incompatibility with the feature [strident]), nor to the least sonorant segments in the language, i.e. oral stops.

In the next section, I show that nasal harmony may be induced by nasal stops in Brazilian Portuguese, but not in European Portuguese. This difference may be attributed to the presence versus the absence of the feature [nasal] in nasal stops in the respective languages.

2.2.   Nasal stops and nasal harmony in Brazilian Portuguese and
European Portuguese

Brazilian and European Portuguese both have contrasting oral and
nasal vowels. This is illustrated for European Portuguese by the following examples (data from Costa & Freitas 1999):

(13)   Oral and nasal vowels in European Portuguese

    a. fado   'fate'   c. fũdo   'bottom'
    b. roda   'wheel'   d. rõda   'tour'

In Brazilian and European Portuguese, not only vowels, but also
glides may be nasalized, i.e. a vowel and a glide within the same
syllable share their specification for nasality:

(14)   Nasal vowels and glides in Brazilian Portuguese

    a. p[õj̃]   'put'
    b. m[ẽw̃]   'hand'

In contrast to Brazilian Portuguese, nasal stops in European Portuguese must be preceded and followed by oral vowels:

(15)   No nasal harmony induced by nasal stops in European
      Portuguese

    a. fumo   'smoke'   c. mata   'woods'
    b. dono   'owner'   d. nata   'cream'

Brazilian Portuguese differs from European Portuguese in that nasal
stops always trigger nasal harmony in the former language. More
precisely, in Brazilian Portuguese, a vowel to the left of a nasal stop
is also nasal (data from Wetzels 1997 reported in Costa & Freitas
1999):

(16) Regressive nasal harmony in Brazilian Portuguese

    a. fũmo / *fumo   'smoke'
    b. dõno / *dono   'owner'

The different behavior of nasal stops in Brazilian and European Portuguese with respect to nasal harmony suggests to me that, from a phonological point of view, nasal stops are of the "plain" type (see 12a) in Brazilian Portuguese and of the "light" type (see 12b) in European Portuguese. In Brazilian Portuguese, nasal harmony originates in vowels or in nasal stops and it affects vowels, glides, and nasal stops. This implies that the nasal feature is sensitive to different requirements in both languages. In Brazilian Portuguese the feature [nasal] associates to vowels, glides, and nasal stops under nasal harmony – i.e. to segments specified for [+son][4] – whereas in European Portuguese, nasal stops never bear the feature [nasal] and nasal harmony only affects vowels and glides, i.e. segments specified for [–cons].

2.3. Towards a typology of nasal harmony

Languages vary in terms of where they make a cut between segments that are compatible with the feature [nasal] and segments that are incompatible (see Piggott 1992, Walker 1994).[5] In Applecross Gaelic, for instance, the feature [nasal] is compatible with vowels, glides, liquids, nasal stops, and fricatives, but not with oral stops (e.g. Ternes 1973, van der Hulst & Smith 1982, Piggott 1996). In Acehnese, the feature [nasal] spreads to vowels, /h r w j/, and nasal stops, but not to strident fricatives and oral stops. In Brazilian Portuguese, the feature [nasal] also associates to vowels, glides, and nasal stops and not to fricatives and oral stops, but in European Portuguese, the feature [nasal] only affects vowels and glides, i.e. segments specified as [–cons]. In some languages, no segment is compatible with the feature [nasal]. In section 4, it will be argued that this is the case for High Alemannic and Dutch. Following Walker (1994, 1998), we may thus conclude that there are at least three possible cuts that are related to the level of sonority for compatibility with the feature [nasal]. Below, I indicate the cuts by the marker '#' and the classes of segments at each side of the cuts are defined by the features [son], [cons] and [cont] (e.g. Chomsky & Halle 1968, Clements 1990).

(17) Three possible cuts for compatibility with the feature [nasal]

vowels   # nasals and   # fricatives   # oral
and glides   liquids   stops
[+son, −cons] [+son, +cons]   [−son, +cons]   [−son, +cons]
                                           |
                                       [cont]

See, however, Wiese this volume, who argues that not all points on the sonority hierarchy are represented featurally.

The following tables display the possible and impossible associations of the feature [nasal] in the languages discussed in this paper ('*' indicates an illicit configuration and I tentatively use the feature [liquid] to specify the segments /l/ and /r/):

(18) a. Acehnese and Brazilian Portuguese:

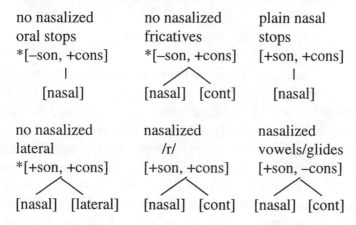

b. European Portuguese:

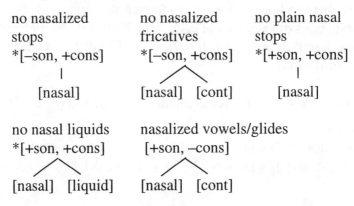

c. High Alemannic and Dutch:

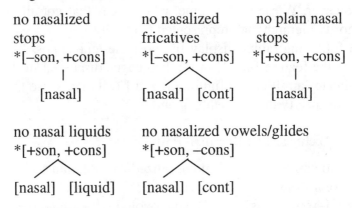

There is no language that differs from, e.g. Brazilian Portuguese only in that the configuration [+son, +cons, nasal] is allowed and [+son, –cons, nasal] is not. In languages with nasal harmony, the nasalizing element is the feature [nasal] and the sonority level plays a role in determining whether or not a segment is affected by the nasalizing element. In itself this is not a new observation (see, for instance, Piggott 1992, Tourville 1991, Walker 1994, 1998). The novel view expressed in the sections above is that the representation of nasal stops may or may not involve the feature [nasal]. There are thus two possible representations of nasal stops (12a versus 12b) and both may be part of the phonology of one language (e.g. Acehnese), or they may help to explain the different behavior of nasality in related languages (e.g. European versus Brazilian Portuguese).

The subsequent sections explore the role and the distribution of the feature [nasal] in morphological processes.

3. Nasal affixation

Nasal affixation is a morphological process which introduces one or more nasalizing features into a morphological domain such as, for instance, a verb stem. I argue that the phonological features SV and [nasal] act as morphological markers in Navajo and Terena. In section 2.3 above, we saw that under nasal harmony, the sonority level expressed by the features [–cons], [+son], and/or [cont] determines whether or not the feature [nasal] associates to a particular segment. In section 3.1, it will be shown that under voicing assimilation, the sonority level expressed by the features [+son] and/ or [cont] also determines whether or not SV actually associates in the environment where this process is expected to apply in Navajo and Southern Paiute. In sections 3.2 and 3.3 I argue that under nasal affixation, the sonority level expressed by the features [–cons], [+son], and/or [cont] crucially determines whether or not the floating features SV and [nasal] associate in certain morphological environments.

3.1. Voicing assimilation in Navajo and Southern Paiute

The Athapaskan language Navajo (Kari 1976, Rice 1993, Sapir & Hoijer 1967, Young & Morgan 1987) displays progressive voicing assimilation, i.e. fricatives are voiced after voiced segments. Consider in this respect that the voiceless fricative /χ/ remains voiceless after /s/ in (19a) and is realized with vocal cord vibration after /z/ in (19b). All underlying voiceless stem-initial fricatives are voiced after voiced segments, i.e. vowels, /l/, /n/, and /z/, but stops are never affected in this position (see [kʰ] in 19c and [t] in 19d):

(19) a. nás - χéés   'I am turning around'
      b. nayííz - γil / *nayííz - χil   'he/she pushed it about'
      c. tèèz - kʰòih   'he has vomited'
      d. shi - titoo - niił   'he will say it to me'

In standard phonological representations, voicing of obstruents is expressed by the feature [voice]. Rice & Avery (1989, 1991), Rice (1993), and Tourville (1991) argue that in languages in which voicing of obstruents and voicing of sonorants is not distinctive, we capture more generalizations if the features [son] and [voice] are replaced by a phonological feature "Spontaneous Voicing" or "Sonorant Voicing" (abbreviated as SV). This feature characterizes voicing in sonorants as well as obstruents. Under this assumption, Rice (1993: 326-328) accounts for the data in (19a-d) as follows. Underlying stem-initial voiceless fricatives receive their voicing by spreading of SV from the preceding segment. In example (19b), for instance, the velar fricative is voiced after voiced /z/. Since Navajo has voiceless aspirated, unaspirated and glottalized stops, but no voiced stops, Rice invokes structure preservation (cf. Kiparsky 1985) to explain why the feature SV may spread to fricatives, but not to stops.

   Now note that a similar process takes place in Southern Paiute, a member of the Numic branch of the Shoshonean language family (Sapir 1930). In this language, we cannot invoke structure preservation to explain the different behavior of fricatives and stops, because all obstruents are underlyingly voiceless. In Southern Paiute, word-initial obstruents always appear voiceless (see 20a-c). Voiceless and voiced fricatives are in complementary distribution after vowels. Voiceless fricatives occur after voiceless vowels (e.g. the bilabial voiceless fricative /ɸ/ in 20c), but never after voiced vowels.[6] In the latter case, fricatives are always realized with voicing. In contrast, voiceless stops may follow both voiceless and voiced vowels (e.g. the phonetically long uvular stop <qq> in 20b, d).

(20) a. sáppI   'belly'   c. sappIɸI   'belly' (abs)
      b. pAqqáŋU 'to kill'   d. navaqqaŋuyïnI 'I kill myself'

In Southern Paiute, there are no underlying voiced obstruents. Thus, structure preservation does not explain why oral stops are never voiced in this language, while fricatives can be. The fact that voiceless stops may follow both types of vowels – whereas the voicing of fricatives is determined by the voicing of preceding vowels – suggests that stops cannot support a feature for voicing under voicing assimilation, whereas fricatives can.

I propose that voicing assimilation in Navajo and Southern Paiute requires an account which makes specific reference to sonority. In particular, I propose that a feature for voicing does not make the feature [son] in the root node superfluous (see also section 3.3 below). I adhere to the traditional view (e.g. Chomsky & Halle 1968) that in some languages, voicing in obstruents is expressed by the laryngeal feature [voice] and I adopt proposals made by, for instance, Piggott (1992) and Rice (1993) that in languages where sonorants can transmit voicing to obstruents, a different feature for voicing is needed. I differ from Piggott and Rice in that I do not assume that this feature replaces [son]. Like [cons], [son] is a binary feature that cannot spread (McCarthy 1988) and that is necessary to describe natural classes. Even in languages where voicing of sonorants and obstruents may be represented by the same feature, it is still necessary to distinguish obstruents from sonorants (cf. section 3.3). In cases where sonorants transmit voicing to obstruents, I assume that sonorants differ from obstruents in that the former are specified as [+son] and the latter as [–son]. When obstruents acquire the feature SV under voicing assimilation from neighboring sonorants, the effect is that they become more sonorous (or vowel-like). I furthermore suggest that the feature SV is sensitive to the degree of sonority of the segment to which it attaches. In particular, the more sonorous a segment is, the more compatible it is with the feature SV. From this it follows that we may find that in some languages, closure in the vocal tract does not contribute enough sonority to bear this voicing specification, whereas some degree of aperture in the vocal tract does. Consider in this respect that in Navajo and Southern Paiute, voicing assimilation is local and requires that an underlying voicing feature (SV) spreads rightward to an adjacent position – as in (21a) – except when that position is not specified for [cont]; see (21b).

(21)   a. Voicing assimilation between continuants

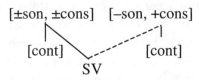

   b. Lack of voicing assimilation

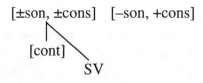

To sum up, in Navajo and Southern Paiute, the feature SV may spread under phonological conditions from voiced segments to fricatives (21a), but not to stops (21b). We will see below that in Navajo, a similar restriction applies under morphological conditions.

3.2. Nasal affixation in Navajo

In Navajo, the perfective of certain verb classes is marked by nasalization of a stem-final vowel and by voicing of a stem-final fricative. The root vowel is nasalized if that vowel finds itself in stem-final position (see 22a where the vowel quality changes as well and where nasalization is marked with a tilde). If the stem in question ends in a fricative, the perfective is marked by voicing of that stem-final fricative (22b). In the Athapaskan languages, laterals are voiceless fricatives (see Rice 1993) and they behave like other fricatives in that they are voiced in the perfective of certain verb classes (see 22c). Stem-final stops are never changed in the perfective, i.e. they remain voiceless (see 22d).

(22) a. -bee   'swim' (stem)   -bíĩ   'swim' (perfective)
      b. -lóós   'lead' (imp.)   -lóóz 'lead' (perfective)
      c. -ʔààł   'chew, eat' (imp.)   -ʔààl 'chew, eat' (perfective)
      d. -ɣáát   'shake out' (imp)   -ɣáát 'shake out' (perfective)

I suggest that the perfective suffix consists of features that increase the level of sonority. In particular, I suggest that the features that mark the perfective are SV for voicing and the feature [nasal] for nasality in vowels.[7] These features need an anchor, i.e. a root node to which they may be associated. Not every root node qualifies as a good anchor, however. The analysis for marking the perfective that I suggest in this paper runs as follows.[8] The suffixal features SV and [nasal] mark the perfective, but – as was the case for SV under voicing assimilation (see section 3.1) – these features cannot associate to a [+cons] root node which is not specified for [cont]. Hence, stops are not affected by the perfective markers SV and [nasal], whereas fricatives are voiced:

(23) a. Voiceless oral stops   b. Voiceless fricatives

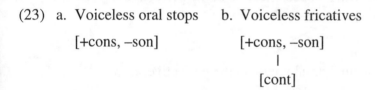

          [+cons, –son]   [+cons, –son]
                                        |
                                     [cont]

      c. No voiced oral stops   d. Voiced fricatives

          *[+cons, –son]   [+cons, –son]
                | ⌒
               SV   SV   [cont]

The suffixal feature SV may associate to consonants represented with the feature [cont] (see 23d). An underlying final voiceless fricative thus acquires the suffixal feature SV in the perfective (see 24b below).

   The reason why the suffixal feature [nasal] is absorbed by word-final vowels, but not by word-final fricatives is that a [+cons] node is not a suitable anchor for the feature [nasal] in this language. In this respect, Navajo resembles European Portuguese (see section 2.2). A

[–cons] root node, on the other hand, is a possible anchor for both SV and [nasal]. The fact that we do not find that vowels preceding final fricatives or stops are nasalized indicates that if the feature [nasal] cannot associate to the right-most element in the perfective, it is better not to realize this feature at all.

In summary, I propose that in Navajo the affixal features SV and [nasal] are associated to the right edge of a stem to mark the perfective. A conflict arises when there is a ban against association of SV and/or [nasal] to the anchor in question. The conflict is resolved in favor of maintaining the ban against association of SV to stops – i.e. consonants which are unmarked for the feature [cont] – and against the association of [nasal] to a segment marked for [+cons]. Segments that occur in word-final position in the perfective form thus have the following specifications for continuancy, voicing, and nasality:

(24) a. word-final stop in the perfective form:
            [+cons, –son] #
      b. word-final voiced fricative in the perfective form:
            [+cons, –son] #

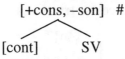

      c. word-final nasal vowel in the perfective form:
            [–cons, +son] #

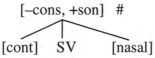

In Navajo, the presence of the features [cont] and [±cons] in underlying representations determines whether neither SV nor [nasal] are associated, or exclusively SV, or both SV and [nasal]. We find the same sensitivity of SV to these features in Southern Paiute (see section 3.1) and the same sensitivity of [nasal] to the feature [+cons] in European Portuguese (see section 2.2).

In Navajo, the feature SV may not spread to voiceless stops under voicing assimilation and neither may the feature SV associate to voiceless stops to mark the perfective. The feature SV may associate to fricatives, but the feature [nasal] may not. The ban against associating SV to obstruents not specified for [cont] is stronger than the wish to mark the perfective by the phonological feature SV. Similar relations between the level of sonority and the features SV and [nasal] exist in other languages and section 3.3 considers nasal affixation in Terena as an example. The correct generalization for Southern Paiute, Navajo, and Terena is: the higher the level of sonority, the more prone the segment is to function as an anchor for the feature SV and/or [nasal].

3.3. Nasal affixation in Terena

In the Arawakan language Terena (spoken in Brazil, see Bendor-Samuel 1960, Piggott 1996, Tourville 1991 and references therein), the first person marker is manifested as nasalization. Nasalization targets the initial segments of words and nasality in vowels and glides must spread rightward. Terena thus exhibits nasal affixation as well as nasal harmony.

Terena consonantal phonemes consist of voiceless oral stops, voiceless fricatives, nasal stops, liquids, and glides:

(25) Terena consonant inventory (Tourville 1991)

	labial	coronal	velar	laryngeal
voiceless stops	p	t	k	ʔ
voiceless fricatives		s š	hy	h
nasals	m	n		
liquids		l r		
glides		y	w	

Voiceless stops appear in onset positions in non-nasalizing environments. Under nasal affixation (to mark the first person singular), they are realized as voiced prenasal stops:

(26) a.   piho   'went' (3rd person)
      b. ^{m}biho   'went' (1st person)
      c.   tuti   'head'
      d. ^{n}duti   'my head'

Fricatives may also appear in the onsets of oral syllables and under nasal affixation they appear as voiced prenasal fricatives:

(27) a.   simoa   'came' (3rd person)
      b. ^{n}zimoa   'came' (1st person)
      c.   šeʔeša   'son'
      d. ^{n}žeʔeša   'my son'

When nasalized, voiceless fricatives are realized as voiced fricatives in Navajo (see 22b, c above). In Terena, voiceless stops and fricatives are realized as voiced prenasal stops and fricatives under nasal affixation. SV associated to [–son] is interpreted as obstruent voicing in Navajo and it is interpreted as prenasalization – with inherent voicing – in Terena:[9]

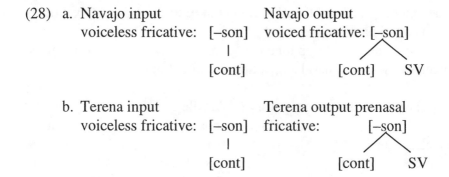

(28) a. Navajo input   Navajo output
         voiceless fricative: [–son]   voiced fricative: [–son]
                              | /\
                           [cont]   [cont]   SV

      b. Terena input   Terena output prenasal
         voiceless fricative: [–son]   fricative: [–son]
                              | /\
                           [cont]   [cont]   SV

Keren Rice (p.c.) suggests to me that voicing may be achieved in obstruents by vocal cord vibration or by extending the resonating cavity, i.e. SV in obstruents may represent voicing or nasal escape of air. In Navajo, SV associated to [–son] is interpreted as vocal cord vibration and in Terena it is interpreted as voicing with nasal escape of air which is perceived as prenasalization. These represent different phonetic choices rather than phonologically distinct entities.

Now consider that glides in Terena appear as onsets (see /y/ in 29a). Under nasal affixation, initial vowels and onset glides can be nasalized (see 29d, b) and they do not block spreading of nasality to following vowels (/o/ in 29b), glides (/y/ in 29d), and nasal stops (/n/ in 29b):

(29) a.   yono   'walked' (3rd person)
        b.   ỹõñõ   'walked' (1st person)
        c.   ayo   'brother'
        d.   ãỹõ   'my brother'

Piggott (1996) assumes that the nasalizing prefix in Terena is a nasal consonant which is unspecified for place of articulation. To prevent a form in which a prefixed /n/ appears – as in *nayo* (for 'my brother') – instead of a nasalized vowel, Piggott (1996) assumes a so-called "ALIGN-IN-ROOT" constraint which says that the morpheme in question should be realized in the root, rather than to the left of the first segment of the root. Contrary to Piggott (1996), I do not assume that the first person marker in Terena is an underspecified segment. Instead, I advocate the position that this morpheme is expressed by the sonority increasing features SV and [nasal] which must ideally both be realized. In this respect, the first person marker in Terena resembles the perfective marker in Navajo. Similar to Navajo, the nasalization process in Terena involves the affixal features SV and [nasal].

The distribution of the feature [nasal] is restricted to the most sonorant segments in Terena, i.e. vowels, glides, the liquid /r/ (but not /l/), and nasal stops. This implies that the wish to realize the feature [nasal] is less strong than the prohibition against association of [nasal] to oral stops and fricatives – i.e. to segments specified as [–son]. Examples (26b, d) and (27b, d) above illustrate that nasal affixation affects the left-most segments of a stem. I suggest that this is due to the fact that in Terena, the affixal feature SV is a prefix which associates to the left edge of stems. We furthermore find that if the feature [nasal] is used as a prefix in Terena, it must spread rightward (see 29b, d). The general claim inherent in my proposal about nasality is that a characteristic property of the feature [nasal] is harmony. At one end of the scale, we encounter languages which allow full nasal fricatives and nasal sonorants and if nasality is realized on one segment, it automatically spreads to adjacent segments which are also compatible with the feature [nasal]. This state of affairs is found in Applecross Gaelic (see Ternes 1973, van der Hulst & Smith 1982, and Piggott 1996, among others). Other languages allow the feature [nasal] to associate to sonorants only and nasality must spread through vowels, approximants, and nasal stops within a given domain (e.g. the word, see the Acehnese examples in 9c,d). Still other languages merely allow nasal vowels and glides. In these languages, the feature nasal always targets every vowel and glide in a particular domain and in section 2.2, we saw that in European Portuguese, the feature [nasal] targets all vowels and glides within a rhyme. Some languages only allow nasal vowels and in section 4, I argue that at the final end of the scale, we find languages which do not allow the feature [nasal] at all.

To illustrate how the proposal mentioned above accounts for the observed data in Terena, consider first the initial syllable of *piho* 'went' in (30a). The initial segment is specified as an obstruent by means of the features [–son, +cons]. In (30b), the affixal feature SV is associated to the left-most segment, which is consequently realized as a prenasal consonant in Terena. There is a ban on the association of the feature [nasal] to obstruents in Terena and for this reason, the affixal feature [nasal] is not realized. If we were to realize the affixal feature [nasal] on the second segment, as in (30c), it would no longer be a prefix, but rather an infix.

(30) a. stem   p   i   + prefix SV_{Af}, $[nasal]_{Af}$
                    | |
            [–son, +cons] [+son, –cons]
                                  |
                               [cont]

b.

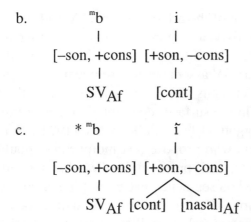

c.

The fact that (30c) is not the actual surface form suggests that if the feature [nasal] cannot associate to the left-most segment, it is better not to realize the affixal feature [nasal] at all.

Now consider that in *ã𝑦̃ɔ̃* 'my brother' (29d), the feature [nasal] spreads rightward. This supports the thesis postulated above that if the feature [nasal] is introduced into a domain, it automatically spreads to adjacent segments that are sonorous enough to bear this feature:

(31)

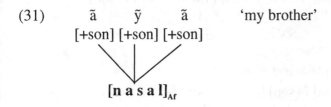

In the examples immediately below, the third person is unmarked. To mark the first person, the left-most vowel is nasalized and the stop or fricative which follows the nasalized vowel is prenasalized:

(32) a. o.to.pi.ko   'chopped' (3rd person)
     b. õ.^{n}do.pi.ko   'chopped' (1st person)
     c. a.hya.ʔa.šo   'desire'
     d. ã.^{n}ža.ʔa.šo   'my desire'

I propose that the occurrence of the affixal features SV and [nasal] in a word is restricted to satisfy a requirement that says that under morphological conditions, SV must be identifiable as an affixal feature. If the affixal feature SV associates to a segment that is under-lyingly specified for SV, its status as a morpheme to express the first person is not identifiable in the surface representation that results. In this respect, I follow Piggott (1996), Pulleyblank (1994), Samek-Lodovici (1993) and others who propose that morphemes should be overtly realized. In Terena, this proposal implies that the affixal feature SV must be realized on segments that are not specified for SV in underlying representations. Hence, the affix SV will associate to the left-most voiceless segment (which will be realized as a prenasal segment as a result). In forms that have an initial segment which is specified for SV in the input representation, SV_{Af} appears on a segment further to the right. For this reason, we find the affixal feature SV associated to the second segment rather than the first in (32b) and (32d). The nasalized form of *otopiko* 'he chopped' (33a) is thus as in (33b):[10]

(33) a.
```
       o       t       o       p       i       k       o
    [+son]  [−son]  [+son]  [−son]  [+son]  [−son]  [+son]
       |               |               |               |
       SV              SV              SV              SV
```

b.
```
       õ      ⁿd      o       p       i       k       o
    [+son]  [−son]  [+son]  [−son]  [+son]  [−son]  [+son]
       \      |       |               |               |
       SV\    SV_Af  SV               SV              SV
          \
          [nasal]_Af
```

Nasal stops do not trigger nasal harmony in Terena. For instance, we do not find that the vowels after the nasal /m/ in *simoa* 'he came' become nasalized. The lack of nasal spread induced by nasal stops indicates that the nasal stop in Terena resembles the light nasal stop in Acehnese and the nasal stops in European Portuguese, i.e. in underlying representations, the nasal stop in Terena is represented without the feature [nasal]. A voiceless oral stop, a prenasal stop and a full nasal stop can thus be represented as follows in Terena:

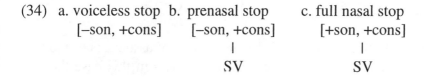

(34) a. voiceless stop b. prenasal stop   c. full nasal stop
       [–son, +cons]   [–son, +cons]   [+son, +cons]
                         | |
                         SV   SV

Since vowels and nasal stops are voiced and involve the feature SV, there is no possibility to show whether the affixal feature SV is realized in the first person in examples such as *áỹõ* 'my brother' and *õmõ* 'I carried'. The affixal feature [nasal] can be overtly realized because there are [+son] segments available as hosts. In *õmõ* 'I carried' the feature [nasal] is not only associated to the left-most vowel, but also to positions to the right.

(35)   õ   m̃   õ   'I carried'

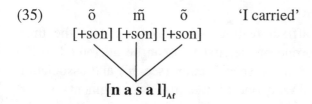

The examples *omo* 'he carries' without nasal harmony and *õmõ* 'I carry' with harmony illustrate that the nasal feature does not originate in nasal stops. When it is introduced into a domain by a morphological process (here to mark the first person), it must spread through vowels, glides, and nasal stops. This implies that even though nasal stops lack a nasal feature in underlying representations (see 34c), they may acquire this feature under nasal harmony (see 35).

    For completeness, we must also consider the effect of nasal affixation in a Terena form with a nasal stop followed by an oral stop somewhere else in the word. An example is *nokone* 'his need':

(36)   n   o   k   o   n   e   'his need'
         [+son] [+son] [–son] [+son] [+son] [+son]
           | | | | |
          SV   SV   SV   SV   SV

To mark the first person, the affixal feature SV associates to the left-most segment which is not specified for SV – in this case the oral stop /k/ – and the affixal feature [nasal] associates to the preceding sonorant segments:

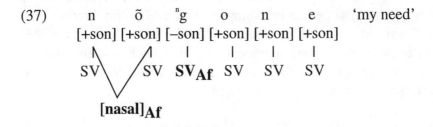

(37)   n   õ   ⁿg   o   n   e   'my need'
         [+son] [+son] [–son] [+son] [+son] [+son]

The reason why the affixal feature SV is associated to the third segment rather than to one of the first two can be attributed to the fact that the latter have an SV specification (see 36) and association of the affixal feature SV to one of the first two segments would prevent the overt realization of this affixal feature. The reason why the feature [nasal] is not associated further to the right than to the third segment, I attribute to (i) a condition that disallows association of [nasal] to a [–son] root node and (ii) a condition against discontinuous association (commonly referred to as "NO GAP", see Archangeli & Pulleyblank 1994).

This section argued that the nasalizing elements in Terena are the sonority increasing features SV and [nasal]. In this respect, Terena resembles Navajo (see section 3.2). The occurrence of the features SV and [nasal] is conditioned by sonority requirements. The affixal feature SV may associate to any segment in Terena, but [nasal] can only be linked to a sonorant segment. In both Navajo and Terena, the feature [nasal] is a morphological marker and its distribution is restricted in that it may never associate to segments specified as [–son]. In this respect, these languages resemble Brazilian Portuguese (see section 2.2). In other languages, the feature [nasal] never associates to any segment. This is the case in languages which do not have nasal harmony, nor nasal affixation. We will see next that in such languages, nasal stops can be epenthetic consonants.

4. Nasal epenthesis

The proposal not to use the feature [nasal] for nasal stops which do not trigger harmony has an interesting pay-off in that it helps to explain nasal epenthesis. Ortmann (1998) proposes that epenthetic segments are "simple" within the phonological system of the language in question in that they require the least amount of featural specification. In some languages, /n/ functions as the epenthetic consonant (henceforth EP). For instance, in High Alemannic – spoken in Switzerland, south west Germany and western parts of Austria – /n/ is inserted between vowels in specific morpho-syntactic contexts (for a complete account the reader is referred to Ortmann 1998). Some examples are:

(38) a. wo   -*n*-   er ko   isch 'when he arrived'
          when EP   he arrived is

     b. grösser wie -*n*- i   'taller than I'
          taller   than EP I

     c. gang zu -*n*- ere   'go to her'
          go   to EP her

     d. säll ha -*n*- i scho   'I have this already'
          this have EP I already

Nasal epenthesis in Dutch is the result of the insertion of a nasal segment in a particular morphological domain in casual speech (Booij 1996). Example (39a) illustrates that the past tense form of a verb ends in Schwa. In fast or informal speech, the consonant /n/ may be inserted between suffixal Schwa and a vowel-initial clitic (see 39b):

(39) a. Ik wilde   dat zeggen   'I wanted to say that'
          [ɪk ʋɪldə dɑt zɛxə]

      b. dat wilde   ik zeggen   'it is that, that I wanted to say'
          [dɑt ʋɪldə ɪk zɛxə]   (careful speech)
          [dɑt ʋɪldə nɪk zɛxə]   (casual speech)

      c. hij wilde   het   'he wanted it'
          [hɛɪ ʋɪldə hət]   (careful speech)
          [hɛɪ ʋɪldənət]   (casual speech)

If the assumption that epenthetic consonants are minimally specified is correct, the fact that /n/ is an epenthetic consonant in High Alemannic and Dutch implies that it is not specified for [nasal]. The interesting prediction that follows from this proposal is that in languages where /n/ is an epenthetic consonant, this consonant will never trigger nasal spread. Moreover, in languages in which every underlying nasal stop triggers nasal harmony, the consonant /n/ is not a possible candidate for epenthesis, because this segment is specified for [nasal] and would therefore not be the minimally specified consonant.

Languages like High Alemannic and Dutch do not have nasal vowels, nasal approximants, or nasal fricatives. Neither does the feature [nasal] seem to have a function in phonological or morphological processes. On the basis of these facts, I conclude that the feature [nasal] never surfaces in their phonology, just like the feature [high tone] does not surface in languages where that feature does not play a phonological role (e.g. English). Nasal stops must somehow be distinguished from oral stops in these languages and since nasal stops are more sonorous than voiced obstruents, the difference may be expressed in phonological representations by the feature [+son]. Thus, in these languages, nasal stops are best represented as the so-called "light" nasal stops in Acehnese (see 12b).

In languages with epenthetic nasals, these particular stops lack the feature [nasal] and, hence, they never trigger nasal spreading. If a nonepenthetic nasal stop does not bear the feature [nasal] either, no nasal stop triggers harmony in such a language.[11] [12]

5. Conclusion

In the literature, it has been proposed that nasal stops can be under-specified for [nasal] in underlying representations (e.g. Rice & Avery 1991, Rice 1993) and that the feature [nasal] is added to the representation by a default rule in phonetic implementation. In this paper, it is argued that the nasal stop may be permanently unspecified for the feature [nasal]. The two possible ways to represent full nasal stops – viz. with or without the nasal feature (cf. 1a versus 1b) – corresponds to different phonological behavior. When nasal stops are specified for the feature [nasal], nasalization is phonologically active in the sense that it triggers nasal harmony. This is the case in, for instance, Brazilian Portuguese. In Terena, full nasal stops do not trigger nasal harmony and they neither block nasal spread when a nasal vowel or a morphological process triggers nasal harmony. This suggests to me that in Terena, nasal stops lack the feature [nasal] in their underlying representations, but they may acquire it in surface representations.

In European Portuguese, nasal stops do not trigger nasal harmony and they block spreading of the nasal feature. In this language, nasal stops are specified as a sonorant stop and the minimal requirement for association of the feature [nasal] in this language is that the anchor be a sonorant continuant. Hence, nasal stops are permanently underspecified for the feature [nasal] and nasalization appears as a phonetic consequence of their specification as sonorant stops, i.e. nasal airflow occurs because [+son] requires airflow across the glottis and noncontinuancy (represented by the lack of the feature [cont]) prevents airflow through the oral cavity.

Walker (1994) already suggested that segments must have some minimum sonority to bear the feature [nasal]. In Acehnese, Brazilian Portuguese, and European Portuguese, nasal harmony is sensitive to the degree of sonority of potential targets and the feature [nasal] spreads from one segment to another until it encounters a node which lacks the degree of sonority demanded in that particular language. Obstruent stops are universally banned from bearing the feature [nasal] because a [–son] node without a feature for oral release, i.e. [cont], has zero sonority.

With respect to nasal affixation, I have argued that the more sonorant a sound is, the better anchor it may be for the features SV and [nasal]. It is more natural for a language to allow the feature [nasal] to associate to roots specified as [–cons] than to roots specified as [+cons]. Also, it is more natural for a language to allow the feature [nasal] to associate to segments specified as [+son] than to [–son, cont] segments. For this reason, we find more languages that have nasal approximants than nasal fricatives. It is against the nature of human languages to allow association of the nasal feature to a [–son] root which does not dominate the feature [cont].

In High Alemannic and Dutch, no segment is compatible with the nasal feature and the feature [nasal] does not play a role in the phonology of these languages. With respect to nasal epenthesis, the assumption is that the epenthetic nasal stop lacks the nasal feature and the interesting prediction that follows from this assumption is that the epenthetic segment cannot induce nasal harmony.

Notes

* First and foremost, I would like to thank Glyne Piggott and Keren Rice with whom I had many interesting and stimulating discussions about the topic of nasality. This paper was presented at the Conference on Distinctive Feature Theory at ZAS in Berlin on 8 October 1999. Special thanks to Peter Avery, Mirco Ghini (✝), Heather Goad, T. A. Hall, Takako Kawasaki, Ursula Kleinhenz, Martin Krämer, Aditi Lahiri, Albert Ortmann, Barbara Stiebels and two anonymous reviewers for critical comments and kind encouragement.
1 Features for place of articulation as well as laryngeal features are ignored here. The representation in (1b) could also be used for laterals, because - according to many approaches to feature theory – laterals are non-continuants. In languages where (1b) represents nasals, the representation for laterals involves an additional feature (presumably [+lateral]).
2 Here and in subsequent examples, syllable boundaries are indicated by a dot.
3 Unfortunately, Durie (1985) does not present examples of final stressed syllables with a nasal vowel and the segment /r/. In the absence of evidence to the contrary, I assume that /r/ is not excluded before nasal vowels. The segments /h r j w/ can be distinguished by their specification for place of articulation, e.g. /h/ lacks a place of articulation, /r/ may be specified as Coronal, /j/ as Dorsal and/or [+front] and /w/ as Labial.

4   Liquids also have the feature [+son], but the feature [nasal] does not associate to this class of segments, presumably due to a co-occurrence condition on features that specify liquids (e.g. [lateral] and/or [rhotic]) and the feature [nasal].

5   Cohn (1993) and Walker (1998) point out that relative sonority may be the only factor that plays a role in determining the compatibility of [nasal] with certain segments in some languages, but in many languages, other factors must also be taken into consideration. For instance, most languages that allow nasal vowels and nasal consonants prohibit nasalized continuants (i.e. approximants and fricatives).

6   In examples (20a-d) from Southern Paiute, stress is assigned to the prefinal syllable. Voiceless vowels are represented by capitals.

7   For another proposal that phonological features act as morphological markers, I refer the reader to Lieber (1987).

8   Rice (1993) proposes that the perfective suffix is a consonant with the feature SV. She argues that since word-final consonant clusters are not allowed in Navajo, this suffixal consonant cannot be syllabified following a fricative and that its root node is therefore deleted, while the feature SV is absorbed by the fricative. Following a vowel, the suffixal consonant receives the feature [nasal] by default. When the suffixal consonant is syllable-final, Rice (1993) assume that the feature [nasal] is absorbed into the vowel by a late rule of nasalization – thus creating a nasalized vowel – and the suffixal consonant is not realized. Rice (1993) has to assume default nasalization to account for the data in (22a), but not for (22b-c) which is *ad hoc*.

9   According to Ladefoged & Maddieson (1996: 119-128), languages that distinguish between voiceless and voiced prenasal consonants are rare. Depending on the language, the representation of a [−son] segment specified for SV may be interpreted as a voiced obstruent (as in Navajo), as a prenasal with voiceless oral release, or as a voiced prenasal (as in Terena). I assume that the feature [spread glottis] distinguishes aspirated and unaspirated prenasal stops in languages which have this contrast.

10 To distinguish the features SV and [nasal] that are present in the stem from the suffixal features **SV** and **[nasal]**, the latter are printed in bold type. In the representations in (33a, b), (35) and (37), I abstract away from the feature [cons].

11 To distinguish nasals from laterals in such languages, the laterals must be specified by an additional feature. The prediction is that in these languages, assimilation from /n/ to /l/ may take place (/n/ + /l/ →[ll]). Conversely, in languages where nasal stops are specified as [nasal] to distinguish them from laterals, we may find that /l/ assimilates to /n/ (/n/ + /l/ → [nn]).

12 One of the reviewers pointed out to me that it is concievable that there is a language with epenthetic nasal stops as well as underlying, i.e. non-epenthetic

nasal stops in which the latter are specified for the feature [nasal]. In such a language, non-epenthetic stops should trigger nasal spreading and the epenthetic nasal stops should not.

References

Archangeli, Diana and Douglas Pulleyblank
    1994   *Grounded Phonology*. Cambridge, Massachusetts: The MIT Press.
Bendor-Samuel, John T.
    1960   Some problems of segmentation in the phonological analysis of Tereno. *Word* 16: 348-355.
Booij, Geert
    1996   Cliticisation as prosodic integration: the case of Dutch. *The Linguistic Review* 13: 219-242.
Chomsky, Noam and Morris Halle
    1968   *The Sound Pattern of English*. New York, Evanston, and London: Harper & Row.
Clements, G. N.
    1990   The role of the sonority cycle in core syllabification. In: J. Kingston and M. Beckman (eds.), *Papers in Laboratory Phonology I: Between the Grammar and Physics of Speech*, 283-333. Cambridge: Cambridge University Press.
Clements, G.N. and Elizabeth Hume
    1995   The internal organization of speech sounds. In: John A. Goldsmith (ed.), *The Handbook of Phonological Theory*, 245-306. Oxford: Basil Blackwell.
Cohn, Abigail
    1993   The status of nasalized continuants. In: Marie K. Huffman and Rena A. Krakow (eds.), *Phonetics and Phonology 5: Nasals, Nasalization and the Velum*, 329-367. San Diego: Academic Press.
Costa, João and M. João Freitas
    1999   On the representation of nasal vowels: evidence from Portuguese children's data. Paper presented at GALA'99, Potsdam.
Durie, Mark
    1985   *A Grammar of Acehnese*. Verhandelingen van het Koninklijk Instituut voor Taal-, Land- en Volkenkunde 112. Dordrecht: Foris.
Hulst, H.G. van der and Piggott, G.L.
    1995   Locality and the nature of nasal harmony, ms., Leiden University & HIL and McGill University.

Hulst, Harry van der and Norval Smith
  1982   Prosodic domains and opaque segments in autosegmental theory. In:
            Harry van der Hulst and Norval Smith (eds.), *The Structure of
            Phonological Representations* (Part II), 311-336. Dordrecht: Foris.
Kari, James, M.
  1976   *Navajo Verb Prefix Phonology*, New York: Garland.
Kiparsky, Paul
  1985   Some consequences of Lexical Phonology. *Phonology Yearbook* 2:
            83-136.
Ladefoged, Peter and Ian Maddieson
  1996   *The Sounds of the World's Languages.* Oxford: Blackwell.
Lieber, Rochelle
  1987   *An Integrated Theory of Autosegmental Processes.* Albany: Sate
            University of New York Press.
McCarthy, John J.
  1988   Feature geometry and dependency: a review. *Phonetica* 43: 84-108.
Ortmann, Albert
  1998   Consonant epenthesis: its distribution and phonological specifi-
            cation. In: Wolfgang Kehrein, and Richard Wiese (eds.), *Phonology
            and Morphology of the Germanic Languages*, 51-76. Tübingen:
            Niemeyer.
Piggott, G.L.
  1992   Variability in feature dependency: the case of nasality. *Natural
            Language and Linguistic Theory* 10: 33-77.
  1996   Licensing and alignment: a conspiracy in harmony, ms., McGill
            University, Montreal.
Poser, William J.
  1982   Phonological representations and action-at-a-distance. In: Harry van
            der Hulst and Norval Smith (eds.), *The Structure of Phonological
            Representations* (Part II), 121-158. Dordrecht: Foris.
Pulleyblank, Douglas
  1994   Neutral vowels in Optimality Theory: a comparison of Yoruba and
            Wolof, ms., University of British Columbia.
Rice, Keren D.
  1993   A reexamination of the feature [sonorant]: the status of 'sonorant
            obstruents'. *Language* 69: 308-344.
Rice, Keren and Peter Avery
  1989   On the interaction between sonorancy and voicing. *Toronto Working
            Papers in Linguistics* 10: 65-82.
  1991   Laterality and coronality. In: C. Paradis and J. F. Prunet (eds.),
            Phonetics and Phonology 2: The Special Status of Coronals, 101-
            124. San Diego: Academic Press.

Samek-Lodovici, Vieri
    1993   Morphological gemination crosslinguistically, ms. Rutgers Univer-
            sity.
Sapir, Edward
    1930   The Southern Paiute language (Part I): Southern Paiute, a
            Shoshonean Language. *Proceedings of the American Academy of
            Arts and Sciences* 65: 1-296.
Sapir, Edward and Harry Hoijer
    1967   *The Phonology and Morphology of the Navaho Language*,
            University of California Publications Linguistics 50, Berkeley and
            Los Angeles: University of California Press.
Steriade, Donca
    1993   Closure, release, and nasal contours. In: Marie K. Huffman and Rena
            A. Krakow (eds), *Phonetics and Phonology 5: Nasals, Nasalization
            and the Velum*, 401-470. San Diego: Academic Press.
Ternes, Elmar
    1973   *Phonemic Analysis of Scottish Gaelic. Forum Pheniticum* I,
            Hamburg: Helmut Buske Verlag.
Tourville, José
    1991   Licensing and the representation of floating nasals. Ph.D. disser-
            tation, McGill University, Montreal.
Walker, Rachel
    1994   Hierarchical opacity effects in nasal harmony: an optimality-
            theoretic account. *Proceedings of ESCOL 94.*
    1998   Nasalization, neutral segments, and opacity effects. Ph.D. disser-
            tation, University of California, Santa Cruz.
Wetzels, Leo W.
    1997   The lexical representation of nasality in Brazilian Portuguese.
            Probus 9.
Young, Robert W. and William Morgan Sr.
    1987   *The Navajo Language; A Grammar and Colloquial Dictionary*,
            revised edition, Albuquerque: University of New Mexico Press.

Patterns, pervasive patterns and feature specification*

K. David Harrison and Abigail Kaun

1. Introduction

In this paper, we explore how surface apparent patterns can lead speakers to posit underspecification in lexical entries. Further, we show that current interpretations of Lexicon Optimization (Prince and Smolensky 1993), in particular that of Archiphonemic Underspecification (Inkelas 1995), incorrectly predict the distribution of underspecification in lexical entries. We present new data and advance two theoretical claims bearing on the above issues. First, we claim that predictably alternating feature values are not necessarily underspecified. In support of this claim we introduce patterns of reduplication in Hungarian word games. Second, we claim that segments that never alternate may still be underspecified. In support of this claim we introduce vowel harmony patterns from Tuvan (or Tyvan), a Turkic language of Siberia. Both claims demonstrate that the incidence of underspecification is neither that which is predicted by Archiphonemic Underspecification, nor that predicted by earlier Autosegmental models. We point the way toward a revised model that would diagnose environments in which underspecification occurs. The model is designed to allow for a principled distinction between pervasive patterns that give rise to underspecification, and other patterns that do not.

Transparency to spreading (or assimilation), susceptibility to spreading, failure to initiate spreading and various other types of behavior prompted analysts working within a derivational model of phonology to hypothesize that certain featural specifications are absent for the relevant segments throughout at least a portion of the phonological derivation. Contrastive Underspecification (Steriade 1987) and Radical Underspecification (Archangeli 1984) were the dominant formal models designed to predict in a principled manner the incidence of underspecification. Contrastive Underspecification theory posited non-contrastiveness as the criterion for potential underspecification. A feature value might be missing from underlying representations if it failed to serve a contrastive function for the segment class in question. Under Radical Underspecification, the commitment to a redundancy-free lexicon had the consequence of eliminating all predictable feature values from underlying representations.

Within Optimality Theory (OT), Richness of the Base specifically rules out the systematic exclusion of featural specifications from input representations (Prince and Smolensky 1993, Smolensky 1995). The input space is assumed to be infinite, thus unrestricted. The lexicon, by contrast, is assumed to be finite. A learner's construction of lexical representations is guided by Lexicon Optimization (Prince and Smolensky 1993), which heavily favors fully specified inputs. It is assumed that a speaker will choose the most harmonic (i.e. the fullest) input-to-output mapping. Outputs can be mapped to fully specified inputs without the accrual of gratuitous faithfulness violations. Given two competing input forms, one fully specified and one partially specified, the fully specified alternative will be preferred, all else being equal. The OT model nevertheless leaves room for the possibility that partially underspecified lexical entries will on occasion be posited.

Archiphonemic Underspecification (Inkelas 1995) seeks to predict when underspecified inputs will in fact be deployed. It demonstrates that the principles of Lexicon Optimization dictate that predictable feature values will be underspecified only when they enter into surface alternations. Underspecification will arise only in instances where there are fully regular and predictable alternations, as the following schematic shows:

(1)	Alternating	Non-alternating
Predictable	underspecified	specified
Unpredictable	specified	specified

In a backness harmony language like Turkish, for instance, only those vowels that are involved in allophonic alternations will be underspecified for backness in lexical entries. In the words given in (2), all post-initial vowels agree in backness with the initial vowel.

(2)   Two words of Turkish
    a. kilim-im   b. kɨlɨc-ɨm
        'rug-1'   'sword-1'[1]

However, it is only the suffix vowels that both alternate and have a predictable value for backness. Archiphonemic Underspecification predicts that only they will be underspecified for backness, as indicated in (3):

(3)   Assumed Lexical Representations

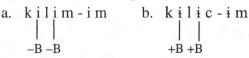

a. k i l i m - i m   b. k ɨ l ɨ c - ɨ m
      | | | |
    −B −B   +B +B

This model essentially claims that harmony targets only suffix vowels in Turkish, because it is only for suffix vowels that a backness value lacking in the input representation is introduced in the corresponding output. Root vowels, whether harmonic or not, will be fully specified (and presumably identical) in input and output representations. Root vowels, on this view, even though they may appear trivially to obey harmony, cannot be thought of as undergoing harmony. Clements and Sezer (1982: 226), motivated by entirely different theoretical considerations, take a more flexible position, stating simply that "...the burden of proof is on the linguist who wishes to demonstrate that roots [in Turkish] are governed by vowel harmony at all."

In section 3.1 we introduce vowel harmony patterns from Tuvan. These demonstrate that speakers can underspecify not only alternating vowels in affixes but also non-alternating vowels within roots. The Tuvan data are corroborated by speakers' distinct treatment of harmonic and disharmonic roots in two other vowel harmony languages: Finnish and Turkish. The patterns that we discuss for all three languages indicate that harmony is indeed active within roots. We offer evidence of the type called for by Clements and Sezer

(1982) to challenge the predictions of Archiphonemic Underspecification.

Before turning to the harmony data, we first discuss Hungarian word game data in which full specification allows for the only satisfactory account of the observed patterns. The Hungarian data are problematic for Archiphonemic Underspecification because while the game forms require across-the-board full specification, only a subset of the relevant segments are predicted by the model to be fully specified.

2. Predictable and alternating segments are not necessarily underspecified

2.1. Hungarian word games

Hungarian is relevant to the present discussion because Hungarian vowels exhibit a number of predictable feature values, some of which participate in alternations and others which do not. Those that enter into surface alternations are predicted by Archiphonemic Underspecification to be underspecified in lexical entries, while those that maintain a fixed, non-alternating value are predicted to be fully specified.

The vowel inventory of Hungarian is given in (4). Vowel length is contrastive, as shown. Crucial to the argument developed below is the fact that the long and short variants of the vowels represented by orthographic <e> and <a> are qualitatively quite distinct. Long mid [eː] alternates with short low vowel [æ], and long unrounded [ɑː] alternates with the short rounded vowel [ɔ]. The predictably alternating pairs are enclosed in boxes below.

(4)   Hungarian Vowel Inventory

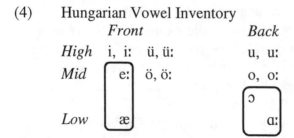

Within the frameworks of both Contrastive Underspecification and Radical Underspecification, these quality differences would be probable candidates for underspecification due to their predictability from length. Quantity is demonstrably contrastive for the vowel system of Hungarian as a whole. In Optimality Theory, however, the principles of Lexicon Optimization lead us to expect the accompanying quality differences to be explicitly recorded in lexical entries when they do not enter into surface alternations. Only in cases where surface alternations do occur does the model predict underspecification.

In certain nouns, the vowel of the final syllable is at times short, and at other times long, as we shall show. For the majority of vowels, this length difference does not substantively affect vowel quality, however for the vowels indicated in boxes in the chart in (4) above, the length difference is accompanied by the expected quality differences. Thus, vowels in the first syllable of so-called 'shortening bases' (Whitney 1949) are long when the noun is unaffixed, but short when certain affixes are added, e.g. *uːr* 'master,' and *urɔk* 'master-PL,' *urɔ* 'master-3,' and *eːr* 'vein,' but *æræk* 'vein-PL' and *æræi* 'vein-3.' In another class of nouns, the vowel of the final syllable is short when unaffixed, but long when certain affixes are added, e.g. *kæfæ* 'brush,' but *kæfeːk* 'brush-PL' and *fɔ* 'tree,' but *faːk* 'tree-PL.' Note, however, that it is not the case that all affixes trigger length alternations of these types of stems. It is instead particular morphemes that have this property.

There are also stem vowels that resist length alternations entirely. These can be either consistently long or consistently short. For example we finds roots such as *keːp* 'picture' and *haːz* 'house,' which retain their long vowel under plural affixation, yielding *keːpæk* 'picture-PL' and *haːzɔk* 'house-PL' (not *kæpæk* or *hɔzɔk). Similarly, we find roots like *kært* 'garden,' which retain the short vowel under suffixation, yielding *kærtæk* 'garden-PL' (not *keːrtæk*, for example).

For the two alternating noun-classes, Archiphonemic Underspecification predicts underspecification of the predictable vocalic features. The model predicts full specification for the non-alternating classes and for all vowels occurring in pre-final syllables.

Evidence bearing on this prediction comes from a Hungarian reduplicative word game similar to the English 'Ubbi Dubbi' game.[2]
The Hungarian game, known as *Veve*, works as follows.[3] For a given
word, a sequence /-Vv-/ is inserted before the rhyme of each syllable.
The overall quality (feature values for height, backness and rounding)
of the reduplicant V is identical to that of the following vowel. We
report here on two versions of the game (Veve I and Veve II). In both
versions, the reduplicated vowel is always short: this is a 'rule' of the
game. In Veve I, the length (quantity) of base vowels is retained, as
shown in (5).

(5)   Veve I examples

base	*base+reduplicant*	
a. itt	i̲v̲-itt	'here'
b. tiːz	t-i̲v̲-iːz	'ten'
c. sæm	s-æ̲v̲-æm	'eye'
d. eːr	e̲v̲-eːr, *æ̲v̲-eːr	'vein'
e. bɔb	b-ɔ̲v̲-ɔb	'bean'
f. ɑːr	ɑ̲v̲-ɑːr, *ɔ̲v̲-ɑːr	'price'
g. neːvmɑːʃ	n-e̲v̲-eːvm-ɑ̲v̲-ɑːʃ, *n-æ̲v̲-eːvm-ɔ̲v̲-ɑːʃ	'pronoun'

In Veve II, however, all vowels, both reduplicant and base, surface as
short. Some examples of this are shown in (6).

(6)   Veve II examples

base	*base+reduplicant*	
a. itt	i̲v̲-itt	'here'
b. tiːz	t-i̲v̲-iz	'ten'
c. sæm	s-æ̲v̲-æm	'eye'
d. eːr	e̲v̲-er, *æ̲v̲-ær	'vein'
e. bɔb	b-ɔ̲v̲-ɔb	'bean'
f. ɑːr	ɑ̲v̲-ɑr, *ɔ̲v̲-ɔr	'price'
g. neːvmɑːʃ	n-e̲v̲-evm-ɑ̲v̲-ɑʃ, *n-æ̲v̲-æv m-ɔ̲v̲-ɔʃ	'pronoun'

Note that by doing away with all length distinctions, as is done in Veve II, it becomes unclear which portion of the string constitutes the reduplicant, and which constitutes the base. Thus, the reduplicant could be construed as either -Vv- or as -vV-. For concreteness, we will assume that, as in Veve I, speakers of Veve II insert the sequence -Vv-.

Of particular importance arc examples d, f, and g, shown in (5) and (6). In each of these forms the reduplicants contain vowels that never surface outside the context of Veve. The examples in (5d) and (6d) contain short [e] while those in (5f) and (6f) contain short [a]. The examples in (5g) and (6g) contain instances of both of these otherwise non-surfacing vowels.

2.2. A formal account of Hungarian

A Correspondence-based analysis of the pattern (McCarthy and Prince 1995), which we shall adopt herein, might run as follows. First, we represent the absence of [æː], [e], [ɔː], [ɑ] in the general inventory of Hungarian as a constraint on inventory structure, given in (7).[4] (cf. Tableau A, third column)

(7)   INVENTORY STRUCTURE (IS): *æː,*e,*ɔː,*ɑ

Following the analysis of correspondence developed in McCarthy and Prince (1995), we invoke two general faithfulness constraints. The first requires identity between input and output forms with regard to quantity (length).

(8)   IDENT-I/O[LG]: Input-Output Identity for length

Any output vowels that do not match their corresponding input vowel in length will run afoul of this constraint (Tableau A, second column). A second constraint requires identity between input and output forms with regard to quality (i.e. all vowel features other than length).

(9)   IDENT-I/O[QUAL]: Input-Output Identity for quality

Any vowel in either base or reduplicant that does not match the input vowel in all features will violate this (Tableau A, fourth column).

We begin with an account of the basic, non-reduplicated forms. Given that Richness of the Base requires that no restrictions be imposed on input structures, it must be the case that inputs containing vowel qualities that are not part of the Hungarian vowel inventory must be mapped to outputs containing only legitimate vowels. This means that IS must outrank at least one of the two faithfulness constraints.

A general principle of optimality theory is that a given constraint hierarchy must be able to map any input onto some well-formed output. So, for example, an input such as /er/ (which is not an actual or even a possible word of Hungarian, because it contains [e]) will be mapped to the well-formed surface form [ær] if IDENT-I/O[QUAL] is low-ranked (tableau A). Note that while the output [ær] is well-formed and thus a possible word of Hungarian, it is not an actual word.

(10) Tableau A

/er/	IDENT-I/O[LG]	IS	IDENT-I/O[QUAL]
a. eːr	*!		
☞ b. ær			*
c. er		*!	
d. æːr	*!	*	

Alternatively, if IDENT-I/O[LG] is low-ranked, then the surface form [eːr] (corresponding to an actual Hungarian word meaning 'vein') will be selected.

(11) Tableau B

/er/	IDENT-I/O[QUAL]	IS	IDENT-I/O[LG]
☞ a. eːr			*
b. ær	*!		
c. er		*!	
d. æːr	*!	*	*

We have shown that there is more than one constraint ranking that will give rise to a licit vowel on the surface when the input contains a vowel that violates the inventory structure constraint. The difference between Veve I and Veve II demonstrates that at least two distinct rankings are posited by speakers of what would appear to be the same dialect of Hungarian (i.e. educated Budapest). Speakers of Veve I invoke the general constraint ranking in tableau A while speakers of Veve II invoke that in tableau B. The full rankings for Veve I and Veve II are given in tableaux C and D respectively.

Two additional correspondence-theoretic (McCarthy and Prince 1995) constraints will be posited to characterize the patterns of Veve. These require the base and the reduplicant to be identical in quantity and quality, respectively. Note that 'base' refers to the *surface* form, which the reduplicant must resemble, and not to the input (underlying) form. Identity between base and reduplicant is thus independent of the degree to which either element is faithful to the input form. In this analysis, we do not invoke a separate constraint on input-reduplicant identity.

(12)   IDENT-B/R[LG]: Base-Reduplicant Identity for length

(13)   IDENT-B/R[QUAL]: Base-Reduplicant Identity for quality

In order to ensure a quality-match between a vowel of the base and its corresponding vowel in the reduplicant, the Veve forms allow otherwise unattested vowels (specifically [e] and [ɑ]) to surface. Base-Reduplicant Identity must therefore outrank IS. For simplicity, we will only consider Veve candidates in which the reduplicant vowel is short. Both documented versions of the game require short reduplicant vowels and we assume that this restriction is undominated. Thus for input /eːr/, there is no possible Veve output [eːveːr].

The constraint rankings are as follows: for Veve I, the faithfulness constraints IDENT-B/R[QUAL] and IDENT-I/O[LG] outrank IS, as shown in tableau C for /eːr/ 'vein.' A single violation of IDENT-B/R[QUAL] is assigned for each vowel in the reduplicant (underlined) that fails to match its corresponding base vowel in one or more features. A violation of IDENT-I/O[LG] is assigned for every vowel in the base (but not in the reduplicant) that fails to match its corresponding input vowel in length. No violations are assigned for a length mismatch between input and reduplicant, as I-R identity is superfluous to the present analysis.

(14)   Tableau C: Veve I with full specification

/Vv, eːr/	IDENT-I/O [LG]	IDENT-B/R [QUAL]	IS	IDENT-I/O [QUAL]	IDENT-B/R [LG]
☞ a. eveːr			*		*
b. æveːr		*!			*
c. ever	*!		**		
d. æver	*!	*	*		
e. evæːr		*!	**	*	*
f. ævæːr			*	*!	*
g. evær	*!	*	*	*	
h. ævær	*!			*	

For Veve II, both base-reduplicant faithfulness constraints outrank IS, as shown. Note that the Input-Output constraint IDENT-I/O[QUAL] dominates IS, giving rise in the optimal candidate (c) to the usually ill-formed surface quality [e].

(15) Tableau D: Veve II with full specification

/Vv, eːr/	IDENT-B/R [LG]	IDENT-B/R [QUAL]	IDENT-I/O [QUAL]	IS	IDENT-I/O [LG]
a. eveːr	*!			*	
b. æveːr	*!	*			
☞ c. ever				**	*
d. æver		*!		*	*
e. evæːr	*!	*	*	**	
f. ævæːr	*!		*	*	
g. evær		*!	*	*	*
h. ævær			*!		*

The word *eːr* belongs to the so-called shortening class (its plural form is *ær-æk*). The root vowel alternates predictably, surfacing as either [eː] or [æ], depending on its length. Archiphonemic Underspecification thus predicts the vowel should be underspecified for some feature(s). Since length is contrastive for the Hungarian vowel system as a whole, we assume that Archiphonemic Underspecification would predict underlying suppression of the quality features (most significantly, the height difference between [eː] and [æ]). If the input for alternating words like *eːr* is underspecified, however, the Veve forms cannot be accounted for. We repeat the above tableaux, this time allowing for the predicted underspecification of vowel quality, indicated in the input below by an archiphone /E/.

(16) Tableau E: Veve I with underspecification

/Vv, Eːr/	IDENT-I/O [LG]	IDENT-B/R [QUAL]	IS	IDENT-I/O [QUAL]	IDENT-B/R [LG]
☞ a. eveːr			*		*
b. æveːr		*!			*
c. ever	*!		**		
d. æver	*!	*	*		
e. evæːr		*!	**		*
☞ f. ævæːr			*		*
g. evær	*!	*	*		
h. ævær	*!				

(17) Tableau F: Veve II with underspecification

/Vv, Eːr/	IDENT-B/R [LG]	IDENT-B/R [QUAL]	IDENT-I/O [QUAL]	IS	IDENT-I/O [LG]
a. eveːr	*!			*	
b. æveːr	*!	*			
☹ c. ever				**!	*
d. æver		*!		*	*
e. evæːr	*!	*		**	
f. ævæːr	*!			*	
g. evær		*!		*	*
💣* h. ævær					*

Under this scenario, the Veve I grammar shown in tableau E has no basis for choosing between candidates (a) *eveːr* and (f) *ævæːr*, due to the fact that IDENT-I/O[QUAL] does not assign any violations. Similarly, the Veve II grammar in tableau F selects (h) *ævær*, shown with a 'bomb', as a better candidate than the attested (a) *ever*, shown with a 'sad face'. The adoption of underspecified representations thus fails in this case to select the attested output.

Finally, Hungarian children reportedly play a word game in which they sing a ditty (18) while replacing all the vowels with a single vowel. The replacement vowel may be any vowel from the Hungarian inventory. The real song goes like this:

(18)   seːp   ɔz   itsi   pitsi   nöːj   tsipöː
        beautiful that   teeny   tiny   woman's   shoe
        'Teeny tiny women's shoes are beautiful.'

Given a replacement vowel [ɔ], the song is sung as follows:

(19)   sɔːp ɔz ɔtsɔ pɔtsɔ nɔːj tsɔpɔː

Given replacement vowel [æ], it sounds like this:

(20)   sæːp æz ætsæ pætsæ næːj tsæpæː

In 'itsi pitsi,' vowel quality may be changed, but the vowel quantity of the input is always preserved. This scenario potentially yields all four of the IS violations listed in (7). In (19) and (20), IS violations are presumably assigned for long [ɔː] and long [æː]. If the replacement vowel were instead [a] or [e], then IS violations would be incurred for each occurrence of short [a] and [e].

The 'itsi pitsi' facts raise the same problem for Archiphonemic Underspecification we exposed in Veve. Namely, no surface difference between putatively specified and underspecified vowels (i.e. predictably alternating and non-alternating) can be discerned. To the contrary: Across-the-board full specification is required. One might attempt an explanation of such word games based on the claim that a reduplicative game, as a morphological process, requires that the input contain a well-formed (i.e. fully specified) word. On this view, underspecified inputs such as those in tableaux E and F would never be submitted to the grammar for analysis.

This explanation cannot be correct, however, as we will show in the remainder of this paper. In the harmony cases to be discussed below, we show that speakers' performance in novel reduplicative tasks indicates that underspecified inputs are indeed utilized. Moreover, the particular distribution of underspecified features is explicitly not that which the principles of Lexicon Optimization and Archiphonemic Underspecification would lead us to expect.

3. Predictable but non-alternating segments may be underspecified

We will present empirical evidence from three vowel harmony languages – Tuvan, Finnish, and Turkish – which poses a further problem for the predictions of Archiphonemic Underspecification. In these languages, we argue, predictable segments must be underspecified even though they are non-alternating. If non-alternating segments are underspecified then alternation is not an adequate diagnostic of underspecification. Our claim that speakers underspecify non-alternating segments rests on the different patterning of harmonic vs. disharmonic vowels in the novel context of reduplication and re-harmonization.

3.1. Tuvan reduplication

Tuvan (Anderson and Harrison 1999) has an eight-vowel inventory, plus contrastive length.

(21)   Tuvan vowel inventory

	Front		*Back*	
High	i	ü	ɨ	u
Non-high	e	ö	a	o

Like most Turkic languages, Tuvan enforces strict backness harmony: only front vowels [i ü e ö] or back vowels [u ɨ a o] may co-occur within a word. Backness harmony is fully productive within roots and affixes. Nonetheless, the language tolerates some disharmony in loanwords, native compound forms, and in one exceptional non-alternating morpheme. Tuvan also has rounding harmony, simply characterized by two basic principles: (i) the vowels [ö o] may not occur in post-initial syllables, and (ii) a high vowel must be rounded [ü u] when it follows any rounded vowel [ü u ö o], otherwise it must be unrounded. As we will show, harmonic and disharmonic vowels pattern differently under reduplication. Our claims about underspecification and harmony rest on this difference in patterning. In this paper, we limit our attention to backness harmony. The interaction of rounding harmony with reduplication is considerably more complex (Harrison 1999, Kaun 2000), but consistent with our general analysis.

Tuvan has a morphological process of full reduplication (Harrison 1999, 2000). For example *nom* 'book' when reduplicated becomes *nom-nam* 'books and the like'. Its use is restricted, however, to a subset of speakers, to a special register, and to certain dialects. Thus, not all native speakers have been exposed to this type of reduplication. Nonetheless, the process is sufficiently transparent that we were able to teach it to both adults and young children in a matter of seconds. Speakers who had just learned the rule were able to produce novel reduplicants, and their output matched that of speakers who use reduplication regularly. The potentially *novel* character of reduplication for some speakers will be central to our argument.

Reduplication takes the entire base and repeats it, while replacing the vowel of the initial syllable. The replacement vowel is a pre-specified [a], except when the base vowel happens to be [a], in which case the replacement vowel is [u] (22i, j).

(22)   Full reduplication of monosyllabic bases
        base   *base + reduplicant*
   a.   nom   nom-nam   'book'
   b.   er   er-ar   'male'
   c.   seːk   seːk-saːk   'mosquito'
   d.   is   is-as   'footprint'
   e.   ög   ög-ag   'yurt'
   f.   süt   süt-sat   'milk'
   g.   qɨs   qɨs-qas   'girl'
   h.   xol   xol-xal   'hand'
   i.   at   at-ut   'name'
   j.   aːr   aːr-uːr   'heavy'

There is clearly a faithfulness relation between the base and reduplicant: except for the replacement vowel, the two are always identical.

3.2. Tuvan re-harmonization

However, reduplicated polysyllabic roots (along with any suffixal morphology) may surface as considerably less faithful to their bases. In polysyllabic forms, post-initial vowels generally agree in backness with the replacement vowel. Note that since the replacement vowel is either [a] or [u], it is always [+back]. To achieve this agreement, speakers subject post-initial vowels to re-harmonization. To call attention to potential re-harmonization effects, we underline all post-initial vowels in reduplicants.

(23) Full reduplication of polysyllabic bases with re-harmonization
  a. idik   idik-ad̤ik (*ad̤ik)   'boot'
  b. fiːdik   fiːdik-faːd̤ik (*faad̤ik)   'video cassette'[5]
  c. teve   teve-tav̲a (*tav̲e)   'camel'
  d. tevelerim   tevelerim-tav̲al̲ar̲im (*tav̲el̲er̲im)   'camel'(PL-1)

Disharmonic segments, whether native or borrowed, fail to undergo re-harmonization, and remain disharmonic.

(24) Full reduplication of polysyllabic bases with no re-harmonization
  a. maʃina   maʃina-muʃ̲in̲a   'car'
                   (*muʃ̲ina, *muʃ̲un̲a)
  b. ajbek   ajbek-ujb̲ek (*ujb̲ak)   'Aibek' (name)
  c. ʒiguli   ʒiguli-ʒag̲ul̲i   'Zhiguli' (car)
                   (*ʒag̲ul̲i,*ʒag̲ul̲u)
  d. aːl=ʒe   aːl=ʒe-uːl=ʒe̲ (*uːl=ʒa̲)   'yurt' (=ALL)[6]

3.3. A formal analysis of Tuvan

Adopting an Optimality Theoretic framework, we model Tuvan harmony and reduplication with the following constraints.

> REPLACE.V1: Morphological vowel replacement rule
> ALIGN[BK]: Backness Harmony
> IDENT-I/R: Input-Reduplicant Identity
> IDENT-B/R: Base-Reduplicant Identity

The first of these, REPLACE.V1, is a Tuvan-specific morphological constraint that simply requires the speaker to replace the vowel when doing reduplication. The actual choice of replacement vowel, as we have argued elsewhere, falls out from general markedness constraints (Harrison 1999, 2000). The alignment constraint is adopted from Smolensky (1993). Though it employs the metaphor of 'aligning' underlying features with the edge of the word domain, it could be equally well construed as a garden-variety constraint on surface well-formedness. We will thus assign an alignment violation in the tableaux below to vowel segments which fail to agree in backness with a vowel in an adjacent syllable. The identity constraints, adopted from McCarthy and Prince (1995), require the surface form of the reduplicant to be identical with the *input* form and the *base* (surface form), respectively.

To begin, let's consider an input form such as *idik* 'boot.' In accord with the predictions of Lexicon Optimization, we assume a fully specified representation for this harmonic form, even though the backness value of the second vowel is predictable on the basis of the backness of the initial vowel. For *idik*, as for all harmonic words, the following constraint ranking allows us to capture the pattern of re-harmonization:

(25) REPLACE.V1 » ALIGN[BK] » IDENT-I/R, IDENT-B/R

Later, we will have cause to modify this ranking (28, 29). But first, to show how the constraints interact, consider Tableau G, where we have included all constraints except for REPLACE.V1 (the Tuvan-specific morphological constraint).

(26) Tableau G: Harmonic form with fully specified input.

/ i d i k, RED/ ǀ −B	ALIGN[BK]	IDENT-I/R	IDENT-B/R
a. idik-adik	*!* [7]	*	*
☞ b. idik-adïk		**	**

The attested output form can only emerge if the harmony constraint ALIGN[BK] outranks both faithfulness constraints. This is due to the fact that the unattested candidate (a) is more faithful to the input, both in terms of IDENT-I/R and IDENT-B/R. Re-harmonization under reduplication provides ample evidence for the undominated status of the harmony constraint.

But for a disharmonic form with a fully specified input, the ranking shown in (25) selects the wrong candidate, as shown in tableau H. Note that for disharmonic forms, we assess a violation of

ALIGN[BK] for each vowel that fails to align its underlying backness specification within its harmony domain (here, the base or the reduplicant, taken separately, cf. endnote 8).

(27) Tableau H: Disharmonic form with fully specified input.

/a j b e k, RED/ | | +B −B	ALIGN[BK]	IDENT-I/R	IDENT-B/R
☹ a. ajbek-ujbek	***!*	*	*
☞* b. ajbek-ujbak	**		**

The attested disharmonic candidate (a) should win, but does not (☹). Instead, the unattested candidate (b) wins (☞*). For candidate (a) to win, the harmony constraint must rank below at least one of the faithfulness constraints. We thus propose an alternative ranking in which ALIGN[BK] ranks below input-reduplicant faithfulness. Again, we assume a fully specified input.

(28) Tableau I: Disharmonic form with fully specified input (new ranking)

/a j b e k, RED/ | | +B −B	IDENT-I/R	ALIGN[BK]	IDENT-B/R
☞ a. ajbek-ujbek	*	****	*
b. ajbek-ujbak	**!	**	**

This ranking correctly selects the attested disharmonic form. We are thus faced with a ranking paradox by which harmonic and disharmonic sequences seem to require separate constraint rankings (i.e. separate grammars). This apparent paradox may be resolved if we allow harmonic words to be represented by underspecified inputs (contra the predictions of Lexicon Optimization and Archiphonemic Underspecification).

(29)   Tableau J: Harmonic form with underspecified input

/i d i k, RED/ | –B	IDENT-I/R	ALIGN[BK]	IDENT-B/R
a. idik-adik	*	*!*	*
☞ b. idik-adık	*		**

Since disharmonic forms do not undergo re-harmonization (tableau H), while harmonic ones do (tableau G), we have assumed the former are fully specified for the harmonic feature and the latter are partially underspecified. Underspecification thus has a desirable result in that it obviates the need to posit separate constraint rankings for various subsets of the lexicon. Partial underspecification has the following consequence, illustrated in tableau J. A faithfulness violation is incurred only for the vowel of the initial syllable in each candidate. The underspecified, non-initial vowels undergo 'cost-free' re-harmonization (candidate b). In tableau I, on the other hand, both vowels are fully specified such that an output which obeys harmony (candidate b), does so at a cost, namely the violation of input-reduplicant faithfulness. The same disparity in the treatment of harmonic and disharmonic vowels is found in Finnish (section 3.4) and Turkish (section 3.5).

3.4. A Finnish word game

Facts similar to those of Tuvan have been documented in a Finnish reduplicative word game known as *kontti kieli* 'knapsack language' (Campbell 1986, Vago 1988). The game adds the word *kontti* 'knapsack' after a word, then preposes the initial (C)V sequences of the two words. Speakers then re-harmonize the remaining vowels according to front/back harmony, with the exception of the neutral [e] and [i]. As in Tuvan, speakers re-harmonize harmonic segments (30a, b), but consistently fail to do so with disharmonic ones (30c, d). Potential re-harmonization targets are underlined in the data below.

(30)   Finnish *kontti kieli*

    a. mitä kontti   → ko-ta mi-ntti(*ko-tä)
        'what' 'knapsack'

    b. sikiö kontti   → ko-kio si-ntti (*ko-kiö)
        'embryo' 'knapsack'

    c. konglööri kontti   → ko-nglööri jo-ntti (*ko-ngloori)
        'juggler' 'knapsack'

    d. manööveri kontti   → ko-nööveri ma-ntti (*ko-nooveri)
        'maneuver' 'knapsack'

Note that root vowels of Finnish never alternate except within the special context of *kontti kieli*. These results show that in the novel context of a language-external word game, speakers treat harmonic and disharmonic segments differently. Campbell (1986) used this to argue for the psychological reality of a rule of vowel harmony within Finnish, even in the face of numerous surface counter-examples to harmony. From our perspective, the Finnish data are comparable with Tuvan and may be analyzed in the same way, with the same implications.

We have claimed that speakers of vowel harmony languages such as Tuvan and Finnish underspecify predictable but non-alternating segments within roots. This claim entails that vowel harmony must be an active process even in cases where it appears to be little more than a static, phonotactic pattern. In Tuvan and Finnish, we have presented evidence that the quality of root vowels is established by means of alignment (Kaun 2000), except in the cases of disharmonic roots. We turn now to Turkish, where we extend our argument that harmony (rendered formally as alignment) actively determines feature values of all harmonic segments, even those that never enter into surface alternations. We argue that Turkish vowel co-occurrence patterns within roots are not merely static, phonotactic patterns but active harmonic processes that have psychological reality and accessibility for speakers.

3.5. Turkish root harmony

Turkish has both backness harmony and a vowel inventory like that found in Tuvan, but it lacks a Tuvan or Finnish-style reduplication process that would subject roots to novel alternations. Turkish root vowels thus never alternate in any context. As a pilot study, we taught a Tuvan-style reduplication rule to three speakers of Turkish. The speakers were instructed to replace the initial vowel of a set of 40 Turkish words (real lexemes of Turkish, both harmonic and disharmonic) with [a] or [u]. After making the replacement, they could then make any other changes – or no changes at all – to the reduplicant. The resulting form (the reduplicant) was to be a nonsense word that 'sounds like a Turkish word.' The speakers produced multiple reduplicants for some bases; they then selected the best-sounding ones. Preliminary results of our pilot study show effects quite similar to those of Tuvan. The Turkish speakers showed a clear preference for re-harmonizing harmonic words according to the pervasive pattern of backness harmony (31a, b). But they generally failed to re-harmonize disharmonic words (31c, d). Starred forms given below show speakers' failure to apply backness harmony to reduplicants. We emphasize that the pilot results lack any statistical significance; they are merely presented here as a model for future experimentation.

(31) Turkish novel reduplication

a.	kibrit	→	kabrit (*kabrit)	'match'
b.	bütün	→	batin (*batün, *batin)	'whole'
c.	mali	→	muli (*muli *mulü)	'Mali'
d.	butik	→	batik (*batik)	'boutique'

Our Turkish speakers, like Tuvan or Finnish speakers, apparently manipulated underlyingly unspecified segments by re-harmonizing them in this novel, reduplicative context. A fuller study of Turkish speakers' harmony preferences under reduplication might thus provide additional empirical evidence that speakers of harmony languages underspecify predictable but non-alternating segments. If they do so, it might, we hypothesize, be in response to an observed harmonic pattern attested in most (but by no means all) lexemes. We hypothesize that the presence of a pervasive pattern of vowel co-occurrence in roots, in combination with regular alternations in suffixes is sufficient to drive speakers to posit a general system of vowel harmony that obtains across both roots and affixes.

4. Systematicity vs. idiosyncrasy

We have shown that feature values, though they may be both predictable and alternating, are not necessarily underspecified. This was the case in Hungarian. Moreover, we have shown that feature values that are predictable but non-alternating may be underspecified. This was the case in the harmony patterns of Tuvan, Finnish, and Turkish. These findings indicate that Inkelas' schematic chart (1) depicting the distribution of underspecification must be revised as follows:

(32)	Alternating	Non-alternating
Predictable	underspecified or specified	specified or underspecified
Unpredictable	specified	specified

Given the indeterminacy of this revised model in predicting the exact distribution of underspecification, we propose an alternative and more flexible model represented in (33). This schematic differs from Inkelas' in several respects. First, for 'alternating' and 'non-alternating,' we substitute 'systematic' and 'idiosyncratic.' Secondly, rather than construing these as discrete categories, we recognize that they constitute a continuum. We do the same for the categories 'predictable' and 'unpredictable'.

(33)	Systematic	Idiosyncratic
Predictable	underspecified	specified
Unpredictable	specified	

Between the poles of systematic and idiosyncratic, and similarly between the poles of predictable and unpredictable, there is, we predict, an identifiable boundary (shown as a thick, shaded line above). Outside this boundary, speakers will cease to deploy underspecification.

It is not yet clear how far along the Systematic-Idiosyncratic continuum a particular pattern may progress before speakers are no longer tempted to view the pattern as predictable. Harmony languages, we have observed, tolerate a considerable amount of disharmony (the unpredictability factor introduced by disharmonic lexemes or morphemes) while still retaining an overall systematicity (the harmony system as a whole). We thus pose the question, "what counts as a *pervasive* pattern?" The real empirical challenge lies in mapping out the two continua and in demonstrating that a given (pervasive) pattern fits at a certain point along them. We have proposed the location of several such patterns herein.

The vowel quality-length connection in Hungarian is indeed predictable. However, the incidence of alternation is idiosyncratically conditioned by word-class. Thus, our model predicts full specification in Hungarian. In Tuvan, Turkish, Finnish, and other harmony languages, predictability is manifested in both alternating and non-alternating segments. Nonetheless, a pervasive pattern permeates the language as a whole. This sort of systematicity correlates with underspecification, we claim. Idiosyncrasy in these harmony languages is limited to an exceptional class of disharmonic foreign borrowings and a very restricted class of non-alternating morphemes. For idiosyncratic/unpredictable vowels in these classes, we of course predict full specification.

In addition to the cases we have discussed in this chapter, our model allows languages to be located at different points along the continua. For example, we would expect a language having strict vowel co-occurrence patterns like those of Turkish and Tuvan, but lacking any affixal morphology at all, to exhibit underspecification of predictable feature values. Over time, we might expect a language to shift its position along the continua. This is, we hypothesize, what has taken place in Uzbek, a Turkic language that appears to be in the process of losing its vowel harmony system. As a greater proportion of disharmonic words enters the language, the vowel harmony pattern in Uzbek becomes less systematic and more idiosyncratic. As this occurs, speakers may at some point cease to consider the pattern predictable and will no longer posit underspecification.

Our goal is to construct a model that will allow us to characterize precisely the circumstances under which speakers will posit abstract lexical entries. This research program, which we have referred to as *pattern-responsive lexicon optimization*, is outlined here and in Harrison and Kaun (2000). An adequate model, we propose, should anticipate speakers' propensity to underspecify in response to pervasive, surface-true patterns (the prime example being vowel harmony), and their propensity to fully specify in response to more limited or idiosyncratic patterns.

Notes

*   We would like to thank the participants at the Conference on Distinctive Feature Theory (October 1999) at ZAS Berlin for their insightful comments on an earlier version of this paper. We also wish to acknowledge the contributions of our many Tuvan, Hungarian and Turkish language consultants. Funding for fieldwork in Tuva in 1998 was provided by the International Research and Exchanges Board (IREX).
1   The tag '-1' denotes first person (singular). All tags herein follow the EURO-TYPE Guidelines of the Committee on Computation and Standardization, European Science Foundation (1993).
2   'Ubbi Dubbi' is an English speech disguise game that was propagated by the 1970's children's television show 'Zoom,' which aired in the United States. The game works by inserting [ʌb] before the rhyme of each syllable within a word.
3   We would like to thank our Hungarian consultants Ms. B. Ürögdi and Mr. B. Varady for their patience and generosity in helping us document Hungarian word games.
4   We find violations of IS in the context of Veve as we have just seen, where short [e] and [ɑ] are allowed to surface. Such violations are observed elsewhere in Hungarian: for some speakers foreign diphthongs are realized as long monophthongs, e.g. *europa* → [æː] ropɔ, and *automata* → [ɔː]tomɔtɔ. Here we find long vowels [æː] and [ɔː] surfacing despite their violation of IS.
5   Note that accidentally harmonic loanwords e.g. *fiːdik* (23b) also undergo re-harmonization, even though they may violate other phonotactic constraints of the language. For instance, Tuvan has no native phoneme [f], however the

loanword *fi:dik* 'video cassette' is fully harmonic and treated like any native, harmonic word with respect to re-harmonization. This shows that an analysis invoking two grammars, one for native vocabulary and one for borrowed or foreign vocabulary, is untenable.

6   The Tuvan Allative marker /=tʃe/ is an enclitic.

7   We assess violations of ALIGN[BK] within the domain of the base or reduplicant, taken separately. For example *idik-adik* accrues just two violations, one for each vowel in the reduplicant (underlined). If a disharmonic base and reduplicant e.g. *ajbek-ujbek* (27a), were counted together as a single domain, there would be more violations, but the same candidates would win out.

References

Anderson, Gregory D. S. and K. David Harrison
    1999   *Tyvan*. [Tuvan] Languages of the World/Materials, vol. 257. München: LINCOM Europa.

Archangeli, Diana
    1984   Underspecification in Yawelmani phonology and morphology. Ph.D. dissertation, MIT, Cambridge, Mass.

Campbell, Lyle
    1986   Testing phonology in the field. In: John J. Ohala and Jeri J. Jaeger (eds.) *Experimental phonology*, 163-186. Orlando, Florida: Academic Press.

Clements, George N. and Engin Sezer
    1982   Vowel and consonant disharmony in Turkish. In: Harry van der Hulst and Norval Smith (eds.) *The Structure of Phonological Representations Vol. II*, 213-255. Dordrecht: Foris.

Harrison, K. David
    1999   Tuvan reduplication and harmony. *Proceedings of the Berkeley Linguistics Society 25. Parasession on Turkic, Dravidian and Caucasian Linguistics*.

    2000   Topics in the phonology and morphology of Tuvan. Ph.D. dissertation, Yale University, New Haven, Conn.

Harrison, K. David and Abigail Kaun
    2000   Pattern-responsive lexicon optimization. *Proceedings of NELS 30*.

Inkelas, Sharon
    1995   The consequences of optimization for underspecification. *Proceedings of NELS 25*.

Kaun, Abigail
    2000   Rounding harmony. In: Bruce Hayes, Robert Kirchner and Donca Steriade (eds.) *The Phonetic Basis of Phonology*. Cambridge: Cambridge University Press. (forthcoming)

McCarthy, John and Alan Prince
    1995   Faithfulness and reduplicative identity. In: Jill Beckman, Suzanne
                Urbanczyk, and Laura Walsh (eds.) *University of Massachusetts
                Occasional Papers in Linguistics 18: Papers in Optimality Theory*,
                249-384. Amherst, Mass.: GLSA.
Prince, Alan S. and Paul Smolensky
    1993   Optimality theory: constraint interaction in generative grammar. Ms.,
                Rutgers University, Rutgers, N.J. and University of Colorado at
                Boulder, Boulder, Col.
Smolensky, Paul
    1993   Harmony, markedness and phonological activity. Paper presented at
                the Rutgers Optimality Workshop-1, Rutgers University.
    1995   The initial state and "richness of the base" in Optimality Theory.
                Technical report, Cognitive Science Department, Johns Hopkins
                University, Baltimore, Md.
Steriade, Donca
    1987   Redundant values. *Papers from the Twenty-Third Regional Meeting,
                Chicago Linguistic Society* 2: 339-62. Chicago: Chicago Linguistics
                Society, University of Chicago.
Vago, Robert
    1988   Vowel harmony in Finnish word games. In: Harry van der Hulst and
                Norval Smith (eds.) *Features, Segmental Structure and Harmony
                Processes, Part II*, 185-205. Dordrecht: Foris.
Whitney, Arthur H.
    1949   *Colloquial Hungarian*. London: Routledge.

Phonetic implementation of the distinctive auditory features [voice] and [tense] in stop consonants*

Michael Jessen

1. General introduction

While feature theory since Chomsky and Halle (1968) is primarily guided by the articulatory perspective, there have been a number of contributions in the recent past in which the auditory/perceptual perspective of distinctive features is explored further (among others, Kingston and Diehl 1994; Flemming 1995; Harris and Lindsey 1995; Traill 1995; Silverman 1997; Boersma 1998). An important landmark in the study of the auditory/perceptual correlates of features is the work of Jakobson and colleagues, including Jakobson, Fant, and Halle (1952; cf. Ohala 1999), Jakobson and Halle (1961, 1968), and Jakobson and Waugh (1987). Evidence from acoustic phonetics is an important prerequisite to the study of auditory/perceptual features and feature correlates. It is only on the basis of reliable acoustic data that one can proceed with auditory modeling, categorical perception experiments, and related methods. Acoustic data also allow inferences on many details of the articulation process (see Stevens 1997), but there are some areas where the articulation-to-acoustics mapping is very complicated (e.g. velum lowering and its acoustic consequences). Taking into account acoustic patterns leads to a more general issue: which kind of data constitutes the empirical basis of phonological analysis? There is no doubt that phonological analysis requires information on phonetic categories, including segments as well as prosodic units such has syllables, feet, and tones. Most of these categories can be symbolized with the *International Phonetic Alphabet*, which is also based on the articulatory perspective. It is also possible to allow data of a more gradient kind to enter phonological analysis. As explored (among others) by phonologists and phoneticians working in the framework of Laboratory Phonology (see Pierrehumbert, Beckman, and Ladd 1996) these are data from all domains of experimental phonetics (as well as from psycho- and neurolinguistics), which includes acoustic phonetics and speech perception research. Such a Laboratory Phonology approach is also adopted in this paper.

The present study provides a literature review and presents some new proposals on the features [voice] and [tense] (plus, more pre-liminarily, [checked]). Different acoustic correlates of these features will be discussed in detail and their relation to the articulation and perception level will be examined. This focus on acoustic feature correlates is intended as a contribution to the exploration of "auditory representation in phonology" (Flemming 1995). At the current stage of research on this topic there is still insufficient differentiation between the acoustic, the auditory, and the perceptual level, and some authors classifiy purely acoustic properties (such as formant frequencies in Hertz) as auditory. But despite the fact that there is some restructuring from the acoustic to the auditory, and again from the auditory to the perceptual level, which needs much more research, it is reasonable to begin the exploration of auditory pho-nology with a careful study of the acoustic level. It is for this reason that the term "auditory" is used in the title of this paper in spite of the fact that most attention will be spent on acoustic data. But when possible, information from perception experiments will be provided as well. The articulatory perspective will also be discussed. This is done with a focus on those articulatory principles and strategies that lead to implementation of the acoustic/ auditory/ perceptual goals (cf. Perkell et al. 1995) which constitute the definition of the distinctive features and their correlates proposed here. For example, oral cavity enlargement through larynx lowering is a strategy in the implemen-tation of the auditorily important voicing during closure pattern of [+voice] stops.

The primary perspective of this study is a paradigmatic one, i.e. a focus on contrasts (in the sense of phonemic oppositions). Most data available in the literature on the topic of this paper come from phonetic studies of minimal pairs in which the relevant sounds occur in a prosodically prominent position. There is less data available on allophonic variation in prosodically weak position and other syntagmatic phenomena, which will be addressed only marginally in this paper.

The general account presented here has been published earlier in Jessen (1998). However, the present paper presents a number of modifications and provides further evidence and motivation from a number of languages. The focus of this paper lies on *stops*, comprising mainly plosives, but also – briefly towards the end of the paper – extrapulmonic stop consonants such as clicks, ejectives, and implosives. More discussion of the implementation of [voice] and [tense] in fricatives, vowels, and other sounds is found in Jessen (1996, 1998).

2.   Introduction to [voice]

Among the features [tense] and [voice] it is the latter which has received more acceptance in the literature. But even the feature [voice] has been subject to controversy, including the question as to which part of the articulation-to-audition continuum it should address. Chomsky and Halle (1968: 327) define [–voiced] sounds as those realized with glottal opening. (Glottal opening is an efficient means of preventing voicing, at least in obstruent production.) A different but related proposal is made by Halle and Stevens (1971), who define voiced obstruents as those produced with slack vocal folds, as opposed to voiceless obstruents, which are produced with stiff vocal folds. The former vocal fold configuration enhances voicing, whereas the latter inhibits it. Due to this specific principle of voicing regulation Halle and Stevens rename the voicing feature "[stiff/slack vocal cords]" (or more appropriately "[stiff/slack vocal *folds*]" in Stevens 1977). Both Chomsky and Halle's and Halle and Stevens' definition make reference to glottal configurations that contribute to the occurrence or non-occurrence of voicing. Since these configurations are aspects of the articulatory make up of voiced vs. voiceless sounds, the voicing feature, if defined in these two particular ways, is appropriately classified as an articulatory feature. It is also appropriately classified as a "laryngeal feature" (see Clements 1985; Lombardi 1991), since the articulatory activities addressed in these feature definitions are focused on laryngeal physiology.

In contrast to these articulatory definitions of the voicing feature we find others in the literature that focus on the acoustics or audition. Jakobson, Fant, and Halle (1952: 26) characterize voicing in stop production auditorily as the presence of a "buzz" and acoustically as the presence of a harmonic sound source with a strong low-frequency component, commonly known as the voice bar (likewise Jakobson and Halle 1968). They also mention periodic vibration of the vocal folds as a correlate of [+voice] and classify this as an articulatory definition (in their terminology, a definition which refers to the "production" level or the "genetical" level; see Jakobson, Fant, and Halle 1952 and Jakobson and Halle 1968, respectively). This is correct insofar as vocal fold vibration is an activity that is detectable not only in acoustic terms, and therefore audible and measurable with acoustic phonetic methods. It is also manifested in purely movement-oriented terms, which can be measured, for example with electroglottography or fiberoptic methods. But Boersma (1998: 16) makes an important point when he says that: "If we define voicing as the vibration of the vocal cords, we are talking about the *perceptual* feature [voice], which refers to a high degree of periodicity in the sound" [emphasis mine] (the same point is made by Ladefoged 1997: 611–612). This argument is based on the well-known fact that in order to achieve vocal fold vibration several often independent articulatory gestures need to be properly coordinated. These include the above mentioned factors of vocal fold slackness and adduction, but also factors such as sufficient subglottal pressure and mechanisms of oral cavity enlargement (see Westbury 1983). Thus, on the level of the articulatory gestures vocal fold vibration is not a unitary phenomenon. Since more than laryngeal activity is necessary to produce and maintain voicing in obstruent production, it is phonetically not entirely correct to classify an auditorily defined feature [voice] nor one defined with respect to vocal fold vibration as a laryngeal feature (Stevens and Keyser 1989).

Since the focus of this paper is on auditory features we will concentrate on the auditory conceptualization of [voice], provided among others, by Jakobson and colleagues. In more recent times the auditory side of [voice] has been explored further by Kingston and Diehl (1994, 1995). According to their proposal the feature [voice] dominates "immediate perceptual properties" (IPP), which in turn dominate several "subproperties". One of the IPPs they propose is the "low frequency property". This IPP not only dominates the sub-property closure voicing (i.e. the classical "harmonic voice source" correlate of [voice]) but also the subproperties low F0 and low F1 at vowel onset. As expressed by the term "low frequency property", all three of these subproperties have in common that they present themselves to the listener as the presence of periodic energy with an amplitude maximum in the low-frequency domain of the spectrum. This proposal by Kingston and Diehl is based on a set of carefully designed speech perception experiments (see Kingston and Diehl 1994, 1995 for further literature). Their account has the advantage that languages can be analyzed with the feature [voice] even if the actual presence or absence of closure voicing is not always available, as long as other subproperties are available to cue the relevant contrast. The same reasoning will be applied here as well. But differently from Kingston and Diehl (1994, 1995), aspiration will be analyzed not as a correlate of [voice], but rather as a correlate of [tense].

3. Introduction to [tense]

In Jakobson, Fant, and Halle (1952), Jakobson and Halle (1961, 1968), and Jakobson and Waugh 1987) increased duration is mentioned as probably the most important auditory foundation of the feature [+tense], especially when this feature is applied to consonants ([tense] is also relevant for vowels). The importance ascribed to duration is furthermore evident by the fact that Jakobson and Halle (1968: 428) see a connection between the segmental feature [tense] and the prosodic quantity feature.

Aspiration is mentioned as one of the correlates of the feature [+tense].[1] As will be made more explicit (see in particular sections 5 and 12), the importance of aspiration as a correlate of [tense] can be seen in its contribution to the durational organization of the consonant (also pointed out by Fant 1960: 224). Another property of stop production that can make a tense stop longer than a lax one is an increased closure duration. The difference between long and short stop closure can potentially be increased to the level of a geminate/ simplex distinction (Jessen 1998 for more on this point). Thirdly, we should consider the possibility that the auditory impression of a short closure might be enhanced by an increased duration in the preceding vowel and a long closure impression by a short preceding vowel. This would make short preceding vowel duration another correlate of the specification [+tense] in stops (Jakobson and Halle 1961; Jakobson and Waugh 1987: 140). This correlate is particularly salient and reliable in word-final /p t k/ vs. /b d g/ in English. Adopting [tense] is one way of accommodating the proposal by some phone- ticians that duration and timing should play a more important role in phonology (Kohler 1984; Port 1996).

The feature [tense] (or the terms "fortis/lenis" which are often used synonymously with "tense/lax") has not received much popu- larity since the fifties and sixties. But more recently one can observe a renewed interest in this feature, especially in the study of German and Germanic languages (e.g. Kohler 1984; Braun 1988; Goblirsch 1994; Iverson and Salmons 1995; Jessen 1996, 1998; van Rooy 1999, van Rooy & Wissing this volume). (It needs to be mentioned, however, that the particular interpretation of the tense/lax feature differs among these and other sources.)

Among the more widely accepted features in current feature the- ory the closest equivalent to [tense] are the features [(spread) glottis] (Halle and Stevens 1971) and [asp(irated)] (Lombardi 1991, 1995). Both of these features make reference to phonemic distinctions between aspirated and unaspirated stops.[2] As far as fricatives and sonorants are concerned, [spread] and – in a perhaps more abstract sense – [aspirated] can also be used to represent voicelessness (Halle and Stevens 1971; Clements 1985; Rice 1988; Lombardi 1991). One major difference between the features [tense] and [spread]/[asp] lies in the scope of possible phonetic correlates of these features. This scope is narrower in the case of [spread]/[asp], where in stop production the focus is on aspiration, whereas in the case of [tense] aspiration is covered together with other durational events of the consonant and its surroundings. With a wider scope of implementations it is possible or at least more likely to achieve invariance (see section 14). While [tense] is preferred over [spread] and [asp] here and in Jessen (1998), several of the proposals on the correlate structure of [tense] that will be made in this paper are also of relevance for phonologists and phoneticians who prefer [spread] or [asp] over [tense] or [fortis].

4. A new model of [voice] and [tense]

In Jessen (1998) a new model was presented in which the acoustic/ auditory correlates of the features [tense] and [voice] were spelled out, and where both the differences and the similarities of these features were made explicit. Figure 1 presents the model of Jessen (1998: 270), but with a number of modifications.[3]

According to the model presented in Figure 1 (see next page) a distinction is made between "basic correlates" and "non-basic correlates". The basic correlates are unique to [tense] and [voice]. The idea behind the term "basic" is that these correlates have particularly high contextual stability and perceptual saliency. *Contextual stability* means that in many contexts in a language (often the clear majority) the relevant distinction is expressed by the correlate whose status is classified as basic. For example, in German the difference between /p t k/ and /b d g/ is expressed in almost all contexts as a significantly longer aspiration for the former than the latter set (Jessen 1998, incl. further references). One important way of showing that a correlate has high *perceptual saliency* is that manipulation of that correlate alone in a speech perception experiment leads to categorical perception.[4]

The basic correlates are also crucial as diagnostics for the question of whether a given language with a two-way distinction that can roughly be transcribed as /b d g/ vs. /p t k/ (or in some cases /p t k/ vs. /pʰ tʰ kʰ/) makes distinctive use of either [tense] or [voice]. If there is a distinction between long aspiration in /p t k/ and essentially no aspiration and at most unstable voicing in /b d g/ an analysis with [tense] is most plausible; if the distinction is one between full or almost full closure voicing in /b d g/ and essentially voiceless unaspirated /p t k/ the most plausible analysis is with [voice]. (This evaluation works particularly well in utterance-initial position.) The former situation is for example most common among the Germanic languages (excluding Dutch, Afrikaans, and Yiddish) and the latter among the Slavic and Romance languages. This diagnostic has to be properly combined with contextual stability and perceptual saliency. Thus, if both full voicing in /b d g/ and aspiration in /p t k/ are found in some context one has to examine whether in general it is the aspirated/unaspirated distinction or the voiced/voiceless distinction which is employed in the larger set of contexts and which is most salient perceptually. For example, in German both an aspiration distinction and a voicing distinction occurs word-medially before schwa (e.g. in *Lake* 'brine' vs. *Lage* 'situation, location'). But generally the aspiration distinction is found in more contexts than the voicing distinction in German, and in an experiment where voicing and aspiration are manipulated independently in minimal pairs like the one mentioned, the perceptual contribution of aspiration is far greater than the one of voicing (Jessen 1998: 285–289; see also Kohler 1979). Of course, languages might also employ three- or four-way systems, like Thai or Hindi, in which case both [tense] and [voice] are employed.

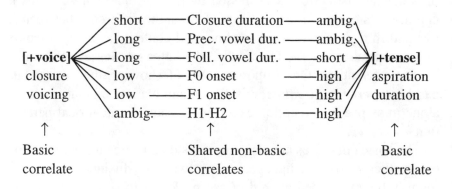

Figure 1.

Figure 1. Model of the range of acoustic/auditory correlates of [tense] and [voice]

The non-basic correlates are correlates of [tense] and [voice] which have less perceptual saliency and less contextual stability than the basic correlates (section 13). It is proposed here that these non-basic correlates are the same for [voice] as for [tense]. The non-basic correlates have the function of supporting the basic correlate or replacing it in those contexts where the basic correlate is weak or unavailable. If both the basic and the non-basic correlates of a feature are taken into account, all the contexts are covered in which the phonemic distinction at hand occurs. This way the features achieve invariance, that is, in each context at least one of the correlates is available for the implementation of the contrast. Invariance is also meant to imply that a feature has a definition that generalizes across all the different correlates, or to speak with Jakobson, that it has a common phonetic denominator (section 14). For example, the feature [tense] has different durational correlates (aspiration duration, closure duration, etc.); thus the common phonetic denominator is duration in general (or properties derived from or serving aspiration duration – the basic correlate of [tense]). Figure 1 also shows the polarities in which the correlates are operative (e.g. whether [+voice] stops have higher or lower F0 onset than [–voice] stops).[5] In the following sections each of the correlates of [tense] and [voice] will be addressed in more detail.

5. Aspiration duration

In Figure 1 aspiration duration is specified as the basic correlate of [tense]: tense stops have a long and clearly perceptible aspiration phase, whereas lax stops have only short aspiration, or probably on the perceptual level no aspiration at all. For a language analyzed with [tense] it is expected that the contextual stability of an aspiration distinction is higher than the one of a voicing distinction (in the latter case analysis with [voice] is more appropriate). On the basis of the contextual stability criterion it is appropriate to employ [tense] for the representation of /b d g/ vs. /p t k/ for instance in the Germanic languages Icelandic, Danish, German, and English.[6]

One well established way of measuring aspiration duration is through the notion of positive VOT (Lisker and Abramson 1964), which is the temporal interval from stop release to voicing onset in the following vowel.[7] In many perception studies it has been shown that manipulation of positive VOT leads to categorical perception of word-initial /p t k/ vs. /b d g/ in English (see Harnad 1987 for some of the literature). In most of these perception studies aspirated stops have been synthesized with aspiration noise during the interval between release and voice onset (Kluender, Lotto, and Jenison 1995 for illustration). The perceptual importance of the amplitude of this aspiration noise has been demonstrated by Repp (1979). Fischer-Jørgensen (1968: 83) makes a terminological distinction between "open interval", which is the distance from release to vowel onset, and "aspiration", which in addition to a long open interval requires noise during that interval.

The fact that aspiration duration (synthesized with positive VOT) leads to categorical perception motivates the classification of this property as a basic correlate. One might ask what it is that makes aspiration duration such a perceptually important event. More specifically, we can ask why aspiration duration is more important perceptually than other durational correlates of [tense]. There is reason to assume that the auditory system is particularly sensitive to events that follow (rather than precede or coincide with) the silence or low amplitude associated with stop closure. This makes stop release a very salient perceptual event (see Silverman 1997: 40–42). This principle would imply more auditory acuity in processing aspiration duration than in processing closure duration or the duration of the preceding vowel. The same general insight is also captured in Kingston's (1985, 1990) "binding hypothesis" (cf. also Keating 1990).

Another reason might lie in the fact that the sheer magnitude of the duration difference between /b d g/ vs. /p t k/ is usually higher for aspiration duration than for closure or preceding vowel duration. For example, in the pooled German data presented in Jessen (1998) aspiration of /p t k/ intervocalically before schwa was 60 milliseconds long, while aspiration duration of /b d g/ had a 22 ms magnitude (p. 86). In the same context, closure duration was at 84 ms for /p t k/ and 58 ms for /b d g/ (p. 89). This demonstrates a larger aspiration than closure duration difference (a still greater difference is found in a stressed syllable). Furthermore, the aspiration durations of /b d g/ are much closer to zero than their closure durations. From an auditory perspective both of these aspects suggest that the listener makes an essentially categorical difference between the presence of aspiration in /p t k/ vs. its absence in /b d g/. Closure duration differences, on the other hand, are more likely to be processed in gradual terms, i.e. as different values on a continuum of durations (likewise preceding vowel duration).

6. Closure voicing

Figure 1 specifies the occurrence of voicing during closure as the basic correlate of [voice]. As with the basic correlate of [tense], both contextual stability and perceptual saliency should be discussed as criteria in support of this choice. For a language properly analyzed with [voice], like for example Spanish or Russian, we expect that in utterance-initial position /p t k/ are essentially unaspirated and /b d g/ are reliably realized with voicing during closure. In terms of VOT the former set has zero or short-lag VOT, while the latter is realized with negative VOT (prevoicing). Now, if /b d g/ are voiced in a context that is as unfavorable for the occurrence of voicing as utterance-initial position (cf. Kingston and Diehl 1994), then it is very likely that voicing in /b d g/ is also found word-medially between vowels or in many other positions adjacent to voiced sounds (see also Keating, Linker, and Huffman 1983). For /b d g/ to be produced with pre-voicing in utterance-initial position the speaker needs special configurations of oral cavity enlargement (such as tongue root advancement, larynx lowering, slackening of the vocal tract walls), in addition to vocal fold slackening, a certain level of subglottal pressure, and other factors; this might not be necessary for voice production in intervocalic position (see Halle and Stevens 1971; Westbury 1983). In other words, occurrence of prevoicing in utterance-initial /b d g/ is a good predictor of high contextual stability of closure voicing in the language, because the speaker makes an active effort to provide all the gestural configurations necessary to produce closure voicing in a context where passively no voicing would occur in /b d g/ (Westbury and Keating 1986). In this sense [+voice] is the marked value of [voice] (in obstruent production), just like [+tense] with the active glottal spreading gesture necessary for aspiration is the marked value of [tense]. Despite the effort to produce voicing in /b d g/, it is conceivable that even in a language with [voice] these sounds can become voiceless in contexts that present a particularly great challenge to the occurrence of voicing. This can be the case in adjacency to voiceless sounds or at the end of an utterance. Given Kingston and Diehl's (1994, 1995) proposal it is possible that other properties (some of the non-basic correlates in Figure 1) take over in such cases, just like other properties than aspiration might take over in contexts unfavorable for the occurrence of aspiration in a language with [tense].

Having examined contextual stability of closure voicing we need to consider perceptual reasons that would motivate assigning basic status to this correlate of [voice]. Notice that full categorical perception is achieved with manipulation of voicing duration alone in a [voice] language, i.e. with a continuum between long (pre)voicing and essentially voiceless unaspirated productions (e.g. Abramson and Lisker 1973 and Williams 1977 on Spanish; Barry 1991 on Russian). In wideband spectrograms voicing during closure in stop production is visible as what is often referred to as the "voice bar". As the acoustic result of forming an oral closure for the production of /b d g/, the energy in all parts of the spectrum except for the low-frequency band that contains the fundamental undergoes extensive damping. Due to this damping process all that is accessible to the listener during closure is a quasiperiodic structure in the lowest components of the frequency range. It can be hypothesized that the lack of energy in higher frequencies provides an ideal perceptual background upon which the presence of low-frequency periodic structure, i.e. closure voicing, can be detected easily. This figure-ground relation between the voice bar and the lack of energy in other parts of the spectral range could facilitate the perception of the voiced/voiceless distinction as a categorical difference. Without the need to compare amplitude levels in different frequencies of the spectrum the listener can easily determine whether there is a voice bar during closure or not. With other correlates of [voice], such as low F0 or F1 values in the adjacent vowel (see below), categorical feature detection is less plausible.

The method of measuring closure voicing as negative VOT is a special case of measuring the amount of closure that is covered by voicing (word medially this is often referred to as "voicing into closure" if less than the entire closure is voiced). This measurement method makes reference to the temporal amount of voicing during closure (see also Shih and Möbius, in press, and further references therein, for automatic voicing detection with ESPS/Waves). To fully understand the perception of voicing it is also necessary to consider the *amplitude* of voicing. Stevens et al. (1992), who investigate the perception of voicing in fricatives (the situation for stops is probably similar), estimate that if the amplitude of voicing during closure drops below a level of 10 dB less than the voicing amplitude of the adjacent vowel, voicing is no longer perceptible. The active maneuvers to enhance closure voicing, mentioned earlier, will ensure a sufficiently large voicing amplitude, but if voicing occurs passively this is much less likely or will only be relevant for a small portion of closure. Even voiceless stops usually have a certain amount of voicing into closure, but it is passively created and probably not loud, nor long, enough to be perceived. These considerations add to the plausibility of a categorical difference based on closure voicing. In languages with [voice], /b d g/ are fully (or near-fully) voiced at a clearly perceivable amplitude level, whereas /p t k/ have at best some passive voicing, which is too short and too weak to be perceived at all. (In Jakobson and Halle 1968 the amplitude aspect of voicing is accounted for by classifying [voice] among the "sonority features".)

7. F0 onset

F0 onset (the fundamental frequency at the onset of and a number of periods into the following vowel) has been listed in Figure 1 as a correlate of both [tense] and [voice]. The connection between aspiration, as the basic correlate of [tense], and F0 onset is made through the aerodynamic hypothesis of F0 perturbation. According to this hypothesis (as far as the aspirated/unaspirated distinction is concerned) aspirated stops induce increased fundamental frequency values in the first periods of the following vowel relative to un-aspirated stops because the high airflow associated with aspiration creates an increased Bernoulli force, which in turn leads to more rapid glottal closure formations and therefore a higher vibration rate of the vocal folds at the early part of the following vowel. Hombert, Ohala, and Ewan (1979), in evaluating this and other hypotheses of F0 perturbation, are rather skeptical about the aerodynamic hypo-thesis. Some recent relevant evidence comes from Mei (2000), where the amount of glottal opening at the first five periods into the vowel following German tense and lax obstruents was correlated with F0 of the same periods (data and procedures of the underlying transillumi-nation study are described in Jessen 1998: Chapter 7). Concentrating on aspirated /p/ and /t/ before schwa and /i/, it turned out that there was a gradual decline of similar shape in both F0 and glottal opening at vowel onset with good temporal alignment. Significant corre-lations from 0.4 and 0.42 between F0 and glottal opening were obtained when data were pooled across periods and repetitions (after tense fricatives even correlations up to 0.63 where obtained). Since the degree of glottal opening stands in a fairly direct relationship to the amount of transglottal airflow and since the connection between aspiration and glottal opening is well established, these results of Mei (2000) support the aerodynamic hypothesis and the status of F0 as a correlate of aspiration and thereby of [tense]. Along the same lines, it is interesting to examine the results of Löfqvist, Koenig, and McGowan (1995) where after American English aspirated /p/ they found with most speakers a decline in open quotient (Fig. 5) and in F0 (Fig. 7). However, the decline of OQ was steeper and shorter than the one of F0. This raises some scepticism against the aerodynamic hypothesis, since the decline in OQ, as a fairly direct index of aero-dynamic influence, was shorter in scope than the observed F0 perturbation effect according to that study.

One method of observing the influence of an aspiration difference on F0 onset without interference from a voicing difference is to look for languages with a two-way opposition that have a pure aspiration-based distinction without optional voicing in /b d g/, and to determine whether there is still a difference in F0 onset between the two stop categories. Examples of languages with this profile are Cantonese (Zee 1980), Mandarin Chinese (Iwata and Hirose 1976; Shimizu 1996: 56–58), and Danish (Jeel 1975; Petersen 1978, 1983). These languages with a strict aspiration-based difference in the stop system show higher F0 onset after aspirated than after unaspirated stops. But the difference can be quite small and, in the case of Danish, counterexamples are possible (cf. Fischer-Jørgensen 1968). Another way of isolating the influence of aspiration from that of voicing is by looking for speakers and contexts where /b d g/ are systematically voiceless while /p t k/ are aspirated. Along these lines there is evidence from German that a certain (though mostly small) expected difference in F0 onset can be attributed to the influence of an aspiration-based distinction without interference from voicing (Jessen 1998; see the data for speakers MJ and MA in Chapter 4). A similar pattern can be observed in the English data presented in Kingston and Diehl (1994: 433–434).

The connection between closure voicing, as the basic correlate of [voice], and F0 onset is established through the vocal fold tension hypothesis of F0 perturbation (see Halle and Stevens 1971; Hombert, Ohala, and Ewan 1979). This hypothesis states that relatively low F0 in the following vowel is a carryover effect from vocal fold slack-ness, which is necessary for actively maintaining closure voicing in voiced stops. On the basis of this hypothesis Halle and Stevens (1971) proposed the feature [slack vocal cords]. Conversely, relative-ly high F0 after voiceless stops results from vocal fold stiffening, which is a means of inhibiting closure voicing. For that configuration Halle and Stevens proposed the feature [stiff vocal cords]. The specific predictions on laryngeal physiology that this hypothesis makes could not always be verified experimentally (Keating 1988 for discussion), but the results of Löfqvist et al. (1989) are supportive. There is good evidence in the literature that in languages with a pure voiced/voiceless distinction (thus without interference from an aspiration distinction) F0 is higher after voiceless than voiced stops. Languages in which this is the case include French (Hombert and

Ladefoged 1977; Jun 1996) and Japanese (Kawasaki 1983; Shimizu 1989, 1996: 27–31).[8]

From these and other sources one gets the overall impression that the connection between a voicing distinction and F0 is stronger than the connection between an aspiration distinction and F0, although both exist. In general this indicates that the connection between the shared non-basic correlates of [tense] and [voice] is not necessarily as symmetrical as is suggested in Figure 1. Evidence for a strong connection between [voice] and F0 onset is also found in Xhosa (Jessen and Roux to appear, including further literature). Xhosa has a three-way contrast among stops (and clicks) between an aspirated category, a "voiced" category, and a third one that varies between ejective and plain realization. (In addition, Xhosa has a bilabial implosive.) The voiced stops are usually not produced with any more than the short and weak closure voicing that is also found in the other sets (Jessen 1999a). The most salient property that distinguishes the voiced stops from the other two cognates is a strong and temporally stable F0 depression effect on the following vowel (Jessen and Roux to appear). In an analysis of Xhosa with the features proposed in this paper it is clear that the feature [tense] is needed for the representation of aspiration. This leaves [voice] for the representation of voiced stops despite the fact that closure voicing, i.e. the basic correlate of that feature, is not employed. Instead, it is one of the non-basic correlates (F0 onset) that probably carries most of the perceptual load and has most contextual stability (except for the implosive, where [+voice] is implemented with closure voicing; this case also provides additional evidence for the necessity of having [voice] in Xhosa). This suggests that non-basic correlates can be phonologized to a level of importance otherwise limited to the basic correlates. The analogical case for [tense] lies in gemination (phonologization of closure duration), which argues for a stronger connection of closure duration with [tense] than [voice] (see section 10).

8. F1 onset

F1 frequency at the onset of and some periods into the following vowel is another parameter that is a correlate of both [tense] and [voice]. The connection between F1 onset and [tense] is through its basic aspiration correlate, like it was the case with the F0 onset correlate. Higher F1 after aspirated stops compared to unaspirated stops is the result of a number of interrelated factors. Firstly, aspiration causes at least a partial masking of the formant transitions, including the rising F1 transition from the low F1 target of the stop (oral constriction leads to low F1) to the higher F1 target of the following vowel (most clearly in /a/). Therefore, at the time where aspiration ends, F1 is relatively high. Secondly, F1 is raised due to the influence of the trachea as a resonator. This tracheal coupling occurs due to the glottal opening gesture in aspirated stops and is still detectable at vowel onset. Tracheal coupling is also the reason for a broadening of F1 bandwidth. Broadening the bandwidth of a formant reduces its amplitude and therefore its perceptibility. This is a factor that enhances the overall masking effect of aspiration on formant transitions and leads to the fact that F1 is relatively high once the acoustic influence of aspiration and its underlying glottal opening gesture has terminated or reached a minimum (see Stevens 1998: section 8.3). One case is reported in Fischer-Jørgensen (1968), where voiceless unaspirated stops in Danish were produced with long rising F1 transitions (suggesting low F1 at vowel onset), while voiceless aspirated stops were produced without or with shorter F1 transitions (suggesting higher F1 onset). Evidence for higher F1 after voiceless aspirated than voiceless unaspirated stops is also presented for Mandarin Chinese by Shimizu (1996: 61–63).

The connection between F1 onset and [voice] can be made through the coarticulatory effects of the cavity-enlarging maneuvers that are necessary for actively maintaining voicing during closure (Fischer-Jørgensen 1968: 92; Trigo 1991). Tongue root advancement and larynx lowering, which are among the most effective means of oral cavity enlargement, both have a lowering effect on F1. Like with the influence of vocal fold slackening on F0 onset, it can be assumed that there is carryover coarticulation from the closure interval, where the adjustments are needed, to the early part of the following vowel. Crucial evidence comes again from Fischer-Jørgensen (1968), where it is reported that F1 starts higher after the voiceless unaspirated stops of French than after the voiced stops of that language. This effect was also found, though on a non-significant level, for Japanese by Shimizu (1996: 34–37).

Another possible explanation for the connection between F1 onset and [voice] derives from the fact even in pure voiced/voiceless systems positive VOT is usually longer in the voiceless than the voiced stops, though of course the difference is not nearly as strong as in aspirated/unaspirated distinctions (Fischer-Jørgensen 1968 on French; Alghamdi 1990: 133–141 on Arabic; Shimizu 1996: 23–27 on Japanese; Ernestus 2000: 205–208 on Dutch). This VOT difference can be attributed in large part to the stronger burst expected in voiceless than voiced stops, which depends on the higher intraoral air pressure found in the former than the latter stop category (see Dixit and Brown 1978). This burst interval in voiceless stops could create the same kind – though not the same magnitude – of a masking effect on F1 formant transition that was mentioned above for aspirated stops.[9]

9. H1-H2

The difference between the amplitude of the first harmonic (the fundamental) and the amplitude of the second harmonic is a parameter that captures voice quality variations. Relatively high levels of H1-H2 are indicative of breathy voice (see Klatt and Klatt 1990; Stevens and Hanson 1994). Whereas true breathy voice also contains aperiodic energy at the frequency level of the third formant and higher, there is also a weaker kind of breathy voice, often referred to as "slack voice" (Ladefoged and Maddieson 1996: 63–66) or "lax voice" (Kingston et al. 1997), which has no striking turbulence at higher frequencies, but which still shows the increased H1-H2 values.

Aspirated stops show increased values of H1-H2 at the onset of the following vowel (incl. a number of periods into that vowel) compared to unaspirated stops in English and German (Chapin Ringo 1988; Ní Chasaide and Gobl 1993; Jessen 1998: 115).[10] This occurrence of an interval of breathy voice after aspirated stops can be explained by the influence of the large glottal opening gesture associated with aspiration (see Dixit 1989). Usually the adduction phase of this glottal opening gesture is not complete at vowel onset, so that there is a temporal interval during which voicing associated with the vowel occurs together with transglottal turbulent airflow associated with a yet incompletely closed glottis (Löfqvist and McGowan 1992). For German this is supported by the fact that glottal opening at vowel onset is significantly larger after /p t k/ than after /b d g/ (Jessen 1998: 338). The resulting mixture of voicing from the following vowel with aspiration turbulence from the preceding stop results in a kind of breathy voice quality that is similar to the one found in intervocalic /h/ (Stevens 1998: 445–465), which is frequently voiced in German and English. This association between aspiration and H1-H2 makes high H1-H2 a correlate of [+tense]. Though no data are known to the author from a two-way system that is strictly based on aspiration, the confounding influence of voicing can be dismissed by the fact that two of six German speakers in Jessen (1998: Chapter 4), all of which showed higher H1-H2 after aspirated /p t k/ than /b d g/, produced /b d g/ consistently without voicing. In Mei (2000) correlations between glottal opening and the voice quality parameters described in Sluijter et al. (1995) were determined on the basis of a study of German obstruents (Jessen 1998: Chapter 7). Temporal alignment between the decline of glottal opening and of H1-H2 into the vowel after aspirated /p t/ was very striking, the shape (steepness, etc,) of the fall was similar, and significant correlations between 0.72 and 0.75, depending on the type of vowel, were obtained between glottal opening and H1-H2 (cf. section 7 for the same methodology with F0).[11] This result presents clear evidence for the association between H1-H2 and the glottal opening gesture necessary in aspirated stops.

The association between H1-H2 and [voice] is ambiguous. Ní Chasaide and Gobl (1993) measured (among other voice quality parameters) H1-H2 (reported by them as H2-H1) in the [voice] languages Italian and French and in the [tense] languages Swedish and German (also in English, but with less explicit documentation). The strongest effects were found for German and Swedish, where increased H1-H2 associated with /p t k/ could be attributed primarily to aspiration. For French and Italian the magnitude of any differences between /p t k/ and /b d g/ was much smaller than in the Germanic languages. Where such differences existed, the direction of the effects was usually the same as in German and Swedish, i.e. higher H1-H2 associated with /p t k/ than with /b d g/ (but on p. 311 they mention a counterexample). This would suggest that relatively low H1-H2 is a correlate of [+voice] and relatively high H1-H2 a correlate of [–voice]. Increased H1-H2 in voiceless stops might result as a carryover effect from the activity of the cricothyroid muscle (CT), which is activated with the goal of stiffening the vocal folds to inhibit voicing during closure (cf. Löfqvist et al. 1989 and section 7). Discussing falsetto voice, Laver (1980) states that the substantial CT activity that this register requires not only increases F0 but also "results in the vertical cross-section of the edges of the vocal folds becoming thin", whereby "the glottis often remains slightly apart" (p. 108). This in turn can lead to mild breathiness and show up as increased H1-H2. The connection between F0 raising and increased open quotient (commonly understood as the articulatory cause of increased H1-H2; Klatt and Klatt 1990) is established in the intonation experiments of Pierrehumbert (1989), Koreman (1996: 154–158), and Marasek (1997: 149).

But there is also evidence that exactly the opposite associations apply, namely an association of [+voice] with *increased* H1-H2. One such case occurs in Xhosa (see Denning 1989 for examples from more languages). As mentioned in section 7, the voiced stops (and clicks) of Xhosa do not have reliable closure voicing and instead they are differentiated from the other two series by tonal depression. In addition to tonal depression, the voiced stops often induce H1-H2 values early in the following vowel of a magnitude equal to or higher than the high H1-H2 values expectedly found after the aspirated stops (Jessen and Roux to appear). Spectrographically, turbulence noise at F3 is rare with the voiced stops. Therefore the voice quality associated with the voiced stops in Xhosa is more adequately classified as "slack voice" than "breathy voice". A similar case exists in Shanghai Chinese (Ren 1992). One reason for the occurence of slack voice in the voiced stops of Xhosa and Shanghai probably lies in a strong larynx lowering gesture, which has a primary effect of F0 lowering and a secondary one of additional vocal fold slackness (Stevens 1998: 466). With a high degree of vocal fold slackness there is probably some leakage of (mildly) turbulent airflow through the glottis (cf. Kingston 1985: 7), hence an increase in open quotient and H1-H2. This is addressed in more detail in Jessen and Roux (to appear), including a discussion of breathy voice in Hindi.

10. Closure duration

There are two opposite ways in which the duration of stop closure can act as a correlate of [tense]. Firstly, closure duration can be a durational correlate of [tense] that is independent of aspiration. Since [+tense] stops were defined as having longer duration components than [−tense] stops it is expected that closure duration in /p t k/ is longer than in /b d g/. This situation is usually found word-medially in English (Lisker 1986) or German (Jessen 1998), though often only if main stress occurs on the preceding syllable (Davis and van Summers 1989). As was mentioned earlier, gemination could be analyzed as the phonologization of long closure duration in [+tense] stops.

Secondly, closure duration can, metaphorically speaking, sacrifice its own potential as a durational correlate of [tense] for the enhance-ment of aspiration duration. That aspiration can be lengthened by shortening closure has been proposed in association with place-of-articulation differences in closure and aspiration (see Maddieson 1997) and in association with additional factors (see Kohler 1984). When comparing /k/ with /p/, aspiration is usually longer and closure shorter in the former than in the latter case (see Docherty 1992: 130–140 for discussion). If it is assumed that the duration of the glottal opening gesture and its coordination with respect to closure onset is roughly constant, shortening closure, as in /k/, has the effect that stop release occurs early in relation to the location of maximum glottal opening. This lengthens the time after release during which the glottis is open, leading to an increase in aspiration duration (Cooper 1991; Jessen 1999c for transillumination evidence). The reciprocal relation between closure and aspiration duration can also be relevant for the distinction between /b d g/ and /p t k/. Hutters (1985) reports that aspiration is particularly long in Danish compared to other languages. At the same time closure duration is quite short, to the effect that closure in /p t k/ is systematically shorter than in /b d g/ in Danish (see also Fischer-Jørgensen 1980). Danish would constitute a serious problem if one was to interpret long closure as a constant attribute of [+tense] stops (as discussed by Braun 1988: 99). Particularly long aspiration values (often above 100 ms) are also reported for the voiceless aspirated stops of Hindi (Kagaya and Hirose 1975 and in particular Benguerel and Bhatia 1980), Mandarin Chinese (Iwata and Hirose 1976 on Speaker A), as well as the (voiceless) aspirated stops and clicks of the Nguni languages Swati (Kockaert and Godwin 1997) and (for several speakers of) Xhosa (Jessen 1999a, incl. further references). In these languages the (voiceless) aspirated category is also the one with usually the shortest closure durations, which is the same pattern as in Danish. (In Hindi, even *voiced* aspirated stops have shorter closure duration than voiced unaspirated stops; this is also shown for Owerri Igbo by Ladefoged and Maddieson, 1996: 62.). It is quite possible that longer closure in /b d g/ than /p t k/ is found frequently in those languages in which /b d g/ are systematically or predominantly voiceless. In addition to Danish, this is the case also in Swati, Xhosa, and Mandarin. Lack of voicing in /b d g/ firstly puts a higher burden on aspiration duration in distinguishing /p t k/ from /b d g/ and secondly frees /b d g/ from the pressure of maintaining short closure for the sake of maintaining voicing during closure (to be discussed now).

If dealing with a language in which /b d g/ are systematically voiced and /p t k/ voiceless unaspirated, i.e. a language with [voice], closure duration is not ambiguous. In this case closure in voiced stops is shorter than in voiceless stops (see Laeufer 1992 for French; Alghamdi 1990: 110–114 for Arabic; Tsuchida 1997: 111–119 for Japanese). This pattern can also be observed in the 4-way system of Hindi, where voiced stops (both aspirated and unaspirated) have shorter closure than their corresponding voiceless stops (Kagaya and

Hirose 1975; Benguerel and Bhatia 1980). That closure duration should be shorter in voiced than voiceless stops makes sense when taking into account the well-known constraints of voice production in obstruents. Together with cavity enlargement and other maneuvers, mentioned earlier, keeping closure short is another way of preventing the reduction of a transglottal pressure drop, which would lead to the cessation of voicing during closure. From a perceptual point of view, any reduction of closure duration leads to an increase of the percentage of voicing during closure. As reviewed by Kingston and Diehl (1995), there are general auditory interactions between the perception of "pulsing duration" (corresponding to voicing duration) and "gap duration" (corresponding to closure duration).

11. Preceding vowel duration

It has been observed that there is the tendency for an inverse relation of closure duration and the duration of the preceding vowel; where the former tends to be relatively long the latter tends to be relatively short, and vice versa (Port and Dalby 1982; Kohler 1984, incl. previous literature). According to this pattern preceding vowel duration as a correlate of [tense] would inherit the ambiguity of closure duration mentioned earlier, and in fact this seems to be the case. In word-medial post-stress position closure duration in /p t k/ is longer than in /b d g/ in English and German; this is also a context in which vowel duration is systematically longer before /b d g/ than /p t k/ (Davis and van Summers 1989; Jessen 1998: 62–64 for review). Word-medially before stress, on the other hand, closure duration shows no systematic effects in English, neither does preceding vowel duration (Davis and van Summers 1989). Consider also those languages where closure duration is systematically shorter in /p t k/ than in /b d g/ for the sake of enhancing aspiration duration. In Hindi both voicing and aspiration lead to a reduction of closure duration relative to the voiceless and unaspirated cognates (Kagaya and Hirose 1975; Benguerel and Bhatia 1980). Consistently with the expected inverse relation of closure and preceding vowel duration, both voicing and aspiration increase the duration of the preceding vowel (Maddieson and Gandour 1977).[12]

To the extent that preceding vowel duration depends on closure duration the value of preceding vowel duration as a correlate of [tense] can be fairly indirect. While for example short closure in /p t k/ is a way of enhancing aspiration duration, which is the basic correlate of [tense], long preceding vowel duration in this case has no direct connection to aspiration, only an indirect one mediated by closure duration. More interesting is the case where closure is longer in /p t k/ than /b d g/ as a [+tense] correlate. In that case short preceding vowel duration enhances long closure duration by providing an inverse background. Such a figure-ground relation probably sharpens the cue value of closure duration on the perceptual level (Kluender, Diehl, and Wright 1988; but cf. Fowler 1992). As suggested by Port and Dalby (1982) the inverse relation of closure duration and preceding vowel duration also is a means of keeping the cue value of closure duration despite the variability induced by variations of prosody and speech rate that influence the temporal organization of an utterance.

A particularly salient case of shorter vowel duration before /p t k/ than /b d g/ is found word-finally in English. It appears that this difference in English is more salient than can be explained by the inverse pattern with closure duration alone (Luce and Charles Luce 1985). Instead it seems that along with tonal depression and gemination this is another case where a non-basic correlate has phonologized, except that this case of phonologization is limited to a specific context (cf. Laeufer 1992 for a different interpretation). According to de Jong (1991), reduced vowel duration before word-final /p t k/ compared to /b d g/ in English is achieved primarily by increasing the speed of the closing gesture and secondarily by beginning this closing gesture relatively early.[13]

That preceding vowel duration is also a correlate of [voice] is shown in languages with a pure voiced/voiceless system. Data from Russian (Chen 1970), Arabic (Alghamdi 1990: 87–90), and Japanese (Tsuchida 1997: 111–119) show that in these languages vowels before voiced stops are longer than vowels before voiceless stops. Chomsky and Halle (1968: 301) explain longer vowel duration before voiced stops by the additional time it takes to shift from the "spontaneous" voicing pattern of sonorants to the more challenging voicing mode in obstruents. Referring to Halle and Stevens (1967) they point out that obstruent voicing has a longer open phase of the glottal cycle than sonorant voicing. That this is the case has been confirmed in more recent experimental work (Gobl, Ní Chasaide, and Monahan 1995; Koreman 1996: 128–132). Chomsky and Halle claim that this increased open phase enhances voice production in obstruents. However, a longer glottal opening phase in voice production also leads to an increase in transglottal air flow, which threatens closure voicing, since it creates an early buildup of intraoral air pressure (Kingston 1985: 7). It is more likely that the different voicing modes in obstruents and sonorants are a passive effect of the presence vs. absence of oral constriction on vocal fold vibration, rather than something that is controlled actively (Bickley and Stevens 1987). If this is the case there is no sense in which the glottal vibration patterns in obstruents need to be actively prepared during the preceding vowel (cf. Chen 1970; Lisker 1974 for further discussion and criticism of different explanations for the vowel duration difference). It seems most plausible instead that the reason why vowels are longer before voiced than voiceless stops lies in the interaction with the shortness of the following closure and the mentioned perceptual figure-ground effect. Hence, the basic explanation for differences in preceding vowel duration seems to be the same no matter whether long preceding vowel duration is a correlate of [–tense] or of [+voice].[14]

12. Following vowel duration

It has been observed for English that /p t k/ causes decreased duration values as compared to /b d g/ not only in the preceding vowel but also in the following vowel (Allen and Miller 1999, incl. further references). Trying again to isolate the influence of aspiration from that of voicing it turns out that this effect is found both in pure voiced/voiceless distinctions, such as in French (Fischer-Jørgensen 1968) and Arabic (Alghamdi 1990: 133–141) and in typical aspirated/unaspirated distinctions such as in Danish (Fischer-Jørgensen 1968, 1980). (However in Mandarin, according to Iwata and Hirose 1976, following vowel duration differs only slightly and counter to expectation in their native subject.)

An explanation for this effect is most straightforward with respect to the influence of aspiration. Since aspiration of /p t k/ is largely superimposed on the temporal interval during which voiced vowel formant transitions would be visible in corresponding /b d g/, it is expected that vowels after aspirated /p t k/ are shorter than after /b d g/ roughly by the amount of time occupied by the transitions. Or to put it differently, one might expect that the amount of time occupied by the aspiration phase is taken away fully from the duration of the following vowel (voiced formant transitions are usually assumed to be part of the vowel, but aspiration part of the preceding stop). However, this is not the case; the time interval by which the following vowel is reduced in aspirated stops is much less than the duration of aspiration (see Allen and Miller 1999 for illustration). Hence, aspiration makes its own temporal contribution to the utterance and only takes away a small part of the following vowel. (This in itself is a good argument for the feature [tense], its definition in terms of duration, and the prominent role of aspiration as a correlate of that feature). But the remaining small vowel duration difference can quite plausibly be attributed directly to the influence of aspiration. Since aspiration duration is the basic correlate of [tense] the duration of the following vowel can clearly be identified as a correlate of this feature. Reduced vowel duration after aspirated stops can also be understood as a means of making aspiration duration perceptually more salient by letting it appear longer relative to the following vowel context.

It is more difficult to understand why following vowel duration should also be a correlate of [voice]. It was mentioned in section 8 that even in pure voiced/voiceless systems positive VOT is longer in the voiceless than the voiced stops, though the magnitude of this effect is much smaller than in aspirated/unaspirated distinctions. As with the explanation offerered for the vowel-shortening effect of aspiration, the burst interval of voiceless stops could take away time from the following vowel, thereby making the vowel shorter than after voiced stops, where the burst is shorter.

In addition to these explanations, that are based on the idea that the duration of the burst or aspiration phase takes away part of the duration of the following vowel, it is also possible to use the same explanation as for the duration of the preceding vowel. Like with preceding vowel duration, variation in the duration of the following vowel could be analyzed as a means of enhancing the closure duration correlate of [tense] and [voice]. (Though in aspirated stops this effect is weak at best since aspiration intervenes between closure and the following vowel.)

13. Reduced contextual stability and perceptual saliency in non-basic correlates

Based on high contextual stability and perceptual saliency, closure voicing was analyzed as the basic correlate of [voice] and aspiration duration as the basic correlate of [tense]. It remains to be determined in which sense and to what extent the shared non-basic correlates of [voice] and [tense] are contextually less stable and perceptually less salient. Starting with the former criterion the case is rather clear for closure duration and preceding vowel duration. If the relevant stop occurs utterance-initially these parameters are not defined. Yet closure voicing and aspiration duration can be measured very well, as shown by Lisker and Abramson (1964). Word-initially within an utterance closure duration is defined, but it is doubtful whether the duration of any existing preceding vowel across the word boundary is relevant. These examples indicate that contextual stability is in the order aspiration dur./voicing > closure dur. > preceding vowel dur. For the remaining non-basic correlates contextual stability seems to be high, since in most cases the relevant stop is followed by a vowel. However, the stops can also occur finally and in consonant clusters. And one should also keep in mind that prosodic, vowel-inherent, and other factors can pose further challenges to contextual stability, which are not found or are less striking with closure voicing and aspiration duration. For example, the cue value of F1 onset can be limited if the following vowel is /i/ or /u/; in that case F1 is low and there will be only a limited frequency range for the expression of stop-induced F1 differences. An analogous situation occurs in intonational contexts where F0 is very high or very low; again it might be difficult to express stop-induced F0 differences. The cue value of preceding or following vowel duration might be reduced if the vowel is very short to begin with for either vowel-inherent or prosodic reasons. Similar effects are expected to occcur with H1-H2, which among other variables is influenced by prosodic factors (Pierrehumbert and Talkin 1992).

Turning to perceptual saliency, it has been shown that the basic correlates lead to full categorical perception. The perceptual value of the non-basic correlates is often limited to their potential of shifting the perceptual boundary in a continuum of the basic correlates. For example, if two aspiration duration continua are synthesized, one in which F1 onset is appropriate for /p t k/ and one in which it is appropriate for /b d g/, categorical perception is achieved with both aspiration duration continua, the only difference being that the 50% crossover point from 100% perceived /b d g/ to zero percent /b d g/ is shifted towards longer aspiration values if F1 is low than if it is high (cf. Kluender 1991). The same kind of trading relation was also observed with aspiration duration and F0 onset (Haggard, Summerfield, and Roberts 1981; Abramson and Lisker 1985; Diehl and Molis 1995) and with aspiration duration and H1-H2 in English (Chapin Ringo 1988). In all these cases aspiration duration has more perceptual saliency than F1 onset, F0 onset, or H1-H2. This becomes clear if one were to reverse the situation by creating a full F0, F1, or H1-H2 continuum, trying to limit aspiration to the role of the factor that shifts the crossover point. The result would probably be that a synthetic stop with a long aspiration value appropriate for /p t k/ is predominantly perceived as /p t k/ even if F1 onset, F0 onset, or H1-H2 are appropriate for /b d g/. Or to put it differently, F0, F1, or H1-H2 manipulations do not lead to categorical perception if aspiration duration is not sufficiently ambiguous to "permit" it (see Abramson and Lisker 1985).

As far as closure duration and preceding vowel duration is concerned it seems at first as if they behave differently than F1, F0, and H1-H2, since they have been shown to lead to full categorical perception (often with both closure and vowel duration varied together). But here one has to carefully examine the fate of the basic correlates. Kohler (1979), for example, shows that the interaction between closure and preceding vowel duration leads to categorical perception if in German pairs like *leiden* 'suffer' vs. *leiten* 'lead' no aspiration difference occurs (this happens when both stops are released directly into the syllabic realization of the following nasal). But Kohler emphasizes that as soon as an aspiration difference occurs (when schwa appears between stop and nasal) aspiration immediately assumes the role of the most powerful cue to the tense/lax distinction. Cases like this (see also footnote 13) seem to indicate that the non-basic correlates closure and preceding vowel duration can unfold their potential for categorical perception only if the basic correlates are ambiguous or unavailable. Also notice, again, that both closure duration and F0 can phonologize, in which case the basic correlates are gone and categorical perception rests exclusively on the non-basic correlates.

14. The common phonetic denominator of [tense] and [voice]

It was suggested that the correlates of a feature should have something in common phonetically. Rather than making a list of unconnected feature correlates it is important to provide phonetic arguments for why certain properties and not others act as correlates of a particular feature.

For [tense] it was claimed that duration is the common denominator, the feature value [+tense] being implemented with relatively longer duration than [−tense]. This is very clear in the case of aspiration duration. Also closure duration can implement [tense] directly, which happens in those cases where it is longer in /p t k/ than /b d g/. This includes the case where closure duration has phonologized into a phonemic geminate/simplex distinction (also included are geminate/simplex distinctions in fricatives and sonorants, and length distinctions in vowels). Where instead short closure duration enhances long aspiration duration the role of closure duration as a correlate of [tense] is indirect, since in that case it is promoting the aspiration duration correlate of [tense], rather than acting as an independent correlate of this feature. A similar situation occurs with preceding and following vowel duration, which is usually shorter for [+tense] stops than [–tense] stops. These are durational modifications of the context that enhance the perception of the duration of the stop and its components. The status of F0 onset, F1 onset, and H1-H2 as correlates of [tense] is different from that of the other correlates since they are not defined in durational terms. Their connection with [tense] is through the basic aspiration duration correlate of this feature. As has been shown in detail in the preceding sections, high F0 onset, F1 onset, and H1-H2 are all the consequence of aspiration. The duration of the following vowel is also a correlate that is primarily caused by aspiration, specifically its temporal aspect, and it might make aspiration perceptually more salient.

For [voice] we can identify Kingston and Diehl's (1994, 1995) "low frequency property" as the common denominator. The basic correlate closure voicing, as well as the non-basic correlates low F0 onset, low F1 onset and high H1-H2, are all manifestations of low-frequency dominance in the spectrum (however, we saw that the status of H1-H2 is ambiguous). The situation is more difficult for the non-basic correlates that are defined in durational terms. Their value as correlates of [voice] is of a more indirect kind. Short closure enhances the production and perception of full closure voicing, i.e. it assists in the optimal functioning of the basic correlate of [voice]. Preceding and following vowel duration, in turn, enhance the closure duration correlate.

15. Summary

With a focus on the acoustic/auditory aspect of speech communication and on the production and perception of phonemic distinctions (distinctive function) this paper has explored the phonetic implementation of the features [voice] and [tense]. While the first of these features is adopted by many phonologists (though with often very different definition and coverage), the latter has been met with much skepticism in the past. Thus, one purpose of this paper has been to reintroduce the feature [tense] and to put it back on the market of currently discussed features. In reaction to implicit or explicit opinions in the literature that [tense] should not be used because it is phonetically vague and abstract, it has been shown here that [tense] is no less phonetically motivated than the more widely accepted feature [voice]. The second purpose of this paper was to propose a new model of feature implementation in which basic feature correlates, which are unique to a feature, are distinguished from non-basic correlates, which are shared by different features – often in a complementary manner (e.g. high F0 onset implementing the positive specification of [tense] but the negative specification of [voice]). The notions of contextual stability and perceptual saliency were discussed as important criteria for evaluating the status and functional importance of different feature correlates and for helping to provide an answer to the question of whether the two-way stop distinction in a particular language is more appropriately analyzed with [voice] or with [tense]. The non-basic correlates support the basic feature correlates and can even replace them in contexts and situations where the basic correlates are unavailable. In the extreme case this can lead to the phonologization of non-basic correlates; tonal depression like in Xhosa and gemination like in Swiss German are examples of the phonologization of the non-basic correlates F0 onset and closure duration, respectively. It was emphasized that the set of correlates of a feature should be grouped together with phonetic criteria, i.e. that there should be a common phonetic denominator.

16. Future research: The status of [checked]

Among the different ways in which the present proposal could be extended in future research particular emphasis should be given to an analysis of the feature [checked]. The Jakobsonian set of features [tense], [voice], and [checked] corresponds closely to the set of "laryngeal features" [spread]/[asp], [voice]/[slack], and [constricted] in feature geometric models (see Lombardi 1991). It would be important to work out the similarities and differences between the articulatory-based laryngeal features and the three most closely corresponding auditory features. In this section some suggestions shall be made about how the phonetic implementation of [checked] might look like.

Jakobson and Halle (1968: 430) define checked as opposed to unchecked sounds as showing "higher rate of discharge of energy within a reduced interval of time (vs. lower rate of discharge within a longer interval), with a lower (vs. higher) damping." They also say that "checked phonemes are implemented in three different ways – as ejective (glottalized) consonants, as implosives or clicks" (see also Jakobson 1968). This definition of [+checked] applies most straight-forwardly to the loud and salient bursts that can usually be observed in ejectives and in clicks. In terms of the model of feature represen-tation presented in Figure 1, burst amplitude can be classified as the basic correlate of [checked].

In addition to (or occasionally instead of) a loud burst ejectives can have a relatively long portion of silence or near-silence after the burst, which is quantifiable as long positive VOT (Jessen 1999a for data and further literature). Since ejectives are also voiceless and thus preceded by voiceless closure, the preceding and following silence provides the ideal background for the perception of the burst.

In clicks we need to consider that in the case of the "affricated" or "noisy" types (see Ladefoged and Maddieson 1996: Chapter 8) the burst is not short and thus does not literally fit the reduced interval of time criterion. It is perhaps promising to concentrate on the high amplitude of the burst as the correlate of [+checked] and be less explicit about its duration and amplitude rise/fall time. Auditorily there is a trade off. Short duration and a fast on- and offset of the burst lead to a sharper auditory response (see Silverman 1997: 40–42), but if too short the burst cannot be optimally processed, given the limited temporal resolution of the auditory system. Long duration of a burst, on the other hand, will clearly be above the auditory threshold and it would permit the perceptual integration of length and amplitude (cf. Turk and Sawusch 1996), but long duration also reduces the auditory sharpness of the signal, due to habituation.

In contrast to ejectives and clicks, implosives have no salient bursts at all. In Xhosa it was found that compared to all other stop types implosives usually had the weakest bursts (Jessen 1999a). Part of this is due to the fact that the implosives are usually voiced – if not always fully then at least towards the end of closure. Voiced stops have low intraoral air pressure, which keeps burst amplitude low as well. Furthermore, larynx lowering in implosives leads to low and even sometimes negative intraoral air pressure. Due to their weak bursts, the feature [+checked] cannot be implemented with its burst amplitude correlate in the case of implosives. But two other observations concerning the Xhosa data suggest an alternative. Firstly, positive VOT was shorter in the implosives than in the other stop series and often approached zero (Jessen 1999a). Secondly, examination of spectrograms revealed that the onset of the vowel after implosives was quite abrupt throughout the frequency range. This observation is confirmed by the finding that implosives had the tendency for relatively low H1-H2 values at vowel onset (Jessen and Roux to appear). This corresponds to Jakobson and Halle's "low damping" criterion (cf. Ladefoged, Maddieson, and Jackson 1988). This spectral sharpness of vowel onset is enhanced by the short or absent distance between burst and voice onset, so that effectively and auditorily the burst constitutes the left boundary of the vowel. This sharpened vowel onset can be covered by Jakobson and Halle's notion of high energy discharge within a short time span. In contrast to ejectives and clicks, implosives show a quick rise, but no equivalent fall in amplitude.

The same kind of situation occurs in the Korean fortis stops. Like implosives, these are produced with short VOT, very low amplitude rise time (i.e. a high degree of abruptness) into the following vowel, and a tendency for low H1-H2 at vowel onset (Han and Weitzman 1970; Jun 1998; cf. also Lee 1990). Thus, the Korean fortis stops are another candidate for the specification [+checked] (cf. Jessen 1998: Chapter 5, incl. more literature).

Taken together it seems that the feature [checked] can be analyzed within the same framework as the features [voice] and [tense]. Like the other features, [checked] has a unique basic correlate – burst amplitude. It also has non-basic correlates that are probably drawn from the same pool of correlates also employed by the other two features. One correlate that was discussed here is H1-H2. Amplitude rise time at vowel onset could be another of these shared non-basic correlates (cf. Fischer-Jørgensen 1968; Debrock 1977). In a more in-depth analysis it is necessary to investigate the connection of the remaining non-basic correlates in Figure 1 to the checked/non-checked distinction.

When considering [checked], a first look should also be taken at how this distinctive feature would interact with [voice] and [tense] in the expression of the possible relevant oppositions in languages. A preliminary proposal along these lines is presented in Table 1 (cf. Ladefoged 1973; Lombardi 1995).

Table 1. Auditory feature combinations for selected sound oppositions

	[tense]	[voice]	[checked]
1. plain stops	–	–	–
2. voiceless aspirated stops; voiceless geminate stops	+	–	–
3. voiced unaspirated stops; voiceless unaspirated stops with slack voice	–	+	–
4. ejectives; Korean fortis stops; voiceless implosives; plain clicks	–	–	+
5. voiced aspirated stops; voiced geminate stops	+	+	–
6. voiced implosives; voiced clicks	–	+	+
7. voiceless aspirated clicks	+	–	+
8. voiced aspirated clicks	+	+	+

In Table 1 the full range of combinations of the three features is exploited. If for any of the possible combinations in 1 to 8 more than one sound type occurs (separated by a semicolon) it is meant to imply that either these sound types cannot occur in opposition within the same language or that at least one further feature is needed to distinguish them. Although plus- and minus values are used, the proposal is also compatible with the privative feature interpretation of Lombardi (1995) (however, in Jessen 1996 it is shown that [tense] behaves in a binary fashion when applied to vowels). Plus-specifications are the marked value of an opposition, minus-specifications the unmarked value.

Some of the feature choices in Table 1 are similar to those in Lombardi (1995) if [asp] is substituted for [tense] and [constricted] for [checked], and these choices require little explanation. But others are different, due to deviations in scope of [tense] and [checked] from [asp] (or [spread]) and [constricted], respectively. Table 1 omits some details mentioned in Lombardi (1995) and mainly concentrates on those aspects that crucially distinguish her (primarily) articulatory feature system from the present auditory one. Hence, the content in Table 1 is only a sketch of a more comprehensive proposal.

Rows 2 and 5 express the claim that aspirated stops and geminates of the same voicing status cannot contrast within the same language. Further discussion of that position is provided in Jessen (1998). Gemination was discussed in this paper as a way of phonologizing closure duration as a correlate of [tense].

Row 3 groups together voiced stops and voiceless unaspirated stops with slack voice. The latter category is found in Shanghai Chinese and Xhosa. Tonal depression (low F0 onset) together with slack voice (realized with increased H1-H2) in these languages can be understood as the phonologization of non-basic low frequency properties as correlates of [voice].

Row 4 groups both ejectives and the fortis stops in Korean into one feature combination. As discussed earlier in this section, the ejectives are the more prototypical instantiation of checked stops since they use the basic burst amplitude correlate. The rare voiceless implosives are also listed here. Consider the case of Lendu, which has an opposition between voiced and voiceless implosives (Demolin 1995). Since Lendu does not have ejectives it is conceivable that the voiceless implosives of that language receive the same feature combination as the ejectives of other languages. This view is also expressed, with illustration from Igbo, by Ladefoged (1973).

Following Jakobson, clicks are also analyzed as [+checked]. If ejectives and plain clicks have the same combination of the three features used here, they must be distinguished by a fourth one because, clearly, there are languages in which ejectives and clicks occur in opposition. This additional feature might come from the domain of the place features. Traill (1995) uses Jakobsonian place features such as [grave] and [compact] in the representation of clicks, which is compatible with the auditory feature account presented in this paper. One case explored in Jessen (1999b) is the contrast between the alveolar click [!] and the velar ejective [k'] found in Xhosa. Both are specified with the same combination of auditory place features [+grave, +compact]. But it is reported in Jessen that there is a strong tendency for [!] to have lower spectral energy distribution and auditory tonality than [k'], so that the Jakobsonian tonality feature [flat] was proposed to represent the difference. Two other reported cases of oppositions between auditorily similar clicks and ejectives are lateral click vs. lateral ejective affricate, occurring in Hadza (Sands, Maddieson, and Ladefoged 1993) and Sandawe (Wright et al. 1995), and dental click vs. dental/alveolar ejective affricate, occurring in quite a number of Khoisan languages (see, e.g. Traill 1985; Vossen 1986). Here the question is whether the speakers of these languages themselves manage to keep the distinction, given the auditory similarity of these contrasts. For the latter one, Traill and Vossen (1997) mention cases of click loss, whereby the dental click was replaced by the dental ejective affricate.

In row 6 implosives and voiced clicks receive the same feature representation. There is clear evidence that these sound classes either do not cooccur at all within the same language or that if they do another feature is available to keep them apart representationally. Khoisan languages, as reported among others by Beach (1938) on Nama and Korana, Snyman (1980) on Zhulhõasi and another !Xũ dialect, Traill (1985) on !Xóõ, and Vossen (1986) on //Ani, have no implosives. This also holds for Hadza (Sands, Maddieson, and Ladefoged 1993) and Sandawe (Wright et al. 1995), where language classification is less clear. For all among these languages that have voiced clicks (which is not the case in Nama/Korana and Sandawe) the voiced clicks are without ambiguity specified [+voice, +checked, –tense], due to the lack of implosives. Dahalo, a Cushitic language, has two implosives and a few clicks, but no voiced ones (Maddieson et al. 1993), so again no ambiguities arise. In the Southern Bantu languages, according to Doke (1954: 36), two language groups have implosives but no clicks (Chopi, Shona), two have clicks but no implosives (Sotho, Tsonga) and only one has both (Nguni). The only implosive found in Nguni (including Xhosa, discussed earlier) is the bilabial one. Voiced clicks do occur, but bilabial clicks are systematically excluded. Since, as proposed by Jakobson (1968) for Zulu, the implosive is labial and the voiced clicks are non-labial the distinction between the two can be represented with a place feature.

Row 7 classifies aspirated clicks as tense and checked. Such a feature combination has no correspondence at all in the feature system of Lombardi (1995). There the combination *[+asp, +constricted] is in principle ruled out because that combination would denote glottal spreading and constriction at the same time (in analogy to the impossible combination *[+high, +low] in vowels). But in the auditory feature system used here, tenseness and checkedness constitute independent dimensions and can be combined. What is subject to controversy, however, about the classification in row 7 is the underlying assumption that aspirated stops are phonologically monosegmental, rather than consisting of a click segment and another segment that constitutes the aspiration accompaniment. Given the richness of possible click accompaniments in Khoisan languages (see Ladefoged and Traill 1994) a phonological analysis can hardly work without assuming that at least some combinations of clicks and their accompaniments are more than monosegmental (discussed in detail by Traill 1985: Chapter 5). That also holds for the present feature analysis when taking into account that some clicks have ejective accompaniments (Ladefoged and Traill 1994). In a monosegmental analysis it would be hard to accommodate two specifications for checkedness in sequence within the same segment – one for the click and one for its ejective accompaniment. (Jakobson 1968 attempted a fully monosegmental account for Korana, but he was not confronted with all the range of possibilities in Khoisan languages, reported later in work such as Traill 1985.) But if bisegmental analyses with some clicks are necessary why should aspirated clicks be monosegmental? As a phonetic argument it can be pointed out that in Xhosa the principle of reducing closure in order to increase aspiration holds not only for aspirated stops (where monosegmental status is not controversial) but also for aspirated clicks in a completely parallel fashion (Jessen 1999a). But more research is necessary. Among other things, it should be explored whether concepts of nonlinear phonology, such as two-root structures, branching below the root node and so forth can resolve the issues addressed here and, more generally, to what extent feature geometry can and should also be used with auditory features.[15]

Row 8 represents voiced aspirated clicks. These only occur in a small subset of click languages. They are reported in Zhulhõasi (Snyman 1980) and !Xóõ (Traill 1985) (see also Ladefoged and Traill 1994, Table VIII for the category "voiced velar plosive followed by aspiration"). If plus-values in Table 1 represent markedness it is expected that the treble marking in row 8 represents a sound type that is very rare among the world's languages. In general, Table 1 provides a fairly accurate model of the cross-linguistic frequencies of the sound classes addressed there (cf. Maddieson 1984). Clearly, the fully unmarked plain stops in row 1 are the most frequent stop type. Stops with one mark (rows 2 to 4) are less common but still widespread (more precisely, this holds at least for one of the stops per row). This is clear for voiced and aspirated stops, but is also the case for ejectives, which "are not at all unusual sounds, occurring in about 18 percent of the languages of the world" (Ladefoged and Maddieson 1996: 78). The stops with two marks (rows 5 to 7) are less frequent and have some areal concentration, and, again, the ones in row 8 with three marks are very uncommon and have a strong areal focus.

Having demonstrated that the set of features [tense], [voice], and [checked], might be sufficient to represent all the relevant oppositions in languages, this paper shall end by emphasizing again the auditory perspective of feature theory. The feature [tense] was defined in terms of duration, [voice] in terms of frequency ("low frequency property"), and [checked] in terms of amplitude. With this distribution of correlates all the three major acoustic and auditory dimensions are employed. This means that the entire auditory space is utilized and that the three features [tense], [voice], and [checked] show maximal auditory dispersion within this space. This maximal dispersion makes sense when considering that, depending on the language, the listener might be confronted with the task of keeping apart sounds specified for two or perhaps all three of these features.

Notes

* A previous and slightly expanded version of this paper was presented in the Stuttgart phonetics working papers AIMS (Arbeitsberichte des Instituts für Maschinelle Sprachverarbeitung) Vol. 6, No. 2. Thanks for comments to Greg Dogil and members from the phonetics group in Stuttgart, and to Mirjam Ernestus. I also appreciate the comments of two anonymous reviewers on the first version of this paper. My phonetic research on Xhosa and my study of the literature on clicks and related topics at University of Stellenbosch during the 1998/99 academic year has made it possible to reexamine some of the crucial issues addressed in this paper, allowing me to improve my proposal in Jessen (1998). For that opportunity financial support from the Alexander-von-Humboldt Foundation and from the Research Unit for Experimental Phonology at University of Stellenbosch (Director: Justus C. Roux) is gratefully acknowledged.

1 That aspiration is understood as a correlate of [tense] in the writings of Jakobson and colleagues is mentioned in Jakobson and Waugh (1987:140), but is otherwise more apparent from the application of the feature [tense] than from its definition. For its application see, for example, Jakobson (1968), where the aspirated stops and clicks of Zulu are analyzed as [+tense] (see also the connection drawn in that paper between the feature [tense] and Trubetzkoy's aspirated-unaspirated distinction). There is also the remark in Jakobson, Fant, and Halle (1952: 38) that if a language uses both [voice] and [tense], the latter is implemented with aspiration. For its definition there are some uncertainties in Jakobson, Fant, and Halle (1952) and Jakobson and Halle (1968). In the statement by Jakobson, Fant, and Halle (1952: 36) that tense stops are produced with greater "strength of the explosion" than lax stops it is not clear whether they actually mean aspiration or rather the transient and frication phase of the stop without its aspiration phase; and if they mean aspiration it is not clear whether they find the amplitude characteristics of aspiration more important than its durational characteristics. In Jakobson and Halle (1968: 431) it is unclear whether they want to capture aspiration with their phrase "heightened air pressure", although from Jakobson (1968) it becomes apparent that they do. But firstly, the term is rather vague, since it does not say whether subglottal or supraglottal air pressure is meant, and secondly, there is less than convincing empirical support for a connection between aspiration and increased sub- or supraglottal air pressure; supraglottal air *flow* is much more appropriate (see Dixit and Brown 1978; Dixit and Shipp 1985; Dixit and Brown 1985). According to Dixit and Shipp (1985) the connection between subglottal air pressure and aspiration actually seems to be the opposite from what might be expected; it tends to be lower rather than higher in aspirated stops. This is problematic also for Chomsky and Halle's (1968) feature [heightened subglottal pressure].

2   The features [spread] and [asp] both refer to aspiration but they differ in their
    location on the articulation-to-audition continuum. The feature [spread] is arti-
    culatory and refers to a glottal opening gesture, which is found in aspirated
    stops (see Dixit 1989). Its classification as a "laryngeal feature" is phonetically
    motivated, since glottal opening is an entirely laryngeal phenomenon. The
    feature [asp] is more to the acoustic/auditory end of the continuum. In articu-
    latory terms it is not unitary, since in addition to a glottal opening gesture stop
    aspiration also requires certain configurations of oral-laryngeal coordination
    (see Löfqvist and Yoshioka 1981). It is, for example, possible to increase
    aspiration by reducing closure duration (this will be addressed again later).
    Since not only laryngeal but also supralaryngeal activity is involved, classi-
    fication of [asp] as laryngeal feature might be motivated by phonological
    arguments (see Lombardi 1991), but it is not entirely correct on phonetic
    grounds.

3   Contrary to Jessen (1998: 270), *burst amplitude* is no longer included as a
    correlate of [tense] or [voice] in Figure 1. Aerodynamic factors favor a small
    burst amplitude in voiced stops and a large one in aspirated stops (see Jessen
    1998: 262f., 271). Empirical support for higher burst amplitude in aspirated
    than unaspirated stops does in fact exist, but with much overlap (see Wu and
    Xu 1987; Khachatryan and Airapetyan 1987; Braun 1988:156-158). In a
    voiced/voiceless system like in French it is difficult methodologically to
    separate burst amplitude from voicing amplitude (Fischer-Jørgensen 1968). Slis
    & Cohen (1969) do report higher burst amplitude in voiceless than voiced stops
    in Dutch but are not specific as to how this measurement problem was
    addressed. Rather inconclusive results on burst amplitude in /b d g/ vs. /p t k/,
    with at most a slight tendency for higher values in the latter set, are also
    reported for English by Zue (1976: 64, 68) and Edwards (1981: 541), where
    however the influence of voicing and aspiration might be confounded (see also
    Braun 1988: 81-83 for further discussion of and literature on burst amplitude).
    In the final section of this paper burst amplitude will instead be interpreted as
    the basic correlate of [checked], based on the hypothesis that this correlate
    plays a much more important role in the expression of clicks and ejectives than
    in the expression of voicelessness and aspiration.

    As a second difference to Jessen (1998), the duration of the following
    vowel is introduced here as a new correlate of [tense] and [voice]. Thirdly,
    breathy phonation will be replaced by the more general correlate H1-H2. Next,
    the polarity of closure duration with respect to [tense] is left open; as will be
    explained later, tense stops can have either longer or shorter closure than lax
    stops. Ambiguous correlate values are also proposed for preceding vowel
    duration as a correlate of [tense] and H1-H2 as a correlate of [voice]. Finally,
    the distinction between "substitute correlates" and "concomitant correlates",
    proposed in Jessen (1998), is eliminated here.

4   The association between contextual stability and perceptual saliency that is
assumed here is also apparent in the contributions to feature theory by Kenneth
Stevens and Sheila Blumstein in a number of papers (see Stevens and Blumstein 1981 for overview). One goal of Stevens and Blumstein is to find acoustic
properties of phonemic distinctions that are both invariant (i.e. which have
maximal contextual stability) and also high in perceptual saliency, evidenced,
among other things, through categorical perception.

5   In this paper features are mentioned without plus- or minus specification if they
are addressed in general terms and with such a specification if a particular
feature value is addressed. Thus, notationally features are treated as binary
here. The question of whether [tense] and [voice] are binary or privative will
not be addressed here (see Jessen 1996 for some discussion).

6   Still, there can be different degrees of the contextual stability of aspiration
compared to voicing. With respect to the Germanic languages mentioned here,
the situation is most straightforward in Danish and Icelandic, where voicing in
/b d g/ is not an option and the contrast between /b d g/ and /p t k/ is one of
aspiration, including in some cases preaspiration (Pétursson 1976; Hutters
1985). (This excludes cases of lenition in Danish, where the opposition is no
longer confined to stop production; cf. Jakobson, Fant, and Halle 1952: 5–6.)
In German voicing in /b d g/ is an option, and is frequently found in intervocalic position. But, as mentioned earlier, voicing in /b d g/ is clearly
outnumbered by aspiration /p t k/ in terms of the contexts in which /b d g/ vs. /p
t k/ is possible. The most important contributing factor to this situation comes
from the fact that aspiration in a stressless syllable with schwa in the nucleus is
possible in German (Jessen 1998: Chapters 2, 3). This is different in English
(esp. American), where /p t k/ in stressless syllables are mostly unaspirated
(see, however, cases like *butter* produced with aspiration by many British
English speakers). But even small degrees of prominence, such as in *rapid* can
lead to aspiration (in this case of /p/), and therefore an aspiration-based
difference (Lisker 1986; Davis and van Summers 1989; cf. also Iverson and
Salmons 1995). Like in German, /b d g/ are very often voiceless in utterance-
initial and post-voiceless position (Docherty 1992: 121–122). Word-finally in
English neither voicing nor aspiration seem to be particularly reliable in their
occurrence and the duration of the preceding vowel is the most important
carrier of the distinction (see Docherty 1992: 120). So overall it is likely that
the contextual stability of an aspiration-based distinction is higher than that of a
voicing-based distinction in English.

7   There are however some disadvantages with this way of capturing aspiration
and with the VOT measure more generally. Firstly, positive VOT is insensitive
as to which acoustic information occurs during the interval between release and
voicing onset. In aspirated stops this interval is filled with aspiration noise, but
in ejectives with long VOT there is essentially silence between release and

voicing onset. In languages where these two sounds contrast the presence or absence of aspiration is important information for the listener (see Cho and Ladefoged 1999, incl. further references). Secondly, vowel onset (e.g. beginning of F2) might be better motivated than voicing onset; perceptually the first glottal vibration(s) without voiced excitation of the upper formants might be difficult to perceive (Lisker and Abramson 1964: 416; Fischer- Jørgensen and Hutters 1981). Thirdly, aspiration in the voiced aspirated sounds of Hindi cannot be captured with VOT alone (Ladefoged et al. 1976; Keating 1990; Lombardi 1991; Davis 1994). In these cases, but maybe also in English, it is better to look for an acoustic event that captures the end of aspiration turbulence (this is also advocated by Künzel 1977: 43–46 and Braun 1988: 115 for German). Furthermore, VOT is not defined (at least not straightforwardly) in fricatives and sonorants with voiced/voiceless distinctions. Finally, VOT (including negative) VOT is defined well in utterance-initial context, but less so or not at all in other contexts. For example, in utterance-final position aspiration can only be measured with respect to the end of aspiration turbulence.

8 French is discussed here as a language that employs [voice]. (In Jessen 1998 the matter was left open.) Some authors have pointed out that the voiced stops and fricatives of French are occasionally devoiced and that therefore classification of French with a tense/lax feature is more appropriate than with a voiced/voiceless feature (Debrock 1977; Jakobson and Waugh 1987:141; see also Temple 1999 for devoicing of /b d g/ in French). The same point has been made for Spanish and Portuguese by Veloso (1995), although traditionally one would think of these languages as employing a clear voiced/voiceless distinction. These arguments crucially depend upon the lack of invariant closure voicing in the voiced obstruents of these languages. However, with the model presented in Figure 1, closure voicing in /b d g/, though expected in the majority of cases, might occasionally be replaced by other correlates of [voice]. That is, a language can still be analyzed with [voice] even if /b d g/ are not always realized with closure voicing. The point is to look for evidence that the speakers of a language with [voice] attempt active voicing in /b d g/, even if they do not always succeed. This is opposed to speakers of languages with [tense], where voicing in /b d g/ occurs only if it is "for free", such as in intervocalic position (Westbury and Keating 1986), and where inevitably the contextual stability of closure voicing will be much lower. Very important in this context is the finding that languages with [voice] usually use regressive voicing assimilation in obstruent clusters, specifically that speakers of these languages tend to express voiceless-voiced clusters as voiced-voiced (Iverson and Salmons 1995; Wissing and Roux 1995, van Rooy & Wissing this volume). As pointed out by Kohler (1984) and van Rooy (1999: 86–87) regressive voice assimilation in these cases can be understood as a strategy of expanding the duration of closure voicing of the second member of the cluster

and therefore enhancing its perception. It is also a way of simply eliminating the threat to closure voicing posed by a preceding voiceless sound. Of course this is done at the expense of the lexical voicing value of the first member of the cluster (i.e. voicing neutralization in syllable-final or, according to Lombardi 1991, non-syllable initial position).

9 The F1 onset correlate can also be understood as a reflection of different degrees of speed in the formation and release of stop closure (cf. Kohler 1984; de Jong 1991). Fast release would be reflected as fast F1 transition into the following vowel, causing relatively high F1 onset after release/aspiration. In this interpretation high F1 results from a production strategy with the goal of creating relatively long closure duration, which has its own potential as a correlate of [voice] and [tense] (section 10). In other words, making the transition into the following vowel fast leaves more time for stop closure, given an equal amount of time. (The same principle applies to fast transitions out of the preceding vowel into the stop.)

10 For Swedish Ní Chasaide and Gobl (1993) show an even stronger effect on the preceding vowel than on the following one, whereas the opposite was the case in German. The effects in Italian and French, to be discussed shortly, are also stronger on the preceding vowel. For this reason the question of where H1-H2 is measured, whether preceding or following the stops, is left unspecified in the naming of this feature correlate. With F1 and especially F0, on the other hand, it appears that the following vowel is more affected by the influence of the stop distinction than the preceding one, therefore the name "F0, F1 *onset*" for the feature correlates. But it should be kept in mind that even with F0 and F1 there can be an effect on the preceding vowel. For example, Kohler (1982) shows higher F0 before /p t k/ than /b d g/ in German and Kohler et al. (1981) show higher F1 before /p t k/ than /b d g/ in French. There is also evidence for higher F1 before word-final /p t k/ than /b d g/ in English (Walsh and Parker 1983).

11 Interestingly, Mei (2000) found as a tendency that the best correlations were obtained between glottal opening and (a normalized as well as an unnormalized version of) H1-A1 (A1 = amplitude of the first formant). For that result data from lax stops and from tense/voiceless and lax/voiced fricatives had been included as well. Exactly that association between H1-A1 and glottal opening is predicted by Sluijter et al. (1995).

12 It is probably reasonable to restrict measurements of preceding vowel duration to word-medial position and to avoid measurements across word-boundary (like for example measuring the duration of <ay> in *say bill* vs. *say pill*). For Danish, where many of the correlates of [tense] without the confounding influence of voicing are available through the work of Fischer-Jørgensen, this means that no opportunity for the measurement of preceding vowel duration arises, since /b d g/ are not realized as stops word-medially (see Jakobson, Fant,

and Halle 1952). In Chinese similar problems occur, due to phonotactic constraints.

13 This exaggerated vowel duration difference might be explained as follows. Final stops in English can be produced without release, in which case aspiration duration, the basic correlate of [tense], is not defined acoustically. If word-final position coincides with utterance-final position closure duration is not accessible either to the listener (again, given the case of unreleased stops). Perhaps because of this possibility that final stops are produced without release in English (often also with glottalization) and of the possibility that word-final position coincides with utterance-final position, preceding vowel duration is acoustically and perceptually most reliable even in cases of fully released and utterance-medial final stops, where closure and aspiration duration are defined. Consistent with these considerations, a negative correlation between release duration and the size of voicing-induced differences in preceding vowel duration has been observed for French by Laeufer (1992).

   In German the (word-medial) vowel duration effect is weaker than in English word-final position, but it is still stronger than explainable by variations in closure duration alone (Braunschweiler 1997). Braunschweiler claims that longer vowel duration before /b d g/ compared to /p t k/ in German is actively created by a phonological rule.

14 Despite all the confirming evidence there are also exceptions to the expected association between [voice] and preceding vowel duration. Keating (1985) did not find a significant vowel duration difference before voiced and voiceless stops in Polish. (She also mentions counterexamples from Czech and Arabic, both of which are [voice] languages; but cf. Alghamdi 1990, mentioned above.) But in Polish she did find the expected pattern that closure duration is significantly longer in the voiceless than voiced stops of a [voice] language. This shows again that the inverse relation between closure and preceding vowel duration is not more than a tendency and that these correlates are dissociable. It also suggests that closure duration is the more reliable cue to [voice] than preceding vowel duration. This makes sense when expecting that in the unmarked case the correlates of a feature associated with a phoneme are manifested within the temporal scope of that phoneme (or, more precisely, during that part of the phoneme where the temporal scopes of the correlates of its features show maximal overlap). The same might apply to preceding vowel duration in [tense] languages, but in the case of English word-final stops preceding vowel duration is more important than closure duration.

15 A bisegmental analysis is also indicated for the "voiced ejectives" of Zhulhõasi (as proposed by Ladefoged and Maddieson 1996: 80f.). In the feature system of Table 1 they would have to take the slot of the implosives if analyzed monosegmentally, which would be problematic in view of the fact that Zhulhõasi also has homorganic voiced clicks.

References

Abramson, Arthur S. and Leigh Lisker
  1973   Voice-timing perception in Spanish word-initial stops. *Journal of Phonetics* 1: 1–8.
  1985   Relative power of cues: F0 shift versus voice timing. In: Victoria A. Fromkin (ed.), *Phonetic Linguistics: Essays in Honour of Peter Ladefoged*, 25 33. Orlando, etc.: Academic Press.
Alghamdi, Mansour M. A.
  1990   Analysis, synthesis and perception of voicing in Arabic. Ph.D. dissertation, The University of Reading.
Allen, S. Sean and Joanne L. Miller
  1999   Effects of syllable-initial voicing and speaking rate on the temporal characteristics of monosyllabic words. *Journal of the Acoustical Society of America* 106: 2031–2039.
Barry, S. M. E.
  1991   Temporal cues in the perception of the voicing contrast in Russian. *Proceedings of the International Congress of Phonetic Sciences* 12, 5: 58–61.
Beach, D. M.
  1938   *The Phonetics of the Hottentot Language*. Cambridge: Heffer.
Benguerel, André-Pierre and Tej K. Bhatia
  1980   Hindi stop consonants: an acoustic and fiberscopic study. *Phonetica* 37: 134–148.
Bickley, C. A. and Kenneth N. Stevens
  1987   Effects of a vocal tract constriction on the glottal source: data from voiced consonants. In: T. Baer, C. Sasaki and K. S. Harris (eds.), *Laryngeal Function in Phonation and Respiration*, 239–253. Boston, etc.: College-Hill Press.
Boersma, Paul
  1998   *Functional Phonology. Formalizing the Interactions between Articulatory and Perceptual Drives*. The Hague: LOT.
Braun, Angelika
  1988   *Zum Merkmal "fortis/lenis". Phonetische Betrachtungen und instrumentalphonetische Untersuchungen an einem Mittelhessischen Dialekt*. Stuttgart: Steiner.
Braunschweiler, Norbert
  1997   Integrated cues of voicing and vowel length in German: a production study. *Language and Speech* 40: 353–376.

Chapin Ringo, Carol
   1988   Enhanced amplitude of the first harmonic as a correlate of
            voicelessness in aspirated consonants. *Journal of the Acoustical
            Society of America* Suppl. 1, 83, S70 [Abstract].
Chen, Matthew
   1970   Vowel length variation as a function of the voicing of the consonant
            environment. *Phonetica* 22: 129–159.
Cho, Taehong and Peter Ladefoged
   1999   Variation and universals in VOT: evidence from 18 languages.
            Journal of Phonetics 27: 207–229.
Chomsky, Noam and Morris Halle
   1968   *The Sound Pattern of English.* Cambridge, Mass./London: MIT
            Press [second printing, 1991].
Clements, George N.
   1985   The geometry of phonological features. *Phonology Yearbook* 2:
            225–252.
Cooper, André M.
   1991   An articulatory account of aspiration in English. Ph.D. dissertation,
            Yale University.
Davis, Kate
   1994   Stop voicing in Hindi. *Journal of Phonetics* 22: 177–193.
Davis, S. and W. van Summers
   1989   Vowel length and closure duration in word-medial VC sequences.
            Journal of Phonetics 17: 339–353.
De Jong, Kenneth
   1991   An articulatory study of consonant-induced vowel duration changes
            in English. *Phonetica* 48: 1–17.
Debrock, Mark
   1977   An acoustic correlate of the force of articulation. *Journal of
            Phonetics* 5: 61–80.
Demolin, Didier
   1995   The phonetics and phonology of glottalized consonants in Lendu. In:
            Bruce Connell and Armanda Arvaniti (eds.), *Phonology and
            Phonetic Evidence. Papers in Laboratory Phonology IV,* 368–385.
            Cambridge, etc.: Cambridge University Press.
Denning, Keith
   1989   The diachronic development of phonological voice quality, with
            special reference to Dinka and the other Nilotic languages. Ph.D.
            dissertation, Stanford University.
Diehl, Randy L. and Michelle R. Molis
   1995   Effect of fundamental frequency on medial [+voice]/[–voice] judg-
            ments. *Phonetica* 52: 188–195.

Dixit, R. Prakash
  1989   Glottal gestures in Hindi plosives. *Journal of Phonetics* 17: 213–237.
Dixit, R. Prakash and W. S. Brown
  1978   Peak magnitudes of supraglottal air pressure associated with affricated and nonaffricated stop consonant productions in Hindi. *Journal of Phonetics* 6: 353–365.
  1985   Peak magnitudes of oral air flow during Hindi stops (plosives and affricates). *Journal of Phonetics* 13: 219–234.
Dixit, R. Prakash and Peter F. MacNeilage
  1980   Cricothyroid activity and control of voicing in Hindi stops and affricates. *Phonetica* 37: 397–406.
Dixit, R. Prakash and Thomas Shipp
  1985   Study of subglottal air pressure during Hindi stop consonants. *Phonetica* 42: 53–77.
Docherty, Gerard J.
  1992   *The Timing of Voicing in British English Obstruents.* Berlin, etc.: Foris.
Doke, C. M.
  1954   *The Southern Bantu Languages.* London: Oxford University Press.
Edwards, Thomas J.
  1981   Multiple features analysis of intervocalic English plosives. *Journal of the Acoustical Society of America* 69: 535–547.
Ernestus, Mirjam
  2000   *Voice Assimilation and Segment Reduction in Casual Dutch. A Corpus-Based Study of the Phonology-Phonetics Interface.* Utrecht: LOT.
Fant, Gunnar
  1960   *Acoustic Theory of Speech Production.* The Hague: Mouton [second printing, 1970].
Fischer-Jørgensen, Eli
  1968   Voicing, tenseness and aspiration in stop consonants, with special reference to French and Danish. *Annual Report of the Institute of Phonetics of the University of Copenhagen* 3: 63–114.
  1980   Temporal relations in Danish tautosyllabic CV sequences with stop consonants. *Annual Report of the Institute of Phonetics of the University of Copenhagen* 14: 207–261.
Fischer-Jørgensen, Eli and Birgit Hutters
  1981   Aspirated stop consonants before low vowels, a problem of delimitation – its causes and consequences. *Annual Report of the Institute of Phonetics of the University of Copenhagen* 15: 77–102.

Flemming, Edward
    1995   Auditory representations in phonology. Ph.D. dissertation, UCLA.
Fowler, Carol A.
    1992   Vowel duration and closure duration in voiced and unvoiced stops:
            there are no contrast effects here. *Journal of Phonetics* 20: 143–165.
Gobl, Christer, Ailbhe Ní Chasaide and Peter Monahan
    1995   Intrinsic voice source characteristics of selected consonants.
            Proceedings of the International Congress of Phonetic Sciences 13,
            1: 74–77.
Goblirsch, Kurt G.
    1994   Fortis and lenis in Standard German. *Leuvense Bijdragen* 83: 31–45.
Haggard, Mark, Quentin Summerfield and Martin Roberts
    1981   Psychoacoustical and cultural determinants of phoneme boundaries:
            evidence from trading F0 cues in the voiced-voiceless distinction.
            Journal of Phonetics 9: 49–62.
Halle, Morris and Kenneth N. Stevens
    1967   On the mechanism of glottal vibration for vowels and consonants.
            MIT Research Laboratory of Electronics Quarterly Progress Report
            85: 267–271.
    1971   A note on laryngeal features. *MIT Research Laboratory of
            Electronics Quarterly Progress Report* 101: 198–213.
Han, M. S. and R. S. Weitzman
    1970   Acoustic features of Korean /P, T, K/, /p t k/ and /p^h, t^h, k^h/.
            Phonetica 22: 112–128.
Harnad, Steven (ed.)
    1987   *Categorical Perception. The Groundwork of Cognition.* Cambridge,
            etc.: Cambridge University Press.
Harris, John and Geoff Lindsey
    1995   The elements of phonological representation. In: Jaques Durand and
            Francis Katamba (eds.), *Frontiers of Phonology: Atoms, Structures,
            Derivations*, 33–79. Harlow: Longman.
Hombert, Jean-Marie and Peter Ladefoged
    1977   The effect of aspiration on the fundamental frequency of the
            following vowel. *UCLA Working Papers in Phonetics* 36: 33–40.
Hombert, Jean-Marie, John J. Ohala and William G. Ewan
    1979   Phonetic explanations for the development of tones. *Language* 55:
            37–58.
Hutters, Birgit
    1985   Vocal fold adjustments in aspirated and unaspirated stops in Danish.
            Phonetica 42: 1–24.

Iverson, Gregory K. and Joseph C. Salmons
1995   Aspiration and laryngeal representation in Germanic. *Phonology* 12: 369–396.
Iwata, Ray and Hajime Hirose
1976   Fiberoptic acoustic studies of Mandarin stops and affricates. *Annual Bulletin. Research Institute of Logopedics and Phoniatrics. University of Tokyo* 10: 47–60.
Jakobson, Roman
1968   Extrapulmonic consonants: ejectives, implosives, clicks. In: *Selected Writings 1: Phonological Studies*, 720–727. The Hague: Mouton.
Jakobson, Roman, Gunnar Fant and Morris Halle
1952   *Preliminaries to Speech Analysis.* Cambridge, Mass.: The MIT Press [sixth printing, 1965].
Jakobson, Roman and Morris Halle
1961   Supplement tenseness and laxness. In: Jakobson, Fant and Halle 1952 (1965), 57–61.
1968   Phonology in relation to phonetics. In: Bertil Malmberg (ed.), *Manual of Phonetics*, 411–449. Amsterdam: North Holland.
Jakobson, Roman and Linda R. Waugh
1987   *The Sound Shape of Language.* Berlin, etc.: Mouton de Gruyter [second edition].
Jeel, Vivi
1975   An investigation of the fundamental frequency of vowels after various Danish consonants, in particular stop consonants. *Annual Report of the Institute of Phonetics of the University of Copenhagen* 9: 191–211.
Jessen, Michael
1996   The relevance of phonetic reality for underlying phonological representation: the case of tense versus lax obstruents in German. In: Ursula Kleinhenz (ed.), *Interfaces in Phonology*, 294–328. Berlin: Akademie Verlag.
1998   *Phonetics and Phonology of Tense and Lax Obstruents in German.* Amsterdam/Philadelphia: Benjamins.
1999a   An acoustic study of distinctive stop types and click accompaniments in Xhosa. Ms. University of Stuttgart.
1999b   Implications for feature theory from the phonetics of contrasting stop types and click accompaniments in Xhosa. Ms. University of Stuttgart.
1999c   Redundant aspiration in German is primarily controlled by closure duration. *Proceedings of the International Congress of Phonetic Sciences* 14, 2: 993–996.

286   *Michael Jessen*

Jessen, Michael and Justus C. Roux
    to appear Voice quality differences associated with stops and clicks in Xhosa.
               Journal of Phonetics.
Jun, Sun-Ah
    1996   Influence of microprosody on macroprosody: a case of phrase initial
               strengthening. *UCLA Working Papers in Phonetics* 92: 97–116.
    1998   The accentual phrase in the Korean prosodic hierarchy. *Phonology*
               15: 189–226.
Kagaya, Ryohei and Hajime Hirose
    1975   Fiberoptic electromyographic and acoustic analyses of Hindi stop
               consonants. *Annual Bulletin. Research Institute of Logopedics and
               Phoniatrics. University of Tokyo* 9: 27–46.
Kawasaki, Haruko
    1983   Fundamental frequency perturbation caused by voiced and voiceless
               stops in Japanese. *MIT Research Laboratory of Electronics Speech
               Communication Group Working Papers* 3: 55–67.
Keating, Patricia A.
    1985   Universal phonetics and the organization of grammars. In: Victoria
               A. Fromkin (ed.), *Phonetic Linguistics: Essays in Honour of Peter
               Ladefoged*, 115–132. Orlando, etc.: Academic Press.
    1988   A survey of phonological features. Bloomington: Indiana University
               Linguistics Club.
    1990   Phonetic representation in a generative grammar. *Journal of
               Phonetics* 18: 321–334.
Keating, Patricia, Wendy Linker and Mary Huffman
    1983   Patterns in allophone distribution for voiced and voiceless stops.
               Journal of Phonetics 11: 277–290.
Khachatryan, Amalia and Albert Airapetyan
    1987   The main cues differentiating aspirated and unaspirated stops and
               affricates in Armenian. *Proceedings of the International Congress of
               Phonetic Sciences* 12, 1: 341–345.
Kingston, John C.
    1985   The phonetics and phonology of the timing of oral and glottal
               events. Ph.D. dissertation, University of California, Berkeley.
    1990   Articulatory binding. In: John Kingston and Mary E. Beckman
               (eds.), *Papers in Laboratory Phonology I: Between the Grammar
               and the Physics of Speech*, 406–434. Cambridge, etc.: Cambridge
               University Press.
Kingston, John and Randy L. Diehl
    1994   Phonetic knowledge. *Language* 70: 419–454.

1995   Intermediate properties in the perception of distinctive feature
            values. In: Bruce Connell and Armanda Arvaniti (eds.), *Phonology
            and Phonetic Evidence. Papers in Laboratory Phonology IV*, 7–27.
            Cambridge, etc.: Cambridge University Press.
Kingston, John, Neil A. Macmillian, Laura Walsh Dickey, Rachel Thorburn and
            Christine Bartels
1997   Integrality in the perception of tongue root position and voice
            quality in vowels. *Journal of the Acoustical Society of America* 101:
            1696–1709.
Klatt, Dennis H. and Laura C. Klatt
1990   Analysis, synthesis, and perception of voice quality variations
            among female and male talkers. *Journal of the Acoustical Society of
            America* 87: 820–857.
Kluender, Keith R.
1991   Effects of first formant onset properties on voicing judgments result
            from processes not specific to humans. *Journal of the Acoustical
            Society of America* 90: 83–96.
Kluender, Keith R., Randy L. Diehl and Beverly A. Wright
1988   Vowel-length differences before voiced and voiceless consonants:
            An auditory explanation. *Journal of Phonetics* 16: 153–169.
Kluender, Keith R., Andrew J. Lotto and Rick L. Jenison
1995   Perception of voicing for syllable-initial stops at different intensities:
            does synchrony capture signal voiceless stop consonants? *Journal of
            the Acoustical Society of America* 97: 2552–2567.
Kockaert, Hendrick and Denise Godwin.
1997   Voicing status of syllable-initial plosives in siSwati. *South African
            Journal of African Languages* 17: 100–104.
Kohler, Klaus J.
1979   Dimensions in the perception of fortis and lenis plosives. *Phonetica*
            36: 332–343.
1982   F0 in the production of lenis and fortis plosives. *Phonetica* 39: 199–
            218.
1984   Phonetic explanation in phonology: the feature fortis/lenis.
            Phonetica 41: 150–174.
Kohler, Klaus J., Wim van Dommelen, Gerd Timmermann, William J. Barry
1981   Die signalphonetische Ausprägung des Merkmalpaares fortis/lenis in
            französischen Plosiven. Pneumotachographische, palatographische
            und spektrographische Untersuchungen. *Arbeitsberichte des Instituts
            für Phonetik, Universität Kiel* 16: 45–94.
Koreman, Jacques
1996   Decoding linguistic information in the glottal airflow. Ph.D. disser-
            tation, University of Nijmegen.

288   *Michael Jessen*

Künzel, Hermann J.
 1977   *Signalphonetische Untersuchung Deutsch-Französischer Interferen-
       zen im Bereich der Okklusive.* Frankfurt, etc.: Lang.
Ladefoged, Peter
 1973   The features of the larynx. *Journal of Phonetics* 1: 73–83.
 1997   Linguistic phonetic descriptions. In: William. J. Hardcastle and John
       Laver (eds.), *The Handbook of Phonetic Sciences,* 589–618.
       Cambridge, USA/Oxford, UK: Blackwell.
Ladefoged, Peter and Ian Maddieson
 1996   *The Sounds of the World's Languages.* Cambridge, USA/Oxford,
       UK: Blackwell.
Ladefoged, Peter, Ian Maddieson and Michel Jackson
 1988   Investigating phonation types in different languages. In: Osamu
       Fujimura (ed.), *Vocal Physiology: Voice Production, Mechanisms
       and Functions,* 297–316. New York: Raven Press.
Ladefoged, Peter, Kay Williamson, Ben Elugbe and Sister Ann Angela Uwalaka
 1976   The stops of Owerri Igbo. *Studies in African Linguistics* Supplement
       6: 147–163.
Ladefoged, Peter and Anthony Traill
 1994   Clicks and their accompaniments. *Journal of Phonetics* 22: 33–64.
Laeufer, Christiane
 1992   Patterns of voicing-conditioned vowel duration in French and
       English. *Journal of Phonetics* 20: 411–440.
Laver, John
 1980   *The Phonetic Description of Voice Quality.* Cambridge, etc.:
       Cambridge University Press.
Lee, Sook-hyang
 1990   Korean lenis and fortis stops: synthesis and categorical speech
       perception task. *Ohio State University Working Papers in Linguistics*
       38: 105–120.
Lisker, Leigh
 1974   On "explaining" vowel duration variation. *Glossa* 8: 233–246.
 1986   "Voicing" in English: a catalogue of acoustic features signaling /b/
       versus /p/ in trochees. *Language and Speech* 29: 3–11.
Lisker, Leigh and Arthur S. Abramson
 1964   A cross-language study of voicing in initial stops: acoustical
       measurements. *Word* 20: 384–422.
Löfqvist, Anders, Thomas Baer, Nancy S. McGarr and Robert Seider Story
 1989   The cricothyroid muscle in voicing control. *Journal of the
       Acoustical Society of America* 85: 1314–1321.

Löfqvist, Anders, Laura L. Koenig and Richard S. McGowan
1995   Vocal tract aerodynamics in /aCa/ utterances: measurements. *Speech Communication* 16: 49–66.
Löfqvist, Anders and Richard S. McGowan
1992   Influence of consonantal environment on voice source aerodynamics. *Journal of Phonetics* 20: 93–110.
Löfqvist, Anders and Hirohide Yoshioka
1981   Intcrarticulator programming in obstruent production. *Phonetica* 38: 21–34.
Lombardi, Linda
1991   Laryngeal features and laryngeal neutralization. Ph.D. dissertation, University of Massachussetts at Amherst [published 1994, New York/London: Garland].
1995   Laryngeal features and privativity. *The Linguistic Review* 12: 35–59.
Luce, Paul A. and Jan Charles-Luce
1985   Contextual effects on vowel duration, closure duration, and the consonant/vowel ratio in speech production. *Journal of the Acoustical Society of America* 78: 1949–1957.
Maddieson, Ian
1984   *Patterns of Sounds.* Cambridge etc.: Cambridge University Press.
1997   Phonetic universals. In: William. J. Hardcastle and John Laver (eds.), *The Handbook of Phonetic Sciences*, 619–639. Cambridge, USA/Oxford, UK: Blackwell.
Maddieson, Ian and Jack Gandour
1977   Vowel length before aspirated consonants. *Indian Linguistics* 38: 6–11.
Maddieson, Ian, Siniša Spajić, Bonny Sands and Peter Ladefoged
1993   Phonetic structures of Dahalo. *UCLA Working Papers in Phonetics* 84:25–65.
Marasek, Krzysztof
1997   Electroglottographic description of voice quality. Habilitationsschrift (Post-doctoral thesis), University of Stuttgart.
Mei, Junhong
2000   Akustische Korrelate der Glottisöffnung in deutschen Konsonanten. Diplomarbeit (M.A. thesis), University of Stuttgart.
Ní Chasaide, Ailbhe and Christer Gobl
1993   Contextual variation of the vowel voice source as a function of adjacent consonants. *Language and Speech* 36: 303–330.

Ohala, John J.
    1999   Preliminaries to speech analysis (1952). In: John J. Ohala, Arthur J. Bronstein, M. Grazia Busà, Julie A. Lewis and William F. Weigel (eds.), *A Guide to the History of the Phonetic Sciences in the United States*, 64–65. University of California, Berkeley.

Perkell, Joseph S., Melanie L. Matthies, Mario A. Svirsky and Michael I. Jordan
    1995   Goal-based speech motor control: a theoretical framework and some preliminary data. *Journal of Phonetics* 23: 23–35.

Petersen, Niels R.
    1978   The influence of aspiration on the fundamental frequency of the following vowel in Danish: some preliminary observations. *Annual Report of the Institute of Phonetics of the University of Copenhagen* 12: 91–112.
    1983   The effect of consonant type on fundamental frequency and larynx height in Danish. *Annual Report of the Institute of Phonetics of the University of Copenhagen* 17: 55–86.

Pétursson, Magnús
    1976   Aspiration et activité glottale. Examen expérimental à partir de consonnes islandaises. *Phonetica* 33: 169–198.

Pierrehumbert, Janet B.
    1989   A preliminary study of the consequences of intonation for the voice source. *Speech Transmission Laboratory Quarterly Progress and Status Report of the Royal Institute of Technology, Stockholm* 4, 23–36.

Pierrehumbert, Janet B., Mary E. Beckman and D. Robert Ladd
    1996   Laboratory phonology. In: J. Durand and B. Laks, (eds.), *Current Trends in Phonology: Models and Methods*, 535–548. University of Salford: European Studies Research Institute.

Pierrehumbert, Janet B. and David Talkin
    1992   Lenition of /h/ and glottal stop. In: Gerard J. Docherty and D. Robert Ladd (eds.), *Papers in Laboratory Phonology II. Gesture, Segment, Prosody*, 90–117. Cambridge, etc.: Cambridge University Press.

Port, Robert F.
    1996   The discreteness of phonetic elements and formal linguistics: response to A. Manaster Ramer. *Journal of Phonetics* 24: 491–511.

Port, Robert F. and Jonathan Dalby
    1982   Consonant/vowel ratio as a cue for voicing in English. *Perception and Psychophysics* 32: 141–152.

Ren, Nianqi
    1992   Phonation types and stop consonant distinctions: Shanghai Chinese. Ph.D. dissertation, University of Connecticut.

Repp, Bruno H.
  1979   Relative amplitude of aspiration noise as a voicing cue for syllable-initial stop consonants. *Language and Speech* 22: 173–189.
Rice, Keren
  1988   Continuant voicing in Slave (Northern Athapaskan): the cyclic application of default rules. In: M. Hammond and M. Noonan (eds.), *Theoretical Morphology. Approaches in Modern Linguistics*, 371–388. San Diego, etc.: Academic Press.
Sands, Bonny, Ian Maddieson and Peter Ladefoged
  1993   The phonetic structures of Hadza. *UCLA Working Papers in Phonetics* 84: 67–87.
Shih, Chilin and Bernd Möbius
  in press   Contextual effects on voicing profiles of German and Mandarin consonants. In: Andrew Breen, Nick W. Campbell, Jan van Santen and Julie Vonviller (eds.), *Progress in Speech Synthesis II: Proceedings of the Third ESCA/COCOSDA International Workshop on Speech Synthesis*. Berlin: Springer.
Shimizu, Katsumasa
  1989   A cross-language study of voicing contrasts of stops. *Studia Phonologica* 23: 1–12.
  1996   *A Cross-Language Study of Voicing Contrasts of Stop Consonants in Asian Languages*. Tokyo: Seibido.
Silverman, Daniel
  1997   *Phasing and Recoverability*. New York/London: Garland.
Slis, I. H. and A. Cohen
  1969   On the complex regulating the voiced-voiceless distinction I. *Language and Speech* 12: 80–102.
Sluijter, Agaath M. C., Stefanie Shattuck-Hufnagel, Kenneth N. Stevens and Vincent J. Heuven
  1995   Supralaryngeal resonance and glottal pulse shape as correlates of stress and accent in English. *Proceedings of the International Congress of Phonetic Sciences* 13, 2: 630–633.
Snyman, J. W.
  1980   The relationship between Angolan !Xũ and Zul'hõasi. In: J. W. Snyman (ed.), *Bushman and Hottentott Linguistic Studies*, 1–58. Pretoria: UNISA.
Stevens, Kenneth N.
  1977   Physics of laryngeal behavior and larynx modes. *Phonetica* 34: 264–279.
  1997   Articulatory-acoustic-auditory relationships. In: William. J. Hardcastle and John Laver (eds.), *The Handbook of Phonetic Sciences*, 462–505. Cambridge, USA/Oxford, UK: Blackwell.

1998   *Acoustic Phonetics.* Cambridge, Mass./London: The MIT Press.
Stevens, Kenneth N. and Sheila E. Blumstein
1981   The search for invariant acoustic correlates of phonetic features. In:
        P. D. Eimas and J. L. Miller (eds.), *Perspectives in the Study of
        Speech,* 1–39. Hillsdale: Lawrence Erlbaum.
Stevens, Kenneth N., Sheila E. Blumstein, Laura Glicksman, Martha Burton and
        Kathleen Kurowski
1992   Acoustic and perceptual characteristics of voicing in fricatives and
        fricative clusters. *Journal of the Acoustical Society of America* 91:
        2979–3000.
Stevens, Kenneth N. and Helen M. Hanson
1994   Classification of glottal vibration from acoustic measurements. In:
        O. Fujimura and M. Hirano (eds.), *Vocal Fold Physiology: Voice
        Quality Control,* 147–170. San Diego: Singular.
Stevens, Kenneth N. and Samuel J. Keyser
1989   Primary features and their enhancement in consonants. *Language*
        65: 81–106.
Temple, Rosalind A. M.
1999   Phonetic and sociophonetic conditioning of voicing patterns in the
        stop consonants of French. *Proceedings of the International
        Congress of Phonetic Sciences* 14, 2: 1409–1412.
Traill, Anthony
1985   *Phonetic and Phonological Studies of !Xóõ Bushman.* Hamburg:
        Buske.
1995   Place of articulation features for clicks: anomalies for universals. In:
        Jack Windsor Lewis (ed.), *Studies in General and English
        Phonetics. Essays in Honour of Professor F.D. O´Connor,* 121–129.
        London: Routledge.
Traill, Anthony and Rainer Vossen
1997   Sound change in the Khoisan languages: new data on click loss and
        click replacement. *Journal of African Languages and Linguistics* 19:
        21–56.
Trigo, Loren
1991   On pharynx-larynx interactions. *Phonology* 8: 113–136.
Tsuchida, Ayako
1997   Phonetics and phonology of Japanese vowel devoicing. Ph.D.
        dissertation, Cornell University.
Turk, Alice E. and James R. Sawush
1996   The processing of duration and intensity cues to prominence.
        Journal of the Acoustical Society of America 99: 3782–3790.

Van Rooy, Albertus J.
  1999　The relationship between phonetics and phonology: An investigation into the representation of the phonological feature [voice]. Ph.D. dissertation, Potchefstroom University.
Veloso, João
  1995　The role of consonantal duration and tenseness in the perception of voicing distinctions of Portuguese stops. *Proceedings of the International Congress of Phonetic Sciences* 13, 2: 266–269.
Vossen, Rainer
  1986　Zur Phonologie der //Ani-Sprache. In: Rainer Vossen and Klaus Keuthmann (eds.), *Contemporary Studies on Khoisan. In Honour of Oswin Köhler on the Occasion of his 75th Birthday*, Part II, 321–345. Hamburg: Buske.
Walsh, Thomas and Frank Parker
  1983　Vowel length and vowel transition: cues to [±voice] in post-vocalic stops. *Journal of Phonetics* 11: 407–412.
Westbury, John R.
  1983　Enlargement of the supralaglottal cavity and its relation to stop consonant voicing. *Journal of the Acoustical Society of America* 73: 1322–1336.
Westbury, John R. and Patricia A. Keating
  1986　On the naturalness of stop consonant voicing. *Journal of Linguistics* 22: 145–166.
Williams, Lee
  1977　The voicing contrast in Spanish. *Journal of Phonetics* 5: 169–184.
Wissing, Daan and Justus Roux
  1995　The interrelationship between VOT and voice assimilation. *Proceedings of the International Congress of Phonetic Sciences* 13, 1: 50–53.
Wright, Richard, Ian Maddieson, Peter Ladefoged and Bonny Sands
  1995　A phonetic study of Sandawe clicks. *UCLA Working Papers in Phonetics* 91: 1–24.
Wu, Zong-Ji and Yi Xu
  1987　Aspirated vs nonaspirated stops and affricates in Standard Chinese. *Proceedings of the International Congress of Phonetic Sciences* 11, 5: 209–212.
Zee, Eric
  1980　The effect of aspiration on the F0 of the following vowel in Cantonese. *UCLA Working Papers in Phonetics* 49: 90–97.

Zue, V. W.
   1976   Acoustic characteristics of stop consonants: A controlled study.
               Ph.D. dissertation, MIT   [published 1980 by Indiana University
               Linguistics Club].

Distinctive [voice] implies regressive voicing assimilation*

Bertus van Rooy and Daan Wissing

1. Introduction

Two conflicting approaches to the interpretation of the distinctive feature [voice] can be observed. The broad interpretation, originating with Lisker and Abramson (1964) holds that a binary opposition between two plosive categories at the level of phonological representation may be implemented by any two of three phonetic categories, viz. voice onset precedes plosive release (henceforth *negative voice onset time*), voice onset immediately follows plosive release (henceforth *short-lag voice onset time*) and voice onset substantially lags behind plosive release (henceforth *long-lag voice onset time*) (see Lisker and Abramson 1964: 389). The narrow interpretation, already present in the work of Jakobson (1949: 423-424), holds that [voice] is employed as distinctive feature only when actual vocal fold vibration is present in the production of the marked member of the pair voiced/voiceless. In terms of the categories of Lisker and Abramson (1964: 389), the [+voice] member of the opposition pair must have negative voice onset time.

Both of these approaches received new impetus in a number of recent papers. On the basis of phonetic similarities that cannot be ascribed to purely articulatory reasons, Kingston and Diehl (1994: 426-428, 432-439) argue for the broader interpretation. In particular, the lowering and raising effects of [+voice] and [−voice] respectively on the fundamental frequency of adjacent vowels are reported to be similar, independent of the specific phonetic realisation of the distinctive feature opposition. This finding enhances the original proposal of Lisker and Abramson (1964: 385), which aimed at simplifying the labels used, and proposing more precise definitions of the categories involved.

However, a narrower interpretation of [voice] is proposed by Keating (1990), Iverson and Salmons (1995, 1999) and Jessen (1998: 268, this volume). Iverson and Salmons (1995, 1999) argue that a number of phonological processes in Germanic languages (excluding Afrikaans, Dutch and Yiddish) can be accounted for more directly if the feature [spread glottis] (henceforth [spread]), rather than [voice], is adopted for these languages. Phonetically, the majority of Germanic languages do not make consistent use of prevoicing, but rather uses a glottal spreading gesture to oppose marked [spread] phonemes to unmarked ones (see Hutters 1985 for phonetic evidence on this). Iverson and Salmons (1995, 1999) relate the phonological consequences of the feature [spread] to its phonetic properties and show them to be specific to languages with the feature [spread] active, and absent from languages with the feature [voice] as the active feature for obstruent contrasts.

Jessen (1998: 12-13, this volume) reintroduces the notion of relational invariant, which characterised the Prague School approach to distinctive features. On the basis of this, a feature [voice] can only be used if some consistent acoustic outcome is present in all contexts. The use of the feature [voice] for an opposition between a short lag and long lag voice onset is inconsistent with the requirement that a phonological feature must be rooted in some invariant property in all contrastive environments.

Iverson and Salmons (1995, 1999), as well as Jessen (1998, this volume), focus their discussions on languages where either [voice] or some other feature — Jessen uses [tense], Iverson and Salmons use [spread] — is selected by a particular language for a binary opposition. In an earlier paper, Keating (1984) elaborates on the work of Lisker and Abramson (1964), and maintains the use of binary [voice] as super-phonological category for three different phonetic categories. However, Keating (1990) subsequently rejects the use of the broadly interpreted [voice], and proposes to complement a narrowly interpreted [voice] with [spread]. Her motivation comes partly from findings on the phasing of voicing and spreading with the closure and release of plosives respectively, and partly from the need to employ both phonological categories simultaneously to characterise systems with more than two plosive categories that differ only in terms of laryngeal features, such as Hindi (see Golston and Kehrein 1999 for a detailed account of laryngeal contrasts in languages of the world).

In this paper, we offer phonetic and phonological evidence on alternations for the narrow interpretation of [voice]. The contributions of Jessen (1998, this volume) on [tense] in German, and Iverson and Salmons (1995, 1999) on [spread] in Germanic languages more generally, both highlight the advantages of some other feature that complements a narrowly interpreted [voice]. The evidence given by Keating (1990: 325-331) in favour of a narrowly interpreted [voice] has to do with phasing of gestures and representation systems rather than alternations. While we accept the main points of these contributions, further evidence from alternations can strengthen the case for a narrow interpretation of [voice].

The phonological evidence in this paper comes mainly from the process of *regressive voicing assimilation*. Various researchers have remarked that there is a close connection between negative voice onset time in plosives (the narrow use of the feature [voice]) and the occurrence of regressive voicing assimilation (see Westbury 1975; Kohler 1984: 163; Gustafson 1986; Iverson and Salmons 1995: 382; Wissing and Roux 1995). However, a number of complications are noted in the literature, particularly the occurrence of progressive devoicing in Dutch (Trommelen and Zonneveld 1979: 104; Slis 1983, 1986) and Afrikaans (Wissing 1990; Wissing and Du Plessis 1992) in contexts where one would expect regressive voicing assimilation to occur.

The best treatment of regressive voicing assimilation and the complications that arise has been subject to some discussion in recent Optimality Theory research (e.g. Lombardi 1999; Grijzenhout 2000; Grijzenhout and Krämer 2000). If the postulated link between the distinctive feature [voice] and regressive voicing assimilation is valid, then a prediction about constraint ranking within Optimality Theory automatically follows from this. Whatever constraint enforces regressive spreading of the feature [voice] must always outrank faithfulness to underlying voicing for the non-rightmost obstruent(s) in an obstruent cluster, as well as the constraint(s) that enforce final devoicing. However, it appears as if this generalisation is simply treated as one possible ranking in the current literature, with other rankings that prevent regressive assimilation also possible. In addition, various alternative constructs are proposed to account for apparent exceptions such as Dutch progressive devoicing. We will show that the adoption of the narrow interpretation of the feature [voice], something not done in Optimality Theory research so far, greatly simplifies and improves an Optimality account of regressive voicing assimilation.

The paper is organised in the following way. In the next section, evidence from various alternations from a number of languages is presented to support the use of a narrow interpretation of the feature [voice], focussing in particular on regressive voicing assimilation. A strong hypothesis emerges from this discussion, viz. that languages with distinctive [voice] will display regressive voicing assimilation as default option. In the following section of this paper, the hypothesis is tested against empirical data from the second language English (a language without distinctive [voice]) as spoken by native speakers of Tswana. Tswana has distinctive [voice] (as well as distinctive aspiration and ejection), but because of its phonotactic structure that disallows obstruent clusters, it cannot have regressive voicing assimilation. However, if our hypothesis is correct, then Tswana speakers are expected to automatically apply regressive voicing assimilation when speaking second languages with obstruent clusters, such as English.

The optional character of regressive voicing assimilation in Afrikaans and Dutch presents potential counter-evidence to our hypothesis. This phenomenon is explored in section 4 to determine if it does indeed present a problem, or if it does not provide supporting evidence, contrary to first appearances.

In section 5, the advantages of the narrow interpretation for an Optimality Theory account of regressive voicing assimilation, as well as some of the complications treated in the literature, are outlined. The major findings are summarised in the final section.

2.   Phonological alternations and the feature [voice]

Two of the most commonly found alternations that involve the feature [voice] are final devoicing and regressive voicing assimilation. In addition, processes like post-nasal voicing and intervocalic voicing also involve the feature [voice]. These processes are reviewed in this section, to determine how a narrow interpretation of the feature [voice] might improve our understanding of them.

Final devoicing occurs when obstruents in codas are realised as voiceless, but are voiced when they occur in onset positions in other realisations of the same morpheme. Examples are:

(1)   Dutch (taken from De Coninck's 1992 volume of poetry)

Underlying form	Surface forms	Gloss
han/d/	han[d]en	'hands' (pl.)
	han[t]	'hand' (sg.)
lie/v/	lie[v]eling	'(my) love' (N)
	lie[f]	'lovely' (Adv)
gee/v/	gege[v]en	'given'(past participle)
	gee[f]	'give' (1st person sg. pres.)
lee/z/	le[z]en	'read' (infinitive)
	lee[s]	'read' (1st person sg. pres.)
ze/ɣ/	ze[ɣ]en[1]	'say' (infinitive)
	ze[x]	'say' (1st person sg. pres.)

(2)   Polish (from Rubach 1996:70)

sa[d]y	'orchards'	*vs.*	sa[t]	'orchard' (nom. sg.)
ko[z]a	'goat'	*vs.*	kó[s]	'of goats' (gen. pl.)
pra[v]o	'law'	*vs.*	pra[f]	'of laws' (gen. pl.)[2]

An example of final devoicing that is of particular interest to the concerns of this paper is discussed by Rice (1994: 126-127).[3] She provides the following data:[4]

(3)   Koyukon

xæ[ɫ]	'trap'	nəɣæ[l]ə	'your (sg.) trap'
ʔɔ[x]	'snowshoes'	səʔɔ[ɣ]ə	'my snowshoes'
nədə[ɫ]	'it is heavy'[5]		

Koyukon, an Athapaskan language, does not distinguish phonemically between voiced and voiceless fricatives. A variety of allophonic processes take place to assign voicing to fricatives in a predictable manner. On the other hand, Koyukon distinguishes phonemically between aspirated and unaspirated plosives. These are not subject to the allophonic voicing/devoicing processes in the environments where fricatives alternate between voiced and voiceless allophones (Rice 1994: 111-113). Under the wide interpretation of [voice], the plosive contrast should be assigned to the feature [voice], since a binary opposition between short–lag and long-lag voice onset time is regarded as a phonetic realisation of the opposition between [+voice] and [–voice] by Lisker and Abramson (1964: 421-422), Keating (1984: 290-291) and Kingston and Diehl (1994: 426-428). However, Rice (1994: 126-127) assigns the feature [spread] to this opposition, and points out that plosives are not subject to this final devoicing, which is strictly a constraint on the allophonic distribution of the feature [voice], and not of [spread]. This generalisation is lost if the feature [voice] is adopted as distinctive for plosives.

A prediction following from Koyukon final devoicing for the process of final devoicing in general is that the phonologically active feature [voice] is affected, and languages without final devoicing are therefore expected not to have the feature [voice] active, but some other feature.[6] This is still tentative, and various exceptions come to mind, including German, where final fortition takes place,[7] as well as French and Ukrainian, where regressive voicing assimilation takes place, but no final devoicing.

Another process that affects the feature [voice] is post-nasal voicing, and a variety of other processes that serve to prevent nasal + voiceless plosive configurations (see Pater 1999 an overview and some discussion). Vaux (1998: 505-507) presents a very relevant refinement on the traditional interpretation of post-nasal voicing. He points out that fricatives generally do not participate in post-nasal voicing processes. The conceived explanation for this makes use of the feature [cont], where nasals and plosives share the specification [–cont], while fricatives are specified as [+cont]. The feature [+cont] is assumed to block the application of post-nasal voicing.

Vaux (1998: 506) identifies a problem with this view. In the Armenian language New Julfa, post-nasal voicing can be observed, both in the historical development from Classical Armenian and in the synchronic phonology of the language. However, New Julfa exhibits a three-way distinction between (pre-)voiced, voiceless aspirated and voiceless unaspirated plosives, alongside a two-way distinction between voiced and voiceless fricatives. Predictably, fricatives do not participate in post-nasal voicing, but unexpected from the perspective of the analysis that assumes [+cont] as blocking feature, voiceless aspirated plosives are not subject to post-nasal voicing either. Vaux (1998: 506) provides the following data:

(4)	*Classical Armenian*	*New Julfa*	*Gloss*
	ənt̪ saj	ənd̪ za	'gift'
	ankanel	ənganiel	'fall'
	t̪ʃan t̪ʃ	t̪ʃand̪ʒ	'fly'
	ajnteɬ	əndieʁ	'there'
	—	insaf	'justice'
	—	sunsunakviel	'starve'
	—	tʰanχiel	'give false hopes'
	—	semsuri	'type of melon'
	tʰantʰ̬ʃel	tʰantʰ̬ʃin tal	'mutter'
	ʃampʰur	ʃampʰur	'spit'
	jawnkʰ	fiunkʰ	'eyebrow'

Vaux (1998: 507) points out that two assumptions should be made to explain these facts. The feature [spread] is the feature relevant to the distinction between fortis and lenis fricatives, and the same feature [spread] also distinguishes between aspirated and unaspirated plosives. If these assumptions are made, it follows that segments with the marked feature [spread] are immune to post-nasal voicing; thus [spread] rather than [cont] serves as blocking feature.[8] These data provide further support for the need to treat the features [voice] and [spread] as complementary, rather than overlapping, notions. Post-nasal voicing appears to require the absence of the feature [spread] then, and presumably a laryngeally unmarked obstruent that can share the feature [voice] with the adjacent nasal.

Vaux (1998) emphasises that data such as these indicate the need to employ the feature [spread], rather than [voice] for fricatives in New Julfa. This proposal that fortis and lenis fricatives are not always distinguished by the feature [voice] receives phonetic support from research on the phonetic realisation of Dutch fricatives. Slis and Van Heugten (1989: 127-129) find that lenis fricatives in Dutch are seldom fully voiced. The phonemic distinction is cued by differences in duration — the fortis fricatives are longer than the lenis ones. This can be a consequence of the glottal abduction that has to be completed for the fortis fricatives. It can also be interpreted as evidence for an opposition in terms of the feature [tense], for which duration is the primary phonetic cue (Goblirsch 1994: 42; Jessen 1998: 122, this volume). Haggard (1978) finds that lenis fricatives in English are also subject to devoicing, accompanied by some glottal abduction. English fricatives are therefore also candidates for classi-fication in terms of the feature [tense] and not in terms of [voice].

A further case where the narrow interpretation of the feature [voice] is potentially relevant is intervocalic plosive voicing in Korean. Phonetic studies (Jun 1994, 1995) have been conducted to determine the status of 'lenis stop voicing' within phonological theory. Jun (1995: 249-250) argues that it is essentially a phonetic phenomenon following from a general lenition process on laryngeal features in certain prosodic positions, the non-initial position of the so-called accentual phrase.[9] Voice onset time-values for aspirated plosives are also shortened in this position. She explains it as a case of gestural overlap between the plosive and the following vowel, and interprets her data as suggesting that it is a non-categorical, gradual effect. This is so because the various prosodic environments con-dition different degrees of voice onset time-reduction and voicing.

Jun's interpretation is supported by Keating (1996: 268-269), who emphasises this as evidence for the phonetic nature of underspeci-fication. If Korean plosives are unspecified for [voice], then it is possible that phonetic factors may cause voicing, but since it remains non-contrastive, it does not achieve the status of a categorical process. Other phonological features, such as [spread] and [constricted] are required to account for the phonemic contrasts in Korean. A prediction that may follow from Korean intervocalic voicing is that this process is potentially only present in languages where lenis obstruents arc not underlyingly specified for [voice]. As such, it will be an allophonic process, or maybe a redundant process that reinforces the lenis/fortis contrast by voicing the lenis obstruents.

From the above, a variety of tentative predictions follow, indicating that a narrow interpretation of the feature [voice] provides the basis of an explanation of various alternations. Such explanations follow more directly from the feature representation itself, rather than being rule-driven ones (in terms of the rule/representation opposition of Anderson 1985). A negative prediction can be made rather strongly for obstruents without a distinctive feature [voice]: they cannot participate in final devoicing.[10] Also, obstruents marked for [spread] cannot be subject to post-nasal voicing, even if they are unmarked for [voice]. Similarly, a negative prediction can be made for minimal obstruent pairs where one member is marked distinctively for [voice]: intervocalic voicing is unlikely to take place.

The specific alternation that forms the focus of this paper is regressive voicing assimilation. The relationship between feature specification and this alternation is explored in depth in the remainder of this paper. Examples of this process are:

(5) Dutch (from Zonneveld 1983:299)
    dwars-**d**raad   [zd]   'cross-wire'
    meet-**b**and   [db]   'tape-measure'
    sluit-**b**alk   [db]   'gate'
    smelt-**b**eker   [db]   'melting-pot'
(6) Polish (from Rubach 1996:70-71)
    [d]ech   'breath' *vs.* [tx]u   'of breaths' (gen. pl.)
    pokła[d]y   'boards' *vs.* podła[t st]atku 'board of a ship'
    ko[ś]ić   'mow'   *vs.* ko[ź] ba   'mowing'
    no[ś]ić   'carry' *vs.* no[ź ž]e   'do carry' (imper.)

Regressive voicing assimilation occurs widely in Slavic and Romance languages, as well as the Germanic languages Afrikaans, Dutch and Yiddish. Various researchers have remarked that languages with regressive voicing assimilation are characterised phonetically by prevoicing in their phonologically marked [voiced] plosives. Westbury (1975: 139) concludes:

> ... there is a direct and immediate relationship which holds between the nature of a given language's system of VOT [voice onset time] contrast among obstruents and the process of voicing assimilation in obstruent clusters. It is assumed that the acquisition of a specific set of contrasts (in effect, the acquisition of a set of physical gestures) determines the degree to which speakers of a given language may control voicing in a variety of contexts. If this hypothesis is correct, then regressive voicing assimilation in obstruent clusters in CSR [Contemporary Standard Russian] should not be considered a rule of the language.

Similarly, Kohler (1984: 163), Gustafson (1986) and Wissing and Roux (1995) argue that languages with prevoicing (negative voice onset time) in their plosives are the ones that, seemingly always, employ regressive voicing assimilation, while those that do not have consistent prevoicing in their plosives all lack regressive voicing assimilation (as confirmed by Iverson and Salmons 1999 for Germanic languages generally). Thus, as Westbury (1975: 139) argues, this process is not a "rule" of any language, but a universal constraint on languages with a given phonetic property.

This phonetic property is exactly the property that implements the phonological feature [voice] in the narrow interpretation. A strong hypothesis can be postulated: if voicing and tenseness/aspiration are defined in narrow senses, then regressive voicing assimilation is a property of all languages with the feature [voice] as distinctive feature. It appears from the literature that this prediction can be made with more confidence than the other relationships involving the feature [voice] postulated in the preceding discussion. Evidence suggests that final devoicing is rather frequently associated with [voice], but intervocalic voicing and post-nasal voicing can be associated with language types only in stating that they are options available only to certain language types. These two processes constitute true parametric options. However, regressive voicing assimilation and maybe final devoicing approach the status of principles of phonology, rather than simply parameters that may be set in more than one way with roughly equal probability. The challenge that such a relationship between alternations and distinctive features poses to a formal phonological theory such as Optimality Theory, is to incorporate in a natural way, without any need for stipulation, a conditional statement of the form "if X, then Y," in this case "if [voice] is selected as distinctive feature, then regressive voicing assimilation automatically applies in that language."[11]

Before this challenge is taken up in section 5, the hypothesis that distinctive [voice] implies regressive voicing assimilation must be tested. If one only relies on observed phonological distributions of languages, then the hypothesis is supported as long as it is true, but there may be a more conclusive test. CV-languages do not allow obstruent clusters. However, if a CV-language makes distinctive use of the feature [voice] in the narrow sense proposed here, then the prediction is that those speakers will display regressive voicing assimilation as soon as they speak a second language in which obstruent clusters do arise. This possibility is investigated in the next section.

3. Regressive voicing assimilation by native speakers of Tswana

Tswana is a Southern Bantu language from the Sotho family. Like all other Southern Bantu languages, it allows only open syllables, with one small complication − it also allows syllabic nasals. Thus, adjacent obstruents never occur in Tswana, only nasal+obstruent consonant sequences may occur. These sequences are subject to homorganic nasal assimilation, as well as a fortition process during which fricatives harden to affricates and voiced plosives unexpectedly surface as voiceless − the exact opposite of what post-nasal voicing would predict. The fortition process is thoroughly integrated into the morphology of the language, however, and also occurs in instances where a prefix historically had a nasal, but the nasal

disappeared. Examples (taken from Ziervogel *et al.* 1967) of these
processes are:

(7)   Tswana homorganic nasal assimilation and post-nasal
       hardening

        [m+p'ɔna]   [bɔna]
        me+see   see (V)
        'see me'   'see'

        [n+t'irela]   [dira]
        me+work   work (V)
        'work for me'   'work'

        [n+t'umela]   [dumela]
        me+greet   greet (V)
        'greet me'   'Good day! / greet'

        [ŋ   + ku]
        sg. class prefix /n/ + sheep
        '(a) sheep'

All four examples have nasal + obstruent clusters, with the first
three also illustrating post-nasal fortition.

Given these facts about Tswana, there is no obvious reason to
expect the speakers to apply regressive voicing assimilation in their
second language pronunciation, unless, perhaps, the second language
exhibits regressive voicing assimilation. Wissing (1996) establishes
empirically that Tswana speakers apply regressive voicing assimilation when speaking Afrikaans. However, Afrikaans also has regressive voicing assimilation (see section 4.2 of this paper). Thus,
one may conclude from this that regressive voicing assimilation in
Tswana-Afrikaans is a consequence of good acquisition, where the
target language pronunciation has been acquired in a native-like
fashion. For this reason, a better test for the prediction that [voice]
implies regressive voicing assimilation in heterosyllabic obstruent
clusters, is to consider Tswana-English because English has obstru-

ent clusters but generally lacks regressive voicing assimilation. An experiment was designed for this purpose.

3.1. Speakers

Four native speakers of Tswana, two male and two female, partici-pated in the experiment as paid subjects. All four of them are compe-tent speakers of English. None of them have ever studied languages or linguistics after completing school, and none reported a history of hearing loss or speech disorders.

3.2.   Stimuli

Sixteen sentences were constructed, in which the first names and surnames of various fictitious people were inserted. All the names ended orthographically in a voiceless obstruent, while all surnames started with a voiced obstruent in the orthography. We assume that the orthography reflects the phonological representations accurately in these cases. The obstruents used were [b d g v z] as the voiced series and [p t k f s] as the voiceless series. These obstruents were selected because their pronunciation does not present problems to Tswana speakers, unlike the fricatives [ð θ] that are often replaced by [d t] in Tswana-English pronunciation.

Consonants occurred in roughly equal proportions, and each consonant from each series was combined with all the consonants from the other series. Examples of the sentences are:

(8)   His name is Je**ff** **B**rown, not Je**ff** **G**reen.   [f-b], [f-g]
       Please call Pe**te** **V**uyani and Dic**k** **D**ean.   [t-v], [k-d]
       Please write down Flo**k** **Z**uma, not Ste**f** **Z**uma.   [k-z], [f-z]

All the names used in the experiment should be familiar to the subjects. The names were either English names or names typically of English or Afrikaans origin and used as second (Western) names by many black South Africans alongside a first name in the native language. Equal numbers of English and African surnames were used.

Two name and surname combinations occurred in each sentence, giving a total number of 32 cases per reading. Each of the four speakers read the stimulus material twice, for a total number of 256 cases (32 x 2 readings x 4 speakers).

3.3. Procedure

Speakers were seated comfortably in a recording studio. A free-standing microphone (Shure SM48) was placed on a table. The microphone was connected to a computer, on which subsequent acoustic analyses were performed. Subjects were given a sheet of paper with all the sentences on it, and given time to familiarise themselves with the sentences. Thereafter, they were requested to read the sentences at a comfortable rate into the microphone. After completing the first reading, they were given a short break and then proceeded with the second reading. Speakers were asked about the purpose of the experiment afterwards, but none had any idea about the purpose. We are therefore satisfied that subjects did not deliberately try to apply regressive voicing assimilation or prevent themselves from applying the process.

The names and surnames, which were the focus of the experiment, were selected from the recorded data, and stored on CD-ROM. Acoustic analyses were conducted with the programme *Praat*, developed by Paul Boersma from the University of Amsterdam, to determine if actual voicing assimilation occurred between the initial obstruent of every surname and the final obstruent of every first name.

The criteria for classifying an example as an instance of regressive voicing assimilation were strict. Fricatives as the final obstruent of the name had to display voicing periods on the waveform for more than half of the actual duration of the fricative, while the following obstruent (the initial consonant of the surname) had to be voiced as well. For plosives, prevoicing of the final consonant of the name was required, or voicing onset more or less simultaneous with plosive release, and uninterrupted vocal fold vibration through-out the closure of the following sound if it is a plosive. This option is not available for following fricatives, so only prevoiced plosives were regarded as instances of regressive voicing assimilation when the following obstruent was a fricative. No indirect indices of regres-sive voicing assimilation were measured, such as the duration of the preceding vowel, the fundamental frequency or first formant properties of the offset of the preceding vowel, since the narrow interpretation of the feature [voice] dictates that an obstruent can only be classified as voiced when actual vocal fold vibration is present.

3.4. Results

Table I. Summary of results. Presentation of data is pooled across the identity of the lefthand obstruent, which is underlyingly voiceless.

Obstruent cluster	Number of cases	Instances of regressive voicing assimilation	Percentage
C $ z	64	45	70
C $ d	48	28	58
C $ b	40	21	53
C $ v	56	27	48
C $ g	48	21	44
Total	256	142	55

No influence of the leftmost consonant was observed. Neither the manner, nor the place of articulation differed substantially across contexts. As far as the rightmost consonant is concerned, no effect can be attributed to manner of articulation, while the place of articu-lation might have a smallish effect. Alveolars conditioned more assi-milation than labials, which conditioned more assimilation than velars in turn.

The cases where regressive voicing assimilation did not apply were all cases where the underlying form of both consonants sur-faced faithfully. Thus, no progressive devoicing was observed. In about two-thirds of the cases of non-application, the speakers inserted a pause of more than 200ms between the name and surname. Regressive voicing assimilation therefore did not take place across a pause. This is not surprising, and has been reported for many languages. Cohen *et al.* (1959: 46) explicitly point out that assimilation can only be possible when there is no pause between two adjacent obstruents.

3.5. Discussion

The hypothesis that this experiment was designed to test, is that a speaker who has acquired the distinctive feature [voice] for obstruents contrasts, will automatically apply regressive voicing assimilation. The results provide unambiguous support for the hypothesis.

Tswana is a language with negative voice onset time for voiced plosives (Wissing and Roux 1995; Wissing 1996), and thus a language that makes distinctive use of the feature [voice]. The Tswana speakers transferred the negative voice onset time to their English pronunciation in this experiment. At the same time, regressive voicing assimilation occurred in more than half of all the possible cases, while the majority of the remainder had a pause that inherently prevents regressive voicing assimilation to take place. This fact is possibly a result of the unnaturalness of the experimental conditions and does not cast doubt on the validity of the hypothesis.

The finding of this experiment poses a challenge to Optimality Theory. The descriptive generalisation can be made by means of constraints and constraint ranking, but as Westbury (1975: 139) points out, regressive voicing assimilation is not just a "rule" that should be stipulated. It is an inherent consequence, even property, of the distinctive feature [voice]. The challenge of incorporating this into Optimality Theory is taken up in section 5. Before that is done, it is important to consider the optional character of regressive voicing assimilation in Dutch and Afrikaans, which may potentially constitute counter-evidence to the hypothesis.

4. Optional application of regressive voicing assimilation in Dutch and Afrikaans

Regressive voicing assimilation does not consistently occur in Afrikaans and Dutch when two adjacent obstruents occur. Dutch has a categorical exception to regressive voicing assimilation, viz. progressive devoicing when the rightmost obstruent in an obstruent cluster is a fricative, and both languages display competition between regressive voicing assimilation and progressive devoicing in a non-categorical manner. This occurs in all obstruent clusters in Afrikaans, and in obstruent clusters with a rightmost plosive in Dutch.

4.1. Dutch categorical progressive devoicing

Dutch obstruent clusters with a fricative in the rightmost position are illustrated below (examples from Trommelen and Zonneveld 1979: 104):

(9) | *Underlying form* | *Phonetic form* | *Gloss* |
|-----|-----------------|---------|
| | boe/kv/orm | boe[kf]orm | 'book form' |
| | har/tz/eer | har[ts]eer | 'sadness' |
| | han/dv/at | han[tf]at | 'taking hands' |
| | drij/vz/and | drij[fs]and | 'quicksand' |

Dutch phonologists report that regressive voicing assimilation occurs when the rightmost obstruent in a cluster is a plosive (see the data in (5) above), but progressive devoicing occurs when the rightmost obstruent in a cluster is a fricative, as in (9) above.

There is a property of Dutch fricatives that should be considered to understand progressive devoicing in the examples in (9) above. Debrock (1978: 462, 470) and Slis and Van Heugten (1989) report that phonologically voiced fricatives in Dutch are not always phonetically voiced. In fact, Slis and Van Heugten (1989: 127) find voicing for more than 50ms in only about 20% of all possible intervocalic pronunciations of [v] and [z].[12] The velar fricative [ɣ] is subject to dialectal variation, with western Dutch dialects not distinguishing it phonemically from [x], although south east Dutch dialects do maintain this phonemic distinction (Slis and Van Heugten 1989: 130).

If this finding is taken into consideration, it is clear that the occurrence of progressive devoicing in Dutch clusters with a rightmost fricative is a result of the phonetic unavailability of vocal fold vibration to spread leftwards in an obstruent cluster. There is no special need to stipulate devoicing of such clusters, no need for a special phonological rule or constraint to "cause" or "explain" it. Its occurrence is a function of phonetics of the lenis fricative, and not of some extra property of the features [voice] and [cont] in Dutch.

It would be more accurate to use some other feature to express the fortis/lenis opposition in Dutch fricatives. Debrock (1978: 470) regards voicing as an optional, redundant feature of the lenis fricatives, and regards [tense] as the primitive feature. It may even become subject to intervocalic voicing like Korean, which is the more likely source of its voicing when it does occur. It is clear, then, that Dutch obstruent-fricative clusters are not exceptions to the implicational relationship between the distinctive feature [voice] and regressive voicing assimilation, but support this relationship. The moment that the distinctive feature [voice], in the narrow sense, is not distinctive, regressive voicing assimilation does not take place, and can not take place.

4.2. Competition between regressive voicing assimilation and progressive devoicing

On the basis of such an understanding of Dutch progressive devoicing in obstruent-fricative clusters, the data on the optional character of regressive voicing assimilation in obstruent-plosive clusters in Dutch, and in all obstruent clusters in Afrikaans can be considered. A number of researchers on Dutch report that regressive voicing assimilation does not always take place when it is expected to (Loots 1983; Slis 1983, 1986), or does not always lead to the complete voicing of the coda-obstruent preceding a voiced onset-plosive (Van

Dommelen 1983). Summarising across the various findings of Slis (1983, 1986), regressive voicing assimilation takes place only about half of the time it is supposed to in compounds such as those in (5) above. The rest of the time, progressive devoicing takes place.

Burton and Robblee (1997) conduct a similar investigation on Russian, and find that regressive voicing assimilation takes place in about 82% of the cases where it is expected to occur, while progressive devoicing only takes place in about 9% of the possible cases. In the other 9% of the cases, no assimilation takes place. In the case of Russian, it is not difficult to dismiss the exceptions as an experimental artefact or perhaps as typical low-level phonetic variability that need not be accounted for by phonology. However, the pervasiveness of the "exceptions" to regressive voicing assimilation in Dutch requires more serious consideration. More specifically, the difference in the degrees of consistency with which regressive voicing assimilation is applied in Russian and Dutch calls for an explanation. The relevant data to explore this issue is available for Afrikaans, a closely related sister language of Dutch.

In Afrikaans, the systematic distinction between obstruent-fricative and obstruent-plosive clusters is absent. Through the years, Afrikaans phonologists (Le Roux and Pienaar 1928: 167; Wissing 1982: 183-85; Combrink and De Stadler 1987: 78) have reported only the occurrence of regressive voicing assimilation in Afrikaans, but recent acoustic research indicates that progressive devoicing occurs as well (Wissing 1990; Wissing and Du Plessis 1992).

The obstruents of Afrikaans are similar to Dutch, except that the lenis fricatives /z ɣ/ are not phonemic. They have been replaced by the fortis fricatives /s x/. The obstruent inventory of Afrikaans therefore looks as follows:

(10) Voiceless/fortis plosives: p t k (c restricted to diminutives)
      Voiced/lenis plosives: b d
      Voiceless/fortis fricatives: f s x (ʃ marginally present)
      Voiced/lenis fricative: v

The following examples are all possible, and attested, pronunciations of the name and surname of a well-known Afrikaans sports star and TV personality, *Naas Botha*:

(11)   UR   /nɑːs boːta/
        PRs   [nɑːz boːta] (regressive voicing assimilation)
               [nɑːs boːta] (no assimilation)
               [nɑːs b̥oːta] (progressive devoicing)

Data illustrating both voicing processes are as follows:

(12)   a. Regressive voicing assimilation
        /sɛsdə/   →   [sɛzdə]   'sixth'[13]
        /dəs vələm/   →   [dəz vələm]   'It's William'
        /dət beːtər/ →   [dəd beːtər]   'it better'
        /klap dət/   →   [klab dət]   'hit it'

        b. Progressive devoicing
        /sɛsdə/   →   [sɛstə]   'sixth'
        /maxda/   →   [maxta]   'Magda' (first name)
        /dənsdax/   →   [dənstax]   'Tuesday'
        /lifdə/   →   [liftə]   'love' (N)

A close examination of the various acoustic studies on regressive voicing assimilation and progressive devoicing in Afrikaans (Wissing 1990, 1991, 1992a, 1992b; Wissing and Du Plessis 1992; Wissing and Roux 1995), which elaborated on the design of Slis (1983, 1986) for Dutch, reveals the following:

(13)

        a. The occurrence of regressive voicing assimilation and progressive devoicing is not particularly sensitive to the type of obstruent in the rightmost or leftmost position, although plosive-plosive and fricative-fricative clusters are slightly more conducive to regressive voicing assimilation than to progressive devoicing.

b. If the syllable preceding the cluster is stressed, progressive devoicing is favoured, e.g. *Dínsdag* [dənstax] 'Tuesday', but if the syllable after the cluster is stressed, regressive voicing assimilation is favoured, e.g. *Dis Wíllem* [dəz vələm] 'It's William'.

c. Across word-boundaries and compound boundaries, regressive voicing assimilation is more likely to occur, *e.g. glas+deur* [xlazdør] 'glass door', while progressive devoicing is more likely to occur within monomorphemic forms, or across affix boundaries, *e.g. lief+de* [liftə] 'love' (N) (adjective *lief* 'love' + nominalising suffix *-de*).

d. If a pause is inserted between the two obstruents in the cluster, neither process is likely to occur.

e. The sociolinguistic values older and male correlate positively with regressive voicing assimilation, while female and younger speakers are more likely to apply progressive devoicing.

To understand these facts, we need to make a distinction between the function of regressive voicing assimilation and the phonetics that allow such a function to be performed. Gustafson (1986) examines the distribution of regressive voicing assimilation and what he calls 'non-phonemic aspiration' in the languages of the world. Non-phonemic aspiration refers to the process of aspiration in languages like English, where aspiration is not a consistent property of plosives, but one that is particularly important in word-initial position for the distinction between fortis and lenis plosives. Gustafson regards this type of aspiration as non-phonemic, since it does not always realise in plosives in a language like English. This is different from a language like Hindi, which consistently uses aspiration as a contrasting property for different plosive types.[14]

Gustafson (1986: 49-51) points out that regressive voicing assimilation and non-phonemic aspiration serve the same function, namely the maintenance of a contrast between word-initial fortis and lenis plosives in languages with different phonetic properties. Those languages that exhibit regressive voicing assimilation are characterised phonetically by a consistent contrast between negative voice onset time and short-lag voice onset in plosives; languages that select the distinctive the feature [voice] in terms of the proposal put forward in this paper. On the other hand, languages that employ non-phonemic aspiration are characterised by an inconsistent opposition between fortis and lenis plosives from a phonetic perspective. In intervocalic positions, negative voice onset time cues lenis plosives (intervocalic voicing), but elsewhere, the fortis/lenis opposition is cued by short-lag *vs.* long-lag voice onset time. These languages select the distinctive feature [tense] rather than [voice].

Both processes are motivated by the same concern, to preserve the contrast between fortis and lenis plosives in word-initial positions. This contrast is under pressure, because of the difficulty in maintaining obstruent contrasts in clusters. Golston and Kehrein (1999: 27-28) find that languages generally do not contrast laryngeal features in tautosyllabic obstruent clusters (see also Lombardi 1995). Gustafson (1986: 51) points out that the same kinds of pressures operate across syllable boundaries. Therefore, regressive voicing assimilation or non-phonemic aspiration is employed to maintain the integrity of an obstruent in onset-positions, particularly if those positions are also word-initial.

The choice of process — regressive voicing assimilation or non-phonemic aspiration — depends on the phonetics of the language concerned. It is almost a tautology to say that plosives without prevoicing simply cannot spread their voicing to the preceding obstruent, nor can fricatives without sustained voicing spread their voicing to a preceding obstruent. Thus, when regressive voicing assimilation is phonetically impossible, non-phonemic aspiration is implemented instead. Non-phonemic aspiration is the tensing of a marked plosive, without a parallel tensing of an unmarked lenis plosive.

It might be the case that the Afrikaans data exhibit both regressive voicing assimilation and non-phonemic aspiration, or something similar. Before we can investigate this possibility, the feature specification of Afrikaans obstruents needs to be considered. Like Dutch phonologists, Afrikaans phonologists generally assume that [voice] is distinctive in Afrikaans. Prevoicing has been observed by Wissing and Roux (1995: 50) among others. However, Afrikaans speakers have been observed to show inconsistent prevoicing in their plosives. Occasional aspiration has also been observed, even though it is not a consistent property (Wissing and Coetzee 1996). The absence of pre-voicing and the occurrence of aspiration both correlate with the sociolinguistic variables female and young, as well as urban. Thus, some reflexes of an opposition along the dimensions of the feature [tense] can be observed in Afrikaans, as is the case for (at least) Dutch fricatives, as pointed out earlier.

The systematic opposition between fortis and lenis fricatives has also been reduced in the development of Afrikaans from 17th century Dutch. Afrikaans only has one voiced fricative, [v]. The historically voiced/lenis fricatives [z] and [ɣ], both of which are still present in contemporary Dutch, have disappeared in Afrikaans, leaving only the voiceless [s] and [x].

Generally, then, the distinctive feature [voice] is not that well established in Afrikaans and Dutch when compared to Romance and Slavic languages. Furthermore, there appears to be considerable sociolinguistic variability within the Afrikaans speech community, with some speakers organising the fortis/lenis contrast more along the dimensions of [voice], but others along the dimensions of [tense].

If these facts are taken into consideration, then it is expected that some speakers will be more prone to employ regressive voicing assimilation, those whose speech is characterised by a distinctive feature [voice] for their plosives. Other speakers, those whose speech is more properly characterised by the feature [tense], are expected to employ some opposite process. This opposite process is labelled progressive devoicing by most researchers, since they perceive this is the opposite of regressive voicing assimilation, but called non-phonemic aspiration by Gustafson (1986). To maintain consistency between the terminology for features and processes, we propose the label progressive fortition for this process. Therefore, cases in Afrikaans where the opposite of regressive voicing assimilation takes place are regarded as instances of progressive fortition.

Apart from the sociolinguistic variability that characterises the competition between the [voice]-regressive assimilation and [tense]-progressive fortition complexes in Afrikaans, there also appears to be a degree of grammaticalisation (see 13b and 13c above). Regressive voice assimilation is observed across morphologically and syntactically stronger boundaries, while progressive fortition occurs more frequently across affixal boundaries and across syllable boundaries in monomorphemic forms. It appears, then, as if both these processes are gradually being entrenched in the morphonology of Afrikaans, with different demarcation functions.

Further evidence for the competition between the [voice]-regressive voicing assimilation and [tense]-progressive fortition complexes comes from child language acquisition. In current work on the phonetics and phonology of Afrikaans children aged 3-4, we have found very little indication of prevoicing in plosives, and find a complete absence of regressive voicing assimilation. These two observations are not independent: there is little or no regressive voicing assimilation in the speech of Afrikaans children *because* there is little or no prevoicing in their plosives. Deuchar and Clark (1996) study the acquisition of the fortis/lenis opposition in English — a language with distinctive tenseness, and Spanish, a language with distinctive voicing, by a bilingual child. They find that the Spanish-type opposition with prevoicing is acquired later than the English-type opposition. During initial stages, the child employs a tenseness distinction in Spanish as well (Deuchar and Clark 1996: 362). Our preliminary findings concur with the findings on English and Spanish, and also provide indirect support to the hypothesis that [voice] implies regressive voicing assimilation, because the absence of [voice] during Afrikaans acquisition implies the absence of regressive voicing assimilation.

Similar to the progressive devoicing (or more accurately, progressive fortition) in Dutch obstruent-fricative clusters, the competition between regressive voicing assimilation and progressive fortition in Afrikaans, and probably Dutch obstruent-plosive clusters as well, does not provide counter-evidence to the hypothesis that the feature [voice] implies the presence of regressive voicing assimilation in a language. When [voice] is not (consistently) present, then regressive voicing assimilation does not apply. Instead, it appears as if [tense] may substitute as distinctive feature for [voice] under various grammatical and/or sociolinguistic conditions, in which case progressive fortition may appear in place of regressive voicing assimilation.

It appears as if Afrikaans and Dutch represent an intermediate category between the more typical [tense] languages (see Iverson and Salmons 1995, 1999 on the Germanic languages in particular) and the more typical [voice] languages, represented by Slavic languages like Russian and Polish.

If our hypothesis is accepted, a number of problem cases in the research on voicing phenomena within the scope with Optimality Theory disappear. To demonstrate the usefulness of our proposal, then, we turn to these problems in the next section.

5. Regressive voicing assimilation within Optimality Theory

Voicing phenomena, in particular regressive voicing assimilation, have been treated in some detail by Lombardi (1999) and Grijzenhout and Krämer (2000) within the framework of Optimality Theory (McCarthy and Prince 1993; Prince and Smolensky 1993). The basic understanding of regressive voicing assimilation, although subject to minor differences in terminology, is relatively uncontroversial, but will be reviewed first to serve as basis for discussion. Thereafter, problems raised by both papers, in connection with progressive fortition in Dutch as well as apparent exceptions in Germanic languages other than Afrikaans and Dutch will be reviewed, and the solution to these problems presented from the framework of the narrow interpretation of the feature [voice] proposed in this paper.

The obvious treatment of regressive voicing assimilation in Optimality Theory is to formulate a number of constraints relevant to the feature [voice] and establish their ranking (for similar accounts, see Lombardi 1999; Grijzenhout and Krämer 2000; Grijzenhout 2000). A syntagmatic markedness constraint on voicing in adjacent obstruents is necessary to force obstruent clusters to agree in voicing. This constraint can be formulated as follows:

(14)   AGREEOBS[VOICE]: Adjacent obstruents agree in value for the feature [voice].

Like all markedness constraints in Optimality Theory, this constraint expresses a generalisation about surface forms, not underlying forms. The constraint is not partial to either regressive voicing assimilation or progressive devoicing, since the application of both processes will result in obstruent clusters in which all obstruents agree in voicing. Lombardi (1999) points out that the agreement-constraint is not inherently directional. The application of regressive voicing assimilation is a consequence of the various other constraints that co-determine, with this markedness constraint, the selection of the optimal candidate. There is, of course, a universally well-attested paradigmatic markedness constraint against voicing in obstruents. This constraint is the one directly responsible for languages such as Korean that have no voiced obstruents:

(15)   *OBSVOICE: Obstruents are voiceless.

However, to account for languages that allow voiced obstruents at all, a faithfulness constraint on obstruent voicing is required. Lombardi (1999) proposes a general faithfulness constraint on all obstruent voicing, the dialectic opposite of the markedness constraint (15) above:

(16)   FAITHVOICE: Obstruents are faithful to their input voicing.

The interaction between the constraints in (14-16) above will not yield the desired outcome, however. A further constraint is required, one that is position-specific in the sense originally proposed by Beckman (1996): a position that is prominent for some phonological or grammatical reason is subject to stronger faithfulness constraints than other, less prominent positions. Incorporating the insight of Gustafson (1986), which was not expressed with the Optimality Theory-paradigm in mind, an onset-specific faithfulness constraint can be proposed:

(17)   FAITHONSETOBS[VOICE]: Obstruents in syllable onsets are faithful to underlying [voice].

Languages with regressive voicing assimilation as a consistent property, such as Russian or Polish, are subject to the following partial constraint ranking:

(18)   AGREEOBS[VOICE], FAITHONSETOBS[VOICE] » *OBSVOICE » FAITHVOICE

In those cases in Afrikaans and Dutch where regressive voicing assimilation takes place, we assume that the same constraints and ranking must be operative. This is illustrated with an Afrikaans example in (19):

(19)   /dəs vələm/ → [dəz vələm]   'It's William'

Input: /dəs vələm/	AGREEOBS [VOICE]	FAITHONSETOBS [VOICE]	*OBS VOICE	FAITH VOICE
[dəs vələm]	*!		*	
☞[dəz vələm]			**	*
[dəs fələm]		*!		*
[dəz fələm]	*!	*	*	**

One key aspect of our analysis of regressive voicing assimilation is that the ranking responsible for the application of the process must be associated with the distinctive feature [voice] in all cases. Thus, once the feature [voice] is acquired as a distinctive feature, the ranking in (18) necessarily becomes part of his or her phonology. This is illustrated by the Tswana-English data in section 3 above in particular.

To conceptualise this state of affairs requires a somewhat modified understanding of Optimality Theory as well. Not only are the constraints universal, like all Optimality Theory-constraints are assumed to be, but also does this ranking represent a universal ranking schema, of status similar to the schema for emergence of the unmarked phenomena (see McCarthy and Prince 1994).

If this schema is universally accepted, then we have a straightforward account of the occurrence of regressive voicing assimilation in the second-language English of Tswana-speakers, and at the same

time, of the absence of regressive voicing assimilation in languages
like German and English. Only one condition applies, viz. the individual speaker must have acquired the distinctive feature [voice]. A
Tswana-speaker never exhibits regressive voicing assimilation in
his/her first language, since Tswana is subject to phonotactic constraints that disallow obstruent clusters from occurring at all.
However, the typical Tswana-speaker has acquired the distinctive
feature [voice], and when speaking English, the Tswana-speaker will
apply regressive voicing assimilation as soon as he/she has suppres-
sed (demoted) the phonotactic constraints that disallow obstruent
clusters.

For Afrikaans and Dutch, the domain of the faithfulness constraint (17) might be different. Grijzenhout and Krämer (2000)
identify a number of domains that compete for faithfulness in Dutch.
The onset of the prosodic word is identified as a particularly salient
site for faithfulness. It might well be the case that the only variation
allowed across languages is the domain over which constraint (17)
holds. In Afrikaans, it also appears that the relevant domain is the
(morphological, and presumably also the prosodic) word, and not as
general as the onset of every syllable, given that obstruent-initial
suffixes do not compete strongly for faithfulness (see Van Rooy
1999 for full detail of an Optimality Theory-analysis of Afrikaans).

Lombardi (1999) and Grijzenhout and Krämer (2000) both deal
with a case that appears to be problematic for an Optimality Theory-
analysis, viz. the behaviour of obstruent-fricative clusters in Dutch
(see section 4.1). Lombardi (1999) formulates the following markedness constraint:

(20)   Post-Obstruent Fricative Voicing (FRICVOICE):

$$* \; [-son] \begin{bmatrix} -son \\ +cont \\ voice \end{bmatrix}$$

She acknowledges herself that this constraint is not very elegant,
but has to be employed, according to her, otherwise the behaviour of
the obstruent-fricative clusters in Dutch is unaccounted for. In terms
of the ranking (18), this constraint has to outrank all of the

constraints, or at least, crucially, the constraint on voicing in onset positions (17), FAITHONSETOBS[VOICE]. Thus, for Dutch the following ranking is proposed by Lombardi (1999):

(21) FRICVOICE, AGREEOBS[VOICE] » FAITHONSETOBS[VOICE] » *OBSVOICE » FAITHVOICE

In terms of Lombardi's analysis, then, a Dutch from like *raadzaam* 'advisable' would be analysed as follows:

(22) /ra:dza:m / → [ra:tsa:m]   'advisable'

Input: /ra:dza:m/	FRIC VOICE	AGREEOBS [VOICE]	FAITHONSET OBS [VOICE]	*OBS VOICE	FAITH VOICE
[ra:dza:m]	*!			**	
[ra:dsa:m]		*!	*	*	*
[ra:tza:m]	*!	*		*	*
☞[ra:tsa:m]			*		**

Grijzenhout and Krämer (2000) reject this analysis on two grounds. The first reason is its descriptive inadequacy. They do a much more comprehensive analysis of Dutch data and particularly incorporate data from Dutch affixes and clitics into their analysis. They show that obstruent-initial clitics, as well as certain obstruent-initial suffixes, are also subject to progressive devoicing, even if those obstruents are plosives. Consequently, what Lombardi (1999) regards as a process relevant to fricatives only, is much more widespread (Grijzenhout and Krämer 2000: 64-65). Secondly, they appeal to the typological universal that voiced fricatives are much more marked than voiced plosives. To accommodate this observation, they propose constraints on faithfulness of plosives, in this way excluding fricatives (Grijzenhout and Krämer 2000: 71-72). Reformulating one of their constraints slightly for consistency with the formulations in this paper,[15] the constraint for faithfulness in the onset of a prosodic word looks as follows:

(23)   Faithfulness to Plosive [Voice] in Prosodic Word Onset (FAITHPLOSVOICE PWO): Plosives in the onset position of prosodic words should be faithful to their underlying voicing.

This constraint, and similar ones that privilege plosive faithfulness to fricative faithfulness, allows them to account for much more data (see Grijzenhout and Krämer 2000: 71-75 for detail and several tableaux), in a way that makes the situation in Dutch look far less exceptional than the way it appears from Lombardi's (1999) analysis.

While the analysis proposed by Grijzenhout and Krämer (2000) is an improvement on the one of Lombardi (1999), it still fails to account for the fact that in Dutch, it also happens that plosives in the onset of prosodic words devoice. The one important gain of their analysis is to recognise that plosives are much more likely to remain faithful to their voicing. This is of course simply a consequence of the fact that fricatives do not have a distinctive feature [voice] in Dutch, as argued earlier. To remedy the remaining problem in the analysis of Grijzenhout and Krämer (2000), one simply has to recognise explicitly that the constraints on voicing in plosives, both faithfulness and markedness constraints, apply only insofar as the distinctive feature [voice] is present in a specific context.

To account for the variability in Dutch, and in Afrikaans, it is necessary to recognise the role of the distinctive feature [voice]. If a particular obstruent is voiced, then it is potentially a candidate for participation in the process expressed in constraints (14-18). The variability in Afrikaans and Dutch must be regarded as a consequence of the variation that holds for the features [voice] and [tense].

Languages like English and German lack regular application of regressive voicing assimilation because their obstruents are never underlyingly specified for the feature [voice]. This recognition is important for the solution of the other problem that Lombardi (1999) identifies with regressive voicing assimilation. She argues that in English inflections, notably the plural and the past tense, voicing assimilation appears to be progressive, rather than regressive. Thus, in the following cases, her generalisation that voicing assimilation is always regressive as a result of different faithfulness relations appears to be contradicted:

(24)   Plural: cat + /z/   /tz/ → [ts]
        Past tense: walk + /d/   /kd/ → [kt]

To account for these cases, Lombardi (1999) appeals to what she terms Harms' constraint, the notion that sonority considerations rules out the presence of a voiceless obstruent closer to the nucleus of a syllable than a voiced obstruent. Following the arguments of Iverson and Salmons (1999), as well as the present proposal for a narrow interpretation of the feature [voice], English does not have a distinctive feature [voice], and therefore cases like (24) are not related to regressive or any other form of voicing assimilation. English has the distinctive feature [tense], and the suffixes above are simply unmarked for this feature. When they attach to stems with a marked [tense] final obstruent, they come to share this feature with them, in a process that is probably related to progressive fortition that occurs across syllable boundaries in English as well. Again, like progressive fortition in heterosyllabic clusters, it appears as if the direction for tenseness assimilation is progressive in tautosyllabic clusters as well, unlike voicing assimilation that appears to be regressive in all cases.

6. Conclusion

The hypothesis proposed in this paper is that the distinctive feature [voice] automatically entails the presence of regressive voicing assimilation in a particular language, provided that the feature [voice] is interpreted in the narrow sense of the actual presence of vocal fold vibration. This is evident from the widespread occurrence of regressive voicing assimilation in language of the world, that all happen to share the distinctive feature [voice].

In this paper, more conclusive evidence has been presented from the occurrence of regressive voicing assimilation in second language varieties such as Tswana-English, where neither the first, nor the second language, normally has regressive voicing assimilation, but as soon as Tswana-speakers are confronted with obstruent clusters (absent from their first language), they automatically apply regressive voicing. Apparent counter-examples, notably the variability that characterises the application regressive voicing assimilation in Afrikaans and Dutch, have been shown not to contradict the postulated relationship between regressive voicing assimilation and the feature [voice], but actually support the hypothesis.

These insights have been brought to bear on a couple of issues raised in research on regressive voicing assimilation within the framework of Optimality Theory. Certain apparent exceptions to the otherwise elegant analysis of Lombardi (1999) disappear as soon as the narrow interpretation of [voice] is adopted. In addition, the variability in Dutch obstruent-plosive clusters, unaccounted for by Lombardi (1999) as well as Grijzenhout and Krämer (2000), does not render the basic Optimality Theory-analysis problematic. It is the phonetic variability of Dutch, and also Afrikaans, that is responsible for the variability in the occurrence of regressive voicing assimilation.

A number of issues are raised for further consideration. If the postulated relationship between the distinctive feature [voice] and regressive assimilation exists, then the possibility of a similar relationship between the feature [voice] and final devoicing arises. A couple of problem cases appear to violate such a hypothesis, including the reported non-occurrence of final devoicing in languages like French and Ukrainian. The phonetics and phonology of these languages need careful investigation, as it appears from this paper that much of what appears to be variable from a phonological perspective can be explained from a phonetic perspective.

Similarly, the relationship between the feature [tense], or [spread] in the terminology of Iverson and Salmons (1995, 1999), and some complementary processes need to be explored in direct comparison to the feature [voice]. Such an analysis might contribute to a more refined understanding of the relationship between the features [voice] and [tense], and yield further support for the adoption of the narrow interpretation of both features.

Finally, the possibility of distinctive features directly associated with certain phonological processes raises a challenge to Optimality Theory. It has already been shown in this paper that not only must constraints be assumed to be universal, but certain ranking configurations seem to enjoy universal status too. This has implications for the conception of ranking in Optimality Theory, and also for the understanding of language acquisition within the theory.

Notes

* The work in this article is partly based on Van Rooy's Ph.D. dissertation (1999), which was completed under supervision of Wissing. Financial assistance by the Centre for Science Development (CSD) in South Africa towards that study is gratefully acknowledged. All opinions expressed in this paper are those of the authors and should not be imputed to the CSD.
1 For the sake of illustration, we assume the pronunciation [ɣ] for the velar fricative in *zeggen*, which would perhaps be more likely in Belgium and some southern provinces of The Netherlands than [x], which would more likely be found in the central and northern parts of The Netherlands (see Slis and Van Heugten 1989 for detail on this issue).
2 Note that these examples from Dutch and Polish do not constitute cases of intervocalic voicing, since there are instances where a voiceless morpheme-final obstruent remains voiceless even in intervocalic positions. These obstruents are then voiceless in their underlying representations, unlike the underlyingly voiced obstruents in the data in (1) and (2). An example from Dutch is *ka[t]* (sg.) 'cat' which becomes *ka[t]en* in the plural. Examples of voiceless intervocalic obstruents in Polish are in the words *ko[s]ic* 'mow' and *no[s]ic* 'carry' (from Rubach 1996: 70-71).
3 Rice (1994: 126-127) also refers to instances of final devoicing that affect sonorants, resulting in allophonic variation parallel to that of fricatives. These are not considered here.
4 Rice (1994: 126) cites these data from an unpublished MA-thesis by Thompson (1977).
5 [ɬ] is a voiceless lateral fricative, and it has a voiced lateral fricative counterpart [l] in Athapaskan languages (Rice 1994: 108).
6 We believe that the feature [tense] is relevant to the majority of the Germanic languages, where aspiration is present in word-initial position, while the intervocalic distinction is often cued acoustically by reduced aspiration of tense obstruents *vs.* passive voicing of lax obstruents. The feature [spread] should be reserved for languages with consistent aspiration of [+spread] plosives. It might well be that [tense] is a hybrid feature that represents a syncretism of the features [spread] and [voice]. However, the exact nature of this distinction is not relevant to the present discussion. For a more detailed discussion of our own position, see Van Rooy and Wissing (1998), and for a slightly different version of the same kind of idea, see Boersma (1998). For convenience of reference, we will maintain the use of [spread] or [tense] of the original authors

whose work we discuss. When we have to refer to this "other" feature, we will use the informal labels *fortis* and *lenis*, where fortis is likely to be aspirated, and lenis unaspirated, occasionally voiced, but only redundantly so.

7   As pointed out by Iverson (1997), Iverson and Salmons (1999) and Holslinger (2000), German does not have "final devoicing" but rather "final fortition", where the right edge of a word (or syllable) is marked by the feature [spread], a feature that is added, rather than a contrast that is neutralised in favour of the unmarked member. German is therefore also not an exception to our view of voicing and its association with regressive voicing assimilation, since it still has no [voice], therefore it should not have regressive voicing assimilation (Iverson 1997: 263).

8   An anonymous reviewer pointed out that it might well be that the configuration [+spread, +voice] is illicit in New Julfa, and this is the reason why post-nasal voicing doesn't extend to aspirated stops. While this is certainly possible, it would be unfortunate if one has to ascribe the blocking of post-nasal voicing in the same language to two different causes when the two instances appear to be very similar.

9   A slightly modified version of the phonological phrase proposed by Jun to account for the domain of Korean lenition effects. Harris (to appear) points out that laryngeal elements are subject to a variety of lenition effects in non-foot initial positions, including passive voicing.

10 Final fortition is of course not excluded, but it is an entirely different process (see also note 7).

11 As an anonymous reviewer points out, this kind of statement is rather easier to incorporate into more phonetically orientated theories like Articulatory Phonology or Gestural Phonology. However, in the context of the present paper, a secondary goal is to solve problems raised by recent research within Optimality Theory; therefore, the perceived shortcoming specifically in Optimality Theory is regarded as a problem worth highlighting.

12 Slis and Van Heugten (1989) study intervocalic fricatives, because they are the ones most likely to be voiced. In final position, Dutch obstruents are always voiceless, unless regressive voicing assimilation takes place, and in initial position, partial devoicing is more common than in intervocalic positions. Debrock (1978) also emphasizes that lenis fricatives are not consistently characterised by voicing in initial positions.

13 The schwa /ə/ is phonemic in Afrikaans, and functions just as any other vowel phoneme. Importantly, a word can be well-formed with two schwas in two syllables, no need for a full vowel.

14 It is on the basis of the difference between languages with non-phonemic aspiration, like English, and languages where aspiration is more consistent in contrasting contexts, like Hindi, that we argue elsewhere for the need to use both [tense] and [spread] as features – [tense] for English and [spread] for Hindi (see Van Rooy and Wissing 1998). We will adopt the feature [tense] in our

own analyses here and subsequently for languages with non-phonemic aspiration.

15 Grijzenhout and Krämer (2000) consistently use IDENT constraints rather than FAITH constraints, drawing on Correspondence Theory (McCarthy and Prince 1995), one of the versions of Faithfulness within Optimality Theory. In principle, we agree with them on this issue, but have adopted a slightly less complex version of faithfulness in this paper for expository purposes.

References

Anderson, Stephen R.
1985   *Phonology in the Twentieth Century: Theories of Rules and Theories of Representations.* Chicago: University of Chicago Press.
Beckman, Jill N.
1996   Positional faithfulness. Ph.D. dissertation, University of Massachusetts, Amherst.
Boersma, Paul
1998   *Functional Phonology: Formalizing the Interactions between Articulatory and Perceptual drives.* The Hague: LOT.
Burton, Martha W. and Karen E. Robblee
1997   A phonetic analysis of voicing assimilation in Russian. *Journal of Phonetics* 25(2): 97-114.
Cohen, A., C. L. Ebeling, P. Eringa, K. Fokkema and A. G. F. Van Holk
1959   *Fonologie van het Nederlands en het Fries.* [*Phonology of Dutch and Frisian.*] 's-Gravenhage : Martinus Nijhoff.
Combrink, J.H.G. and L.G. de Stadler
1987   *Afrikaanse Fonologie [Afrikaans Phonology].* Johannesburg: Macmillan.
De Coninck, Herman
1992   *Onbegonne werk: gedichten 1964-1982 [Unstarted work: poems 1964-1982].* (4th ed.) Antwerpen: Manteau.
Debrock, Mark
1978   Is the fortis-lenis feature really redundant in Dutch? *Leuvense Bijdragen* 67: 457-472.
Deuchar, Margaret and Angeles Clark
1996   Early bilingual acquisition of the voicing contrast in English and Spanish. *Journal of Phonetics* 24: 351-365.
Goblirsch, Kurt Gustav
1994   Fortis and lenis in standard German. *Leuvense Bijdragen* 83: 31-45.

Golston, Chris and Wolfgang Kehrein
    1999   Laryngeal contrasts. Unpublished manuscript, California State University, Fresno (CA) and Phillips University, Marburg (Germany).

Grijzenhout, Janet
    2000   Voicing and devoicing in German, English and Dutch. Paper presented at the First International Conference on Linguistics in Southern Africa, Cape Town (SA).

Grijzenhout, Janet and Martin Krämer
    2000   Final devoicing and voicing assimilation in Dutch derivation and cliticization. In: Barbara Stiebels and Dieter Wunderlich (eds.), *Lexicon in Focus*, 55-82. Berlin: Akademie Verlag.

Gustafson, Kjell
    1986   Aspiration and voicing assimilation. *Progress Report from Oxford Phonetics* 1:46-54.

Haggard, Mark
    1978   The devoicing of voiced fricatives. *Journal of Phonetics* 6: 95-102.

Harris, John
    To appear Release the captive coda: the foot as domain of phonetic interpretation. To appear in *Papers in Laboratory Phonology VI*. Cambridge: Cambridge University Press. (Available at http://www.phon.ucl.ac.uk/home/johnh/home.htm)

Holslinger, David J.
    2000   Lenition in Germanic. Ph.D. dissertation, University of Wisconsin, Madison.

Hutters, Birgit
    1985   Vocal fold adjustment in aspirated and unaspirated stops in Danish. *Phonetica* 42: 1-24.

Iverson, Gregory K.
    1997   Review of W. Brockhaus, Final Devoicing in the Phonology of German. *American Journal of Germanic Linguistics and Literatures* 9(2): 255- 264.

Iverson, Gregory K. and Joseph C. Salmons.
    1995   Aspiration and laryngeal representation in Germanic. *Phonology* 12: 369-396.
    1999   Glottal spreading bias in Germanic. *Linguistische Berichte* 178: 135-151.

Jakobson, Roman
    1949   On the identification of phonemic entities. *Selected Writings I: Phonological Studies,* 418-425. s'Gravenhage: Mouton.

Jessen, Michael
    1998   *The Phonetics and Phonology of Tense and Lax Obstruents in German.* Amsterdam: Benjamins.

Jun, Suh-Ah
1994   The domains of laryngeal feature lenition effects in Chonnam Korean. *Ohio State University Working Papers in Linguistics* 43: 15-29.
1995   Asymmetrical prosodic effects on the laryngeal gesture in Korean. In: Bruce Connell and Amalia Arvaniti (eds.), *Papers in Laboratory Phonology IV: Phonology and Phonetic Evidence*, 235-253. Cambridge: Cambridge University Press.

Keating, Patricia A.
1984   Phonetic and phonological representation of stop consonant voicing. *Language* 60: 286-319.
1990   Phonetic representations in generative grammar. *Journal of Phonetics* 18: 321-334.
1996   The phonology-phonetics interface. In: Ursula Kleinhenz (ed.), *Interfaces in Phonology*, 262-278. Berlin: Akademie Verlag.

Kingston, John and Randy L. Diehl
1994   Phonetic knowledge. *Language* 70: 419-454.

Kohler, Klaus J.
1984   Phonetic explanation in phonology: the feature fortis/lenis. *Phonetica* 41: 150-174.

Le Roux, T.H. and R. de Villiers Pienaar
1928   *Afrikaanse Fonetiek [Afrikaans Phonetics]*. Cape Town: Juta.

Lisker, Leigh and Arthur S. Abramson
1964   A cross-language study of voicing in initial stops: acoustic measurements. *Word* 20: 384-422.

Lombardi, Linda
1995   Laryngeal neutralization and syllable wellformedness. *Natural Language and Linguistic Theory* 13(1): 39-74.
1999   Positional faithfulness and voicing assimilation in Optimality Theory. *Natural Language and Linguistic Theory* 17(2): 267-302.

Loots, Marijke
1983   Syntax and assimilation of voice in Dutch. In: Marcel van den Broecke, Vincent van Heuven and Wim Zonneveld (eds.), *Sound Structures: Studies for Antonie Cohen*, 173-182. Dordrecht: Foris.

McCarthy, John J. and Alan S. Prince
1993   Prosodic morphology I: Constraint interaction and satisfaction. Unpublished manuscript, University of Massachusetts, Amherst/ Rutgers University.
1994   The emergence of the unmarked: optimality in prosodic phonology. In: M. Gonzalez (ed.), *Proceedings of the North East Linguistic Society* 24: 333-379. Amherst, Mass.: Graduate Linguistic Student Association, University of Massachusetts.

1995   Faithfulness and reduplicative identity. In: Jill Beckman, Laura
            Walsh Dickey and Suzanne Urbanczyk (eds.), *Papers in Optimality
            Theory*. University of Massachusetts Occasional Papers in
            Linguistics 18, 249-284. Amherst, Mass.: Graduate Linguistic
            Student Association, University of Massachusetts.

Pater, Joe
1999   Austronesian nasal substitution and other NÇ effects. In: Rene
            Kager, Harry van der Hulst and Wim Zonneveld (eds.), *The
            Prosody-Morphology Interface*, 310-343. Cambridge: Cambridge
            University Press.

Prince, Alan S. and Paul Smolensky
1993   Optimality Theory: Constraint interaction in generative grammar.
            Unpublished manuscript, Rutgers University/University of Colo-
            rado, Boulder.

Rice, Keren
1994   Laryngeal features in Athapaskan languages. *Phonology* 11: 107-
            147.

Rubach, Jerzy
1996   Nonsyllabic analysis of voicing assimilation in Polish. *Linguistic
            Inquiry* 27(1): 69-110.

Slis, Iman H.
1983   Assimilation of voicing in relation to voice quality. In: Marcel van
            den Broecke, Vincent van Heuven and Wim Zonneveld (eds.),
            Sound Structures: Studies for Antonie Cohen, 245-257. Dordrecht:
            Foris.

1986   Assimilation of voice in Dutch as a function of stress, word
            boundaries, and sex of speaker and listener. *Journal of Phonetics*
            14(2): 311-326.

Slis, I. H. and M. van Heugten
1989   Voiced-voiceless distinction in Dutch fricatives. In: Hans Bennis
            and Ans van Kemenade (eds.), *Linguistics in the Netherlands*, 123-
            132. Dordrecht : Foris.

Trommelen, Mieke and Wim Zonneveld
1979   *Inleiding in de Generatieve Fonologie [Introduction to Generative
            Phonology]*. Muiderberg: Coutinho.

Van Dommelen, Wim A.
1983   Some observations on assimilation of voicing in German and Dutch.
            In: Marcel van den Broecke, Vincent van Heuven and Wim
            Zonneveld (eds.), *Sound Structures: Studies for Antonie Cohen*, 47-
            56. Dordrecht: Foris.

Van Rooy, Bertus
   1999   The relationship between phonetics and phonology: an investigation into the representation of the phonological feature [voice]. Ph.D. dissertation, Potchefstroom University.
Van Rooy, Bertus and Daan Wissing
   1998   On the relationship between voicing, aspiration and tenseness. *South African Journal of Linguistics* Supplement 36: 101-124.
Vaux, Bert
   1998   The laryngeal representation of fricatives. *Linguistic Inquiry* 29(3): 497-511.
Westbury, John R.
   1975   The status of regressive voicing assimilation as a rule of Russian. *Texas Linguistic Forum* 1: 131-144.
Wissing, Daan
   1982   *Algemene en Afrikaanse Generatiewe Fonologie [General and Afrikaans Generative Phonology].* Johannesburg : Macmillan.
   1990   Progressiewe stemassimilasie –'n 'nuwe' Afrikaans fonologiese reël [Progressive voicing assimilation – a 'new' Afrikaans phonological rule]. *South African Journal of Linguistics* 8(2): 88-97.
   1991   Regressiewe stemassimilasie in Afrikaans: ses hipoteses eksperimenteel getoets [Regressive voicing assimilation in Afrikaans: six hypotheses tested experimentally]. *South African Journal of Linguistics* Supplement 11: 132-156.
   1992a   Vowel duration in Afrikaans: the influence of postvocalic consonant voicing and syllable structure. *Journal of the Acoustic Society of America* 92(1): 589-592.
   1992b   Stemassimilasie en segmentsterktehierargieë in Afrikaans [Voicing assimilation and segment strenght hierarchies in Afrikaans]. *South African Journal of Linguistics* Supplement 13: 121-134.
   1996   Regressiewe stemassimilasie in die Afrikaans van Tswanamoedertaalsprekers [Regressive voicing assimilation in the Afrikaans of Tswana mother tongue speakers]. *South African Journal of Linguistics* 14(4): 150-153.
Wissing, Daan and Andries Coetzee
   1996   Die akoestiese eienskappe van stemlose eksplosiewe in Afrikaans [The acoustic properties of voiceless plosives in Afrikaans]. *South African Journal of Linguistics* Supplement 34: 63-82.
Wissing, Daan and Hans du Plessis
   1992   Die fonologie van –de en –te in Afrikaans [The phonology of –de and –te in Afrikaans]. *South African Journal of Linguistics* Supplement 13: 185-204.

Wissing, Daan and Justus Roux
  1995   The interrelationship between VOT and voice assimilation. In Kjell
           Elenius and Peter Branderud (eds.), *Proceedings of the 13th International Conference of the Phonetic Sciences,* Volume 1, 50-53.
           Stockholm.
Ziervogel, D., J. A. Louw, J. A. Ferreira, E J. M. Baumbach and D. P. Lombard
  1967   *Handboek vir die Spraakklanke en Klankveranderinge in die
           Bantoetale van Suid-Afrika [Handbook of the Speech Sounds and
           Sound Changes of the Bantu Languages of South Africa].* Pretoria:
           Unisa.
Zonneveld, Wim
  1983   Lexical and phonological properties of Dutch voicing assimilation.
           In: Marcel van den Broecke, Vincent van Heuven and Wim Zonneveld (eds.), *Sound Structures: Studies for Antonie Cohen,* 297-312.
           Dordrecht: Foris.

The phonology of /r/*

Richard Wiese

1. Introduction

Phoneticians and phonologists have always referred to a type of sound segment symbolized by "r", and recognized that this comes in various varieties. The IPA-system recognizes at least eight such kinds of "r", which can be very different from each other. The problem then is this: what makes the unity of these r-sounds, or rhotics? Ladefoged and Maddieson (1996) in their survey of r-sounds conclude that there is no phonetic basis for a unity within this otherwise well-motivated class, and see only a historical and orthographic basis for referring to a group of r-sounds. The present paper will first show that the variation of r-sounds, within and across languages, is indeed impressive. But the evidence for "r" from phonological patterns in the languages of the world is so strong that we cannot leave the matter here.

I will then discuss a few possible ways of capturing "r", and will conclude that the common core for all the possible realizations of /r/ is most likely to be found in terms of syllable prosody, in particular with reference to the sonority hierarchy. However, the conception of the sonority hierarchy needs to be revised in order to allow for a characterization of /r/ in terms of this concept. While previous conceptions of the sonority hierarchy define the hierarchy in terms of segmental features, the present revision proposes an abstract ordering relation independent of segmental features, especially major class features. If this view turns out to be correct, it has consequences for the understanding of the definition of segments in terms of basic features.

2. The paradox

It appears to be a fairly innocent question to ask what an r-sound is. If we approach the question by assuming that symbols based on the Roman letter "r" are commonly used to denote r-sounds[1], we may derive at the following table, a subset of the table of consonants in the IPA notation; version of 1996. That is, the IPA notation provides, in a first approximation, 7 different symbols for rhotics. The set of sounds enumerated in (1) will serve as a preliminary starting point for the discussion to follow.

(1)   Simple IPA symbols used for r-sounds

	Dental/Alveolar/Postalveolar	Retroflex	Uvular
Trill	r		R
Tap or Flap	ɾ	ɽ	
Fricative			ʁ
Approximant	ɹ	ɻ	

In addition to these seven symbols, the IPA notation recognizes a dental/alveolar lateral flap: ɺ, and a diacritic for rhoticity, to be added to vowel symbols as such: ɚ, e˞, a˞, etc. The list of rhotics provided by Ladefoged and Maddieson (1996: 216) is very similar; they do not include the rhotic vowel and use [ʁ] for a uvular approximant instead of a fricative (as does Walsh Dickey 1997: 14). Note that even with these extensions, we have not arrived at a complete list of rhotics. For example, there is no simple symbol in (1) for the uvular approximant, although there is very likely to be such a non-rolled, non-fricative r-sound, for example in Standard German (prevocalically; according to a number of descriptions; see Hall 1993 or Wiese 2000). If [ʁ] is used for the approximant, the question arises whether the uvular fricative is a rhotic as well. By using diacritics, such additional sounds can be described, in this case as [ʁ̝].[2] Of course, there may not be any logic behind the use of the letter *r* in this system of notation, and indeed we will see immediately that other segments are treated as rhotics as well. Conversely, there is no compelling reason to assume that all r-like symbols are indeed used for members of the class of rhotics.

To increase the confusion, it must be pointed out that there is a sufficient number of sounds which are treated ambiguously: on some occasion, they are assigned to the class of r-sounds, and on other occasion, they are assigned to some other class of segments. For example, [χ] is interpreted either as a voiceless fricative or as a rhotic – see Dutch, which has this fricative, but which also has similar or identical r-sounds (Booij 1995: chapter 2.3). Note also that [ʁ], the voiced uvular fricative, is included among the r-sounds in the IPA table, while its unvoiced counterpart, [χ], is not. Apparently, it is not possible to say whether all voiced and voiceless uvular fricatives are r-sounds or not (see below for more discussion of fricatives as rhotics). Restricting r-sounds to voiced consonants would be only partially correct, as r-sounds can be voiceless, often through assimilation and sometimes as a voiceless (or aspirated) /r̥/ contrasting with voiced /r/ (as in Sedang, Irish, Ingush; see Ladefoged & Maddieson 1996: 236-237 for details).

In a similar vein, [ɾ] and [ɽ] are interpreted as either a rhotic tap/flap or as just a tap/flap – cf. English (tap/flap) to Spanish, where the same symbol stands for a rhotic tap/flap. In other words, it looks as if segmental properties do not lead to an unambiguous decision whether some sound is a member of the class of r-sounds or not. It is this observation that I will expand upon in the analysis below. There are in fact more candidates for r-sounds, for example the bilabial trill [ʙ] and the labio-dental approximant [ʋ]; see discussion below and more examples in Wiese (to appear). Just to mention one of these: Ladefoged (1993: 169) lists the voiced bilabial trill [ʙ] among the "types of *r*", while Ladefoged and Maddieson (1996: 216) in an otherwise very similar table of r-sounds do not mention this sound. Obviously, (1) lists those r-sounds which happen to be symbolized by some variant of the letter *r* in the main consonant table of the IPA. It is unclear whether there is any deep significance attached to this difference in symbolization.[3]

The important question to be answered, of course, is whether there is any common denominator to the sounds commonly (though not unambiguously) identified as rhotics. The set of rhotics could comprise either the sounds listed in (1) or a modified version of this

set. Alternatively, the whole question is moot. Based on the generalizations noted in (3) below and on the discussion in section 5, this
paper will arrive at the conclusion that there is indeed a phonological
class of rhotics, following work by Hall (1997) and Walsh Dickey
(1997). Other questions to be answered consequently are the following: if there is a class of rhotics, what is the property shared by all
its members? Why is the alveolar trilled [r] generally regarded as the
prototypical r-sound? Why is there so much synchronic and diachronic variation within the set of rhotics?

The question of the defining property of r-sounds is not identical
to the question what the defining property of a typical major class in
phonology is. Major classes such as consonants, vowels, obstruents,
or approximants are indeed hard to define phonetically. But it is not
clear at all whether r-sounds are major classes in this sense. The
languages of the world typically contain exactly one r-sound. Maddieson (1984: 83) gives the following statistics for the number of r-
phonemes in his data base of 317 languages:

(2)   Number of r-phonemes in languages (absolute/%)

0	1	2	3	>3
74/23.3	183/57.7	51/16.1	8/2.5	1/0.3

There is, as this table demonstrates, a clear preference for a language
to have exactly one r-phoneme. In addition, deviations from this preference are minimal: 1 r-phoneme ±1 per language accounts for 97%
of the language sample. This fact contrasts with the large number of
available sounds in the class. Further generalizations from Maddieson's survey are the following: apical or alveolar trilled [r] is the
dominant r-sound; languages with more than one r-phoneme typically distinguish these by manner, and not place, of articulation; no
language in this database has more than four r-phonemes. [4]

If there are at least eight or nine different r-sounds which are
identified in a fairly unproblematic manner, it should be possible to
state a reasonably precise definition of what an r-sound is. But this is
by no means the case. As a second look at table (1) shows, there cannot be a common property of r-sounds in terms of the articulatory
classification on which the IPA table is based, because neither

manner of articulation nor place of articulation are constant. And for none of the relevant rows (manners) or columns (places) in table (1) do we find exclusively r-sounds in their respective rows/columns.

Is there more hope in finding an acoustic property distinguishing all r-sounds from all other sounds? This question is discussed at some length by Ladefoged and Maddieson in the relevant chapter of their survey of the *Sounds of the World's Languages* (Ladefoged and Maddieson 1996: chapter 7), largely based on a study by Lindau (1985). While previous studies had identified a lowering of the third formant as a possible acoustic feature of r-sounds, Lindau demonstrates that this is by no means true for all r-sounds. Their conclusion is therefore completely negative – there is no known acoustic property of this sort. Ladefoged and Maddieson (1996: 215) begin their discussion by stating: "The terms rhotic and r-sound are largely based on the fact that these sounds tend to be written with a particular character in orthographic systems derived from the Greco-Roman tradition, namely the letter 'r' or its Greek counterpart rho." After discussing what they regard as the complete set of r-sounds and their possible properties they concur with Lindau (1985: 166): "There is no physical property that constitutes the essence of all rhotics." A refutation of this negative conclusion is not known to me.

Ladefoged and Maddieson (1996: 245) end their discussion as follows: "Although there are several well-defined subsets of sounds (trill, flaps, etc) that are included in the rhotic class, the overall unity of the group seems to rest mostly on the historical connections between these subgroups, and on the choice of the letter 'r' to represent them all." In place of an unambiguous featural characterization of the class of r-sounds, there is only a "family resemblance", in that members of one subclass share properties with members of some other subclass. In this way, all subclasses are related to at least one other subclass in a network of shared properties; see Lindau (1985: 167). Walsh Dickey (1997), confirming the observation that there is no unique property shared by all rhotics, takes up the notion of family resemblances between different types of rhotics and argues that the phonetic basis of rhotics consists not in a single phonetic property but in a set of related properties. It remains to be seen whether there is a non-arbitrary way of establishing such "polymor-phous categories" (Walsh Dickey 1997), given that possibly all phonetic categories can be interpreted as being related in one way or other. In other words, it is hard to see how an unambiguous class of rhotics is established in this way. Furthermore, Walsh Dickey (1997: section 3.3) acknowledges that the unity of rhotics is to be found in a phonological categorization (for a discussion of Walsh Dickey's treatment of rhotics see section 3.2).

In striking contrast to this negative conclusion (shared by Schiller 1999), it is equally true that phonological unity of the r-sounds can be demonstrated. The most obvious generalizations for r-sounds are the following (in part also recognized by Ladefoged & Maddieson 1996: 216; see also Hall 1997: 108 and Walsh Dickey 1997: section 3). Maddieson (1984: 82) presents other generalizations on r-sounds, which will be discussed in section 3.4.

(3)   Generalizations on /r/

i. The position in the phonotactic patterns of languages: r-sounds are vowel-adjacent elements in the syllable, occurring between vowels and other consonants in the same syllable (if such clustering is possible in a particular language). The pattern is: CrVrC.

ii. r-sounds, while non-syllabic consonants in general, often have a syllabic variant. It appears that languages which allow for sylla-bic consonants at all will allow for syllabic /r/.[5]

iii. Rhotics of one type often alternate with rhotics of another type (synchronically or diachronically). While alternations with other segments occur as well, the frequency and range of rhotic-inter-nal alternation is noteworthy and is found in families which are otherwise quite diverse; see Walsh Dickey (1997: section 3.3) for examples.

iv. If a rhotic alternates with another rhotic in terms of stricture, the phonotactics of these r-sounds does not change; see below for examples, especially from French and German.

v. Phonological constraints and other generalizations such as those in i. to iv. above can refer to /r/ without any reference to the type of /r/ in question, see discussion of the /rVr/-constraint in Dutch below (section 4.2) and the positional restrictions on rhotics in Australian languages noted by Walsh Dickey (1997: section 3.3).

The paradox, then, is this: how can a completely heterogenous class of sounds, with apparently no identifiable common property, function as a unit in the languages of the world? Or, in other words: is /r/ a fiction? Given present knowledge and the state of the art, it is clear that the unity of rhotics can only be found in their phonological behavior. But to the extent that current phonological theory relies on featural specifications of units and classes of such units, there must be some featural account of rhotics.

One possible move in order to simplify the system of r-sounds would be to argue that some subsets of the consonants considered in (1) are not part of the rhotic system at all. For example, one could exclude uvular consonants from the class. However, there are reasons beyond tradition and common phonetic and linguistic usage to keep uvular trills, approximants and even fricatives in the class. For the uvular trills and approximants, it appears that languages which include such a segment in their phonemic inventory, do not show the alveolar r-sound otherwise found in most languages. Given that most languages have a rhotic in their phonemic repertoire, it is plausible to assume that the questionable uvular sound is to be interpreted as this rhotic sound. The languages with uvular trills reported in the UPSID data base (Maddieson 1984) are Batak, French and German. None of these languages has a coronal (dental, alveolar, retroflex) rhotic. Curiously, the claim that rhotics in French and German are predominantly trills, can well be questioned (see below).

A second move in the same direction would be to argue that all *fricatives* should not be regarded as rhotics at all.[6] However, this move is problematic for two reasons: first, the variation (synchronic and diachronic, free or contextual) noted above often involves fricatives. This is particularly obvious for languages in which /r/ is or may be a uvular sound, such as in German, French or Portuguese. For all of these languages, fricatives are undoubtedly among the allophones or alternants noted; for French and German see below in (9) and (16), for Portuguese see Walsh Dickey (1997: section 3.3.3). Second, there are (admittedly few) languages in which a fricative is the primary or even only variant of the r-phoneme. Such languages include the eight languages noted by Maddieson (1984) to employ a voiced coronal fricative r-sound.[7] Finally, as noted above, some languages contrast voiced and voiceless rhotics (/r̥/ in contrast with /r/). While information is not always available, it is plausible to assume that the voiceless rhotics in these languages are to be interpreted as fricatives; see Ladefoged and Maddieson (1996: sections 7.5, 7.6). The voicing contrast found for a few languages also seems to make it impossible to restrict rhotics to voiced segments.

3.   Possible features of /r/

To address the question of adequate feature specifications of r-sounds, I first discuss some accounts presented in the phonological literature so far. As the need for identifying rhotics as a class largely follows from the fact that there are phonological generalizations to be captured, it is hopefully the case that the features necessary are to be found in proposals from the domain of phonology, because the concept of the natural class is prominent in most, if not all, phonological theories. As we have seen in section 2, straightforward phonetic features (articulatory or acoustic) are not available, anyhow. Furthermore, as noted by Hall (1997) and Walsh Dickey (1997: section 3.3), there is surprisingly little discussion of the feature or the features of /r/. In the following, it is assumed that rhotics may range from vocalic to fricative. This is important, as there are different solutions available if, in particular, fricatives are excluded from consideration. However, I have just argued that rhotics may be fricatives. This discussion is continued in section 4.1 below.

3.1 Naive full specification

A first approximation would be to look at the prototypical /r/, namely the dental/alveolar trilled consonant [r]. Features of this sound could be as in (4), where it is irrelevant whether a purely segmental feature structure of the SPE-type is chosen, or whether some more elaborate autosegmental structure of features (Feature Geometry; see, e.g., Clements 1985, McCarthy 1988, Halle 1995 is adopted.

(4) Features of /r/, full specification:

[+cons, +cont, +son, –lateral, +coronal, –nasal]

All of the specifications here are necessary to distinguish [r] from some other sound. However, this is obviously not a viable solution for the general problem. The feature specification in (4) is simply not true for the majority of cases listed in (1) and those discussed elsewhere. (4) may be a specification for the prototypical /r/, but clearly not for the whole class. Furthermore, only [+cont] (see discussion in section 3.3), and [–lateral] seem to hold for all realizations of /r/. Even nasal /r/ has been reported for a few languages; see /r̃/ in Waffa as described by Cohn (1993).

3.2 The direct approach

3.2.1 The feature rhotic

A direct attack on the problem is proposed by Lindau (1985) and Hall (1997). While Lindau tentatively suggests the use of a feature [rhotic] as a cover feature, and does this in full acknowledgement of the impossibility of a phonetic grounding (see section 2 above), Hall (1997: chapter 4) proposes to turn the problem into a virtue, and to acknowledge a phonological feature [rhotic] because of the obvious generalizations dependent on it. Hall's main concern in this chapter is the status of coronal rhotics and their featural description (within a study of coronals in general), but he argues that the phonological generalizations valid for r-sounds require access to the r-sounds as a class.

According to this proposal, r-sounds are [+rhotic], and it is this specification which allows a comprehensive reference to r-sounds or rhotics. However, calling rhotics [+rhotic] is potentially just a termi-nological move. First, [rhotic] works more like a cover feature, one with no phonetic correlate and no basis identifiable in the data. Second, it is therefore of no help in deciding which segments belong to the class of r-sounds and is problematic for the ambiguous sounds mentioned at the end of section 1. All we can say is that a questionable sound such as the tap [ɾ] or the bilabial trill [ʙ] is either [+rhotic] or not. It is even unclear how this assignment affects the sound in question. In other words, the proposal is more a restatement of the problem than a solution for it. We should therefore look at further approaches which are both viable and enlightening.

3.2.2 Rhotics as place of articulation

A further approach to characterize rhotics with a set of standard features is that of Walsh Dickey (1997: chapter 3). In her study of rhotics, she proposes to define the class of rhotics by place features alone. Rhotics are, according to her study, sounds with a non-primary Laminal node. This Laminal node is dominated by an Apical node, which is in turn dominated by a Coronal node, see (5a) for the respective feature tree. Furthermore, uvular rhotics are assumed to have the structure in (5b). The presence of a secondary Laminal node is common to all rhotics, and separates them from all other classes of sounds.

(5) Features of /r/, Walsh Dickey (1997):

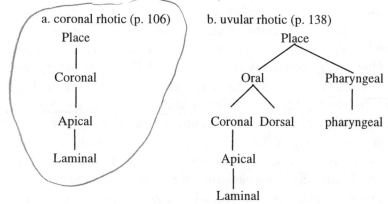

Walsh Dickey's reason for postulating the Apical node is the observation that coronal rhotics are predominantly apical (and not laminal!, see below). The reason for postulating the additional Laminal node is that, according to her view, rhotics resist rules of palatalization because they are palatal already. And since "Palatalization is secondary laminality" (p. 105), the presence of this node follows.

As seen in the structures in (5), the model allows for a complex stacking of place features. Expressing the distinction between primary and secondary features by making the latter dependent of the former is a standard move in models of Feature Geometry. But in this model, features can also be dependent of themselves (Laminal dominates Laminal, p. 119), and seemingly contradictory features (such as Apical and Laminal) can both be present in a single segment; see (5). The first possible objection to the model under consideration therefore is that this system of hierarchical place features overgenerates vastly. The domination of features by themselves is apparently unrestricted (Dorsal dominates Dorsal, p. 67), as is the depth of the stacking.[8] The model thus allows for far more place distinctions than commonly made, and it allows for the descriptions of articulations which are probably impossible.

Secondly, the unexceptional presence of a Laminal node (the defining feature for rhotics in this model!) is in striking contrast to the assertion that rhotics are generally non-laminal: "Apical rhotics are abundant; laminal rhotics are avoided." (Walsh Dickey (1997: 98)). As noted above, the reason for its presence is the tendency for rhotics to resist palatalization. But, as Walsh Dickey notes, this is just a tendency, and there may well be other reasons for the observation.[9] One other account is proposed by Hall (2000), who argues that the resistance of rhotics to palatalization lies in the fact that (coronal) rhotics are apicals, while palatalized sounds are normally laminal. It is this clash with markedness principles which makes palatalized rhotics rare. A further problem with the Laminal node lies with uvular rhotics. These are equipped with the structure displayed in (5b), which not only illustrates the multitude of stacked place features in this approach. As Walsh Dickey (1997: 98) admits, there is no evidence for the presence of the secondary Laminal node in the case of uvular rhotics.

Thirdly, Walsh Dickey's claim that r-sounds interact exclusively with front, but not with back, vowels, can also be questioned. Her examples (Walsh Dickey 1997: 98) all refer to coronal rhotics. It is questionable whether uvular rhotics are to interact with front vowels as well. In fact, Krämer (1979) demonstrates a backing influence of German uvular /r/ on preceding vowels. Furthermore, retroflex rhotics tend to lead to backness of vowels as well (see Kingston and Cohen 1992), and trills or flaps have been shown to *lower* a preceding vowel; see Bhat (1974: 76f.). There is no explanation in this model for the widely documented lowering and/or backing effects.

Fourthly, the proposal presupposes that rhotics are never fricatives (Walsh Dickey 1997: 98). Rhotics are always liquids, and the feature [liquid] is incompatible with fricatives. But at the same time, Walsh Dickey (1997: 71) acknowledges that 3.5% of all rhotics in the database by Maddieson (1984) are in fact fricatives. This issue remains unresolved.

Finally, the proposal sketched in (5) is in striking contrast to the observation that the generalizations on rhotics, as noted above, are primarily of a *phonotactic* or *prosodic* nature. Why should such generalizations depend on a very specific configuration of place features?

3.3 Underspecification

A further approach which seems promising at first glance is to remove all variable information from the feature specification of /r/. In such an underspecification approach, one would look for the small set of features common to all occurrences of /r/ and then provide all additional values by means of universal and/or language- and context-specific rules. Looking back at the features in (4), it appears that [+cont] is a possible candidate for such an underspecified featural characterization of /r/.

(6) Features of /r/, underspecification:

[+cont]

The reasoning behind this proposal is not, of course, that only /r/ is [+cont], but that, plausibly, all types of /r/ are [+cont], with one possible exception to be discussed below, and that the feature-filling rules needed for /r/ can be kept apart from those filling in specifications for other continuants. (As noted in section 3.1, r-sounds are also [–lateral] and (mostly) [–nasal]. But an approach to /r/ based on these two specifications would probably not be very illuminating.) A complete underspecification model will have to specify the set of rules deriving at the full specification, in this case of the particular r-sound or r-sounds in the language under discussion.

Are all r-sounds [+cont]? The possible counter-example would be the tap/flap variety of /r/.[10] There is little discussion of features of tap/flaps in general, but Hall (1997) explicitly argues that they are [–cont], a view also assumed by Bhat (1974: 86). For Hall, this is one reason for his "retreat" to a feature [rhotic].

From her phonetic studies of r-sounds, Lindau (1985) argues differently. She observes that taps are like single-phase trills in terms of closure and opening phases:

(7)   Lindau (1985: 166):

> "The taps look very much like the closure phase of a trill. An average apical tap lasts 20 msec. [...] Each closure phase of an apical trill also lasts about 20 msec, based on the average from twenty-five speakers of six languages. From an acoustic point of view, a trill can be regarded as a series of taps. A tap is also frequently a variant of a trill, particularly in intervocalic position."

Presumably, if trills are [+cont], and if taps take up a subduration of trills, then taps should be [+cont] as well. In addition, there is the observation that taps/flaps are often realized as trills if stressed or emphasized. Bhat (1974: section 3.1.2) lists several languages in which this is the case. It is unlikely that this change is one from [–cont] to [+cont], rather, which trills and flaps/taps provide the strong vs. weak elements on a strengthening/weakening scale. I therefore assume that taps/flaps share continuancy with other rhotics. [+cont] can then be used as a possible common demonitor of all r-sounds. However, as many other sounds (such as all vowels) are [+cont] as well, this specification is not the distinctive feature for the class of r-sounds.

There is a second problem in the underspecification approach to r-features. Full-fledged underspecification systems (first explored by Kiparsky 1982 and Archangeli 1984) require a rich hierarchy of serially-ordered specifications. This problem, identified before in the use of underspecification, is particularly pressing for a segment which is as highly variable as the r-sounds. For example, Wiese (2000: chapter 6) in an attempt to characterize the German consonant and vowel system in a radically underspecified featural description, needs a complex battery of various types of feature-filling rules in order to provide a full specification, even for a single language. The full range of such rules is needed for the derivation of various allophones of /r/. Furthermore, rule-ordering paradoxes arise, which require rules applying early in the derivation to refer to the output of other rules which are otherwise required to apply later in the derivation.

As pointed out by T. A. Hall, the underspecification solution starting from just the specification [+cont] (see 6) will also fail for a language with more than one rhotic. In conclusion, it must be said that an underspecification solution to the r-paradox seems, if feasible at all, to require a high degree of rule-ordering, including the acceptance of problematic ordering relationships, even ordering paradoxes.[11] In addition, the underspecification approach, though it acknowledges the segmental instability of rhotics, has no account for the prosodic unity of its members. Using other less radical versions of underspecification theory, such as Contrastive Underspecification Steriade (1987), evades some of these problems, but leads to others. In particular, it seems impossible to underspecify /r/ to a degree that all and only variants of it are included. That is, it is of no help in giving a general characterization of r-sounds. The use of privative features instead of largely binary features, as in Wiese's account (Wiese 2000: chapter 6), might be advantageous, but would still not completely solve the problem.

One further approach might be sought in the model of Articulatory Phonology; see Browman and Goldstein (1986) or Browman and Goldstein (1992). Indeed, Schiller (1999: 277) argues that different variants of uvular (!) German /r/ can be described with reference to "a post-dorsal constriction gesture of the tongue". But this is obviously not a characterization of r-sounds in general. Given that r-sounds do not seem to have a common property in terms of articulatory gestures, it is hard to see how Articulatory Phonology could provide a better basis for the characterization of r-sounds.

3.4 A prosodic approach

For a final solution, let us return to the observations on /r/ made in (3i-v). On closer inspection, none of these generalizations mentions any segmental features of the type discussed in the preceding proposals. Rather, reference is made here to the *phonotactic* properties of r-sounds in general, and to the general instability of /r/ with respect to any segmental properties. Taking this observation serious, it is only logical to argue that the "essence" of /r/ lies not in its segmental features, but exactly in the domain of its distributional patterning: */r/ is a prosody.*

More precisely, /r/ relates to the make-up of syllables in a very direct way. It is this property which is constant across r-sounds, and it should thus be taken as the defining property of the class as a whole. (8) states this position directly:

(8)   A prosodic definition of /r/:

/r/ is the point on the sonority scale between laterals and vowels.

/r/ is related here to the sonority scale or hierarchy, as widely discussed in the phonological literature since the early work by Sievers (1901) and Jespersen (1904). According to this conception, the sonority hierarchy defines an ordered scale of sound classes. The relative order of sounds in a syllable is such that high-sonority items are always closer to the peak of the syllable than sounds lower on this scale. There are actually two claims made in (8): first, /r/ must be seen as a constant point of its own on the sonority scale, and second, this is a plausible, if not the only, answer to the question for the defining property of rhotics.

The first of these claims can be substantiated by reference to French. Standard French /r/ can be a uvular approximant or a fricative; see (9a). In other varieties, /r/ is predominantly a fricative; see (9b).

(9)   Two types of French /r/: Tranel (1987: 143)

a. "constrictive *r* is the one characteristic of standard French. ... This type of *r* is generally voiced and non-fricative. However, ... it is devoiced when it immediately follows a voiceless stop or fricative in the same word. The devoicing is partial if the *r* precedes a vowel (as in *quatre ans* 'four years' and *présent* 'present'), complete otherwise (as in the sentence *ils sont quatre* 'there are four of them')."

b. "In southwestern France, a voiceless and very fricative back *r* is commonly found."

However, the manner of articulation of French r-sounds as sketched in (9) is completely irrelevant for their phonotactic combinatorial possibilities. French allows for (a subset of) obstruent-sonorant clusters in onset positions, while obstruent-obstruent clusters are not admitted. However, /r/ occurs in such consonant clusters irrespective of its properties in terms of voicing and degree of closing, as shown in (10).[12]

(10) Obstruent-r clusters in French:

    a. Standard French *frais, cru, trois*: fʀɛ, kʀ̥y, tʀ̥wa
    b. Southwestern French *frais, cru*, trois: fχɛ, kχy, tχwa

In other words: while obstruent-r clusters freely occur even with fricative /r/, other obstruent-fricative clusters (ks, tf, ps, kf, etc.) are not generally allowed in a syllable onset of French. We may draw the conclusion that devoiced or fricative /r/ occurs in positions which are generally restricted to those of sonorant consonants. /r/ in French is/can be a fricative, but does not behave as such in the phonotactics. Phonotactically, it behaves as predicted by (8). French /r/'s pattern distributionally like sonorant consonants, even when they are not sonorants, segmentally.[13]

In his survey of r-sounds, Maddieson (1984: 82) lists a number of generalizations which hold for the majority of r-sounds in his sample. The first and most widely true of these is the following: "An r-sound is most likely to be voiced." which holds for 97.5% of his 316 languages. This observation (as well as others put forward by Maddieson) looks very much like a statement on the segmental, and not prosodic, content of rhotics. However, it is obvious that there is a relationship between the feature of voice and the sonority rankings of sound classes, such that voiced sounds are generally inside voiceless sounds within a syllable. It is less clear whether the implication needs to be seen as an implication from voicing to sonority or vice versa. That is, rhotics might be overwhelmingly voiced *because* they are high on the sonority hierarchy, and not vice versa.

Two observations have been made at this point. One is that the quality (and thus, sonority in the standard sense) of /r/ varies from fricative to vocalic. The other is that the sonority hierarchy, as generally conceptualized, relates to exactly these qualities. The conclusion from these two statements then seems to be that /r/ cannot systematically and uniquely be related to the sonority hierarchy. /r/ cannot be assigned a single point on the sonority hierarchy, because it varies precisely in the properties which are relevant for the assignment to particular points in this hierarchy.[14] This conclusion, clearly expressed by Schiller (1999), though with respect to other languages, seems inevitable given standard assumption about the sonority hierarchy. Let us therefore inspect the sonority hierarchy more closely.

4. /r/ and the Sonority hierarchy

To briefly recapitulate the status and function of the sonority hierarchy, we start by looking at this concept as in the proposal by Clements (1990). According to this specific instantiation of the general concept, five major classes of sounds are brought into an order, such that all obstruents are minimally sonorous, while all vowels are maximally sonorous. /r/ is of course part of the class of liquids.

(11)   A minimal sonority hierarchy (Clements 1990):

obstruent < nasal < liquid < glide < vowel

To be sure, there are several problems relating to a syllable-structure account relying on a sonority scale. One of these problems is how to account for complex segments, such as affricates, pre- and post-nasalized obstruents, doubly-articulated sounds, etc.[15] For present purposes, I will assume that most of these cases can be handled by assigning a sonority value not to a phonetic segment, but to a more abstract position in a syllable, such as a C-node or V-node (see Clements and Keyser (1983), and subsequent work). Complex segments are structures in which more than one segment is assigned to a single such node. Other structures apparently violating the sonority hierarchy in (11) can often be treated in terms of "extrasyllabicity", the idea that at word edges, some segments are not part of syllables, and thereby not subject to the requirements of the sonority hierarchy, as in the English word *strict*, where initial /s/ and final /t/ may be treated as extrasyllabic elements of this sort.

The type of sonority hierarchy exemplified in (11) relies on the distinctions which can be expressed by commonly used segmental features, features such as [cons], [nasal], [son], etc.; see, for slightly different proposals, Giegerich (1992: 192), Blevins (1995: 211), Wiese (2000: 261). However, not all of the relevant classes are distinguished without problems by such features; see the discussion bclow.

4.1 Revisions

Going beyond the hierarchy in (11) may be necessary, though. There are two arguments from German for giving /r/ a place of its own within the sonority hierarchy. First, /r/ can occur beween vowels and /l/ in the coda, and /l/ can occur between vowels and nasals in the coda, as shown in (12). Reverse orders (/lr/ or /nl/ in the coda) are impossible, and therefore, if /r/ is higher in sonority than /l/, and /l/ is higher than nasals, the clustering is "explained" by reference to this hierarchy.

(12)   r/l/Nasal-distinctions in German:

	a. r/l		b. l/nasal	
	Kerl	'bloke'	Köln	'name, Cologne'
	Quirl	'beater'	Schelm	'rogue'
	Kasperl	'name'	Halm	'stalk'

Second, in certain clusters at right edges the sonorant consonants of German can be syllabic. This is obligatory for /r/ (see 13a), but optional for the remaining sonorants, i.e., /l/ and the nasals (see 13b, c), where the syllabic sonorants alternates with a schwa-sonorant sequence. Again, it looks as if /r/ is closer to vowels than other sonorant consonants, and the sonority hierarchy expresses this generalization. The alternation between syllabic consonants and schwa in (13b, c) is not completely free, but subject to conditions of register, types of segments and tempo. But this variation does not exist for the realization of /r/ in most variants of German; /r/ is always syllabic, a sound symbolized as [ʁ], [ɚ] or [ɐ] (and not a sequence of some vowel plus /r/).

(13)   Syllabic consonants in German

    1. obstruent-/r/

Vater	[faːtɐ]	'father'
Wasser	[vasɐ]	'vase'

    2. obstruent-/l/

Scheitel	[ʃaɪtəl]/[ʃaɪtl̩]	'parting'
Rassel	[ʀasəl]/[ʀasl̩]	'rattle'

    3. obstruent-nasal

leiten	[laɪtən]/[laɪtn̩]	'lead (verb)'
lassen	[lasən]/[lasn̩]	'let'

Let us assume that some extensions of the minimal sonority hierarchy in (11) are necessary, in particular for languages allowing complex onsets and codas, such as the Germanic languages. /r/ will then have a specific place of its own on the sonority hierarchy, namely the one specified in (8). A final detail concerns the relationship between /r/ and glides. Glide-r sequences behave differently from other vowel-r sequences. Diphthongs plus /r/ are heterosyllabic, as shown in (14a), and contrast in this respect with high vowel-r sequences, which are tautosyllabic.

(14)   vowel-r sequences

a. diphthong		b. high vowel		
Feier	[faɪ.ɐ]	'party'	für	[fyːɐ̯]	'for'
Feuer	[fɔɣ.ɐ]	'fire'	vor	[foːɐ̯]	'before'
Bauer	[baʊ.ɐ]	'farmer'	Bar	[baːɐ̯]	'bar'

The conclusion may be that /r/ and glides are mutually exclusive in a syllable position Kahn (1976), Rice (1992), Hall (1992b), Wiese (2000) – at least in English and German.[16] Accounting for these observations leads to an extended sonority hierarchy, which uses smaller classes of sounds in order to describe some of the phono-

355 of the paper

tactic possibilities; see (15). I will assume for the rest of the paper that this scale is the most appropriate one for German.

(15) An extended sonority hierarchy (Wiese 1988: 91, Wiese 2000, Hall 1992a):

obstruent < nasal < lateral < **/r/** < glide < vowel

As for the realization of /r/ in terms of manner features, German is not very different from French, insofar as fricative versions exist as well.[17] There is a colloquial variant of German in the Lower Rhine area which has distinct uvular fricative r-sound in the position after a short vowel as in (16b). Data are from Hall (1993: 92); Schiller (1999) provides phonetic confirmation for the empirical claim that the r-variant is indeed a fricative. In other variants, /r/ is vocalized in the same context (16a); as shown in (16c), the fricative is voiceless if preceded by a short vowel and followed by a voiceless coronal obstruent.

(16) Postvocalic /r/ in Standard German (a.) and Lower Rhine German (b., c.)

a.	vocalic		b. voiced fricative		c. voiceless fricative		
Kerl	[keɐl]	'bloke'	[kɛʁl]	'bloke'	hart	[haχt]	'hard'
Zorn	[tsɔɐn]	'anger'	[tsɔʁn]	'anger'	Mord	[mɔχt]	'murder'
Arm	[ʔaɐm]	'arm'	[ʔaʁm]	'arm'	Hirsch	[hɪχʃ]	'deer'

As is the case for French, German fricative /r/ has just the phonotactic possibilities as any other type of /r/. As shown by the examples in (16b), it even occurs before /l/ and before nasals in a syllable coda. This is just another example of the paradox noted before. It should also be noted that Lower Rhine German has vocalic variants of /r/ along with fricative versions, providing further evidence that there is no fundamental distinction between the fricative and the other variants of the rhotic.

In the case of German, however, fricative /r/ is derived by rule. It is therefore possible to argue that the fricative version is a surface phenomenon of obstruentization only, and that rhotics must be characterized on some other level of representation, one in which rhotics are *not* fricative. Such a position faces two problems: first, there are languages in which the r-sound appears predominantly as a fricative; some versions of French (see 10) provide one example; other examples have been listed in note 8 below. A straightforward exclusion of these languages seems unwarranted.

The second problem is of a theoretical nature. So far, I have largely avoided the question on which level of representation rhotics can and must be characterized, where "level" is to be understood as the input or output of rule-application in derivational phonology. A possible move in order to unify rhotics with respect to their segmental definition would be to argue that rhotics are not identical to their surface form. Rather, they behave in a unified way on deeper representations. According to this conception, those rhotics which are fricative on the surface could be excluded from further consideration. Whatever the correct answer is going to be, it seems problematic to argue that rhotics exist exclusively on non-surface levels. First, there are languages in which rhotics are predominantly fricative. A learner of such language would have to derive the underlying non-fricative representation of such a rhotic from a principle saying that the frication property is to be ignored. Second, it might be problematic to claim that a phonologically relevant property can be exclusively non-surface. Even without denying that there are mismatches between deep and surface representations (as in the case of alternations), the total *exclusion* of a phonological property from surface representations constitutes a more drastic step. But restricting the sonority hierarchy to non-surface representations would directly imply such a surface-free solution.

There seems only one way to acknowledge these observations and considerations in total, and, at the same time, to keep the sonority hierarchy as part of a surface form: we must give up the idea that points on the sonority hierarchy are defined in terms of fixed segmental features. As such a definition is not even possible for /r/, some other way of defining the points on the sonority hierarchy must be devised.

The proposal to be made here is that the sonority hierarchy is nothing but an abstract ordering of points on a scale. The positions are defined not by their inherent segmental features (which seems impossible, at least in the case of /r/), but by nothing than their relative position in the scale. As seen above, on the basis of the evidence from German, six such positions are well-motivated. I leave open whether simpler or more expanded scales are needed for other languages.[18]

(17) An abstract sonority hierarchy:

   P1 < P2 < P3 < **P4** < P5 < P6

The definition of /r/ may now be made on the basis of (17). /r/ is a position on an abstract sonority scale, namely the one between that for /l/ and glides, the position highlighted in bold in (17). This definition is completely distinct from any of the segmental definitions, either of those discussed in section 3 or of any other imaginable one. In other words, under this conception of the sonority scale, it is not the features and natural classes defined by them which constitute the basis of the points on the scale. Rather, the points on the scale (as defined by the ordering relation) are primes which define classes – at least for /r/. I leave open the question whether other or even all points on the sonority scale should be reinterpreted in a similar way. Given the problems with features such as [cons] or [vocalic] (see discussion by Hume and Odden 1996), the possibility clearly exists. Note also that the glide/vowel-distinction made in the sonority scales in (11)/(15) is often interpreted as a difference in syllable prosody alone, one that is largely independent of any segmental features. This would then provide another example of sonority difference which is purely prosodically-based. Furthermore, Grijzenhout (this volume) argues that the feature [nasal] is absent for one type of nasal stop. In such a case, this feature is unavailable for determining the sonority value of the respective segment.

In a way, the revision of the sonority hierarchy proposed in (17) also constitutes a possible answer to the frequent criticism raised against the concept of the sonority hierarchy (Ohala 1990, Butt 1992, Schiller 1999), to the effect that the whole concept is circular and against the facts. The circularity arises from the fact that the sequencing of segments within syllables is supposed to derive from the sonority hierarchy, which in turn is constructed on the basis of observed sequential patterning. The counterfactual nature of the hierarchy relates to phenomena as those discussed above: an /r/ patterns like other rhotics, even if a fricative; at edges, clusters occur even though not admitted by the hierarchy.[19] If we remove segmental features from the hierarchy, but leave the notion of relative ordering intact, large parts of that criticism do not apply anymore. The circularity is avoided because sonority classes in the sense of (17) are based on the observable sequential patternings alone. At least the sonority class of r-sounds need not be defined by means of segmental major class features, as is the case for earlier proposals such as (11) or (15).

Finally, the approach proposed here allows for a prediction with respect to the sounds identified as ambiguous ones in section 2. Sounds are treated as rhotics if in the respective prosodic slot; otherwise they are not. Segmentally, they may be identical. It is for this reason that sounds alternating with clear rhotics are often interpreted as rhotics as well, even if they seem unlikely as rhotics if seen by themselves. An example of this usage is Scottish Gaelic [ðʲ], which is treated as the a rhotic by Ladefoged *et al.* (1998), because it appears as the palatalized variant of /r/.

4.2 The Dutch /rVr/-constraint

As a final example for the particular, but quite systematic, behavior of /r/, I turn to a particular constraint on /r/ discussed in relation to the phonology and morphophonology of Dutch. First, words in Dutch, as shown in (18a), cannot contain the sequence /rVr/, where V stands for any short vowel, including schwa. Second, there are allomorphies of the agentive/inhabitant suffix, which surfaces as either *-er*, *-der*, or *-aar*, i.e., that is, as three allomorphs in complementary distribution.[20]

(18) Impossible words in Dutch:

   a. */rur/, */rar/, */ror/, etc.

b. *-er* after stem ending in stressed syllable with final
consonant except for /r/: speel-er/*scheer-er 'player/shaver'
-der after stem ending in stressed syllable with final /r/:
scheer-der/*speel-der 'shaver/player'
-aar after stem ending in unstressed syllable:
wandel-aar/*scheer-aar/*speel-aar 'walker/shaver/player'

There are several different proposals for the adequate treatment of the phonotactic constraint(s) responsible for the pattern; see Booij (1995: chapter 3.5.4), Booij (1998), Plag (1998) for discussion. They differ in detail, but commonly rely on a constraint avoiding identical elements within some domain (OCP-effect). The point to be made in the present context is that the avoidance of /rVr/ is completely independent of the particular realization of /r/. First, variants of Dutch allow for different types of /r/, both alveolar and uvular, and of various manners of articulations (see Reenen 1994, Velde & Hout 1999). But there is no evidence at all that the /rVr/-constraint depends in any way on the details of r-realization. Second, differences in the realization of the first and the second /r/ in the crucial structure (rVr) can exist in Dutch and are also irrelevant. This set of facts argues for two points: first, we note once again the unity of /r/. In order to express the constraint at all, reference to /r/ "as such" is necessary. Second, the irrelevance of segmental features of /r/ is obvious again too. The unity of /r/ should therefore be sought in some other domain. The observation that discussion of the Dutch /rVr/-constraint correctly neglects segmental details of r-realization is mirrored on a more general level: Maddieson (1984: 78) reports that in 10.8% of his sources, manner of articulation was simply not reported for /r/.

5. Conclusions and problems

In summary, the conclusions of the present article can be drawn as follows:

1. Being an /r/ is what matters in a phonological system, while the type of /r/ in terms of segmental features is often systematically irrelevant (and subject to wide variation and rapid change).

2. Synchronic and diachronic changes in r-quality are frequent and ubiquitous and do not affect the phonological system.

3. On the other hand, /r/ is non-arbitrary in terms of its phonotactic patterning. Its constant appearance between vowels and other consonants leads to the conclusion that /r/ is a prosody.

4. /r/ is therefore best defined as a point on the sonority scale. This point can be located precisely through observable sequential patterns of sounds within the syllable.

5. The concept of the sonority scale needs to be revised. Points on the sonority scale are nothing but relative positions on this scale, not to be defined by segmental major class features.

This conception of /r/ and of the sonority scale has some further consequences for the view one might have of major classes. Although I stated that r-sounds as a class are not directly comparable to other major classes (such as vowels or obstruents), it is obvious that these major classes also relate to the sonority hierarchy in a direct way. It is therefore conceivable that major classes can or must be defined in prosodic terms. This revision could be based upon the sonority hierarchy or some other prosodic concept, such as the sub-constituents of the syllable. It is quite conceivable that the standard view of segment classes is ultimately inadequate and should rely not so much on strictly segmental features than on prosodic structure and conditions.[21] One question in this context is whether the laterals (the class of /l/-sounds) are to be interpreted in a similar fashion or not. At present, I have nothing to say on this question.

Another consequence of the present proposal might be a new view on rhotacism. A rhotacism in the sense of "some sound turns into /r/" should then be seen not as a segmental change, but as a change in terms of points on the sonority hierarchy. Such rhotacisms have been reported for Old High German, Old English (see discussion by Howell 1991), and for the group of languages called Italic (see Coleman 1992: 244). Significantly perhaps, rhotacisms in West Germanic languages have often been termed "sonorization".

Perhaps needless to say, there are some obvious and not so obvious problems with the present proposal. One question which comes to mind is how to treat those /r/'s which do not fit the phonotactic pattern claimed to exist for /r/. In particular, some initial r-sounds, as in Polish or Russian, seem hard to accomodate to the solution proposed. Polish, for example has one /r/ which can also appear in the following contexts (with '[' denoting a left word-boundary):

(19)   r-obstruent clusters in Polish

[rt, [rd, [rdᶻ, [rv, [rž, [ržn, [ržń

In these clusters, taken from Rochoń (2000: chapter 3.1.1), /r/ clearly precedes an obstruent. However, as these clusters are restricted to word-initial position, an analysis of extrasyllabicity is strongly supported; Rochoń (2000: chapter 3.3) provides more pieces of evidence for such an analysis. One consequence of a structure in which a segment is extrasyllabic is that syllable-related principles, such as the sonority sequencing, are simply not applicable. However, if /r/ is a point on the sonority scale, then what is an extrasyllabic /r/? This leads to an important point of clarification, and perhaps of limitation:

The main proposal of this paper is that the rhotics as a class are to be characterized as a prosody, crudely put, as P4. However, this is no substitute for the need to give a featural specification to individual phonemes /r/ in a language. Let us suppose a prototypical language, namely one with CV-and CVC-syllables only, and with one phoneme /r/. Saying that this /r/ is characterized as P4 is of no consequences for its phonotactic behaviour, and as /r/ appears in the same slot as all other consonants, it does not distinguish it from any other consonants either. This individual consonant needs to be described by adequate feature specifications, and any variation of this r-sound too. In the same manner, an account of Polish phonology needs to give a featural description of the phoneme /r/ in this language, and it is this /r/

which we can refer to in a discussion of ist clustering properties. This does not mean that the phonotactic properties of /r/ are irrelevant (once /r/ is part of a syllable).

A final aspect of /r/ is the fact that vowels can be rhotacized or r-coloured. What, then, is a rhoticized vowel? If /r/ is related to a position on the sonority hierarchy distinct from the positions for vowels, as claimed in this paper, it seems there is no room here for vowels which are r-sounds at the same time. (Syllabic /r/'s as in 13-14 are a different matter, they just require an /r/ to appear in the nucleus. The fact that /r/ can often be syllabic is an argument for a sonority-related description of /r/.) For the time being, I will argue that the exclusion of rhotacized vowels from the description is in fact a welcome result. Rhotacized vowels have been described as being very similar to retroflexion. They are articulatorily as diverse as retroflexion is in general (Ladefoged and Maddieson 1996: 313-14). It therefore seems much more appropriate to equate "rhotacized" vowels with retroflex place of articulation, on which I have nothing to say, than with /r/. There is an acoustic similarity between some (but not all!) r-sounds and retroflexion, namely the lowering of the third formant. This may be the reason that such vowels are called "rhotacized", but it is perhaps not a sufficient reason for equating rhotacized vowels and r-sounds.

Notes

* I have to thank many people for providing useful input to this paper, in particular my colleagues in Marburg, and especially Wolfgang Kehrein. The audiences at the Berlin *Conference on Distinctive Features Theory* and at a colloquium in Düsseldorf have also been very helpful in formulating the ideas of the present paper. I thank the editor and an anonymous reviewer for important suggestions.

1   In the following, I use the terms "r-sound" and "rhotic" interchangably. I will also use "/r/" as a symbol referring to a sound from this class without any commitment as to its precise quality.

2   The diacritic symbol "ˌ" lowers the referent of its main symbol. Thus, fricative [ʁ] is lowered here to a more open approximant. Conversely, the IPA notation also uses a raising symbol "ˌ" and gives "ɹ = voiced alveolar fricative" as an example. If raising and lowering symbols convert between approximants and

fricatives, the notation seen as an over-all descriptive system becomes redundant and ambiguous in several respects.

3   On the other hand, it is clear that the IPA notation tends to use simple letters of the Latin alphabet for unmarked and common sounds. The symbols are not chosen arbitrarily.

4   The one language with 4 r-phonemes in table (2) is Irish Gaelic, which can be analyzed in different ways. Bammesberger (1982) and Chiosáin (1994), e. g. assign two /r/-phonemes to Irish Gaelic from very different perspectives. Other r-sounds seem to be rule-based alternants. Walsh Dickey (1997: chapter 3) presents more statistical results on rhotics.

5   Bell (1978: 169), in his survey of syllabic consonants, notes that there are more languages in his sample with syllabic nasals than with syllabic liquids (laterals and rhotics). But he also notes (p. 171) that syllabic nasals and syllabic liquids may have different origins: syllabic liquids arise as a consequence of vowel reduction, syllabic nasals do not.

6   Maddieson (1984) tentatively admits coronal rhotics as fricatives (8 languages in his sample), but excludes uvular fricatives from the class of rhotics. He points out (p. 80) that the inclusion of voiced coronal fricatives in the class of rhotics may, in the sources, be based on phonotactic considerations.

7   The languages in Maddieson's sample are the following: Azerbaijani, Sa'ban, Karen, Kabardian, East Armenian, Araucanian, Chukchi, Burushaski.

8   The same place nodes are also allowed either to be sisters of each other (Coronal and Dorsal in 5b and similarly for laterals, Walsh Dickey 1997: 71), or to be daughters of each other (Dorsal below Coronal as velarization, p. 6). The number of possible place distinctions is therefore staggering. Hall (2000: section 2.3) presents a partially similar set of critical remarks on this model.

9   Palatalized rhotics are represented (Walsh Dickey 1997: 71) by the node Laminal being dominated by another Laminal node. Such a recursive stacking of place features is regarded as marked and therefore rare.

10 Ladefoged (1993: 168) and others argue that taps (as in Spanish) and flaps (as in American English) are different sounds. For present purposes, the distinction can be ignored.

11 Given that German has a rule of r-Vocalization refering to the syllable rhyme, possible further complications arise in the respective ordering of segmental rules and rules of prosodic structure assignment.

12 No attention is paid to the correctness of the vowel qualities in (12b).

13 This puzzle has been observed by others before, see, e.g., Roca and Johnson (1999: 80): "What is interesting, indeed puzzling, is that all the phonetically quite different *r*s function similarly in the respective phonological systems. In

particular, they tend to function like sonorants, even when they are not so phonetically, undoubtedly the reason they are generally construed as rhotics."

14 One possible move to avoid the problem might be to restrict the sonority hierarchy to a more abstract level of representation, such as the level of underlying forms. But first, it is unclear whether the unity of /r/ in terms of segmental features exists here. Second, this raises all sorts of questions on the role of the syllable in underlying representations.

15 For an overview and discussion of such complex segments from African languages, see Clements (1999).

16 This does not hold for Scandinavian languages, for example Icelandic.

17 The wide-ranging variation of /r/ in German is also surveyed by Kohler (1995: chapter 6.1.1.6), Schiller (1999) and Wiese (to appear). Kohler (1995: 153) asserts that a phonetic characterization of the phoneme /r/ in Standard German is not possible, confirming the present point of view even for a single language. Itô and Mester (2000) add an interesting observation on the behaviour or German /r/ in loan-word phonology: words such as English *story* may be used in German in three different pronunciations: sto[r]y, sto[ʀ]y, [ʃ]to[ʀ]y, that is, with or without nativized SC-cluster and with or without a nativized r-sound. But the fourth logical possibility, *[ʃ]to[r]y, is not acceptable. In other words, the r-sound is adapted to the German variant much more easily than the s-sound (preceding /t/), again confirming the point that the r-sound is more variable than other sounds.

18 In any case, expansion or simplification is more readily available for this type of sonority scale than for previous proposals which are based on segmental features.

19 The latter problem may be relegated to some notion of extrasyllabicity at edges. I do not wish to claim that all criticisms of the sonority hierarchy are crucial counterarguments against the concept itself.

20 There are also lexical exceptions, such as *leraar* 'teacher'. I thank an anonymous reviewer for important suggestions for this set of examples.

21 For one attempt in this direction, see Golston and Hulst (2000).

References

Archangeli, Diana
    1984   *Underspecification in Yawelmani Phonology and Morphology.* Cambridge, Mass.: MIT Press.
Bammesberger, Alfred
    1982   *Essentials of Modern Irish.* Heidelberg: Winter Verlag.

Bell, Alan
   1978   Syllabic consonants. In: Joseph H. Greenberg (ed.), *Universals of Human Language*, 153-201. Stanford: Stanford University Press.
Bhat, D.N.S.
   1974   The phonology of liquid consonants. *Working Papers on Language Universals* 16: 73-104.
Blevins, Juliette
   1995   The syllable in phonological theory. In: John A. Goldsmith (ed.), *The Handbook of Phonological Theory*, 206-244. Oxford: Blackwell.
Booij, Geert E.
   1995   *The Phonology of Dutch*. Oxford: Clarendon Press.
   1998   Phonological output constraints in morphology. In: Wolfgang Kehrein and Richard Wiese (eds.), *Phonology and Morphology of the Germanic Languages*, 143-163. Tübingen: Niemeyer.
Browman, Catherine P. and Louis M. Goldstein
   1986   Towards an articulatory phonology. *Phonology Yearbook* 3: 219-252.
   1992   Articulatory phonology: an overview. *Phonetica* 49: 155-180.
Butt, Matthias
   1992   Sonority and the explanation of syllable structure. *Linguistische Berichte* 137: 45-67.
Clements, George N.
   1985   The geometry of phonological features. *Phonology Yearbook* 2: 223-250.
   1990   The role of the sonority cycle in core syllabification. In: John Kingston and Mary E. Beckman (eds.), *Papers in Laboratory Phonology I: Between the Grammar and Physics of Speech*, 283-333. New York: Cambridge University Press.
   1999   Phonology. In: Bernd Heine and D. Nurse (eds.), *African Languages: An Introduction*. Cambridge: Cambridge University Press.
Clements, George N. and Samuel J. Keyser
   1983   *CV-Phonology: A Generative Theory of the Syllable*. Cambridge, Mass.: MIT Press.
Cohn, Abigail C.
   1993   The status of nasalized continuants. In: Marie K. Huffman and Rena A. Krakow (eds.), *Nasals, Nasalization, and the Velum*, 329-367. (*Phonetics and Phonology* 5.) San Diego: Academic Press.
Coleman, Robert
   1992   Italic languages. In: William Bright (ed.) *International Encyclopedia of Linguistics*, 241-245. Oxford: Oxford University Press.

Giegerich, Heinz J.
    1992   *English Phonology. An Introduction.* Cambridge: Cambridge University Press.
Golston, Chris and Harry van der Hulst
    2000   Stricture is structure. In: Ben Hermans and Marc van Oostendorp (eds.), *The Derivational Residue in Phonological Optimality Theory*, 153-173. Amsterdam, Philadelphia: John Benjamins.
Hall, T. Alan
    1992a   Syllable final clusters and schwa epenthesis in German. In: Peter Eisenberg, Karl-Heinz Ramers and Heinz Vater (eds.), *Silbenphonologie des Deutschen*, 208-245. Tübingen: Narr.
    1992b   *Syllable Structure and Syllable-Related Processes in German.* Tübingen: Max Niemeyer Verlag.
    1993   The phonology of German /ʀ/. *Phonology* 10: 83-105.
    1997   *The Phonology of Coronals.* Amsterdam, Philadelphia: John Benjamins.
    2000   Typological generalizations concerning secondary palatalization. *Lingua* 110: 1-25.
Halle, Morris
    1995   Feature geometry and feature spreading. *Linguistic Inquiry* 26: 1-46.

Howell, Robert B.
    1991   *Old English Breaking and its Germanic Analogues.* Tübingen: Niemeyer.
Hume, Elizabeth and David Odden
    1996   Reconsidering [consonantal]. *Phonology* 13: 345-376.
Itô, Junko and Armin Mester
    2000   Covert generalizations in Optimality Theory. Unpublished ms., Santa Cruz
Jespersen, Otto
    1904   *Lehrbuch der Phonetik.* Leipzig, Berlin: Teubner.
Kahn, Daniel
    1976   Syllable-based generalizations in English phonology. Ph.D Dissertation, MIT.
Kingston, John and Avis H. Cohen
    1992   Extending articulatory phonology. *Phonetica* 49: 194-204.
Kiparsky, Paul
    1982   From cyclic phonology to lexical phonology. In: Harry van der Hulst and N. Smith (eds.), *The Structure of Phonological Representations*, 131-175. Dordrecht: Foris.
Kohler, Klaus J.
    1995   *Einführung in die Phonetik des Deutschen.* Berlin: Erich Schmidt.

Krämer, Wolfgang
1979   *Akustisch-phonetische Untersuchunge zum vokalischen /R/-Allophon des Deutschen.* Hamburg: Buske.
Ladefoged, Peter
1993   *A Course in Phonetics.* Fort Worth, etc.: Harcourt Brace Jovanovich.
Ladefoged, Peter, Jenny Ladefoged, Alice Turk, Kevin Hind and St. John Skilton
1998   Phonetic structures of Scottish Gaelic. *Journal of the International Phonetic Association* 28: 1-41.
Ladefoged, Peter and Ian Maddieson
1996   *Sounds of the World's Languages.* Oxford: Blackwell Publishers.
Lindau, Mona
1985   The story of /r/. In: Victoria A. Fromkin (ed.), *Phonetic Linguistics: Essays in Honor of Peter Ladefoged*, 157-168. New York: Academic.
Maddieson, Ian
1984   *Patterns of Sounds.* Cambridge: Cambridge University Press.
McCarthy, John J.
1988   Feature geometry and dependency: a review. *Phonetica* 45: 84-108.

Ní Chiosáin, Máire
1994   Irish palatalisation and the representation of place features. *Phonology* 11: 89-106.
Ohala, John J.
1990   Alternatives to the sonority hierarchy for explaining segmental sequential constraints. In: Michael Ziolkowski, Manuela Noske and Karen Deaton (eds.), *Papers from the 26th Regional Meeting of the Chicago Linguistic Society*, 319-338. 2, Parasession on the syllable.) Chicago: Chicago Linguistic Society.
Plag, Ingo
1998   Morphological haplology in a constraint-based morpho-phonology. In: Wolfgang Kehrein and Richard Wiese (eds.), *Phonology and Morphology of the Germanic Languages*, 199-215. Tübingen: Max Niemeyer.
Reenen, Pieter van
1994   Driemaal /r/ in de Nederlandse dialecten. *Taal en Tongval* 46: 46-72.
Rice, Keren D.
1992   On deriving sonority: a structural account of sonority relationships. *Phonology* 9: 61-99.
Roca, Iggy and Wyn Johnson
1999   *A Course in Phonology.* Oxford: Blackwell Publishers.

Rochoń, Marzena
    2000   *Optimality in Complexity: The Case of Polish Consonant Clusters.*
            Berlin: Akademie-Verlag.
Schiller, Niels
    1999   The phonetic variation of German /r/. In: Matthias Butt and Nanna
            Fuhrhop (eds.), *Variation und Stabilität in der Wortstruktur: Unter-*
            suchungen zu Entwicklung, Erwerb und Varietäten des Deutschen
            und anderer Sprachen, 261-287. Hildesheim u. a.: Olms.
Sievers, Eduard
    1901   *Grundzüge der Phonetik. Zur Einführung in das Studium der Laut-*
            lehre der indogermanischen Sprachen. Leipzig: Breitkopf & Härtel.
Steriade, Donca
    1987   Redundant values. In: Anna Bosch, B. Need and E. Schiller (eds.),
            Papers from the Parasession on Autosegmental and Metrical Phono-
            logy, 339-362. Chicago: Chicago Linguistic Society.
Tranel, Bernard
    1987   *The Sounds of French. An Introduction.* Cambridge: Cambridge Uni-
            versity Press.
Velde, Hans van de and Roeland van Hout
    1999   The pronunciation of (r) in Standard Dutch. In: Renée van Bezooijen
            and René Kager (eds.), *Linguistics in the Netherlands 1999*, 177-
            188. Amsterdam: John Benjamins.
Walsh Dickey, Laura
    1997   The phonology of liquids. Ph.D. Dissertation, University of Massa-
            chusetts.
Wiese, Richard
    1988   *Silbische und Lexikalische Phonologie. Studien zum Chinesischen*
            und Deutschen. Tübingen: Max Niemeyer Verlag.
    2000   *The Phonology of German.* Oxford: Oxford University Press.
    to appear The unity and variation of (German) /r/. In: Hans van de Velde and
            Roeland van Hout (eds.), *r-atics: Sociolinguistic, Phonetic and Pho-*
            nological Characteristics of /r/. Brussels: Institut des Langues
            Vivantes et de Phonétique.

Index of languages

Index of subjects